SRI AUROBINDO'S

Savitri

A STUDY OF THE COSMIC EPIC

SRI AUROBINDO'S

Savitri

A STUDY OF THE COSMIC EPIC

PREMA NANDAKUMAR, PHD

wisdom tree

SRI AUROBINDO SOCIETY

This edition published in 2011 by Wisdom Tree in collaboration with Sri Aurobindo Society, Pondicherry (www.sriaurobindosociety.org.in).

ISBN 978-81-8328-175-1

Published by
Wisdom Tree,
4779/23, Ansari Road,
Darya Ganj, New Delhi-2
Ph.: 23247966/67/68
wisdomtreebooks@gmail.com

Printed in India at Print Perfect

TO THE MOTHER

The luminous heart of the Unknown is she,
A power of silence in the depths of God

It is time some genius appear to reconstitute
the shattered picture of the world.
He should live in the continual presence of
all experience, and respect it; he should
at the same time understand nature, the
ground of that experience; and he should
also have a delicate sense for the ideal
echoes of his own passions, for all the
colours of his possible happiness.
All that can inspire a poet is contained in
this task, and nothing less than this task
would exhaust a poet's inspiration.
We may hail this needed genius from afar...
we may salute him, saying:

Onorate l'altissimo poeta.

Honour the most high poet, honour the highest
possible poet.

George Santayana

CONTENTS

PREFACE TO THE THIRD EDITION

The first edition appeared on 24 November 1962 and the second on 24 November 1985. Apparently the Mother has willed a twenty-three-year gap between editions for *Sri Aurobindo's Savitri: A Study of the Cosmic Epic* (earlier titled *A Study of Savitri*)! Her grace has sustained me throughout my life. When my father, Prof K.R. Srinivasa Iyengar, communicated to her that a panel of three examiners from England had recommended the award of the degree of Doctor of Letters summa cum laude for my thesis, *A Study of Savitri*, she gave instructions for its publication immediately. Sri K.D. Sethna read the manuscript and suggested some improvements which were carried out. For me it was all too sudden, dream-like, when I received the hard-bound copy, which was followed by several generous reviews in leading magazines. Writing in Modern Language Review, Prof. Vivian de Sola Pinto observed:

> Dr Nandakumar's English style is fluent, always readable and sometimes eloquent. Her book is based on a wide literary culture … All students of the work of Aurobindo and indeed of the spirit of modern India must be grateful to Dr Nandakumar for this intelligent and sympathetic guide to the masterpiece of a poet whose work is still too little known outside India.

During the last fifty years, *Savitri* has been increasingly gaining its rightful space in Indian academia. Several dissertations have been submitted in various universities with signal success. Eminent orators like Ambalal Purani and M.V. Nadkarni have taken the epic poem all over India and abroad to enthusiastic audiences. Innumerable books on *Savitri* have been published. There are also websites exclusively devoted to studying the poem. And yet I have been repeatedly asked for copies of my book which apparently continues to be of significant help to the student of Sri Aurobindo's epic. This is how Sri M.L. Himatsingka kindly acceded to my request and brought out a paperback edition in1985.

For the last fifteen years and more, the book has remained out of print, though the demand has continued. I am grateful to Sri S.G. Gautam for initiating the idea of this new edition. I was delighted when Sri Vijay of Sri Aurobindo Society came forward to set off the process for its publication. This I do consider as a direct ray of grace from the Mother as the book is being issued during the golden jubilee of the Society. It has also been a joy to work with the young and enthusiastic helpers in the task of production, Krishna, Gita and Vilasni. Nandita Jaishankar's attention to detail as an editor has been of great help. I am deeply thankful to Shobit Arya and Sapna Rangaswamy for publishing the book under the auspices of Wisdom Tree.

My mother, deeply devoted to *Savitri* which was her life's companion, was looking forward to this new edition when she merged with the Mother in 2007. Her angelic spirit is sure to be delighted for she was always my first reader and critic and tireless correspondent. My husband Nandakumar, and our children Ahana, Bhuvana and Raja have been the source of light and laughter in my life. It is a special joy to thank them formally.

Though I have published several books after *A Study of Savitri*, this work remains very close to my heart. The work gave me the honour of being the first student to take up the epic for doctoral study. I owe to my father all that is in it. I can see and hear my father in the book, as he explained to me the poem, helped me plan the work and guided me to the right books on literature and philosophy in the Andhra University Library. He patiently corrected my manuscript, cheered me up when I felt despondent and curbed my enthusiasm for a flowery style. When the first edition was in the press, he went through the proofs with me which was in itself a lifetime's education.

Indeed I see my entire life in this book ever since father read the complete *Savitri* at home using the one-volume university edition which had been published in 1954. And the two days in November 1959 when Ambalal Purani kept the 1000-strong student-listeners of Andhra University in the Erskine Square mesmerised by his speeches on Sri Aurobindo and *Savitri*. The audience with the Mother after my thesis had brought me the doctoral degree, the publication of the book, my post-doctoral work on Sri Aurobindo and Dante Alighieri growing out of one section in this book, my days spent in reading Sri Aurobindo and writing about him guided gently by my father are all entwined in its pages. It is all due to Mother's grace and I bow to her in gratitude.

Merging into the folds of *Savitri* one can feel spirituality as a tangible experience for the epic never fails us. Every reading opens yet another brave new world! I was a teenager when I used to accompany my father in his daily walks, and listened to him reciting 'The Symbol Dawn' while we watched the sun rise above the Bay of Bengal:

> The brief perpetual sign recurred above.
> A glamour from unreached transcendences
> Iridescent with the glory of the Unseen,
> A message from the unknown immortal Light
> Ablaze upon creation's quivering edge,
> Dawn built her aura of magnificent hues
> And buried its seed of grandeur in the hours.

More than half a century later, I marvel how *Savitri* has been a guardian "angel of the way" for me, and I have not lost any of the hope, the wonder and the faith instilled in me by my father in those early days of studying the poem. Towards the Greater Dawn then!

Prema Nandakumar

PREFACE TO THE SECOND EDITION

Long out of print, *A Study of Savitri* now comes out again, and I am grateful to Sri M.L. Himatsingka, the indefatigable and dedicated spirit behind All India Books and VAK: The Spiritual Bookshop for it. Doubtless several books on *Savitri* have appeared during the last two decades, notably by M.P. Pandit, Rohit Mehta, Syed Mehdi Imam, and Rameshwar Gupta; but I have also been receiving all these years repeated queries regarding the reissue of my work. I therefore venture to think that it has, perhaps, a place of its own in the growing critical literature on *Savitri*, and deserves this new lease of life.

I may add that, following this work and helped by a UGC post-doctoral Senior Fellowship for three years (1967-70) at Andhra University, I completed a comparative study of Dante's *The Divine Comedy* and Sri Aurobindo's *Savitri*. It appeared first serially in *Sri Aurobindo Circle Annual* (1972-78) and later in book form (1981).

But *Savitri* remains inexhaustible, embodying in its nectarean message "an immortal Sunlight radiating over the future". And our 'critiques' are no more than humble approaches and offerings. In the end one surrenders to the poem itself, and its alchemic power and glory.

Prema Nandakumar

PREFACE TO THE FIRST EDITION

This book is substantially the same as the thesis for which the Andhra University, on the unanimous recommendations of a Board consisting of Professors Vivian de Sola Pinto, H.O. White and T.J.B. Spencer, awarded the Degree of Doctor of Philosophy on me at the Annual Convocation held in December 1961. The present publication has been kindly sponsored by the Andhra University, with the help of a grant-in-aid from the University Grants Commission (UGC), and I am duly grateful to both my Alma Mater and the UGC for thus facilitating the publication of this book so soon after the award of the Degree.

During the last several months I have been asking myself why, having wavered for quite some time between Virginia Woolf and *Savitri* as my subject for the PhD course, I finally chose the latter. I should perhaps say rather that whereas I chose Virginia Woolf, *Savitri* chose me. Sir Aurobindo's portraits adorn the walls of my parental home, and I have grown up in silent and reverent admiration of the Master. As a girl I was once privileged to visit the Sri Aurobindo Ashram at Pondicherry. And which Hindu girl reacts otherwise than with love and gratitude towards the mythic heroine, *Savitri*.

That I should wish to study Sri Aurobindo's *Savitri* was thus not surprising: what was really surprising was that I took so long to reach a decision which, once made, seemed altogether the right thing. My first postgraduate enthusiasm had been the great Tamil poet, Subramania Bharati, some of whose poems I translated into English and published as *Bharati in English Verse*. Now Bharati had been Sri Aurobindo's intimate friend at Pondicherry for about ten years, and what could be more appropriate than my turning from Bharati to Sri Aurobindo?

There has been no end to my good fortune. Firstly the subject itself, which I now think is the greatest—the most inspiring—that a woman, at any rate a Hindu woman, could think of or write about. Secondly, I have had constant advice and help from my father, Prof K.R. Srinivasa Iyengar, who is not only the author of the standard biographical study of Sri Aurobindo but is also one of the eminent authorities on the subject. Thirdly, the UGC were good enough to award a research scholarship that enabled me to prosecute my studies without saddling myself with teaching duties.

Fourthly, in November 1959, Mr A.B. Purani the author of the only book on Sri Aurobindo's *Savitri* was our guest for a few days and gave on 25 November an inspiring lecture in the University on *Savitri*. Having been closely associated with Sri Aurobindo for about thirty years, Mr Purani is one of the very few people who can talk with real authority on the Master's thought and message. I was privileged to discuss the plan of my book with him, clear up several of my difficulties, and even to look into some of his private lecture notes on *Savitri*. Finally, certain review-assignments by Madame Sophia Wadia for the *Aryan Path* and the *Indian P.E.N.* enabled me during the last few years to read and write about Sri Aurobindo's posthumous publications—notably *Ilion* and the plays—while Sri Nolini Kanta Gupta, Secretary of the Sri Aurobindo Ashram, gave me no small encouragement by publishing my first essay on *Savitri* ('The Exordium') in the quarterly journal, *The Advent*.

On the other hand, the more I studied, the more I began to feel bewildered. *Savitri* is a colossal poem of nearly 24,000 lines. The mere attempt to 'understand' it left me often despairing whether I would ever be able to bring my project to some sort of conclusion. I was for a while quite lost in Aswapati's 'Worlds', and the 'Descent into Night' was a terrible experience. But I persevered and my father was always there to help me whenever I floundered. The collateral studies took me to vast new oceans of knowledge. There were Sri Aurobindo's own works, formidable in their bulk and weight and manifoldness of knowledge. I was advised to read Evelyn Underhill's classic treatise on mysticism, and this took me to other books on mysticism and the great mystics. I also took deep draughts from the springs of modern English and American poetry. Browsing in the University library, I read whatever seemed to have relevance to my subject in its wider perspective, and took numerous notes and carefully card-indexed them. As the months passed I had the feeling of a person who has foolishly ventured far into the sea and finds, whichever way he turns, nothing but an endless expanse of water. The shore seems to be nowhere.

I could have gone on reading and taking notes for a lifetime, for one subject led to another and to another still, and all seemed relevant enough to the study of a 'Cosmic' epic like *Savitri*. But I realised at last that I must really put my notes in some order, plan my book and start writing it. First I attempted a verse play on the Savitri theme, more as an exercise in understanding and interpretation than as a serious literary effort. Next I turned to Part II of the present thesis. Mr Purani's 'Summary' was very useful, of course, but since he is a tried *sadhak* or initiate of Sri Aurobindo's yoga, many things that are perhaps self-explanatory to him seemed at first puzzling in the extreme to me. But repeated re-readings enabled me to complete this Part which is more or less a critical synopsis of the poem. I now turned to the original legend in the *Mahabharata* and made my own rendering, though I found the prose versions of Pratap Chandra Roy and John

Brough as also the verse renderings of Sir Edwin Arnold, Romesh Chunder Dutt and Toru Dutt useful for one reason or another.

Parts of the chapter 'Overhead' Poetry and *Savitri* were presented as a paper before the English Faculty Research Seminar on 12 March 1960. The final chapter on *Savitri* as a 'Cosmic Epic' took me to other epics, ancient and modern, and I had an enchanting time exploring these 'realms of gold'. Dante, among the poets of the past, comes closest to Sri Aurobindo, and I found the essays on Dante by T.S. Eliot and Allen Tate the most illuminating, though Charles Williams is very good too. Of the moderns, Ezra Pound and Nikos Kazantzakis challenge comparison with Sri Aurobindo as epic poets. I have therefore made an attempt to see both the *Cantos* and *The Odyssey: A Modern Sequel*, in relation to *Savitri*. Last to be written was the first chapter on Sri Aurobindo's life and work: while writing it I was conscious of what I had already written in the later chapters, and hence some points have been only glanced at since they are anyhow dealt with in fuller detail at the appropriate places later on.

My main difficulty has been narrowing down the subject and at the same time setting it in the right backgrounds. This is no study of Sri Aurobindo or of his philosophy or yoga or politics, not even a study of his poetry as a whole. The single poem, *Savitri*, is the subject; and Sri Aurobindo's life and thought, his philosophy and yoga and politics and his other poems, are brought in only to make the appreciation of *Savitri* easy or complete. But *Savitri* is an epic in the English language, and it cannot be studied in a cultural vacuum. *Savitri* by itself, *Savitri* in relation to Sri Aurobindo's life and work, and *Savitri* in relation to the currents of human thought and experience of all times: such are the three ascending terms in the argument that I have tried to present in the following pages.

Sri Aurobindo's yoga and his philosophy were no 'freaks' but are paralleled by similar (though not identical) realisations and leaps of thought elsewhere. Thus, while claiming outstanding genius and originality for Sri Aurobindo, I have been at some pains to show that, far from being a 'crank' or a 'case', he was generally in the line of the great mystics, philosophers and poets of the world. For example, when I had almost completed my thesis, I came across Pierre Teilhard de Chardin's *The Phenomenon of Man*, and I was surprised to find striking similarities between his and Sri Aurobindo's speculations, to which I have drawn attention in the course of the first chapter.

In The 'Legend' and the 'Symbol', I have tried to show that Sri Aurobindo's *Savitri*, massive though it is in conception and impressive in execution, is in its main ingredients implied in the old legendary story, even as the colossal Indian banyan tree is essentially implied in its tiny seed. As regards the symbolism, I have striven to show that Sri Aurobindo has drawn freely from the rich storehouse of Vedic symbolism and fused the many derived symbols into a single new blaze of revelation. In 'Overhead' Poetry and *Savitri*, again, I have endeavoured to show that as 'overhead' poetry involves, first 'thematic content', second 'language' or verbal expression, and finally 'rhythm', in *Savitri* the 'content' is mainly Sri Aurobindo's own yogic experiences (including the journey in consciousness and the spiritual struggles in the mystic's 'Dark Night of the Soul'), the language is symbolic, often drawing upon the Vedic symbolism, and the rhythm is iambic blank verse, but with an Upanishadic and Kalidasian force and finish.

But 'overhead' poetry is not, after all, a wholly new bag of poetical, tricks, but rather the pushing up of certain possibilities in all great poetry to a further height and consistency of profoundly moving utterance. This point too I have tried to make in the course of the chapter, with illustrations from poets of the ancient and the modern world. Finally, in *Savitri*: A Cosmic Epic, I have done my best to show that *Savitri* is an epic of the soul with a range that is truly cosmic, and that, while it recalls for one or another reason many of the epics of the past and of the present-day world, still the *Divina Commedia* comes nearest to it in its scope and depth and quality of its poetic utterance. The essence of the celebrated Gayatri (or Savitri) mantra is that by meditating on Savitri the adorable Supreme Creator of the Universe, the devotee invokes the intercession of that Power to awaken the veiled indwelling Effulgence to guide the mind towards the Truth. The Supreme Creator is also the veiled slumbering Effulgence; as a result of the divine intercession, what is slumbering is awakened, what is veiled is revealed, and man returns to the sovereignty of the Spirit. Sri Aurobindo is thus able to make his poem at once the story of Savitri and Satyavan, and the story of Man in the Universe: in short a human and a cosmic epic in one.

I realise now that it was vain on my part to have supposed that what Sri Aurobindo took some decades to compose could be 'studied' and the results of the study presented in easy critical categories. But I derive much encouragement from the concluding remarks in Mr Patrick Cruttwell's recent article on 'Makers and Persons':

> ...two very general caveats for the critic, which are also caveats, to a slightly lesser degree, for the common reader. The first is that we ought to make quite sure, before we undertake the microscopic investigation of a writer, that he is, for ourselves, worth investigating—which means, that we have enjoyed and been impressed by his work. And the second caveat is that the ways in which the person affects and is revealed in his creations are enormously varied and subtle; the evidence, however lavish, is never, in the nature of things, complete; and it behoves us, therefore, however fearless we may be in our pryings, to be cautious in our conclusions. [1]

I can at least say that I have genuinely enjoyed, and have often been overwhelmed by *Savitri*; I can also say that after all this exploration and scrutiny, I still feel that there is a lot more to know, that all the 'facts of the case' are not ready to hand; and if the poem intrigues me still in many places, if I feel constantly baffled, the reason may very well be that I do not know all the facts, that perhaps I have not even had the patience or perseverance to look for them in the right places. The poetry of *Savitri* is the reality, my critical study is but an illusion, but I hope, an illusion not wholly unrelated to the Reality!

Savitri is poetry and philosophy, and is based on Sri Aurobindo's own yogic experiences and realisations. The appreciation of a poem like *Savitri* must accordingly involve special difficulties. In the 'Preface' to his thoughtful work, *Dante the Philosopher*, M. Etienne Gilson writes:

> When a philosopher discusses literature he often reveals a want of taste, but when a man of letter discusses ideas he sometimes reveals a want of precision. By helping one another we shall perhaps draw nearer to that state of grace in which love increases as understanding becomes clearer, and understanding is all the clearer as love is the more profound. Great writers expect no less of us, for their ideas are bound up with their art, and their very greatness consists in the fact that after they have gone their thoughts remain inseparable from the manner in which they have expressed them. [2]

Being neither a philosopher nor a litterateur but only a hesitant student attempting the double approach, it is possible that my argument lacks 'precision' and 'taste' both; but at least I have not failed to hanker after 'that state of grace' to which M. Gilson refers. Again and again, amidst others, two names—Dante and Sri Aurobindo — are brought into juxtaposition in my thesis, sometimes deliberately and sometimes by accident, as it were; and re-reading the whole thesis, I ask myself whether the crest of the winding argument is not, in effect, to hail *Savitri* as a modern *Divine Comedy*.

If *Savitri* the epic is poetry and philosophy fused with mystic experience, its central character is the blessed feminine herself, woman pictured not only as beauty and love but also as strength and will. The good wife is verily man's *shakti,* all the reservoirs of his strength, and not just the 'weaker' sex; not frailty but strength is the mark of woman: such is the inspiring Hindu conception of the role of woman as wife as it finds expression in the *Mahabharata* story. The German poet, Rainer Maria Rilke, explaining the whole 'meaning and purpose' of his *Malte Laurids Brigge*, once asked in the course of a letter:

> ...how is it possible to live, when the very elements of this life are unintelligible to us? When we're everlastingly inadequate in love, uncertain in resolve, and incapable in the presence of death, how is it possible to exist?[3]

These—the first and last things are the very issues treated in Sri Aurobindo's *Savitri*, and Savitri is the answer to our 'existential' problem. Yoga leads to right knowledge, and right knowledge makes right action possible. Savitri is an example of a woman who is not 'inadequate in love', who is not 'uncertain in resolve', and who is not 'incapable in the presence of death'. She bravely faces the 'existential' problem and masters it; she is the redeemer of her husband, and she is the redeemer of the world. There is, indeed, no heroine in the world's literature who is quite as adorably human and at the same time as lovably divine as Savitri. It was thus with sure insight that Sri Aurobindo has made this archetypal woman as wife and *shakti* the theme of his loftiest poetical flight.

There is another circumstance, too, about this poem that deserves emphasis here. *Savitri* is the work of an Indian poet in the English language, a fact that must have a challenging significance today. Anglo-Indian literary relations are an absorbing subject and call for separate examination. But here one or two points are particularly relevant. The British political connection has ceased, but English has still a place in India. India's elder statesman, Mr C. Rajagopalachari, has acknowledged that English is the gift of the Goddess Saraswati to India. And Mr Sisirkumar Mitra writes:

> Now a word about English. This remarkable language, already international, has rendered signal service to the cause of India's unity, her nationalism and her independence, and occupies, in her everyday life, a place of importance, perhaps no whit less great than did Sanskrit or Pali, each in its own day...If English is the greatest gift of England to India, India's greatest gift to English, and through it, to the world is Sri Aurobindo's masterpiece, *The Life Divine* and his sublime epic,

> *Savitri*, through which he has sent forth his divine message to humanity. [4]

Sri Aurobindo spent his impressionable years in England—Manchester, London, Cambridge—and he was thus ideally equipped to be the builder of the bridge of understanding between the people of the West and the East. Even so accomplished a writer as Sri Aurobindo, to whom English was like a mother tongue, is bound to wield the language with a significant difference. But such differences will only serve to enrich the language, not impoverish it. As a writer declared in the *Times Literary Supplement*, the 'centre of gravity' had shifted and "while we are busy 'consolidating', a brand new 'English' literature will be appearing in Johannesburg or Sydney or Vancouver or Madras."[5] He might have added "or Pondicherry".

Another writer, Ronald Nixon (now Sri Krishnaprem), has also expressed the opinion that, "The English language has been given to the world and its usage and limits can now no longer be determined exclusively by the ears of the Islanders whose tongue it originally was. Those who would remain sole rulers of their language must abjure empire."[6] Indian English at its best—like American English—has a distinctive quality of its own, for it cannot escape being influenced by the climate—physical, intellectual, spiritual—of India. Nothing therefore is of happier augury for the future of human solidarity and harmony than the fact that Sri Aurobindo, an Indian among Indians, a Rishi in the tradition of Vamadeva and Yajnavalkya, nevertheless chose English as the natural medium of expression to communicate his thoughts and visions to the world.

The appearance of *Savitri*, therefore, is an auspicious omen of incommensurable potency. The recurrent symbol in the poem is Dawn—Dawn now defeating Darkness, Dawn now paving the way for the Noon of the future. And *Savitri* may very well herald the dawn of a new and a better world, 'a new heaven and a new earth'. Savitri herself is the Dawn: "Dawn of the luminous journey, Dawn queen of truth, large with the Truth, how wide is the gleam from her rosy limbs—Dawn divine who brings with her the heaven of light."[7]

I have already recorded my debt to my father. His personal library of Aurobindonian literature has been of ready use to me; he has also permitted me to make use of the letters in his possession as also certain private notes and unpublished articles. We have read the more difficult parts of *Savitri* together and discussed the planning of my book. He has read the first drafts of my chapters as they were written and made suggestions towards their improvement with regard both to the argument and the style. I am also deeply grateful to Professor Vivian de Sola Pinto (University of Nottingham), Professor H.O. White (Trinity College, Dublin) and Professor T.J.B. Spencer (University of Birmingham), and to three friends at the Sri Aurobindo Ashram—Mr A.B. Purani, Mr M.P. Pandit and Mr K.D. Sethna—for their generous appreciation and helpful criticisms, which have enabled me to revise and make improvements in the 'copy' before sending it finally to the press.

For the rest, my debt to the various authorities is indicated, generally in the 'Select Bibliography', and particularly in the references. I have, almost as a general rule, avoided referring to my authorities with prefixes like Mr, Dr, or Prof, for obvious reasons; this in no way implies want of respect or courtesy to them on my part. I have referred to the dates of publication in the references only if the books are not listed also in the 'Select Bibliography' with all the necessary details. Again, I have given the dates, not necessarily of first publication, but of the publication of the actual edition or impression used by me. With regard to the spelling of proper names and the transliteration of Sanskrit words, I have tried to be consistent, though it is too much to hope that I have been entirely successful. Also, the epigraphs at the head of the three Parts of the thesis are based on Sri Aurobindo's renderings of the respective verses from the *Rig Veda*, and in fact, I have throughout given extracts only from his versions of the Veda, the Upanishads and the *Gita*.

I also wish to place on record my gratitude to the Manager and Staff of Sri Aurobindo Ashram Press for the care, patience and devotion with which they have produced this book with so attractive a get-up. I have indeed received unstinted help and encouragement from so many quarters, and if my *A Study of Savitri* still falls far short of the ideal, it can only be because of my own limitations of which I am only too conscious. I may, however, take consolation from the words of the Master: "If thy aim be great and thy means small, still act; for by action alone these can increase to thee."

Prema Nandakumar

PART I

TOWARDS *SAVITRI*

Beholding
the higher Light
beyond the darkness
we came
to the divine Sun
in the Godhead,
to the highest
Light of all.

Rig Veda

SRI AUROBINDO: HIS LIFE AND WORK

I

INTRODUCTION

When I behold thy face, 'mid bondage, pain and wrong
And black indignities, I hear the soul's great song
Of rapture unconfined, the chant the pilgrim sings
In which exultant hope's immortal splendour rings,
Solemn voice and calm…the spirit of Bharat-land,
O poet, hath placed upon thy face her eyes afire
With love, and struck vast chords upon her vibrant lyre. [1]

Such was Rabindranath Tagore's homage to Aurobindo Ghose in 1907. The occasion was the arrest and imprisonment of Aurobindo in connection with his editorship of the nationalist paper, *Bande Mataram.* Twenty-one years later, on 29 May 1928, Rabindranath saw Sri Aurobindo again in his ashram at Pondicherry, and left the following record of his meeting:

> At the very first sight I could realise that he had been seeking for the soul and had gained it, and through this long process of

> realisation had accumulated within him a silent power of inspiration. His face was radiant with an inner light and his serene presence made it evident to me that his soul was not crippled and cramped to the measure of some tyrannical doctrine, which takes delight in inflicting wounds upon life.
>
> I felt that the utterance of the ancient Hindu *Rishi* spoke from him of that equanimity which gives the human soul its freedom of entrance into the All. I said to him, 'You have the Word and we are waiting to accept it from you. India will speak through your voice to the world, *Hearken to me*...
>
> Years ago I saw Aurobindo in the atmosphere of his earlier heroic youth and I sang to him, 'Aurobindo, accept the salutations from Rabindranath.' Today I saw him in a deeper atmosphere of reticent richness of wisdom and again sang to him in silence, 'Aurobindo, accept the salutations from Rabindranath.' [2]

Tagore was an international figure, a Nobel laureate and twelve years Sri Aurobindo's senior in age. The 'homage' is, therefore, all the more striking. Sri Aurobindo was not like other men. The heroic fighter of 1907 had become, by a mysterious process of spiritual alchemy, the *rishi* of 1928. He had indeed become the Soul of India.

Again, Henry Miller has recorded that, "the experience which stands out most strongly in my mind is the reading of Romain Rolland's two volumes on Ramakrishna and Vivekananda."[3] Sri Ramakrishna Paramahamsa was a god intoxicated man, a saint who seized the Kingdom of Heaven by violence. Swami Vivekananda was his principal disciple and interpreter, his spiritual heir and his tempestuous St Paul. Sri Aurobindo continued, and in a way completed, their work. Romain Rolland himself described Sri Aurobindo as, "the most noble representative of this great Neo-Vedantic spirit...the foremost of Indian thinkers,"[4] and also as, "the completest synthesis that has been realised to this day of the genius of Asia and the genius of Europe," and as the last of the great *rishi*s who held "in firm unrelaxed grip, the bow of creative energy."[5]

Tagore and Rolland, one an Indian and the other a Frenchman, have thus greeted Sri Aurobindo in almost identical terms. Another Frenchman, Paul Richard, said before a Japanese audience after meeting Sri Aurobindo:

> The hour is coming of great things, of great events, and also of great men, the divine men of Asia. All my life I have sought for them across the world, for all my life I have felt they must exist somewhere in the world, that this world would die if they did not live. For they are its light, its heat, its life. It is in Asia that I found the greatest among them—the leader, the hero of tomorrow. He is a Hindu. His name is Aurobindo Ghose.[6]

Years later, after the publication of Sri Aurobindo's philosophical treatise, *The Life Divine*, Sir Francis Younghusband hailed it as "the greatest book which has been produced in my time".[7] And writing about its author the *Times Literary Supplement* under the editorship of D.L. Murray said:

> He is not an armchair philosopher, but a man who, having led a life of intense activity, has retired to brood over it, if one may say so of a Hindu, in the dim light of a Gothic cathedral. In fact, he is a new type of thinker, one who combines in his vision the alacrity of the West with the illumination of the East. To study his writings is to enlarge the boundaries of one's knowledge.[8]

Not only did Sri Aurobindo combine the spiritual fervour of Ramakrishna with Vivekananda's intellectual vigour, he also brought the East and the West into full creative partnership. The Hindu brooding in the dim light of a Gothic cathedral: the Indian forging the links between the thought of the East and the thought of the West: the Bengali writing in the English language with a singular mastery of phrase and rhythm: a Lighthouse of the Spirit for the East as well as the West. How shall we account for this truly unusual phenomenon?

II

LIFE-SKETCH

Sri Aurobindo was born on 15 August 1872, an hour before sunrise, in Calcutta. His parents were Krishnadhan Ghose, a physician,and Swarnalata Ghose. Sri Aurobindo's elder brother, Manomohan, became a poet of considerable distinction and a Professor of English. His younger brother, Barindra Kumar, became a revolutionary. Sri Aurobindo's own birth on 15 August 1872 has a double national significance: it was the centenary year of the birth of Raja Rammohan Roy, the Father of Modern India and seventy-five years later, on 15 August 1947, India became a free country. Thus Sri Aurobindo's birthday and India's Independence Day are now being celebrated together.

Sri Aurobindo's father, Krishnadhan, had himself received his higher education in England, and wished his children to have an English education, as far as possible uncontaminated by 'native' ways and 'native' speech. He accordingly sent Sri Aurobindo, along with his elder brothers Benoy Bhushan and Manomohan, to the Loretto Convent School at Darjeeling. Thus, from the age of five, Sri Aurobindo moved mainly with English children and learned to speak English as a matter of course. In 1879, Krishnadhan took his sons to England and left them there to continue their studies. For fourteen years, from 1879 to 1893, Sri Aurobindo lived in England, partly at Manchester, partly in London, and finally at Cambridge.

Since even at home, in India, Krishnadhan had employed an English nurse, Miss Pagett, Sri Aurobindo had no—or very little knowledge of—Bengali when he arrived in England. At Manchester, he stayed with friends of his father, the Rev William H. Drewett and Mrs Drewett, and learned from them Latin, French, history, geography and arithmetic. Even in England, the Ghose boys were carefully insulated, under instructions from their father, from the influence of Indians and Indian ways. Sri Aurobindo and his two brothers grew up practically as English children.

After five years at Manchester, Sri Aurobindo proceeded to St Paul's School, London, in 1884 and remained there for another six years. He was an apt pupil in every way and secured the Butterworth Prize for Literature and the Bedford Prize for History. Dr Walker took personal interest in Sri Aurobindo, impressed by his character and abilities, taught him Greek, and pushed him rapidly into the higher forms. Did the Head Master of St Paul's already see something of Sri Aurobindo's future destiny? Sri Aurobindo's school record mentions the fact that he went up to Cambridge with a scholarship to enter King's. Before leaving for Cambridge, he seems to have acquired a high degree of proficiency in the Classics, some intimacy with French (and, of course, English), and more than a nodding acquaintance with German, Italian and Spanish. He had also begun to write verse in English.

At King's, too, Sri Aurobindo did very well. He had his £80 scholarship, and, having passed his preliminary test for the I.C.S., he had a probationership stipend as well. However, all three brothers —Benoy Bhushan, Manomohan and Sri Aurobindo—were often in difficulty, owing to irregular or insufficient remittances from their father but Sri Aurobindo seems on the whole to have done somewhat better than his two brothers. One of his tutors, G.M.Prothero, certified that, as a student, Sri Aurobindo displayed, "very unusual industry and capacity...Besides his classical scholarship he possessed a knowledge of English literature far beyond the average of undergraduates and wrote a much better English than most young Englishmen."[10]

Oscar Browning remarked that, although he had examined papers at thirteen examinations, he had never during that period seen such excellent papers as Sri Aurobindo's and his 'essay'—a comparative study of William Shakespeare and John Milton—was "wonderful".[11] Sri Aurobindo passed the Classical Tripos in the first division, and also secured a prize for Greek and Latin iambics. Besides he passed the I.C.S. final examinations with credit. Of extra-curricular activity, too, there was much: for example, nationalist speeches at the Indian Majlis and writing poetry. But, from another point of view, it was a life bereft of the usual consolations of a home.

Sri Aurobindo left Cambridge for London in October 1892. He was expected to join the I.C.S., but as he repeatedly failed to appear for the Riding test, he was ultimately disqualified. It is clear Sri Aurobindo himself, "felt no call for the I.C.S. and was seeking some way to escape from that bondage…he managed to get himself disqualified for riding without himself rejecting the Service."[12] A friend, James S. Cotton, now negotiated with the Maharaja of Baroda and secured for Sri Aurobindo a job at Rs 200 per month. This seemed to settle his future, and so he sailed by *S.S.Carthage* and arrived in India early in 1893 and took up his duties in Baroda on 8 February. He moved from the Land Settlement Department, where he had his first assignment, to the Stamps Office, then to the Central Revenue Office and the Secretariat, and so at last to Baroda College, first as Lecturer in French, and later as Professor of English and Vice-Principal.

Fourteen years in England, especially at so impressionable a period of his life, should have completely de-nationalised Sri Aurobindo. This was not how things worked, however; he no doubt grew attached to English and European thought and literature, but not to England or the West; he had no personal ties there.[13] On the contrary, he was happy to be back in India. When he stepped on the soil of India, "a vast calm descended upon him…and surrounded him and remained with him for long months afterwards."[14] He experienced on a later occasion a sense of the vacant Infinite while walking on the bridge of the Takht-i-Suleman in Kashmir, and Mahakali's living presence once filled him with rapture on the banks of the Narmada.[15]

Soon after his return to India, Sri Aurobindo employed special tutors and quickly mastered his mother tongue, Bengali and Sanskrit.

As he was serving in Baroda, it was easy for him to learn Marathi and Gujarati as well. His years at Baroda were years of ceaseless striving and achievement in many fields of activity: teaching, scholarship, political journalism, poetry, Yoga. He dieted on the poets of the West and India, and his library had all the great English poets from Geoffrey Chaucer to Algernon Charles Swinburne. His Bengali tutor, speaking of the 1898-9 period, has recorded that among the English poems on which Sri Aurobindo was then engaged there was one on Savitri also. And, referring to a later period (probably 1905), C.R. Reddy has stated that once A.B. Clark, then Principal of the Baroda College, remarked to him: "So you met Aurobindo Ghose. Did you notice his eyes? There is mystic fire and light in them. They penetrate into the beyond....If Joan of Arc heard heavenly voices, Aurobindo probably sees heavenly visions."[16]

Meanwhile certain developments were taking place in the country and Sri Aurobindo could not be a disinterested spectator. India was the Mother, and foreign rule was a curse. The politicians of the old school, who believed in petitioning to the British rulers to vouchsafe doses of self-government, seemed to be out of tune with the temper of the people. The decision of Lord Curzon's Government to partition Bengal was felt as a blow to the unity of the Bengalees and a challenge to awakened India. Sri Aurobindo had been for some time playing an important part in the behind-the-scenes activities of the Indian National Congress. Now he decided to come into the open, leave the Baroda Service, and take the plunge into politics. He became the de facto editor of the 'extremist' Calcutta daily, *Bande Mataram*. The paper took its name from the opening line of a song in a famous Bengali novel—*Ananda Math* by Bankim Chandra Chatterjee, and meant simply, "Mother, I bow to Thee"! But now it became a rallying political slogan, a powerful battle-cry, and even a potent mantra. As Sri Aurobindo himself remarked:

> The mantra had been given and in a single day a whole people had been converted to the religion of patriotism. The Mother had

> revealed herself. Once that vision has come to a people, there can be no rest,no peace, no further slumber till the temple has been made ready, the image installed and the sacrifice offered. A great nation which has had that vision can never again bend its neck in subjection to the yoke of a conqueror. [17]

Sri Aurobindo simultaneously took charge of the new Bengal National College, though later on he gave up the Principalship to devote himself entirely to politics. He was now content with a salary one-fifth of what he had been drawing at Baroda for some years.

Sri Aurobindo's open involvement in politics lasted about three and a half years, from the middle of 1906 to the beginning of 1910. This included a whole year of incarceration in the Alipore Jail in connection with the Muzzaferpore outrage which had caused the death of two innocent European ladies. A few dates may be given as the significant landmarks of Sri Aurobindo's political period:

August 1906

Sri Aurobindo was in effective charge of both *Bande Mataram* and the Bengal National College.

December 1906

At the Calcutta session of the Indian National Congress, Sri Aurobindo played a prominent part, along with noted fellow Nationalists like Bal Gangadhar (Lokamanya) Tilak and Lala Lajpat Rai.

July-September 1907

Arrested in July but released on bail, Sri Aurobindo stood trial in September with regard to certain articles that had appeared in *Bande Mataram*, but the prosecution failed, and he was acquitted.

December 1907

Sri Aurobindo attended the Surat Congress and in alliance with Tilak and other Nationalist 'Extremists' broke with the Moderates led by Phirozeshah Mehta and G.K. Gokhale, so the Congress ended in a fiasco.

January 1908

Sri Aurobindo was with Yogi Lele for three days in Baroda, and had an ineffable Advaitic-Vedantic experience which enabled him to see, "with a stupendous intensity the world as a cinematographic play of vacant forms in the impersonal universality of the Absolute Brahman."[18] During the next four months, Sri Aurobindo was simultaneously engaged in yoga *and* politics; a union of inner calm and hectic outer activity.

May 1908

On 4 May 1908, Sri Aurobindo was arrested in connection with the Muzzaferpore outrage, and was later moved to Alipore, and placed in solitary confinement.

19 May 1908 to 5 May 1909

The Alipore Bomb Case and the trial of Sri Aurobindo provoked nationwide interest. It was in the course of his solitary confinement in the Alipore Jail that Sri Aurobindo had his great mystic experience —Narayana *darshan*—which he was later to describe in his Uttarpara speech. The prosecution failed once again, and Sri Aurobindo was acquitted and released on 6 May 1909.

30 May 1909

Sri Aurobindo made his celebrated speech at Uttarpara. His new sense of spiritual direction was revealed, not merely by this speech, but also by the two weekly newspapers that he now launched, the *Karmayogin* (in English) and *Dharma* (in Bengali).

25 December 1909

Sri Aurobindo published his 'Open Letter to My Countrymen', which was to be his "last political will and testament", in the *Karmayogin* in case he was deported by the Government.

February 1910

Sri Aurobindo secretly left British India and reached the French settlement of Chandernagore, near Calcutta.

April 1910

Leaving Chandernagore, Sri Aurobindo reached Pondicherry, another French possession but further to the South of India, on 4 April, and remained there—his place of retreat, his cave of *tapasya* [19]—till he passed away in the early hours of 5 December 1950.

The period of Sri Aurobindo's active participation in politics was short, yet he shot to prominence quickly, and his words moved men's hearts more than the proverbial trumpet. His direction of *Bande Mataram* was an illustrious page in the history of Indian journalism. Not only did he wield a brilliant pen in political controversy, but his pen also did him yeoman's service in political, philosophical and literary exposition. Some of his poetry and translations were published—the five-act blank verse drama, *Perseus the Deliverer*, *Vidula* or 'The Mother to her Son' (from the *Mahabharata*) in *Bande Mataram*, and *Baji Prabhou* in *Karmayogin*. At the time of publication, all these had a pointed political appeal. In the play the stress was on the word 'deliverer'; Vidula exhorts her son to fight while Baji lays down his life in defence of his country. Several of Sri Aurobindo's unpublished writings, including poems, were taken away by the police and filed among the 4,000 exhibits in the Alipore Case. Many are totally lost, but some have been recently recovered and posthumously published.[20]

The Alipore Trial served in no small measure to make Sri Aurobindo's name a household word in India. Having sensationally demolished the prosecution's case against Sri Aurobindo, his counsel C.R. Das, a great name in Indian politics during the 1920s, ended his moving peroration as follows:

> ...Long after the controversy will be hushed in silence, long after this turmoil, this agitation will have ceased, long after he is dead and gone, he will be looked upon as the poet of patriotism, as the prophet of nationalism and the lover of humanity. Long after he is dead and gone, his words will be echoed and re-echoed, not only in India, but across distant seas and lands.

> Therefore, I say that the man in his position is not only standing before the bar of this court, but before the bar of the High Court of History.[21]

Sri Aurobindo continued to be a controversial figure even when he was in prison and when he came out a year later, he was hailed as a prophet, as a leader of humanity. What Tagore says about the prophet and his true role now applied to Sri Aurobindo:

> Then comes the great prophet; and in his life and mind the hidden fire of truth suddenly burns out into flame. The best in the people works for long obscure ages in hints and whispers till it finds its voice which can never again be silenced. For that voice becomes the voice of Man.[22]

Arriving at Pondicherry, which was already a sort of political asylum to several Indian revolutionaries, Sri Aurobindo lived in comparative seclusion after all the blaze of publicity in which he had spent the previous three or four years.

"The lives of the saints", writes William James, "are a history of successive renunciations of complication, one form of contact with the outer life being dropped after another, to save the purity of the inner tone."[23] Schopenhauer adds that, "the more a man belongs to posterity, in other words to humanity in general, the more of an alien is he to his contemporaries."[24] This 'sacrifice' Sri Aurobindo was continually making all his life. Further, to test his power of endurance, he fasted in 1910 for over twenty days. In the Alipore Jail, as a result of fasting for over ten days, Sri Aurobindo lost ten pounds in weight, but otherwise felt stronger at the end of the period. In Pondicherry, his twenty-three-day fast didn't interfere with his full mental and vital vigour and when he broke the fast, he started taking the normal food as before without any problems. Although such austerities didn't really appeal to him, these experiments nevertheless demonstrated that one could, if one wished, draw energy from the vital plane, instead of depending daily on the physical food but of course, this could not go on for ever.

Sri Aurobindo lived in Pondicherry for nearly forty-one years. This was the last, greatest and most unique phase of his life. Here too a few landmarks may be indicated:

4 April 1910

Sri Aurobindo arrived in Pondicherry and stayed at Shanker Chetty's house as his guest till October, when he moved into a rented house, a few disciples gathering around him there.

1910–1914

These were the years of 'silent yoga'. Sri Aurobindo dropped all political activities and felt free to concentrate on spiritual work, seeing clearly that Britain would be forced by the inexorable march of events to concede independence to India. He felt that all human activity was a "thing to be included in a complete spiritual life".[25] In the course of his yoga he was able to posit the dynamic spiritual principle, which he called the Supermind (after *vijñāna* in Sanskrit), and he felt that the way was now open for the emergence of the Gnostic Man or the Superman.

29 March 1914

Madame Mirra Richard (the Mother) meets Sri Aurobindo and recognises him as the Krishna of her visions and spiritual experiences, the Guru she had been seeking all her life.

15 August 1914

Arya, a monthly journal devoted to "a systematic study of the highest problems of existence", was launched on Sri Aurobindo's forty-third birthday. Madame Richard and Paul Richard collaborated in the venture till they were obliged, owing to the exigencies of the war, to leave for France. The main burden of running the journal fell upon Sri Aurobindo, who wrote most of it. After regularly appearing for about six and a half years, the journal ceased publication in 1921.

24 April 1920

Madame Richard came again, after a residence of some years in Japan, and now stayed on. The circle around Sri Aurobindo gradually grew. *Arya* had spread the Aurobindonian message far and wide, and people with a 'call' to yoga were now drawn to Pondicherry.

1 January 1922

The Mother took entire charge of the house occupied by Sri Aurobindo and his disciples. This became the nucleus of the Sri Aurobindo Ashram, exemplifying the old Hindu ideal of *guru-gṛha-vāsa* (living with the teacher). There were 'evening talks', with the disciples gathering round Sri Aurobindo: and the 'talks' covered almost all subjects under the sun.[26]

24 November 1926

This was the day of realisation (*siddhi*), for on that day Sri Aurobindo experienced the descent of a new power of consciousness, the Overmind, which would prepare the ground for the ultimate descent of the Supermind. Sri Aurobindo now completely withdrew into seclusion, leaving the management of the ashram to the Mother. The 'evening talks' and visitors' interviews ceased. The disciples, however, were able to see Sri Aurobindo on certain days in the year—15 August, 24 November, 21 February and 24 April—and receive his blessings.

23 November 1938

There was a relaxation in the rules relating to Sri Aurobindo's complete retirement, "owing to circumstances, inner and outer, that made it possible for him to have direct physical contacts with the world outside."[27] For the past twelve years he had maintained contact, even with his ashram inmates, only through letters. Now some of his disciples at least were able to meet him almost daily, so the 'evening talks' were resumed. The ashram was growing, and so were Sri Aurobindo's and the Mother's responsibilities. On the '*Darshan* Days', however, people from all over India gathered in Pondicherry and received the blessings of the Master and the Mother. All through his Pondicherry period, Sri Aurobindo's literary and spiritual work went hand in hand, his writing appearing first in the *Arya*, then in book form (usually revised), and again, after 1942, in the various journals dedicated to the exposition of his vision of the future.

11 December 1948

The National Prize (for eminent merit in the Humanities) was awarded to Sri Aurobindo in absentia at the Andhra University Convocation. In his citation, the Vice-Chancellor C.R. Reddy said:

> In all humility of devotion, I hail Sri Aurobindo as the sole sufficing genius of the age...He is among the Saviours of Humanity, who belong to all ages and all nations, the Sanatanas, who leaven our existence with their eternal presence, whether we are aware of it or not...His soul is like a star and dwells apart.[28]

5 December 1950

After a brief illness, Sri Aurobindo passed away at 1.26 a.m., his body reposing "in a grandeur of victorious quiet". For the next four days the body seemed "charged with such a concentration of supramental light that there was no sign of decomposition."[29] On 9 December, the body was buried in the ashram premises at 5 p.m.

The above bare recital of the cardinal events of the Pondicherry period of Sri Aurobindo's life is but the mockery of a biography, for the real life of an 'enlightened one' like him is not lived on the outside for the curious eyes of prying men or for cheap reportage. When the body was consigned to its last resting place, the Mother read the following message, which was both a prayer to Sri Aurobindo and a benediction to the assembled congregation:

> To Thee who hast been the material envelope of our Master, to Thee our infinite gratitude. Before Thee who hast done so much for us, who hast worked, struggled, suffered, hoped, endured so much, before Thee who hast willed all, attempted all, prepared, achieved all for us, before Thee we bow down and implore that we may never forget, even for a moment, all we owe to Thee. [30]

Since his passing away the ashram which grew round him at Pondicherry has grown in strength of numbers and in the variety and intensity of its dedicated work. Although the Mother, Sri Aurobindo's spiritual collaborator during the last thirty-five years of his life, has also left her physical body, she still guides the ashram's destiny.

A couple of points should be stressed before we pass on to a brief—necessarily very brief—consideration and "assessment" of Sri Aurobindo's work in many fields of activity. His retirement to Pondicherry, and later complete seclusion in his own ashram, did not mean a divorce from the ways and problems of average humanity. On the contrary in fact; for the very principle of his yoga, "was not only to realise the Divine and attain to a complete spiritual consciousness, but also to take all life and all world activity into the scope of this spiritual consciousness and action and to base life on the Spirit and give it a spiritual meaning." In his retirement Sri Aurobindo kept a close watch on all that was happening in the world and in India and *actively intervened whenever necessary, but solely with a spiritual force and silent spiritual action.*[31] During the Second World War, he advised all support to the Allies, and later, during the Cripps Mission, he advised acceptance of the British offer. The purblind Congress leaders—M.K. Gandhi, Jawaharlal Nehru, A.K. Azad and the rest, though not Rajaji (C. Rajagopalachari)—rejected his advice, with the consequences (one of them being the Partition) that we all deplore.

Although he did not encourage casual visitors, who generally had only a sightseer's interest or a prying journalistic curiosity, on important occasions he relaxed the rule of seclusion. Prominent Nationalist leaders like C.R. Das, the poet Tagore, the educationists James H. Cousins and C.R. Reddy, his former pupil K.M. Munshi, and several others met Sri Aurobindo at Pondicherry and had fruitful discussions with him.

After his interview, James H. Cousins noted: "I retain a flavour of gentleness and wisdom, breadth of thought and extent of experience that marked him out as one among millions."[32] Tagore's impressions have been cited at the head of this chapter. Of the visitors—poets, painters, musicians, politicians, professors, waifs, sadhus, ecstatics, romantics, idealists, capitalists, labourers—who came to see the Master (or the Mother) and remained as permanent *sadhak*s (practitioners of Yoga) there was no end. President Woodrow Wilson's daughter became a permanent inmate of the ashram.

The community grew month by month, and although variety seemed to be the key-note—variety in colour, creed, community, language, race and occupation—the emotional attachment to Sri Aurobindo and the Mother, the feeling of 'belonging' to them, the sense of dedication to their cause, made the *sadhak*s a true community, a family, an ashram and not just a random collection of all sorts of individuals. And the family overflowed the physical limits of the ashram at Pondicherry, for Sri Aurobindo's disciples were—and are—to be found all over India, and the world.

Many were the tributes that were paid to Sri Aurobindo when the news of his passing away was flashed forth on the radio on the morning of 5 December 1950. One English disciple, Norman Dowsett, wrote on *The Immaculate Hour of Passing*:

THEN STILL THE NIGHT

Only the breath of a sigh
Is heard in the leaves,
Only a whispered goodbye
The earth still cleaves;
Only the sound of His flute
Astir on the breeze—
Then still the night—mute
As the silent trees. [33]

And the Indo-Ceylonese poet, J. Vijayatunga, wrote no less feelingly:

Out of Thy love
For God Thou lovedst us with all our weakness
And animality; Thy radiance cut across

The grossness of our lives, and touched dark corners,
Thy wisdom shed drops upon our dry hearts,
Thy glory, wide as the sea, touched the shores of our darkness.
Are we sad today? Is the earth dark without light?
Nay, Master, Thou didst not live in vain
Thy life sublime and austere was not spent
For naught...Holding to the hem
Of Thy garment we shall raise ourselves
To High Heaven, by thy Grace, if not now
In some distant age, and once again
We shall behold Thee, O Master,
Shining with ever greater lustre, shining
Like the Sun, but unafraid we shall reach Thee
And touch Thee, and be burnt in the Fire
Of Thy love. [34]

III

YOGA

There have been great fighters in modern India like Tilak, philosophers like Vivekananda, poets like Tagore, and 'mahatmas' like Gandhi. But Sri Aurobindo was all these, and a yogi as well. To the question, what is yoga, it is not possible to return an easy or facile answer, and unfortunately the word 'yoga' is being bandied about too often and used too indiscriminately.

"Indian Yoga", writes Sri Aurobindo, "in its essence a special action or formulation of certain great powers of Nature, itself specialised, divided and variously formulated, is potentially one of these dynamic elements of the future life of humanity."[35]

Yoga, then, is the technique of bringing out the fullest possibilities of powers already inherent in Nature. It is really a multiform technique, because one or another of the many powers of Nature could be isolated and its fullest potentialities brought out. Man has a body, a mind, a heart—he has a physical, mental and emotional life—he can work, he can think, he can love. He can exercise his will, he can channel his passions. Any one of his faculties or functions could be isolated and perfected, and we would then have the Yoga of Works (Karma Yoga), the Yoga of Knowledge (*Jnana* Yoga) and the Yoga of Love or Devotion (*Bhakti* Yoga). There are other yogas too like *Raja*, *Hatha*, and Tantra, etc. These are really so many 'paths' leading to God or the Life Divine.

Aurobindo took these and other ideas from the older yogas and evolved a dynamic and truly multiform yoga of his own, which he called Integral or *Purna* Yoga. It was not necessary, he thought, to isolate this or that faculty or instrument; all could be simultaneously used to bring about the desired union with God or the desired transformation of man. He developed his ideas, principally in the 1,000-page treatise, *The Synthesis of Yoga*, but also in his other works, and especially in the thousands of letters to his disciples in which he discussed their particular problems in the larger context of the yoga. Many of these letters have been lately arranged and published in two massive volumes, *On Yoga* (Tomes One and Two), which form an indispensable guide to the yoga of Sri Aurobindo. There is also the more succinct *The Mother*, one of the classics on the subject; and there are the records kept by disciples like Purani, Nirod and Dilip of conversations with the Master; and, finally, there are authoritative expositions by the Mother herself, and disciples like Nolini, Rishabhchand and Pandit. Altogether, it is a vast, and still growing, literature.

Writing on the mystic, Jacob Boehme, J.J. Stoudt says that, "he was a prophet in more than a metaphorical sense because he created a philosophy of history more profound than the dated apocalypses of his contemporaries, he saw a new world emerging from a new man, a new level of religious living begetting a new social order, and, so intense had his sunrise to eternity been for him, he gave himself a place in creating this new world."[36] Sri Aurobindo is that kind and order of prophet, in a sense even more absolute perhaps than that intended by Stoudt. In one of his letters, Sri Aurobindo has briefly explained the total aim of his yoga:

> The object of the Yoga is to enter into and be possessed by the Divine Presence and Consciousness, to love the Divine for the Divine's sake alone, to be tuned in our nature into the nature of the Divine, and in our will and works and life to be the instrument of the Divine. Its object is not to be a great Yogi or a Superman (although that may come) or to grab at the Divine for the sake of the ego's power, pride or pleasure. It is not for Moksha though liberation comes by it and all else may come, but these must not be our object. The Divine alone is our object. [37]

Seize the million, the thousands, hundreds, and tens will be incidentally included in the catch. Possess the Divine and be possessed by the Divine; all else come as a matter of course, and no seeming hardship will really matter. "It is only divine Love", Sri Aurobindo wrote in 1934, "which can bear the burden I have to bear, that all have to bear who have sacrificed everything else to the one aim of uplifting earth out of its darkness towards the Divine."[38] Such Love could be a Cross, a pain that is also a joy. One who is capable of such Love—a Buddha, a Christ, or a Sri Aurobindo—is honoured as a Messiah by us who are of the earth because we know that only such a superman can hold the key to the future; but, "whether this means that the human race in general will at some future epoch evolve, reach upward, to his level, who can say?"[39]

In the past there had been great yogis in India. The *Bhagavad Gita* itself, which is as old as the *Mahabharata*, is a great manual of yoga; and many would say that the Raja Yoga of Patanjali, which tries to mobilise psycho-vital, psycho-mental and physico-mental processes on the issue of a rise to a higher consciousness, is *the* yoga. The *Jnana*, Karma and *Bhakti* yogas too have masses of adherents. What, then, is the speciality about Sri Aurobindo's yoga? Not a mere adding up or jumbling together of all these older methods. It is an *integral* yoga.

The others come in, of course, wherever necessary or possible, but there is some other element also.

Sri Aurobindo's yoga is new because its aims are new and it has to employ means that are new. It aims not at, "a departure out of the world and life into Heaven or Nirvana, but at a change of life and existence." The object sought after, "is not an individual achievement of divine realisation for the sake of the individual, but something to be gained for the earth-consciousness"; and in order that this transformation of earth-consciousness may take place, "a method has been pre-conised"[40] which uses the old techniques with a new urgency and motive power. A new principle of instrumentation, namely the Supermind, is to be brought down and made to inhabit and energise the earth consciousness. The physical, vital, mental, all would then come under the supramental influence, just as now the mental consciousness is able—thanks to our arts and sciences—to influence our physical and vital life. Even now the human mind, while it has some influence on our body and passions, is unable to influence the life of the mere animal, except to a very limited extent. The descent of the Supermind, when it takes place, will naturally mean the possibility of a great extension in the power of the human consciousness, far beyond the present power that men have, and the higher mental power a few have. At first only a handful of people will embody this supramental consciousness, but there will be radiating influences which will gradually encompass all earthly life.

While this was the possibility that Sri Aurobindo saw—a possibility that seemed to him an inevitability, while he doubtless experienced in the course of his forty-five years' yoga a power of consciousness denied to average humanity, yet it was not the supramental that he was able to realise but a middle power between the Mind and the Supermind, which he called the Overmind. This was his realisation or *siddhi* on 24 November 1926. "It is only the supramental Force that works absolutely", he wrote in 1935, "because it creates its own conditions. But the Force I am using is a Force that has to work under the present world conditions. It is not the less a Force for that."[41]

Twelve years later, he wrote again that his yoga had enabled him to put only an Overmind force on human affairs, with the result that when it acted in the material world it was, "inextricably mixed up in the tangle of the lower world force that its results, however strong or however adequate to the immediate object, must necessarily be partial."[42] But he had no doubt that, since the Overmind was a realised fact, the Supermind too would be—sooner or later. He refused therefore to be daunted by defeat or by the doom that seemed to hover over man in the atomic age. A few months before he passed away, when conditions were pretty bleak because of the Cold War and the warm Korean War, because of the Indo-Pakistani imbroglio, Sri Aurobindo wrote to a disciple: "I am not disposed even now, in these dark conditions, to consider my will to help the world as condemned to failure."[43] The fact was that, although himself realising the Highest consciousness (including the Supermind), Sri Aurobindo nevertheless found it convenient to bring down only the Overmind into the physical being and consciousness, but even so the Supermind was always behind it. The limitations were apparently self-chosen, the aim being to keep the link with the physical consciousness and use the higher powers from that stand. In this the Overmind helped Sri Aurobindo as a medial force, a bridge, and for the time being he was content to operate from that bridge, to use that force, with the Supermind always poised in the inner being, ready for deployment in an emergency.

It would be clear from the foregoing that Sri Aurobindo's 'retreat' was no running away from the demands of life but rather a different way of confronting life's challenges with a view to mastering them and laying the foundations of a new life here on earth. "My own life and my Yoga", he said once, "have always been, since my coming to India, both this-worldly and other-worldly without any exclusiveness on either side."[44] He has, again, compared his yoga to a battle; and, "its very attempt raises all sorts of adverse forces and one must be ready to face difficulties, sufferings, reverses of all sorts in a calm and unflinching spirit."[45] When one dares into the occult or hidden regions of Nature, the forces of the subtle physical and supraphysical planes are seen to be active—sometimes to help, sometimes to hinder; and hence the need for faith, calm, patience and fearlessness. Yoga, after all, is the razor's edge. Its first taste could be "bitter like poison" on account of the difficulties to be faced and surpassed, but the end would be "sweet as nectar" because of "the joy of realisation, the peace of liberation or the divine *Ananda*."[46]

In the first three parts of *The Synthesis of Yoga*, Sri Aurobindo outlines the dynamics of the three classical paths—the Yoga of Divine Work, the Yoga of Integral Knowledge, and the Yoga of Divine Love, and in the final part describes the Yoga of Self-Perfection which uses all three disciplines in a bold way:

> To arrive by the shortest way at the largest development of spiritual power and being and divinise by it a liberated nature in the whole range of human living is our inspiring motive.
>
> The principle in view is a self-surrender, a giving up of the human being into the being, consciousness, power, delight of the Divine, a union or communion at all the points of meeting in the soul of man, the mental being, by which the Divine himself...shall by the light of his presence and guidance perfect the human being in all the force of the Nature for a divine living...The liberated individual being, united with the Divine in self and spirit, becomes in his natural being a self-perfecting instrument for the perfect outflowering of the Divine in humanity.[47]

The individual should perfect himself first, then seek to perfect the race. The spiritual aspirant who desires self-perfection has to put forth a certain personal effort:

> ...the triple labour of aspiration, rejection and surrender—an aspiration vigilant, constant, unceasing—the mind's will, the heart's seeking, the assent of the vital being...rejection of the movements of the lower nature, rejection of the mind's

> ideas, opinions, preferences, habits, constructions, so that the true knowledge may find free room in a silent mind, rejection of the vital nature's desires, demands, cravings, sensations, passions, selfishness, pride, arrogance, lust, greed, jealousy, envy, hostility to the truth, so that the true power and joy may pour from above into a calm, large, strong and consecrated vital being, rejection of the physical nature's stupidity, doubt, disbelief, obscurity, obstinacy, pettiness, laziness, unwillingness to change, *tamas*, so that the true stability of light, power, *ananda* may establish itself in a body growing always more divine; surrender of oneself and all one is has and every plane of the consciousness and every movement to the Divine and the Shakti.[48]

To aspire for the Divine and only the Divine, to reject from one's life all that is in any way undivine and so make oneself a plastic instrument in the hands of the Divine—this, in a nutshell, is the way of this yoga. Once self-perfection is achieved, one will be able to strive for the perfection of others and the world. It is therefore very truly a self-transforming and world-transforming yoga.

Besides systematically expounding his own yoga in *The Synthesis of Yoga* and some of his other writings, Sri Aurobindo has also given us brilliant commentaries on the *Isha Upanishad* and the *Bhagavad Gita*. Elucidating the last (the eighteenth) stanza of the former, Sri Aurobindo says that, "the sign of right action is the increasing and finally the complete submission of the individual to the divine Will", and in a footnote adds: "Here the offering is that of completest submission and the self-surrender of all the faculties of the lower egoistic human nature to the Divine Will-force."[49]

The *Gita*, of course, is a pocket spiritual encyclopaedia, for all spiritual problems are "briefly but deeply dealt with" in it, and in his *Essays on the Gita* Sri Aurobindo has "tried to bring out all that fully".[50] Almost every great philosopher and thinker in India has commented on the *Gita*, and in our own century Tilak, Gandhi, Sarvepalli Radhakrishnan, Rajagopalachari and Vinoba Bhave—

among others—have made the *Gita* a text (or pretext) to present their own philosophies.

Sri Aurobindo has likewise given an Aurobindonian version of the *Gita*. His writing often rises to heights of poetry, and the last chapter is magnificent. The key stanza in the whole *Gita* is, without question, the sixty-sixth in the last chapter: "Cast away all your dharmas and take refuge in Me alone; there is no need to grieve, for I shall liberate you from all sins." Sri Aurobindo says that these words, "express the most complete, intimate and living relation possible between God and man."[51] Rejection of all dharmas and total surrender to the Divine, such should be the decisive action. The rest would follow, for now the Divine would take up the responsibility. Krishna tells Arjuna in effect:

> This then is the supreme movement, this complete surrender of your whole self and nature, this abandonment of all dharmas to the Divine who is your highest Self, this absolute aspiration of all your members to the supreme spiritual nature…This is the supreme way because it is the highest secret and mystery and yet an inner movement progressively realisable by all.[52]

The three movements of the Aurobindonian yoga, as given in *The Mother*, are Aspiration, Rejection, Surrender. The *Isha Upanishad*, as interpreted by Sri Aurobindo, lays stress on the right Knowledge of the Lord and total submission (or surrender) to Him. In the *Gita*, too, the stress is on aspiration, abandonment (or rejection) and complete surrender. Sri Aurobindo thus traces the seeds of his yoga to the *Gita*, the *Isha Upanishad*, and the Veda generally. Sri Aurobindo's yoga is new in its practical urgency and dynamism, but its strength is that it has its roots in India's spiritual past.

IV

POLITICS

Not much need be said about Sri Aurobindo's politics. While an undergraduate at Cambridge, he was not only an active member of the Majlis but he also joined an Indian Secret Society, functioning from London, known as the 'Lotus and the Dagger'. On his return to India, he contributed a series of articles to the *Indu Prakash*, entitled 'New Lamps for Old', criticising the old leaders for their weak-kneed policy of political mendicancy. His own ideas regarding the emancipation of India were as yet nebulous; there was plenty of idealism and impatience, but little constructive thinking.

It was after his turn to yoga in the early years of the new century that his political ideas began to acquire definiteness and the accents of authority. In fact, he first went to yoga to be able to perfect his instruments so that they might serve the country more efficiently and purposefully. The Curzonian policy of repression and the decision to split Bengal into two halves brought matters to a head. In 1905 Sri Aurobindo wrote the pamphlet, *Bhawani Mandir*, and this 'packet of political dynamite' circulated privately and rattled the bureaucracy. Recovered but recently, the 'scheme' is reproduced in full in A.B. Purani's *Life of Sri Aurbindo,* and reading it today we can see both why Sri Aurobindo could not but write that pamphlet and why the bureaucracy tried to suppress it.

Bhawani Mandir is partly a diagnosis of India's ills and partly the prescription of a radical cure. India's ills flowed from her want of strength; what was the remedy, then? "We have to change our natures, and become new men with new hearts", he said. "Strength can be created only by drawing it from the internal and inexhaustible reservoirs of the Spirit, from that Adya-Shakti of the Eternal which is the fountain of all new existence." In a stirring oration Sri Aurobindo asked for dedicated men, even as Jesus said,

"Follow me, and I will make you fishers of men." "Come then", said Sri Aurobindo,

> ...hearken to the call of the Mother. She is already in our hearts waiting to manifest Herself, waiting to be worshipped—inactive because the God in us is concealed by *tamas*...You who feel Her stirring within you, fling off the black veil of self, break down the imprisoning walls of indolence, help Her each as you feel impelled, with your bodies or with your intellect or with your speech or with your wealth or with your prayers and worship each man according to his capacity. Draw not back...[53]

The practical part of the scheme envisaged the organisation of a band of political *sannyasi*s, dedicated to *brahmacharya* (single-blessedness or celibacy), who would (like the Jesuits of old), be ready to "do or die" (in Gandhi's famous phrase of 1942) for the country. An inaccessible hill-temple dedicated to Bhawani, the Mother as the supreme Shakti, would be the refuge and the training-place of these political knights-errant who would draw their strength, not from the fact of numbers or the possession of arms, but from the home of the Spirit.

The scheme also gave in an appendix, rules for the new order of *sannyasi*s under various heads. Although the scheme may be read today as just an idealistic plan or programme for training a band of selfless, self-perfecting workers dedicated to the service of the country and the community, the Rowlatt Committee Report has recorded that the pamphlet "really contains the germs of the Hindu revolutionary movement in Bengal". Anyhow, soon after writing *Bhawani Mandir*, Sri Aurobindo was in the 'thick of the fight' and no wonder the bureaucracy interpreted the pamphlet in the worst possible light. There was much reading between the lines, and *Bhawani Mandir* was freely (though wrongly) thought to be an invitation to political extremism and even the cult of the bomb.

We have seen, in an earlier section, how Sri Aurobindo's brief sojourn in the political arena was nevertheless a sensational one.

While he was getting deeper into politics, he was at the same time also being drawn more and more towards yoga. The mystic experience at Baroda in January 1908 was a turning point in his life. Henceforth he was in politics, but not quite of it. He was like a man in a trance; he seemed to work and talk as other men but he also seemed to be detached from it all. In 1907 Henry Nevinson had found Sri Aurobindo, "grave with intensity, careless of fate or opinion, and one of the most silent men I have ever known...of the stuff that dreamers are made of..."[54] In 1908 Sri Aurobindo was, if anything, graver and serener, unattached to the ebb and flow of the political flood.

The second great spiritual experience which came to him in the Alipore Jail completed the transformation; from the 'still centre' of detachment he passed on to the circle of purposeful commitment. So far his surface mind had attended to problems like the formulation of a programme for India's regeneration, self-development through self-help—swadeshi, national education, arbitration, etc.—and passive resistance to evil in any of its forms. He did not, of course, make a fetish of the word 'passive'; as K.R. Srinivasa Iyengar points out. "Sri Aurobindo did not rule out violence in all circumstances, but it appeared to him that the bureaucracy, not being of the ruthless Russian kind, could be effectively countered by passive resistance."[55] In many respects—though not in all—the Gandhian 'Constructive Programme' and Civil Disobedience (or *satyagraha*) movements of a later day both flower from the Aurobindonian policies and programmes.

When he came out of prison in May 1909, Sri Aurobindo felt that the movement of national redemption would now take its own proper course and achieve ultimate victory, and he could therefore devote himself entirely to the much vaster problem of human perfection and earth-transformation. But even from his retreat in Pondicherry he had a clear view of the Indian and world situation, and was ready to exert the force that was in his hands—a higher mental or intuitive power of consciousness and, after 1926, an overmental consciousness. Mere words could be misleading, yet the point might be made (hazardous though all such generalisations must be) that the two great creative spirits of modern India—Mahatma Gandhi used *moral* force in politics while Sri Aurobindo used a *spiritual* force, and both sought, in their different ways, to purge politics of its *asuric* and egoistic evils.

V

PHILOSOPHY

In 1934 Sri Aurobindo wrote: "I am supposed to be a philosopher, but I never studied philosophy—everything I wrote came from yogic experience, knowledge and inspiration."[56] Again, declining an invitation to contribute to a volume on 'Contemporary Indian Philosophy', he said that it was "quite impossible for me to write philosophy to order."[57] On a later occasion also, with regard to a statement in an article that he had derived his philosophical technique from Shankara, Sri Aurobindo said:

> That is not true. I have not read much of philosophy. It is like those who say that I am influenced by Hegel. Some even say that I am influenced by Nietzsche...The only two books that have influenced me are the *Gita* and the Upanishads. What I wrote was the work of intuition and inspiration working on the basis of my spiritual experience...Experience and formulation of experience I consider as the true aim of philosophy. The rest is merely intellectual work and may be interesting but nothing more. [58]

Sri Aurobindo's philosophical magnum opus is the luminous and voluminous treatise, *The Life Divine*, a jewel of a title, yet wonderfully apt to describe its total content. It grew out of his experience of the higher planes of consciousness which indicated to him the ultimate possibility of the descent of the Supermind. He sought corroborative evidence in India's ancient scriptures—the Vedas, the Upanishads and the *Gita*—and found it in ample measure. For the rest he had to think out the whole argument and present it in a style that was worthy of the subject. In the first instance it appeared as a sequence of articles in the *Arya*, but subsequently it received careful revision at his hands and appeared in two volumes, each of twenty-eight chapters:

Vol I: 'Omnipresent Reality and the Universe'
Vol II: 'The Knowledge and the Ignorance – The Spiritual Evolution'
Part I: 'The Infinite Consciousness and the Ignorance'
Part II: 'The Knowledge and the Spiritual Evolution'.

The argument, reduced to fundamentals, is simplicity itself. In the first volume, Sri Aurobindo describes the nature or constituents of 'omnipresent Reality', which is made up of two quartets:

A. *Sat* (Existence)
B. *Chit* (Consciousness-Force)
C. *Ananda* (Bliss)
D. Supermind (Real-Idea: *Vijnana*)
D'. Mind
C'. Psyche
B'. Life
A'. Matter

The upper hemisphere or quartet of *Satchidananda* has, in the course of involution—or the descent of consciousness—the phenomenal lapse from undivided to divided existence—become the lower hemisphere of our terrestrial travail made up of Matter, Life, Psyche and Mind. There is a 'veil' now that separates Mind (D') from Supermind, its opposite number in the upper quartet; the creative principle and power of the upper hemisphere, Truth-Consciousness, self-knowledge that is also self-force (D), is both in possession of the essential unity of things and is able out of it to manifest its multiplicity. If humanity and earth-nature are to change decisively, a 'rending' of the 'veil' is necessary, for then the Supermind or the supramental consciousness would operate *here*, even as Mind of the mental consciousness is already operating. Neither the denial of matter through asceticism nor the denial of the Spirit through materialism or hedonism, neither escaping into the upper hemisphere nor absorption in the lower, can solve the age-long problems of mankind. Matter and spirit should be brought into an intimate and integral partnership. Only the Supermind can bring about such a partnership and transformation.

In the first part of the second volume, Sri Aurobindo explains how the Knowledge of the upper quartet became the Ignorance of the lower quartet. Evil and its manifestations are neither eternal undivine powers nor beginningless *maya* but a field of force with a limited validity at the middle mental rung in the stair of consciousness. The dualities are also relativities. Evil will cease when the Ignorance is replaced by spiritual Knowledge. In the second part of the second volume, Sri Aurobindo discusses how this could be achieved. The ascent from Ignorance to Knowledge will be long and slow, and there must be many gradations on the way. In order to reach the Supermind, many levels above the Mind—Higher Mind, Illumined Mind, Intuition, Overmind—will have to be passed. But it can be done, and will be done, leading, "inevitably towards an evolution in the Knowledge, a self-finding and self-unfolding of the Spirit, a self-revelation of the Divinity in things in that true power of itself in Nature which is to us still a Supernature."[59]

The style of *The Life Divine*—if it can be dissociated from the thought—is at once the attraction of the book and also the reason why it exasperates so many readers. J.A. Chadwick (who became Sri Aurobindo's disciple and assumed the name 'Arjava') described the language as 'global', because it tried to express a "global thinking".[60] But once one can surrender to its rhythms, the book really seems to have the "power of creating round us wide circles of peace".[61] Faced by so formidable a revelation, people have been obliged to seek suitable comparisons. D.S. Sarma calls it "a vast philosophical prose epic…on the spiritual evolution of the universe" and describes Sri Aurobindo as "a self-exiled and self-imprisoned Dante" and *The Life Divine* as, "a philosophical *Divina Commedia* having its Inferno in the Spirit's descent into the ignorance of mind, life and matter, its Purgatorio in the ascent to the true knowledge of the so-called Supermind and its Paradiso in the ineffable mysteries of *Satchidananda*. His spiritual guides, his Virgil and Beatrice, are the *Rig Veda* and the *Bhagavad Gita*".[62]

An English critic, G. Wilson Knight, likewise writes: "In reading Sri Aurobindo's colossal work of mystical philosophy, *The Life Divine*, I was continually struck to find how much of his visionary structure was covered by the lucid couplets and fourfold plan of Pope's *Essay*."[63] Besides the *Commedia* and the *Essay on Man*, various other works too, the *Summa Theologica*, for example, have been pointedly compared with *The Life Divine*.

It is thus natural that philosophers should try to see points of resemblance between *The Life Divine* and the thought of other philosophers of the East and of the West. Khalifa A. Hakim finds the great truths of the higher Sufism embodied in Sri Aurobindo's philosophy. S.K. Maitra finds in Sri Aurobindo's thought the "meeting of the East and the West", and he also makes interesting comparisons between Sri Aurobindo and Western thinkers like Plato, Plotinus, Hegel, Hartmann, Bergson, Whitehead and others.[64]

Plato, like Sri Aurobindo, was a seer and a poet, but as a philosopher he was rather less consistent than the Indian thinker. Plotinus' double trinity is paralleled by Sri Aurobindo's double quartets—the upper and the lower hemispheres of omnipresent Reality separated by a veil of obscuration. Whereas the Hegelian dialectic creates the impression that we can reach the Absolute more or less automatically, by sheer power of gravity as it were, in the Aurobindonian view the ascent is not altogether inevitable and is really conditioned by the auspicious descent of Divine Grace at every step of the evolutionary advance. Hartmann's dualism of value and reality is apparently in sharp contrast to Sri Aurobindo's affirmation that value is also Reality.

As for Bergson, although he was a 'volcanic thinker' like Sri Aurobindo, his theory of 'creative evolution' lacks both the comprehensiveness and the logical clarity of the theory of Divine Evolution outlined in *The Life Divine*. Again, while Whitehead was a great system-maker (like Sri Aurobindo) and took (like him all knowledge for his province), his philosophy of organism is but a bloodless and loveless abstraction compared to Sri Aurobindo's philosophy of the Life Divine evolving from the life mundane as we know it. Gathering the threads of his argument, Maitra concludes by saying that Sri Aurobindo has really given us "an outline of future philosophy", touching the whole arc of our being and combining the functions of religion, philosophy, art, poetry, and even dedicated work.

Sri Aurobindo's thought is also likely to provoke comparison with the thought of Gurdjieff, Ouspensky and Berdyaev. The Gurdjieff-Ouspensky system is a Gnostic system, like Sri Aurobindo's. There is thus a superficial similarity between the two systems which is no doubt striking.[65] The Ray of Creation and the Aurobindonian stair of Involution-Evolution seem distantly to resemble each other. In the Absolute, according to Gurdjieff, the three basic forces (active, passive, neutralising) are in perfect harmony; but down the scale of creation (or 'involution', as Sri Aurobindo would prefer to call it), the forces separate, mingle, clash, and the divers worlds—the suns, the planets, etc.—come into being.

But even as evolution is possible and is actually proceeding, it is also possible to go *up* the Ray of Creation and reach the highest state. But the Gurdjieff-Ouspensky system is but a tour de force of the speculative intellect, and does not draw (as Sri Aurobindo's system does) from a fount of personal spiritual experience. There is, says D.S. Savage, a deadness, a lack of a living intuition at the root of

Gurdjieff's Gnosis, whereas Sri Aurobindo's vision of the Supermind is an integral unity of apprehension, "a primary spiritual intuition which is only afterwards elaborated by the reasoning mind."[66] As for Berdyaev, his postulation of Nature's 'transfiguration' is rather suggestive in the context of the Aurobindonian postulation of a supramental transformation of man and Nature. Dorothy M. Richardson the novelist once wrote after reading about Sri Aurobindo's life and thought:

> Has there ever existed a more synthetic consciousness than that of Sri Aurobindo? Unifying he is to the limit of the term. How I wish that the now so widely read Berdyaev could have entered it and found therein the answer to his central problem: that of the seemingly impossible transfiguration of the universe.[67]

Similarly, the theory of the 'Mental Ambience' put forward as a speculative possibility by Viscount Samuel in his modern Utopia, *An Unknown Island*, has a remote resemblance to the Aurobindonian supramental consciousness. But the British philosopher had no personal spiritual experience of anything like the Ambience, though he conceded, in the course of a letter, that while he had no doubt merely put it forward "as a speculation, and not even as a hypothesis, still less as a fact...None the less it may be a fact!" [68]

Again, the recently (and posthumously) published book, *The Phenomenon of Man* by Pierre Teilhard de Chardin provokes comparison with *The Life Divine* at many points. Father de Chardin, a Jesuit was also a hard-headed biologist and palaeontologist, and he saw in man the spearhead of the evolutionary adventure. But his thesis, although sought to be scientifically sustained, is also basically the expression of an intuition.[69] He is not unaware of India's contribution to philosophy:

> India—the region *par excellence* of high philosophic and religious pressures: we can never make too much of our indebtedness to the mystic influences which have come down to each and all of us in the past from this 'anticyclone'. But however efficacious

> these currents for ventilating and illuminating the atmosphere of mankind, we have to recognise that, with their excessive passivity and detachment, they were incapable of building the world. The primitive soul of India arose in its hour like a great wind but, like a great wind also, again in its hour, it passed away. How indeed could it have been otherwise? Phenomena regarded as an illusion (*Maya*) and their connections as a chain (Karma), what was left in these doctrines to animate and direct human evolution? [70]

This is, of course, a misreading of ancient Hindu thought and an equating of Indian philosophy with a caricature of Mayavada and Advaita-Vedanta. Besides, de Chardin could not have written like this, and indeed would have greatly benefited, had he been acquainted with *The Life Divine*. For example, Gerald Bullett is particularly attracted to Sri Aurobindo because he tries to transcend the two 'negations', namely the materialist 'denial' and the ascetic 'refusal'.[71]

Nor was Sri Aurobindo a mere mystic or dreamer. "I think I can say", he writes, "that I have been testing day and night for years upon years more scrupulously than any scientist his theory or his method on the physical plane."[72] It is de Chardin's merit as a thinker that he has seen evolution, not as a one-way traffic, but in relation to involution:

> First let it be noted that, by the very fact of the individualisation of our planet, a certain mass of elementary consciousness was originally emprisoned in the matter of earth, ...By its initial chemical composition, the early earth is itself, and in its totality, the incredible complex germ we are seeking.[73]

Again, later in the book:

> ...if the universe, regarded sidereally, is in process of spatial expansion (from the infinitesimal to the immense), in the same way and still more clearly it presents itself to us, physico-chemically, as in process of organic *involution* upon itself (from the extremely simple to the extremely complex)... [74]

Although Sri Aurobindo and de Chardin do not give an identical.

meaning to 'involution', the resemblance in their systems is striking enough. Further, corresponding to the Aurobindonian concept of the Supermind, de Chardin posits the concept of the Omega point:

> Only one reality seems to survive and be capable of succeeding and spanning the infinitesimal and the immense: energy—that floating, universal entity from which all emerges and into which all falls back as into an ocean; energy, the new spirit; the new god. So, as the world's Omega, as at its Alpha, lies the Impersonal.[75]

There is also in de Chardin's thought the same *apparent* ignoration of the problem of pain and evil that we find in Sri Aurobindo's thought.[76] "We mankind", writes Julian Huxley in his 'Foreword' to de Chardin's book, "contain the possibilities of the earth's immense future, and can realise more and more of them...That, it seems to me, is the distillation of *The Phenomenon of Man*."[77] *The Life Divine* is a more complete and convincing revelation than de Chardin's very thoughtful book, but of both it may be said that they are philosophies of affirmation and philosophies of hope.[78]

These parallels (near or distant, close or vague) between aspects of Sri Aurobindo's thought and the thought of some of the Western thinkers of yesterday or today are interesting mainly because they serve to show that there is nothing purely 'Oriental' or 'escapist' in the Aurobindonian philosophy. Sri Aurobindo felt that "man can never get out of the futile circle the race is always treading, until he has raised himself to a new foundation."[79] Such a foundation would be the supramental—when it can be realised. Sri Aurobindo thus fused in his philosophy his answer to the existential problem and the problem of value, and both in terms of logic. And Sri Aurobindo lived his thought and made it dynamic through his yoga. As the Protestant theologian, Otto Wolff, says: "it is Aurobindo, representing mankind, who takes that next step into evolution...by realising it in his own person...Sri Aurobindo's yogic accomplishment practically and existentially fulfilled is a magnificent contribution to various sciences which, in their way and in the frame of their possibilities, confirm Sri Aurobindo throughout."[80]

Not satisfied with so comprehensive a statement of his philosophy, Sri Aurobindo turned to some of its applications in the fields of social and political organisation, and of art and poetry. *The Human Cycle* is thus a notable little treatise on the psychology of social development. Man's primary urge should be to open to the higher light of the overhead planes of consciousness: to turn to the Divine, to achieve a progressive divinisation of his nature. As he once wrote to his brother Barin: "No one is God but in each man there is a God and to make him manifest is the aim of divine life. That we can all do."[81]

When man so manifests the divine, then his philosophy, art, science, ethics, social existence, and vital pursuits will be, "no longer an exercise of mind and life, carried in a circle, but a means for the discovery of a greater Truth behind mind and life and for the bringing of its power into our human existence."[82] When small collectivities thus organise themselves, it should not be difficult for the ideal of human unity also to be realised on truly spiritual foundations, instead of being sought to be realised (as they now are) through mechanical or semi-legalistic organisations like the old League of Nations or the present United Nations. "Human society", Sri Aurobindo writes, "progresses really and vitally in proportion as law becomes the child of freedom; it will reach its perfection when, man having learned to know and become spiritually one with his fellow-man, the spontaneous law of his society exists only as the outward mould of his self-governed inner liberty."[83] Sri Aurobindo therefore concludes his treatise on *The Ideal of Human Unity* with the affirmation that, while the mechanical means now being adopted to forge world unity will have to be pursued for the time being, a lasting solution can come only when the supramental transformation takes place:

> A spiritual oneness which would create a psychological oneness not dependent upon any intellectual or outward uniformity and compel a oneness of life not bound up with its mechanical means

> of unification, but ready always to enrich its secure unity by a free inner variation and a freely varied outer self-expression, this would be the basis for a higher type of human existence.[84]

VI

POETRY

Last of all, let us turn to the poet. There are a few unusual circumstances here: Sri Aurobindo, a Bengali, brought up both in India and England till his twentieth year in ignorance of his mother tongue, became a classical scholar, and wrote verses in Greek and Latin—and also in English—in his Cambridge days. He had besides an intimacy with several European literatures, and after returning to India, he tried to gain an equal intimacy with Sanskrit, Bengali and some other modern Indian literatures. Apart from the undergraduate Greek and Latin exercises in versification, all Sri Aurobindo's poetry is in English.

The earliest pieces were probably written when he was in Cambridge, and some of the additions to *Savitri* were made a few weeks—almost a few days—before he passed away. This means a career extending over a period of sixty years. He was a poet before he became a teacher, a politician or a yogi and remained a poet all through. His *Collected Poems and Plays* appeared in two large volumes, making a total of over 600 pages, in 1942. Since then *Savitri* with its over 800 pages has been given to us. Of posthumous publications, of course, there seems to be no end. If all were collected together, the plays and poems, including the verse translations, should make the formidable bulk of about 3,000 pages. No mean achievement by any standards whatsoever.

One of Sri Aurobindo's most ardent admirers, particularly of his poetry, begins his study thus:

> How shall we crown Sri Aurobindo? Is he greater as a yogi than as a philosopher? Does the literary critic in him out-top the

> sociological thinker? Does he shine brighter as a politician or as a poet? It is difficult to decide. Everywhere Mount Everest seems to face Mount Everest. But when we study this Himalaya of various extremes of height, the first eminence that strikes us is Sri Aurobindo the poet.[85]

The *first*, as also the *last* eminence; for, if Sri Aurobindo's earliest efforts were the epyllions *Urvasie* and *Love and Death*, his latter-day preoccupation was *Savitri*, the great epic which he left all but complete. The corpus is, even on a first view, rich in variety as it is impressive (and more than impressive) in quantity. There are early lyrics included in *Songs to Myrtilla*, for the most part written during 1890-2, and summed up thus by the author in the *Envoi*:

> Pale poems, weak and few, who vainly use
> Your wings towards the unattainable spheres,
> Offspring of the divine Hellenic Muse,
> Poor maimed children born of six disastrous years!...
> For in Sicilian olive-groves no more
> Or seldom must my footprints now be seen,...
> Me from her lotus heaven Saraswati
> Has called to regions of eternal snow
> And Ganges pacing to the southern sea...[86]

Few certainly, though not perhaps quite pale or weak, these early pieces have a disarming sensibility even when they are derivative, and the memorial pieces—to Goethe, Bankim, Madhusudan, Rajnarain, Parnell—really seem to rise to the occasion. In his later years he wrote numerous lyrics, but more and more these came to be charged with philosophical or spiritual import. There is, on the whole, an unflagging mastery both of language and rhythm. Western and Indian mythology agreeably mingle in a poem like *Who* in which Jupiter figures in one stanza and Brahma in the next, and the rhythm has an anapaestic swing as in:

> We will tell the whole world of His ways and His cunning:

He has rapture of torture and passion and pain;
He delights in our sorrow and drives us to weeping,
Then lures with His joy and His beauty again.[87]

This and the other poems in the volume originally published in 1915 have an intellectual and philosophical rather than a purely poetic cast, though there are also pieces like *The Sea at Night* that are powerfully evocative.

Nine Poems, Six Poems, Poems (1941), Poems Past and Present, Last Poems (1952) and More Poems—not to mention the pieces in quantitative metres—taken together constitute a rich treasure-house of lyric poetry. Even of the latest volume, *More Poems*, a reviewer (usually allergic to Sri Aurobindo) writes: "From imitative exercises which reveal the tutelary inspiration of favourite poets—ancient and modern, Eastern and Western—to the playing of infinite variations on himself as sage and seer, we have here in this small volume gleaming gems scattered by a prodigal hand."[88]

But it is the mystic muse that is most typical of Sri Aurobindo at his best. Mystic experience by its very nature is incommunicable in words, and this is the challenge to the poet; it is also a compulsive need. When the poet is able to find the right rhythm and sound, the right word and symbol, he succeeds in communicating the concentrated essence of his experience. To the poet it is a recordation of his experience; to the reader, an intimation of immortality. Only a few lines can be given here by way of illustration:

In that diamond heart the fires undrape... [89]

A breath, a cry, a glimmer from Eternity's face,
in a fragment the mystic Whole...[90]

Rose of God, damask force of Infinity, red icon of might,
Rose of Power with thy diamond halo piercing the night!
Ablaze in the will of the mortal, design the wonder of thy plan,
Image of Immortality, outbreak of the Godhead in man... [91]

Time waits, vacant, the Lightning that kindles,

the Word that transfigures:
Space is a stillness of God building his earthly abode...[92]

And a huddle of melancholy hills in the distance...[93]

In several of his letters, and more particularly in his book, *The Future Poetry*, Sri Aurobindo has referred to the uniqueness of the mantra, the rhythmic vehicle employed by the Vedic seers to communicate to their hearers the language of the Spirit:

> The poetic vision of life is not a critical or intellectual or philosophic view of it, but a soul-view, a seizing by the inner sense; and the mantra is not in its substance or form poetic enunciation of a philosophic truth, but the rhythmic revelation or intuition arising out of the soul's sight of God and Nature and the world and the inner truth...[94]

The seer is the soul, the creator is the soul, the hearer too is the soul; the mantra is seeing and articulating at once, and, at the other end, hearing and seeing at once. When yoga gave Sri Aurobindo this power of vision, the rhythmic word often came unbidden as it were from the overhead—the above-mental—planes of consciousness, and all he had to do was to listen and to transcribe. "There are poets", he once said, "who neither experience nor even understand what they have written. They merely transcribe."[95] Again, on another occasion, "It is the inner hearing. Sometimes one hears a line, a passage, a whole poem, or sometimes they come down. The best poetry is always written in that way."[96] The lines may be revised later on, to fulfil technical requirements; or one may have to wait, till the right phrase or line comes down again.

All this does not mean that poetry is a wholly unpredictable and illogical thing. It is, however, this intangible soul-quality—not its intellectual or philosophical content—that gives poetry its peculiar power to cause *ananda* or pure aesthetic bliss. In his later years, it was increasingly Sri Aurobindo's practice to listen to the rhythmic word from above or generally try to write from an overmental level. Poems like *Thought the Paraclete* and *Rose of God* and, of course, the greater part of *Savitri* could only have been written from an overhead plane of global consciousness.

Aside from the mystic note (or at least alongside of it, for it is really the Great Bass in Sri Aurobindo's poetry), other notes too are occasionally heard. When Hitler's armies were overrunning all Western Europe in 1940 and the future of civilisation seemed very bleak indeed, Sri Aurobindo indited the powerful *The Children of Wotan*, the opening lines of which may be quoted here:

> Where is the end of your armoured march,
> O children of Wotan?
> Earth shudders with fear at your tread, the death-flame laughs in your eyes.
> We have seen the sign of Thor and the hammer of new creation,
> A seed of blood on the soil, a flower of blood in the skies.
> We march to make of earth a hell and call it heaven.
> The heart of mankind we have smitten with the whip of the sorrows seven;
> The Mother of God lies bleeding in our black and gold sunrise."[97]

When most of the other leaders in India—Hindu and Muslim alike—were seized with a paralysis of the will and hence were unable to give the right lead to the country at the time of the war, Sri Aurobindo saw it at its deepest level as the struggle between the *deva*s (the gods) and the *asura*s (the demons) and would have liked India to throw her weight whole-heartedly on the side of the Allies. Failing in his private attempt to persuade the Congress leaders, he contented himself with exerting his spiritual action on the side of humanity and progress. *The Children of Wotan* is charged with power as well as prophecy, not the less Aurobindonian for being so openly 'political'. Nor is it outdated for the edge of its criticism is directed, not against the Nazi alone, but against all apologists of Totalitarianism; don't the latter still boast wherever they may be entrenched in power:

We mock at God, we have silenced the mutter of priests at his altar.
Our leader is master of Fate, medium of her mysteries.
We have made the mind a cipher, we have strangled Thought with a cord;
Dead now are pity and honour, strength only is Nature's lord.
We build a new world-order; our bombs shout Wotan's peace.

"That strain...was of a higher mood", but happily there are more enjoyable strains as well. One such is the sonnet, *A Dream of Surreal Science:*

One dreamed and saw a gland write Hamlet, drink
At the Mermaid, capture immortality;
A committee of hormones on the Aegean's brink
Composed the Iliad and the Odyssey.
A thyroid, meditating almost nude
Under the Bo-tree, saw the eternal Light
And, rising from its mighty solitude,
Spoke of the Wheel and eightfold Path all right.
A brain by a disordered stomach driven
Thundered through Europe, conquered, ruled and fell.
From St. Helena went, perhaps, to Heaven.
Thus wagged on the surreal world, until
A scientist played with atoms and blew out
The universe before God had time to shout.[98]

Nothing could be lighter in touch, or more serious in import. On the other hand, *The Tiger and the Deer* [99] is a vivid evocation of the Terrible and the Mild, concluding with the prophecy:

The mighty perish in their might;
The slain survive the slayer.

But, perhaps, the most enjoyable of the shorter poems is *Despair on the Staircase* which seems to have unaccountably strayed from T.S. Eliot's *Old Possum's Book of Practical Cats*:

Mute stands she, lonely on the topmost stair,
An image of magnificent despair;
The grandeur of a sorrowful surmise
Wakes in the largeness of her glorious eyes…
Her tail is up like an unconquered flag;
Its dignity knows not the right to wag.
An animal creature wonderfully human,
A charm and miracle of fur-footed Brahman,
Whether she is spirit, woman or a cat,
Is now the problem I am wondering at.[100]

Sri Aurobindo's translations form another distinctive group. There is so much of it that really merits detailed study, though, of course, this is not the place for such an undertaking. Sri Aurobindo seems to have followed no principle of exclusion, for he has turned into English (generally verse, occasionally rhythmic prose) whatever happened to catch his fancy or struck a responsive note in his heart. One of the earliest is from Meleager:

Now lilies blow upon the windy height,
Now flowers the pansy kissed by tender rain,
Narcissus builds his house of self-delight
And love's own fairest flower blooms again;
Vainly your gems, O meadows, you recall;
One simple girl breathes sweeter than you all.[101]

At Baroda naturally his interests first hovered round Sanskrit and Bengali poetry. Renderings from the *Ramayana* and the *Mahabharata*, from Chandidas, Vidyapati, Horu Thakur, Nidhu Babu and others, from Bhartrihari, from the *Sagar-Sangit* of C.R. Das, from the Vedas and the Upanishads, from Bankim Chandra and Dwijendralal Roy—all these make for both variety and volume. Sri Aurobindo was willing to turn his hand to these exercises in translation—more often than not they were "amplified transmutations" rather than mere word-for-word paraphrases—without prejudice to those occasions when the surge of inspiration carried him to the high nodal points of his truly creative work. But there is grace and a sufficiency of emotional intensity even in translations like:

> I did not dream, O love, that I
> Would ever have thee back again.
> The sunflower drooping hopelessly
> Expects no Sun to end her pain.

This is from the early Baroda period, and perhaps not revised for publication (it is from a posthumously published volume), but the touch is light, and the sentiment is sugary. *Vidula* (1907) from the *Udyog-Parva* of the *Mahabharata* has a deeper voice as befits the theme, and *Songs of the Sea* (which belongs to an even later period) are more satisfying still. There are forty pieces in diverse stanza forms and ranging over a whole world of sentiment. "The poet", says Iyengar, "approaches the sea as a friend, as a lover, as a loyal subject, as a devotee, as a shadow that must ever pursue the object, as a waif that would return to the bosom of the mother",[102] and always is the articulation apt and adequate, as for example in the last 'song' of all:

> This shore and that shore—I am tired, they pall.
> Where thou art shoreless, take me from it all.
> Pilot eternal, friend unknown embraced,
> O, take me to thy shoreless self at last. [103]

The most ambitious, perhaps, of the verse translations are from Kalidasa. The rendering of *Meghadutam* in terza rima has so far not been recovered, but one hopes against hope it will be. *The Hero and the Nymph*, a verse rendering of Kalidasa's *Vikramorvasie*, was first published in 1911, and there is no better version—or one as good—in English. The prose patches are racy, and the blank verse is supple, full of modulations, and proves equal to the demands made upon it by Kalidasa. The scene in which the hero, Pururavas, moves distraught because of separation from Urvasie, is a prolonged improvisation, and there are echoes of Lear in the storm-scene:

No, I must permit
The season unabridged of pomp; the signs
Of storm are now my only majesty;
The sky with lightning gilt and laced becomes
My canopy of splendour, and the trees
Of rain-time waving wide their lavish bloom
Fan me…the mountains are my citizens,
They pour out all their streams to swell my greatness…[104]

It is natural to pass on from *The Hero and the Nymph* to Sri Aurobindo's own plays. Of these latter, only one—*Perseus the Deliverer*—appeared in his own life-time. Four other five act plays—*Vasavadutta, Rodogune, The Viziers of Bassora* and *Eric*—and an unfinished play entitled *Prince of Edur* have been published posthumously. It is not surprising therefore that *Perseus* is the maturest, but there are fine things in all the plays.

Perseus rescuing Andromeda from the sea-monster is a classical legend which has inspired poets and dramatists of the ancient as well as modern world. Sri Aurobindo has made the legend, "the nucleus round which there could grow the scenes of a romantic story of human temperament and life-impulses on the Elizabethan model… Time there is more than Einsteinian in its relativity, the creative imagination is its sole disposer and arranger; fantasy reigns sovereign; the names of ancient countries and peoples are brought in only as fringes of a decorative background; anachronisms romp in wherever they can get an easy admittance, ideas and associations from all climes and epochs mingle; myth, romance and realism make up a single whole. For here the stage is the human mind of all times…"[105] These prefatory remarks of the author apply more or less to all five plays, whether they *seem* to have an Indian or an alien origin.

In *Perseus the Deliverer*, Polydaon the priest of Poseidon is the central figure; his very sanctity makes him wrong-headedly to assume (like Raghupati the priest in Tagore's play, *Sacrifice*) a cruel and vengeful role, demanding Andromeda's innocent blood.

The central action of the play is Andromeda's releasing the prisoners in an act of pure compassion. This brings upon her head the wrath of Polydaon and Poseidon. She is chained and exposed to the sea-monster. But at the nick of time Perseus saves her. There are many passages of sustained eloquence, for example Polydaon in his mood of megalomania and Andromeda giving utterance to her despair as she is chained to the rock. Perseus speaks the epitaph over the dead body of Polydaon—an epitaph that would fit other fanatics too, a Hitler for instance! Perseus' also is the closing speech, underlying the evolutionary message of the play:

> ...the ascent is slow and long is Time.
> Yet shall Truth grow and harmony increase:
> The day shall come when men feel close and one.
> Meanwhile one forward step is something gained,
> Since little by little earth must open to heaven
> Till her dim soul awakes into the Light. [106]

Less loaded with 'purpose', *Vasavadutta* is more disarmingly romantic, and harks back to the legend in Somadeva's *Katha-sarit-sagara* ('The Ocean of Story') and the famous play by Bhasa. King Udayan is held prisoner by his rival, King Mahasegn, and Princess Vasavadutta is the jailor. The inevitable happens, the jailor becomes Udayan's slave fulfilling her mother's warning:

> Thou wilt know, my bliss,
> The fiercest sweet ordeal can seize
> A woman's heart and body. O my child,
> Thou wilt house fire, thou wilt see living gods;
> And all thou hadst thought and known will melt away
> Into a flame and be reborn.

Like *Vasavadutta*, *Rodogune* too is good romance and good drama, but unlike it, a tragedy. Rodogune is the darling of romance, in whom beauty and fatality meet; she can dream of happiness, but not attain it. She is a fragrant ineffectual flower crushed to death by the insane rivalry of the brothers, Antiochus and Timocles. Their mother, Cleopatra, the Chancellor, Phayllus, Cleone his sister, are a trio of evil-doers. The undemanding Eunice and the honest nurse, Mentho, brighten the picture, the one by her unselfish love, the other by her fearlessness. Antiochus the hero fails by his own excesses as much as through the perfidy of others and Rodogune dies because she will not—she cannot—survive him. There are echoes of *Anthony and Cleopatra* in lines like:

> O wasp soft-settling, poignant, sting,
> Sting me with bliss until I die of it...[107]
>
> A god ! Yes, I have godlike stirrings in me...[108]

Timocles' song too has a faintly Elizabethan ring:

> Will you bring cold gems to crown me,
> Child of light?
> Rather quick from breathing closes
> Bring me sunlight, myrtle, roses,
> Robe me in delight.
> Give me rapture for my dress,
> For its girdle happiness. [109]

Another play to be rescued from oblivion, *The Viziers of Bassora* (1959) is not the least rewarding of the group of four plays. Less poetic perhaps than *Rodogune*, less fierily pointed with purpose than *Perseus the Deliverer*, and less immediately effective than *Vasavadutta*, the play is nevertheless very readable with its well-constructed plot, its striking characterisation and its significant evocation of atmosphere.

There is a good Vizier and a junior bad Vizier; the former's son, Nureddene, loves the Persian slave-girl Anice-al-jalice, but the bad Vizier creates difficulties. The lovers are obliged to flee to Baghdad, where the great Caliph, Haroun al Rasheed (the Charlemagne of Persian History), conceives an instant liking for them and sets Nureddene on the throne of Bassora. "Romance" the play is called, and romance it is. There is no need to read between the lines for any lurking philosophy. The language has a rich sensuousness that succeeds in vividly evoking the atmosphere of ancient Baghdad and Bassora. Nureddene reminds us of Prince Hal in Shakespeare's *Henry IV*. Almuene the bad Vizier is sinister like Heathcliff, and Fareed is a shadowy Linton. Doonya has maiden-fire, and Anice walks in beauty, literally an "emperor's portion". And Harkoos the Ethiopian eunuch is both long-suffering and witty. As a sample of the quality of the verse, Haroun's speech comes handy:

> Meanwhile remember
> That life is grave and earnest under its smiles,
> And we too with a wary gaiety
> Should walk its roads, praying that if we stumble,
> The All-Merciful may bear our footing up
> In His strong hand, showing the Father's face
> And not the stern and dreadful judge.[110]

The more recently published *Eric* (1960) projects the struggle for power between Eric the elected King of Norway and Swegn, the Earl of Trondhjem. The latter's sister, Aslaug, and his wife, Hertha, come to Eric's court dressed as dancing girls, seeking an opportunity to kill him. But Eric and Aslaug themselves fall in love, and old hatred and new love fight for mastery in the heart and soul of Aslaug. In the symbolic realms of the gods, there is likewise a struggle between Thor the ruthless and Freya the auspicious. Love triumphs, Thor's reign is ended, and Freya's begins; Swegn is captured and pardoned, Aslaug marries Eric, and the people of Norway are assured of a termless period of peace and prosperity. The kernel of the drama is the transformation of Aslaug. Changed herself, she effects a like revolution in Eric as well, who now realises that wisdom and power are *not* enough. Love is the ultimate secret, for it transcends both wisdom and power. In the central scene, she debates the issue between hatred and love:

> Not hate,
> O Eric, but the hard necessity

The gods have sent upon our lives, two flames
That meet to quench each other.[111]

Twice she lifts the dagger to kill sleeping Eric, but she cannot do it; it is the climactic moment in the play. Although the dramatic situation, the vivid characterisation, and the precipitate movement of the action have all an Elizabethan vigour and vivacity, the stress is nevertheless on the poetry, for all—situation, characters, action—are seized poetically, and the "leap of love across the abyss of hate" is presented almost as a lightning flash, a blaze of revelation. [112]

The incomplete play, *Prince of Edur* (1961), is dated 1907, and thus belongs to the early months of Sri Aurobindo's editorship of *Bande Mataram*. It would be reasonable therefore to read in this unfinished play (only three out of the projected five Acts were actually written) some sort of political parable. The story is redolent of the romance and heroism enshrined in the pages of James Tod's *Annals of Rajasthan*.

Bappa among the Bheels is really the Gehelote Prince of Edur, and it is his destiny to get the better of all his rivals and enemies —Toraman the Cashmerean, Pratap of Ichalgurh, and Rana Curran the usurper of Edur—and also to marry Comol Cumary, the Rana's daughter. Is Toraman the puffed-up foreigner with a stranglehold on India? Is Rana Curran the local collaborator, ready to compromise with the enemy on terms however ignoble? Is Pratap the symbol of national self-respect and ineffectual courage? And, is Bappa really the preordained redeemer and 'Man of Destiny'? In Act III, Coomood says: "Tomorrow is the May-feast's crowning day" ; and Acts IV and V should unfold tomorrow's crowning purpose, but the play breaks off when Nirmol Cumary makes her affirmation of faith:

Coomood, our fragile flowers will weave
A bond that steel cannot divide, nor death dissever. [113]

It is clear the play was intended to have a happy ending—a purposeful Hamlet achieving his father's crown and marrying a determined Ophelia! The blank verse is colourful and the imagery is rich, and although we are reading verse that wasn't finally revised, the Aurobindonian touch is unmistakable:

> Dare greatly and thou shalt be great; despise
> Apparent death and from his lifted hand
> Of menace pluck thy royal destinies
> By warlike violence. [114]

A casual by-product of the political period, *Prince of Edur* has undertones that strike responsive chords within, and albeit the play is unfinished, one can infer the conclusion in terms of poetic causality. Love is the supreme reality—although it may assume different forms like compassion, adoration, love of the woman, love of the mother. Be it Andromeda, Vasavadutta, Rodogune, Anice-al-jalice, Aslaug, Comol Cumary, woman is love, and love has its varied forms and potencies. It is always love that sets the pace of the action; and love is a redeeming power, and poetry is the native language of love.

As for the narrative poems, *Urvasie, Love and Death* and *Baji Prabhou*, all belong to the pre-Pondicherry period, at least the first two to the Baroda period. *Urvasie* is an Aurobindonian narrative version of Kalidasa's play, *Vikramorvasie*. The Urvasie myth goes back to the Veda, and it has been treated variously by poets and dramatists. Tagore's lyric, *Urvashi*,[115] has been described as "a sheer melodious and poetic cry", a hymn celebrating the Woman Beautiful, the archetypal Helen, glorious Aphrodite whose virtue, whose *swabhāva*, is "to ravish the soul of Paradise". But Sri Aurobindo's poem is epical in cast, and romantic in its impulsion. *Love and Death* is more compact but no less charged with romantic fervour. Love is the theme of both poems, love that dares everything, and sacrifices everything (except itself). Kshatriya or Brahmin, love is the great leveller. It is the sweet uncalculating madness, but of incalculable value Pururavas and Urvasie, Ruru and Priyumvada, come together, and they perceive that their union is,

> ...magically
> Inevitable as a perfect verse of Veda. [116]

Baji Prabhou, on the other hand, is about war and heroism and sterling patriotism; making their stand in "a tiger-throated gorge", Baji and his band of stalwart warriors resist the invaders and make a Thermopylae of Raigarh. It is Baji's "finest hour"; he has upheld Shivaji's trust, and he has changed a possible Mogul victory to a complete rout.

Love and war: the tried old themes of epic and romance; and in *Ilion* Sri Aurobindo attempted an epic on a much more ambitious scale. Lotika Ghose has recorded that to a query about Sri Aurobindo's poetry Frederic Spiegelberg of the Stanford University answered with the counter-question: "Isn't it entirely Greek?"[117] *Ilion* at least is certainly Greek—though not entirely! While experimenting on classical metres, it was but natural that Sri Aurobindo should feel particularly attracted to the hexameter.

It appears that one of his classmates at Cambridge, Hugh Norman Ferrar, once read out a line from Homer or a line from Arthur Hugh Clough that was typically Homeric which he thought was the most characteristic line, and that gave Sri Aurobindo the swing of the metre.[118]

Beside developing his own theory of true quantity in English, Sri Aurobindo wrote *Ahana* in rhymed hexameters and the epic *Ilion* in unrhymed hexameters. *Ahana* is a sustained and nobly articulate philosophic poem of over 500 lines but cast in the form of a long supplication by humanity followed by Ahana, the Goddess of Dawn, responding, giving the categorical promise: "Lo, I come, and behind me Knowledge descends..."[119]

But *Ilion*, although left incomplete, is superb in its own way. Homer's *Iliad* begins with the tenth year of the siege of Troy and concludes with the death and funeral rites of Hector. The subsequent history of the Trojan War may be pieced together from references in other poems of olden times. The Wooden Horse episode is narrated by Aeneas to Dido in the *Aeneid*. The interval between Hector's death and the burning of Troy was filled with the achievements of Memnon and Penthesilea, the treacherous killing of Achilles by Paris, the quarrel between Odysseus and Ajax, the killing of Paris with the bow of Philoctetes, and other episodes since commemorated in tragedy and heroic poetry.

From the nine Books of *Ilion* now available it is difficult to say how Sri Aurobindo had planned to plot his epic. The editor's prefatory note says that the poem "deals with events on the last day of the siege of Troy". In these nine Books the centre of the action is the issue between Penthesilea and Achilles and the issue is not concluded in Book IX, which is itself extant only as a fragment. In the first Book of the *Aeneid*, Virgil makes Aeneas recall, among other episodes of the Trojan War:

> ...Penthesilea leading the crescent shields of
> The Amazons and storming through the melee like a fire,
> Her bare breast thrusting out over the golden girdle,
> A warrior queen, a girl who braved heroes in combat.[120]

It was thus with a sure sense of epic appropriateness that Sri Aurobindo cast his epic as the clash between Penthesilea and Achilles, even as Homer had concentrated on Hector and Achilles. Probably, *Ilion*, had it been completed, would have ended with the death of Penthesilea at the hands of Achilles and of Achilles at the hands of Paris.

Ilion begins with Achilles sending word to the Trojans that they might still purchase peace with honour if they surrendered Helen and agreed to his own marriage with Polyxena, Priam's daughter. An assembly of the Trojan senators is called—"this last of Ilion's sessions"—and Antenor the aged statesman counsels a policy of lying low and secret preparation. Laocon and Paris, however, counsel defiance as Moloch does in *Paradise Lost*, and so the die is cast. There are partings on the eve of the battle—Anchises and Aeneas, Antenor and Halamus, Paris and Helen, Paris and Cassandra. Meanwhile Achilles has learned of the rejection of his offer and decides upon instant battle. There is a parallel assembly of the Greek chieftains, and after hearing Agamemnon, Menelaus and Odysseus, they too decide to join the fray at Achilles' side. In a short Book Achilles takes leave of his mistress, Briseis. There is also a synod of the gods on Olympus, and the future is dimly determined after a long debate: "And in the noon there was night. And Apollo passed out of Troya."[121] The battle at last begins, and now one side, now another seems to get the upper hand; when the poem abruptly ends, Penthesilea is not dead yet, and Achilles is still alive.

But although incomplete, *Ilion* is an astonishing work. It has a true epic surge, massiveness of conception and splendour of detail in execution. Homer's heroes and heroines, gods and goddesses, reappear somewhat altered in mien and raiment, yet clearly recognisble. And Penthesilea—who is portrayed as an Eastern, even an Indian, warrior-queen—is superb. The debates are elaborated with extravagance in true epic style, and the similes too are characteristically Homeric, at times indeed out Homering Homer without quite ceasing to be Aurobindonian. Even metrically the poem, especially the earlier portion which had received careful revision at Sri Aurobindo's hands, is strikingly articulate, the steady dactylic flow giving it a volume and power of movement not often found in English poetry.[122]

VII

SAVITRI

There remains *Savitri*.

Reading *Ilion* people interject: "Isn't it entirely Greek?" Reading *Savitri* people might likewise exclaim: "How entirely Indian!" These can only be one's first reactions. Closer study must reveal whole new universes of meaning—and this is particularly true of *Savitri*. Gilbert Murray says rightly that, "one cardinal fact about great poetry...is that its main value lies in a process, not in a result...we do not understand a great poem till we have felt it through and as far as possible recreated in ourselves the emotions which it originally carried."[123] And A.E.

Housman says that it is the peculiar function of poetry, "not to transmit thought, but to set up in the reader's sense a vibration corresponding to what was felt by the writer."[124]

The Hindu tradition is to read great poetry—say the *Ramayana*, the *Gita* or the *Bhagavata*—in a mood of reverent attention over a period of years, coming to it again and again, for not in one reading alone can one hope to conquer its heights of significance. *Savitri* too calls for such continuous and reverent study. If it baffles us at first, it may be that it is a new kind of poem, demanding a new alertness in response.

Savitri was begun in the closing years of the last century and concluded about the mid-point of the present century. It is a great Yogi's ripest and completest poetic testament to our time and all time. It is the story of a heroine enshrined in immemorial Hindu legend, and it carries the name of the holiest of Hindu mantras. It spans the past, the present and the future, man, Nature and God; it has an immediate human urgency, and also an enveloping cosmic background. Its very composition is largely the result (so it is confidently claimed) of a new aesthesis with its source of origin located in the overhead planes. In *The Human Cycle*, Sri Aurobindo had written:

> A time comes when the creator of beauty revolts and declares the charter of his own freedom, generally in the shape of a new law or principle of creation, and this freedom once vindicated begins to widen itself and to carry with it the critical reason out of all its familiar bounds. A more developed appreciation emerges which begins to seek for new principles of criticism, to search for the soul of the work itself and explain the form in relation to the soul or to study the creator himself or the spirit, nature and ideas of the age he lived in and so to arrive at a right understanding of his work.[125]

In *Savitri*, Sri Aurobindo declared his charter of freedom, and it behoves the reader of the poem to, "search for the soul of the work itself and explain the form in relation to the soul." This is no easy task, much less a task that can be hurried through, but one can at least approach this task with due humility. "There must be a new extension of consciousness and aesthesis," says Sri Aurobindo elsewhere, "to appreciate a new kind of mystic poetry."[126] At any rate, patience, receptiveness and humility may be expected to pave the way towards an appreciation of this great epic, this symphonic recordation of a great yogi's mystic apprehension of the aspirations and struggles of mankind for defeating death and achieving immortality.

Let us now turn, in the next part, to the poem itself.

PART II

SAVITRI

Meet ye the Dawn
as she shines wide
towards you
and with surrender
bring forward
your complete energy.
Exalted in heaven
is the force
to which she rises
establishing the sweetness;
she makes the luminous worlds
to shine forth
and is a vision
of Felicity.

Rig Veda

THE EXORDIUM

> "If seeds in the black earth can turn into such beautiful roses, what might not the heart of man become in its long journey towards the stars?"
>
> G. K. Chesterton

I

'THE SYMBOL DAWN'

Sri Aurobindo's chosen aim in life was to show earth-bound mortals the path that leads to the Life Divine. It was to illustrate this passage to the earthly paradise that he wrote his epic *Savitri*, a masterpiece of sustained philosophical motivation and steeped in mysticism and yoga *sadhana*.

The well-known story of the young wife, Savitri, who saved her husband from an untimely death, thus scoring a victory over the seeming inexorability of Fate, is here swathed in the robes of Vedantic metaphysics and given a poetic reincarnation. Savitri thus evokes, not only the heroic girl-wife of immemorial legend, but also our Universal Mother who bears with infinite patience and immaculate strength the trials and tribulations of mortality and succeeds in the end in vouchsafing immortality to the children of the earth.

This ambrosial story is unfolded to the *sahṛdaya* through a succession of images and symbols. Sri Aurobindo's poem opens, as a literary epic usually does, on the crucial day that is to witness the central act of the epic. The past is mapped out in a sudden flashback, the future will be summed up later. The present is what matters, and the poem is concerned with it.

Savitri, the princess of Madra and darling daughter of King Aswapati, has married the exiled King Dyumatsena's dear son, Satyavan. She is living in the forest with her husband and his elders, sharing uncomplainingly their austere life. Between Savitri and Satyavan a true marriage of minds has been effected. Satyavan is blissfully happy; Savitri too, but her joy is marred by the uneasiness which has been caused by her knowing the approaching end—the fate of Satyavan—as warned by the celestial bard, Narad. Thus the young wife perforce leads a two-fold existence, outwardly serving her elders and preserving an angelic calm, but inwardly dreading the Day and its ominous consequences. And the Day has now arrived. The poem starts here:

Night is fleeing and Dawn is approaching.

It was the hour before the Gods awake.[1]

It is an arresting opening, instinct with immeasurable significance. This first canto evokes the 'symbol dawn' and dwells on its varied filiations with life and the spiral of Consciousness. The whole canto is so charged with mystic symbolism that, in a manner of speaking, it is dense and not easily penetrable. Such poetry makes its impact on us by sudden illuminations rather than by the dull steady light of a logical sequence of ideas. A vision is presented to us, and it slowly grows and expands its orbit. First there is the Night—it is pitch dark, for generally the hour immediately preceding Dawn is the darkest of the hours of darkness. Yet, through this dense night, peep the rays of twilight. Presently Dawn envelops the world in a maze of hazy light, and darkness withdraws quiveringly, like the demoness Lankini leaving her guardianship of Lanka's gates with the approach of the

Sun-like resplendent Hanuman. The process is simultaneous—light coming and darkness retreating and vanishing. And Dawn heralds the Day, even as Aruna heralds Surya.

This sublime picture of Dawn is verily infused with the symbolism of growth in consciousness: that is, Woman inconscient waking up from her stupor and becoming slowly transformed into the superconscient goddess. Sri Aurobindo's aim in retelling the familiar story of Savitri is to show how the mind that at first partakes of the inconscience of the lowest depths or rungs of life, passes through successive stages of evolution, and at last attains the highest, the Superconscient. In the first canto itself Sri Aurobindo hints at these vistas of higher consciousness, leading man from the lowest to the topmost rung of the evolutionary ladder.

The key symbol is Dawn. It is preceded by Night which is both silent and grim:

> Almost one felt, opaque, impenetrable
> In the sombre symbol of her eyeless muse
> The abysm of the unbodied Infinite...[2]

There is a shower of diction evoking the deep, impenetrable, lethargic, sombre, incomprehensible night. Inconscient matter lies inert, like a coiled pythoness of a woman:

> Its formless stupor without mind or life.... [3]

But in this seemingly 'fathomless zero' lie nevertheless the germs of immortal life. The banian tree waxes immense through centuries in its majestic grandeur. But where lay its beginning? In the tiny seed planted in the womb of the nascent earth! Thus, for the life that ultimately attains the Superconscient, the germ still is the inert, unformed, inconscient matter.[4] This germ stirs to induce the birth of life. The stir is very slight, gentle and almost imperceptible; it is a "nameless movement, an unthought idea." This movement is personified in a "long lone line of hesitating hue" that heralds the coming Dawn; bringing in her wake the promise of the supramental age:

> Dawn built her aura of magnificent hues.... [5]

Earth's children have risen, and they spring to their daily tasks. Savitri too has risen. But although she is in it, she is not of it. When people around her are immersed in their daily tasks, she goes about with her heart rendered numb by the coming ordeal. Her face is calm, and outwardly she is merely the stern daughter of Duty. But:

> A dark foreknowledge separated her
> From all of whom she was the star and stay...[6]

She has to face an ordeal and save Satyavan and safeguard humanity's future, and to accomplish this divine task,

> Unhelped she must foresee and dread and dare. [7]

For Savitri knows that this long-awaited Dawn ushers in "the day when Satyavan must die".

So much for the coming of light and the gathering of consciousness out of night and unformed matter. In this canto Sri Aurobindo uses a carefully balanced structure of symbols to demonstrate the emergence of knowledge from the amorphous matter of ignorance. Three women are introduced in this connection. The swarthy woman, Night; the efflorescent damsel, Dawn; and, mediating between them, Savitri, who is human as well as divine.

Night is like Lankini, the demoness-deity of Ravana's Lanka. It is next to impossible to detect life in any form or cultivate consciousness of any kind in this unintelligible chaos. This woman clad in funereal robes is the denial of all hopes—or so it seems at first. The idea of supramental bliss is incongruous in the context of this impenetrable veil of unfeeling, unintelligible matter. Where, then, is the hope for man—Earth's child—who yearns for the Life Divine, when what he faces is this:

> ...shadow spinning through a soulless Void...? [8]

But this dark mud nevertheless contains the sapling for tomorrow's fresh white lotus.

Presently Earth's child sees the gay dawn approaching, and most welcome is her approach. It is the Goddess Usha who symbolises the Superconscient. Man naturally wants to cast away the badges of temporal limitation that he has been wearing till now, and gather the life eternal that Usha symbolises. She comes bringing with her the "God-touch" that promises Fulfilment and interprets:

> ...a recondite beauty and bliss
> In colour's hieroglyphs of mystic sense...
> ...the lines of a significant myth
> Telling of a greatness of spiritual dawns...[9]

Goddess Usha has come; the seed in the black earth has become the beautiful rose; a sweet odour pervades the earth; early birds are chirping; the far east is presently glowing russet-hued; the wind is fresh and free. Thus the coming of Usha is very auspicious for the mortal who aspires for immortality.

But all is not right with the world which wants to reach God in his Heaven, as it knows not the way. How will the ordinary mortal reach the dizzy heights of the soul's high mountains? How will the sapling inside the mire blow forth a divine lotus? Man is either depressed and rendered hopeless by the gaping mass of inconscient matter that is symbolised through Night, or he is astonished and left helpless by the dazzle of the Superconscient symbolised by the Goddess Usha. Is there no way for the ordinary mortal to cut through the coils of uncivilised demoniac dominations imposed by formless matter and embrace the Life Divine of civilised angelic Brahma-Knowledge? There is, says Sri Aurobindo, and paints in apt poetic hues the sufferings and successes of our Primordial Mother represented in the light-stepping slender-waisted Savitri.

In the first canto itself a hurried but memorable hint of Savitri's life and trial has been given. After all, we know the story of Savitri's struggle and victory. It is this Savitri of popular legend that is seen to forge the link between the inconscient matter and the Superconscient Life Divine. The life-giving rays of the Sun turn the tiny seed buried in the pond into a bright pearly lotus.

Savitri begins her life as an artless innocent princess born amidst wealth and comfort. Then she assumes the role of the Redeemer whose mission is to transform this meaningless mortal life into the purposeful Life Divine. "Savitri is represented in the poem", says Sri Aurobindo, "as an incarnation of the Divine Mother. This incarnation is supposed to have taken place in far past times when the whole thing had to be opened, so as to 'hew the ways of Immortality'."[10]

As a mortal, Savitri weds Satyavan, who symbolises Truth, pure and unsullied. Truth at first succumbs to Death, to the poison of ignorance. Savitri, now the incarnation, roused by this outrage, and armed with Love and Righteousness, wins back Truth (Satyavan), and the couple reunite to inaugurate the Life Eternal on earth.

II

'THE ISSUE'

In the second canto, entitled 'The Issue', we see Savitri very near to the mighty issue between Death ignominious and Life Eternal. Only a few hours, and the issue will be joined between Yama and Savitri. This is the crucial moment in her life. To draw back and leave Fate to its devastating work is out of the question. For, it is she in whom the Universal Mother has descended to save humanity from the blight of terrestrial bondage. To Savitri only one way is possible; that is, to go forward, to struggle, to dare Destiny, whatever the final outcome.

Sages have pronounced that Fate is inexorable; thus failure seems to be more likely than victory. Yet Savitri must issue forth, and not withdraw the step placed forward. So Savitri, called by the peremptory summons of Duty and filled with bottomless compassion, stands on the threshold of the field of Fate, ready for the struggle. A short while from now, Death will claim Truth from Love; and it is no easy task to defeat Death and grasp Immortality. But Savitri does not give way to despair. Unperturbed, like a block of wood,[11] she strengthens herself and awakens her self with indrawn yogic strength from the Divine.

With the Mighty Doom just round the corner, Savitri falls into a reverie, when the near past marches through her memory as a crystallised documentary. Dawn has come to the world; Savitri has risen and is following her daily round of duties as a housewife. While she is at these routine exertions,

> Awhile, withdrawn in secret fields of thought,
> Her mind moved in a many-imaged past.[12]

Savitri's heart aches to think that such a threatened end should have been designed to such a happy life as hers has been. Her memories have not dimmed with the passage of time; on the other hand, in their complete wholeness they lie "mapped to her sun-clear recording view". She glances at her treasure-trove of memorable experiences where everything can be found as fresh as a morning flower:

> From the bright country of her childhood's days
> And the blue mountains of her soaring youth
> And the paradise groves and peacock wings of Love
> To joy clutched under the silent shadow of doom
> In a last turn where heaven raced with hell.[13]

In these five lines are succinctly reviewed the variegated turns of her whole life upto the present. The birth of Savitri; the child-princess; the blushing maiden young; the meeting of Satyavan and the birth of Love; the warning of Narad and the foreknowledge of relentless fate; marriage and the bitter-sweet year that followed it; and now the threatening Doom—everything has been condensed into an incandescent lyrical passage. Savitri's soul is choked as it were at the very thought of possible failure, which must mean Nothingness forever. An intense emotional fever grips her heart and she determines to go on with the struggle. She must win and save Truth; only then can the supramental age be ushered in by means of the union of Love and Truth. Man must ascend the peak of the superconscient, notwithstanding this giant hurdle that is sprawled across the way; and Savitri has come to remove the obstacle, whatever the hazard.[14]

Savitri is here revealed to us, in this intrinsically dramatic situation, as being poised on the peak of perilous uncertainty. After twelve months of blissful married life she has to confront the advancing Fate, a Fate which in itself also foreshadows the coming of a spiritual Dawn. Her mind is torn between dark forebodings and radiant hopes. The clouds are gathering and look dully malicious. Will they send forth a shower of divine light or will they, after all, envelop the whole world in a thick blanket of Darkness? Seized by the uncertainty of the future, a deep oblivion falls upon her mind, obscuring it in dense dark night. Curiously enough this night actually forebodes good. For it is the dark hour before dawn, it is the poison preceding nectar.[15] And so too the spiritual aspirant must needs experience "the dark night of the soul" before participating in the "bliss of Brahman" (*Brahmānanda*):

> An absolute supernatural darkness falls
> On man sometimes when he draws near to God.[16]

It is Savitri's turn now:

> That hour had fallen now on Savitri.[17]

The sweet, the agonised "remembrance of things past" is ended, Savitri is now on the threshold of the future. She is drawing near her eternal home, but she knows not whither lies the path. As for the present, it is a complete void. Neither of the past nor of the future, it is in this present she must face her Task:

> On the bare peak where Self is alone with Nought.[18]

Here she must wrap about her the armour of her yogic strength and

> ...plead her case upon extinction's verge,
> In the world's death-cave uphold life's helpless claim
> And vindicate her right to be and love.[19]

The Supreme Moment has drawn very near; the twelve months of passionate joy have fled like

> A mailed battalion marching to its doom,[20]

and,

> The last long days went by with heavy tramp... [21]

The cast and sound of these lines suggest the relentlessness of Time's march, which seems to have both a bulldozer heaviness and irresistibility. It is as though the sergeant time has given orders for a forward march, and the days pass without flinching or haste, regardless of the hour that conceals within its womb the poison of immitigable Death; or, is it rather going to be the Nectar of Eternal Life?

The days have gone by too soon; alas! Evanescent is earthly joy and beauty. Now that fate has begun its chase, Savitri has withdrawn into herself. About her silence reigns; but silence, when witnessed in her presence, is mystically eloquent. And she stands here serene like a jewel of purest ray. Holy, fair, majestic and, above all, womanly:

> All in her pointed to a nobler kind. [22]

Hers was:

> A body like a parable of dawn
> That seemed a niche for veiled divinity. [23]

Every act of hers—walking, smiling, talking, working—was invested with the liquid purity of Heaven-born Grace.

For this mortal woman has immortality within her; the human child is made of superhuman dimensions. She is of the earth, but not earthy; she is of Heaven, but is no featureless divinity. Rather she is:

> Near to earth's wideness, intimate with heaven,
> Exalted and swift her young large-visioned spirit
> Voyaging through worlds of splendour and of calm
> Overflew the ways of Thought to unborn things.[24]

It is in such a girl that the world-creatrix, the world-saviour, is personified. Possessed of immense reserves of power, Savitri is

> At once...the stillness and the word,
> A continent of self-diffusing peace,

An ocean of untrembling virgin fire:
The strength, the silence of the gods were hers. [25]

Although she is born human to save humanity, yet is she divine in her origins. The ray of divinity issues forth unfailingly through the framework of the mortal being. To this Divine Mother who walks the earth in a mortal garb is given the challenge to meet and master. The issue thus presented to her is:

Whether to bear with Ignorance and Death
Or hew the ways of Immortality,
To win or lose the godlike game for man... [26]

But, then, she is not born to yield the field to Ignorance and Death.

To lead, to deliver was her glorious part.[27]

Hers is the task to unclasp the net that binds this "immense material world" which is really a gaol, and thus release humanity to the freedom of a tremendous spiritual heaven. To break mankind's fetters, "Her single will opposed the Cosmic rule." Savitri is determined to face the issue and strive her uttermost to "stay the wheels of Doom." She is confident in her power, although the issue's result is as yet uncertain. But success is not impossible to achieve. A clicking of the switch can set ablaze a building hung with innumerable bulbs. The first decisive push, the primal force, is what is needed. Once that is accomplished, the force will make instantaneous contacts, and brighten a whole city, thus dispelling darkness and enveloping life with light. So also with this Major Issue.

A prayer, a master act, a king idea
Can link man's strength to a transcendent Force...
One mighty deed can change the course of things;
A lonely thought becomes omnipotent.[28]

Man is mortal no doubt; made of flesh and blood, he has nothing permanent about him; nor anything of superior merit in him—except his soul. The soul is deathless, permanent. It is actually a spark spilt from the Starry Heavens of the Divine Realms. This the soul is the godhead that lodges behind the apparent brute machine. But it lies inert until it is stirred to life and sovereignty. The cobra raises its hood only when it is provoked; to glimpse the beauty and majestic grandeur of a King Cobra, we have first to rouse it.[29] So also with the human soul. When it is prompted by a spiritual struggle it raises from the Nescient unconscious state and draws itself to its full stature of Divinity. Faced with the mighty crisis of the challenge of Death claiming Satyavan (thereby smothering Truth itself), Savitri is called to action, and:

> The great World-Mother now in her arose... [30]

Armed with Righteousness, sustained by Hope, and spurred on by the call of Duty, Savitri like:

> A flaming warrior from the eternal peaks
> Empowered to force the door denied and closed
> Smote from Death's visage its dumb absolute
> And burst the bounds of consciousness and Time.[31]

Such is the grand beginning of Sri Aurobindo's epic. The Dawn of the fated day has arrived, but the spiritual dawn for mankind is yet to come. Meanwhile our compassionate Mother has chosen to struggle with the Enemy. Fortifying herself with the nectarean past and the gains of her yoga, she is now ready to face Death and win back Truth, and rear in our midst a new heaven and a new earth.

BACKGROUNDS AND ANTECEDENTS

Thought's odour is so pale that in the air
Nostrils inhale, it disappears like fire
Put out by water. Drifting through the coils
Of the involved and sponge-like brain it frets
The fine-veined walls of secret mental cells,
Brushing their fragile fibre as with light
Nostalgic breezes: And it's then we sense
Remote presentiment of some intensely bright
Impending spiritual dawn, of which the pure
Immense illumination seems to pour
In upon our existence from beyond
The edge of knowing.

David Gascoyne

ASWAPATI'S YOGA

SECTION A

'THE BOOK OF BEGINNINGS'

I

'THE YOGA OF THE KING: THE YOGA OF THE SOUL'S RELEASE'

The fateful day in Savitri's life has dawned, and she is ready to face the event.

But Savitri—who is she, why is she here, how has the issue been joined? To answer these questions, Sri Aurobindo has to resort to retrospective narration. Time stands still as it were, while our eyes are turned back to view the vasts of the past.

Savitri was born because of a "world's desire". It was her father, King Aswapati, who articulated the "world's desire"; and Aswapati was humanity's advance scout destined to prepare the way for the coming of Savitri.

Aswapati is individual man, he is a king and therefore leader and representative of his race, and he is also the heart of humanity voicing forth its innermost aspiration. Thus his yoga too falls into three stages, and the first stage is the subject-matter of Book I, cantos 3, 4 and 5.

As individual man, Aswapati's first dim spiritual awakening comes when he realises that the body—the material appearance—is not all. Behind the appearance—behind the many layers of appearance—is the reality. Man is neither the beginning nor the end; he comprises the whole gamut from the worm that was to the God that is to be. Earth and Heaven meet in man, and man partly is and wholly hopes to be. Beyond night and twilight and starlight beckons the dawn of a spiritual day. The mystery, the miracle, of "married Earth and Heaven", the mating of finite self with Infinity, is the drama that is being played, and is yet to be concluded.

Now Aswapati "grew into his larger self… (and) saw a greater world".[1] He sees beyond reason and mind, and sees the soul—a whole new world in the spaces of the soul. He establishes occult contact with other beings and other planes—the Many of the phenomenal world—and thus achieves an apparently endless extension of experience, leading upto an almost total comprehension of the material, the measurable, the sensible, and comprising the utmost termini of things, symbols and signs. The soul within grasps the worlds without; the One apprehends and fuses with the Many.

From the individual to the universal; from the universal to the transcendental. Such is the preordained pace of advance. Accordingly Aswapati dares beyond all beyonds, he plunges into the "nameless vast", and is:

> Caught by a voiceless white epiphany
> Into a vision that surpasses forms,
> Into a living that surpasses life,…[2]

This is the formless, immaterial, incommensurable, insensible Nihil, the Void—a pure *pralaya* or deluge—an absolute dissolution of everything. It is indivisible Space-Time, the pure primal stuff of the Cosmos and what's beyond it.

Aswapati presently returns to the phenomenal world, but only after a baptism in the waters of transcendence. His return is a rebirth, or a renewal of life armed with stainless knowledge from the remote ineffable home of Truth. He feels spiritually fresh and strong, even as people feel after a good invigorating bath, a plunge in the waters of the Ganga or a splash under a waterfall. The effects remain, at least for a time. The awakened and purified soul tries to keep in touch with the 'intimations of immortality'. Even the lower reaches of Aswapati's being, having lately experienced a profound sea-change, tingle with a new consciousness of power and joy.

What's the 'use' of this higher knowledge and power? There is a purposeful merging of the higher knowledge and the lower, from which results an integration and an advance. Such advance is also facilitated by lightning streaks of sudden illumination from the 'home-of-all womb-of-all' (in G.M. Hopkins' phrase):

> An ictus of revealing lustre fell
> As if a pointing accent upon Truth,
> And like a sky-flare showing all the ground
> A swift intuitive discernment shone.[3]

Such thrusts of flame kindle the sluggish mind to life, making it scour the vasts between "summit and abyss" and gather knowledge-pearls of incalculable price. Thus awakened, alerted and active, the mind spreads out, the net is heavy with what has come its way and curious man can piece out the design behind the appearance:

> The balance of the world's design grew clear,
> Its symmetry of self-arranged effects... [4]

Now Aswapati has a view of the Tree of Cosmos, spreading "its magic arms through a dream of space". Analogous to, but more elementally all-comprehending than the Aswatha Tree of Indian mythology and the Life Tree Ygdrasil of Scandinavia, this Tree of Cosmos is reared and supported by the Spirit. Aswapati feels intrigued by Creation —its cause, its course, its malady, its cure. The game of Creation is God's "spendthrift work", "a splendid extravagance of the waste of God".[5] Call it divine *lila* or the wondrous play of chance and change!

Aswapati realises that the universe is no "senseless whirl borne round inert on an immense machine". The impress of Shakti the Creatrix is everywhere, however veiled to our eyes. Light is hidden somehow in darkness, life in inconscience, knowledge in ignorance. There has been a 'descent', an 'involution', of God into matter; the ascent, the evolution, from matter to God is proceeding, and must conclude. Life is not unreal, life is not futile:

> Life now became a sure approach to God,
> Existence a divine experiment
> And cosmos the soul's opportunity.[6]

From this first reading of the pages of Omnipresent Reality, from this first inkling into the processes of involution and evolution, Aswapati achieves his "soul's release from ignorance", and his mind and body experience their "first spiritual change".

> A wide God-knowledge poured down from above,
> A new world-knowledge broadened from within:....[7]

He is a new man, poised for the achievement of greater things still, of immeasurable import to him and the world.

II

'THE SECRET KNOWLEDGE'

But before he can dare new spiritual adventures, Aswapati should get to know the bases of the 'Secret Knowledge' that his hoary ancestors—the seers of the Veda, the *rishi*s of the Upanishads—have bequeathed to him. The sacred books point the way. One is encouraged, one is warned. Maps and mariner's compasses have their uses for traveller and voyager. The 'Secret Doctrine' is the spiritual adventurer's map and compass combined. Aswapati therefore turns to the mastery of the 'Secret Doctrine'.

On a height Aswapati stands, and looks "towards greater heights". The dialectic of advance is a singular meeting of opposing movements: there is the climb of consciousness, from the material, vital and mental, to still higher planes; there is the descent of consciousness from the higher—the highest—to the lower realms; and there is the meeting, the fusion, the transformation. All the time there is the veiled Guide or Presence within, who is the 'eyes and ears' of the awakening, the awakened, soul. However, all this is but an occult, not a visible or demonstrable, reality. Yet the drama is played on no far inaccessible stage but *here and now*. As B.P. Wadia once wrote:

> The Occult World is in co-adunition but not in co-substantiality with the human world…it interpenetrates the market place, the highways of traffic…it is where homes are built and families are reared…The birth in the Occult World does not imply a death in this, but rather a higher living on this earth which the Occult World carries within its bosom.[8]

The stage is set here, in our own hearts, in our own souls, "but all is screened, subliminal, mystical… it needs the power of a spiritual gaze."[9] No doubt, the visibly real is the world of the dualities, the purblind meanderings of the Earth-Goddess "across the sands of Time". She dreams vaguely of a better world where death has no sting, desire no pang of unfulfilment, and incapacity no roots. What the Earth-Goddess most needs are mind, will, strength, joy—unqualified, unblemished. The real forces determining our advance are the forces *within*, but we are generally blind to their presence or power. We are alas! out of touch with our "subliminal quiverings"; rather we are slaves, in our daily activities, to our own petty acts, and we are content to be imprisoned in a mental consciousness with its dungeon narrowness and stark obscurity. But what could be, what is to be, is an open book to the immortals, and the power behind them:

> Above the world the world-creators stand,
> In the phenomenon see its mystic source.[10]

In man's darkest extremity, this power will descend to his help; the mind's inner chamber will be charged with a new potency, and all earth will grow "unexpectedly divine".

The human predicament when man has reached the mental stage of his evolutionary career is "an interregnum in Reality", a mid-region, shall we say, between the dusk that has gone and the flame that is to come. In Alexander Pope's words, man finds himself at the fluid junction between two continents:

> Plac'd on this Isthmus of a middle state,
> A Being darkly wise, and rudely great:
> With too much knowledge for the Sceptic side,
> With too much weakness for the Stoic's pride...
> In doubt to deem himself a God, or Beast;
> In doubt his Mind or Body to prefer;
> Born but to die, and reas'ning but to err...[11]

If we concentrate on the present alone, we run the danger of missing both the origins and the ultimates. We have, then, to learn to end the prevalent ignorance, and:

> ...fill the immense lacuna we have made,
> Re-wed the closed finite's lonely consonant
> With the open vowels of Infinity, ...[12]

The gods who inhabit the higher planes enjoy a condition of static perfection, which is in sharp contrast to man's dynamic evolving destiny. In Sri Aurobindo's poem, *The Life Heavens*, there is a significant affirmation:

> I, Earth, have a deeper power than Heaven;
> My lonely sorrow surpasses its rose-joys....[13]

Earth's inhabitant, man, is provoked by the aloofness of the mere gods to exceed himself and them. It is not for him to wail like the Lotous-Eaters about the gods' indifference to human woes. What if they seem careless:

> ...of the grief that stings the world's heart,
> Careless of the pain that rends its body and life? [14]

Man has no need to despair; divine guidance and intervention are not wanting, and "an outstretched Hand is felt upon our lives". Not the gods, but the Power transcending them—even them—is our true guide and helper. It is this secret master of all works—the master who is the actor and the play, the potter and the clay—that really governs the universe and runs this "endless masquerade".[15] And this Power, this master, is *Purusha-Prakriti*, the ineffable Two-in-One:

> ...all is their play:
> This whole wide world is only he and she.[16]

Strange is the relationship between *purusha* and *prakriti*, like word and meaning:

> Happy, inert, he lies beneath her feet:
> His breast he offers for her cosmic dance
> Of which our lives are the quivering theatre,....[17]

Purusha consents to veil himself in ignorance for an uncertain term and play the part *Prakriti* allots to him. Life in matter commences a purblind game, and the first hectic chapters of Evolution come to be scrawled:

> He takes up her powers;
> He has harnessed her to the yoke of her own law.[18]

At last the veiled unconscious *Purusha* awakes to a "memory of Self... the Godhead breaks through the human mould."[19] Although still consenting to be her vassal, he ensures in their collaborative acts an unfolding purpose, a progression towards the heights. Thus, even thus, "in Nature's instrument loiters secret God". Coercing his divinity, God is labouring here in our midst.[20] We are driven to action, shaped, changed and chastened by the Power—the Absolute, the Perfect, the Alone—"who is in us as our secret self". He will recast us into his own mould and raise us to Infinity.

Yet, for the time being, the Dusk is more real than the Dawn. God is veiled and even denied, and the human adventure is timid, halting, subject to evasions, setbacks and retreats. This hesitant voyaging should cease, and the spirit of bold adventure should possess high-souled man. He should leave the familiar coastal regions and venture forth to reach "the islands of the Blest". Beyond the seeming termini of this world must the traveller—the veiled *Purusha*; the insatiable mariner; the indefatigable Odysseus of the occult seas—dare to catch the vision of the blessed Isles, to discover "a new mind and body in the city of God".[21] No sleep, no rest, till the goal be reached!

Purusha and *Prakriti* are entangled here together in a mystic embrace, and they are seemingly lost in this cosmic game of play and clash and new creation.[22] He is Being and Becoming both, Becoming in his entanglement or communion with her, and Being as the one transcendent Reality. The descent (or involution) made, the whole ascent (or evolution) is awaiting splendorous accomplishment.

> For this he left his white infinity
> And laid on the spirit the burden of the flesh,
> That Godhead's seed might flower in mindless Space. [23]

III

'THE YOGA OF THE KING: THE YOGA OF THE SPIRIT'S FREEDOM AND GREATNESS'

Such is the 'Secret Knowledge' Aswapati has received from "timeborn men". He can attempt a bolder assay, a greater spiritual transformation, than the earlier movement of mere "soul's release" (Book I, canto 3). He knows now in fuller detail the long way to be traversed, the signposts, the turns, the clue. And so:

> He found the occult cave, the mystic door
> Near to the well of vision in the soul,
> And entered where the Wings of Glory brood…[24]

He has cut the cord of limited mind that binds him to the earth-crust, and feels free of the burden of human perplexity and frustration. He can read Nature's laws, the necessity behind the play of appearance,

> Resolve its oracle and its paradox,
> Its riddling phrases and its blindfold terms,
> The deep oxymoron of its truth's repliques,... [25]

The riddle of the world unriddles itself to Aswapati, and he grows in puissant understanding. But earth's limitations and failures still cause him intense disquiet and dissatisfaction:

> Here even the highest rapture Time can give
> Is a mimicry of ungrasped beatitudes,
> A mutilated statue of ecstasy,...
> Or a simulacrum of enforced delight
> In the seraglios of Ignorance. [26]

Aswapati is, however, cheered by the thought that man can still work out his destiny, "recreate himself and all around/And fashion new the world in which he lives." [27]

A cleansing retreat is called for, and Aswapati resolutely withdraws into a void, an absolute condition of silence of the mind. Sri Aurobindo is here evidently recalling his own experience at Baroda under Yogi Lele's guidance. It is a unique cathartic or 'beyonding' experience,[28] and Aswapati leaves "earth-nature's summits", mounts "burning like a cone of fire", and quests "for God as for a splendid prey". Although his heady flight is sought to be prevented by "the black Inconscient", Aswapati sweeps on,

> Hearing the echo of his single steps
> In the eternal courts of Solitude. [29]

As Aswapati rises thus above the remote horizons of our familiar consciousness:

> ...to meet him bare and pure
> A strong Descent leaped down. A Might, a Flame,
> A Beauty half-visible with deathless eyes,

A violent Ecstasy, a Sweetness dire,
Enveloped him with its stupendous limbs... [30]

In consequence of this tremendous embrace, he becomes a changed being, breathing "a supernal air", and "the soul and cosmos faced as equal powers".[31] He sees great vistas of possibility opening before him. To Aswapati it seems as though nothing is impossible. Earth's frustrations shall cease. Enfranchised Mind will prove "a mediator divinity", ending the rule of ignorance on earth. Nature with her tantalising magic-ways, the "Circean wonderland" of caprice and perversity, the garish "bizarre kingdom" of man, all submit to the control of Aswapati's "spiritual will". [32]

There is verily an occult world that rules and sustains the phenomenal world of the senses. The movements in the occult world are revealed when we pore within, penetrate into the subliminal consciousness, and establish communication with the innermost truth and power. Nothing then would be beyond our purview or sovereign control.

This occult world stands finally revealed to Aswapati's quickened vision, and:

A giant order was discovered here...
Ascending and descending twixt life's poles
The serried kingdoms of the graded Law
Plunged from the Everlasting into Time,
Then glad of a glory of multitudinous mind
And rich with life's adventure and delight
And packed with the beauty of Matter's shapes and hues
Climbed back from Time into undying Self,
Up a golden ladder carrying the soul,.... [33]

The descending and ascending occult stairs are strangely and tauntingly reminiscent of parallel stairs in the phenomenal world, and invite Aswapati to roam and explore. It is like a vast inverted cone, and there is a steep descent from Spirit's immaculate peaks to the abyss of time, inconscience and ignorance, and there is the complementary ascent back to the peaks; and between the two stairs all the worlds meet and all abide. Aswapati is intrigued, charmed, transported:

> Sunbelts of knowledge, moonbelts of delight
> Stretched out in an ecstasy of widenesses
> Beyond our indigent corporeal range.
> There he could enter, there awhile abide.
> A voyager upon uncharted routes
> Fronting the viewless danger of the Unknown,
> Adventuring across enormous realms,
> He broke into another Space and Time.[34]

The last three cantos of Book I describe the first part of Aswapati's Yoga, and even this falls into two movements, "one a psycho-spiritual transformation and the other a greater spiritual transformation with an ascent to a supreme power."[35] The canto on 'The Secret Knowledge' comes in between appropriately, for the first yogic movement prepares Aswapati for receiving the knowledge, while the knowledge itself becomes a preparation for the second yogic movement. The first dim awakening to the splendours in the firmament of the Spirit has led to a deep thirst for knowledge, and draughts of this nectarean knowledge have given him the vision to see and the wings to reach the Spirit's peaks of beckoning felicity. His further explorations are not for himself alone, but for the benefit of the race as well; he is Aswapati as well as a king, and he cannot forget in his own achieved felicity the still unredeemed Earth and the 'too too sullied' race of Man.[36]

SECTION B

'THE BOOK OF THE TRAVELLER OF THE WORLDS'

In 1936, Sri Aurobindo wrote to one of his correspondents: "There was no climbing of planes there in the first version… I had no idea of what the supramental World could be like at that time, so it could not enter into the scheme."[37] Taking up the poem later, Sri Aurobindo worked into it the *Divina Commedia* of the occult worlds with an elaborate and vivid particularity. The revisions came one upon another, and at one stage Sri Aurobindo wrote: "…the 'Worlds' have fallen into a state of manuscript chaos, corrections upon corrections, additions upon additions, rearrangements on rearrangements out of which perhaps some cosmic beauty will emerge!"[38] Eight years later, in 1946, Sri Aurobindo acknowledged that, "*Savitri* has grown to an enormous length…The small passage about Aswapati and the other worlds has been replaced by a new Book, the Book of the Traveller of the Worlds, in fourteen cantos with many thousand lines."[39] Actually, however, there are now fifteen cantos, and in these is described with a singular vividness Aswapati's spiritual ascent as a typical representative of the race to win the possibility of discovery and possession of all the planes of consciousness.

I

'THE WORLD STAIR'

As Aswapati, tearing from his last terrestrial moorings, plunges into the occult unknown universe of moods, energies, world-shapes and freedom-formulas, he experiences the throb of direct contact with the cosmic play of passion and motion and "self-creation without end or pause". Contradictions merge and mix and cease in a harmony;

"plots of pain and dramas of delight" spin themselves round; all imaginative leaps and fanciful freaks find their realisation there. The ultimate clue of the Word only is missing,

> The integer of the Spirit's perfect sum…
> The absolute index to the Absolute. [40]

Anon Aswapati catches sight of the immense "high-curved world-pile", reared against the base of matter's plinth, and rising "towards breadths immeasurable". The descending stair from the summits of the Spirit to matter's abysses is balanced by this other,

> …single stair to being's goal.
> A summary of the stages of the spirit,
> Its copy of the cosmic hierarchies
> Refashioned in our secret air of self
> A subtle pattern of the universe.
> It is within, below, without, above. [41]

In the occult world, as in the material cosmos, the centre is everywhere, the circumference is nowhere; the fully awakened soul is all the worlds that are, the centre and the circumference as well! The budget of mankind's present discontents and failures is no permanent writ. There is this "ladder of delivering ascent" offering an escape from the abyss into the far plateaus of the Spirit. Man is not abandoned forever to his present fate. The assurance is given that

> This faint and fluid sketch of soul called man
> Shall stand out on the background of long Time
> A glowing epitome of eternity,… [42]

A Seer (the inner Guide) "inspires our ascent", as he now responds to the call of Aswapati too, who bears "the burden of the world's desire". And so Aswapati flies past world after world, and still mounts higher and higher,

> …towards an indiscernible end
> On the bare summit of created things.[43]

II

'THE KINGDOM OF SUBTLE MATTER'

From the kingdom of *gross* matter or the material cosmos of order and harmony, though lacking "the sole timeless word", Aswapati crosses to the world of *subtle* material existence where "dwell earth-nature's shining origins". This is the world of physical mind, or, in other words, the world of matter shot through by the mind:

> The golden issue of mind's labyrinth plots,
> The riches unfound or still uncaught by our lives,
> Unsullied by the attaint of mortal thought
> Abide in that pellucid atmosphere. [44]

It is "the brilliant roof of our descending plane", it is an intermediate power-house or reservoir; almost a world of archetypes, its location and function are best described thus:

> A heaven of creative truths above,
> A cosmos of harmonious dreams between,
> A chaos of dissolving forms below,
> It plunges lost in our inconscient base.[45]

The descent of God from his heights to the depths of gross terrestrial existence implying nescience and inconscience is but one half of the divine play, for this has, as in a rebound, created the possibility —the necessity—for a corresponding ascent as well. A truly mighty partnership is at work here. The plunge into the depths has obscured, not wholly extinguished, the light from above. At present it is true enough that earth-life is tainted by the shadows of defeat. Passion flames up for a while, but an end comes soon—all too soon—to the "sacred orgy of delight". Love fails us, power fails us, and even knowledge fails us. But there is no cause for despair. Rather should we remember that it is an unfinished tale and the best is yet to be:

> Here in a difficult half-finished world
> Is a slow toiling of unconscious Powers;...[46]

Genuine effort at self-exceeding must succeed because it will be met by an answering adequate response from above; the call shall not be in vain, and "the Light now distant shall grow native here". Intimations come even now from the remote halls of Immortality, but as yet they are only:

> ...brief magnificent reminiscences
> And high splendid glimpses of interpreting thought,
> But not the utter vision and delight.[47]

What we need is "a fourth dimension of aesthetic sense" that will ultimately "re-align" our souls to the cosmic wideness. The full possibility of realisation is rendered difficult now because of a blinding or obscuring veil, but even this will be pierced or broken through in the fullness of time.

The world of subtle matter is compact of delight and beauty and love and sweetness,

> ...a miracle of symmetric charm,
> A fantasy of perfect line and rule.[48]

By resolved limitation, it has achieved a limited perfection; there is no looking before and after or a pining for what is not; there is no striving for what is beyond the reach, no hugging of excess and the sad recoil of satiety,[49] all is order and completeness and contentment:

> In their narrow and exclusive absolutes
> The finite's ranked supremacies throned abide;...[50]

This is a stage on Aswapati's journey, not the final destination; and so he looks "beyond for greater light" and resolutely leaves behind "that fine material paradise".

III

'THE GLORY AND FALL OF LIFE'

The passage from the world of subtle matter brings Aswapati to the life-realms, where the 'vital', the principle of life, has full play. The law of life here comprises birth, growth, decay and death. With an endless but blind appetite the life-principle explores all possibilities, regardless of consequences. Change and danger, pain and defeat, are the play-fellows and pests of this region. Here people sit and 'hear each other groan'; dolorous their converse, transient their joy; pure felicity forever eludes. But thought-sick though life be and knotted with failure, yet Life too derives from the Timeless and carries the memory of "a lost world rapture".

Strange that, at the heart of pain, joy—or the hope of joy—should have her sovereign shrine. But so it is indeed. It may be that the visible prospect is barren and bleak. The sky lours, the earth yawns, the end seems sure.

> But near and real to the longing heart
> And to the body's passionate thought and sense
> Are the hidden kingdoms of beatitude. [51]

At first they are dreams, hopes, visions merely; but they signify or embody the shape of things to come.

There is clearly a veil or gulf between earth appearance and the other reality, between 'earth-fact' and 'dream-truth'. This veil once pierced, this gulf once crossed—this must happen sooner or later—the dream would become fact and reality would arrive. The "inscrutable Supermind" would help "the hazardous experimenting Mind" in its endeavours to end the Nescience and reach upto the Truth. All will then be possible. But in the meantime life is tied to the circuit of deception and failure. Life is almost in love with "amorous Death" and sleep imitates "extinction's peace". Man despairs of chastening and harmonising "his cosmos-chaos of personality".

Such alas! is the picture of the fallen state of life. But how to describe the 'other' state, the power and the glory? How to paint the colours of paradisal felicity? How to visualise the splendour of the 'dream-truth'? Aswapati, however, can see this glory unfolding before him:

> There were summit-glories inconceivable,
> Autonomies of Wisdom's still self-rule...
> There sat the oligarchies of natural Law,
> Proud violent heads served one calm monarch brow:
> All the soul's postures donned divinity.
> There met the ardent mutual intimacies
> Of mastery's joy and the joy of servitude
> Imposed by Love and Love's heart that obeys
> And Love's body held beneath a rapturous yoke...[52]

It is the life we know *here*, but purged of all its taints and the limitations of "death, desire and incapacity"; it is life without twist or crookedness, without pain or satiety, but instinct with "heavenly variety". So fashioned in freedom and power, life will "explore the measures of the rhythms of God", and weave,

> ...her wizard wonder-dance,
> A Dionysian goddess of delight,
> A Bacchant of creative ecstasy.[53]

Aswapati, even as he sees this world of bliss, knows "no way to enter into its joy". From the sleep of matter's inconscience has emerged the play of life and the attendant strife of the dualities: mind has sprouted, and with it doubt, and the engines of sorrow and joy. Life as it came from Heaven to colonise the earth had suffered a profound change, and all her sweetness has turned into "a maimed desire", and terrestrial existence, exemplifying the 'Fall of Life', has become but "an episode in an eternal death". Such is the 'evil mystery' of the human lot!

IV

'THE KINGDOMS OF THE LITTLE LIFE'

Life in its heavenly origin is no doubt a principle of pristine purity and power; but as it sinks in the mire of the earth, it cannot help sharing for the nonce somewhat of the dolour and density of the soil. For a while, then, life is inevitably yoked to "an instinct-driven Ignorance", and must perforce draw the heavy chariot of pain; only instinct and sense-perceptions rule the Kingdom of the Little Life. But 'mind' is not long in soliciting and directing life, fitfully and uncertainly at first, but presently with more concerted and ambitious aim. Mind-crowned man has made his appearance on earth, and he is rich in endowments and his life is full of possibilities.

> He becomes a mind, he becomes a spirit and self;
> In his fragile tenement he grows Nature's lord.[54]

From matter to life, from life to mind, and from mind to—he doesn't know yet. There is a continuous striving, there is a progressive effort but the desire is dogged by incapacity, the aspiration is followed (if at all) by only partial achievement. There are random movements, purblind advances; there is progress surely, but along an exasperating zig-zag path of toil and difficulty. Still must the spirit of evolution press on further and further, towards newer and newer horizons:

> Matter dissatisfies, she turns to Mind;
> She conquers earth, her field, then claims the heavens…
> Ascending slowly with unconscious steps,
> A foundling of the Gods she wanders here
> Like a child-soul left near the gates of Hell
> Fumbling through fog in search of Paradise.[55]

Aswapati is eager to mark the steps in the arduous evolutionary spiral. This means really a return to the beginnings, and a survey of the whole track. And so,

> Along swift paths of fall through dangerous gates
> He chanced into a grey obscurity
> Teeming with instincts from the mindless gulfs...[56]

At the very bottom life is intimate with death, indifferent alike to beauty and light. In this nether empire of the little life, there are divers petty kingdoms, each with its own badge of limitation and circumscribed sovereignty.

See life first crawling out from her "cabin of mud" where she had lain mute and rigid for ages. It is a "weird and pigmy world", a world of automatic responses; a world of gropings, wrestlings, false starts and futile results; verily "a vain unnecessary world" marked by "meaningless suffering and a grey unease". Yet Aswapati finds a meaning even in these obscure beginnings of life. Even here the world is somehow charged with the beauty of God. The slime and the mire somehow yield a wondrous progeny.

> The world's senseless beauty mirrors God's delight.
> That rapture's smile is secret everywhere;
> It flows in the wind's breath, in the tree's sap,
> Its hued magnificence blooms in leaves and flowers.[57]

Life in cells, in micro-organisms, in worm, in reptile, in insect—even this life is not devoid of meaning.[58] No doubt about it, Being is involved even in these lower realms and darkened vasts:

> Even in these formless coilings he [Aswapati] could feel
> Matter's response to an infant stir of soul. [59]

In the adjoining second Kingdom of the Little Life, Aswapati marks "a fierier breath of waking life". Here "an insect hedonism" flutters and creeps, and there are "dragon raptures, python agonies", and "great puissant creatures with a dwarfish brain, and pigmy tribes". This is the stupendous "animal experiment". Here within a narrow circuit are packed the ages of Geologic time, the giant lizards and mastodons that have perished without a trace, the mammoths, now only preserved as fossils; these are the mighty that have shortsightedly disinherited themselves.

There are the mammals, too, and early primitive man; creatures of Nature red in tooth and claw, they have been content to work for the body's wants,—"content to breathe, to feel, to sense, to act", no more. Selfhood and Breed (in the elemental sense in which Robert Bridges uses the terms in his poem, *The Testament of Beauty*) spin the animal plot, and primitive man is engaged in grovelling in the "grooves of animal desire". Even when man leaves the jungle and forms community and society, and raises town and fortress, he must needs maim and mangle himself with slaughter, plunder, rape, fire and deceit and so enact the drama of self-wrought misery. The Heroic Age of epic striving and failure and misery is but another milestone on this ambiguous march:

An animal in the instinctive herd
Pushed by life impulses, forced by common needs,
Each in his own kind saw his ego's glass;
All served the aim and action of the pack.[60]

Men and women living in walled-up isolation moan that understanding is difficult; quick to quarrel, they fight among themselves on account of colour, creed, region, or possessions and so, even so, they go round and round 'the prickly pear' and round and round again.

The third of the Kingdoms of the Little Life manifests the emergence of the intellectual man, a 'push' from below facilitated by "a masked intervention from above". The mind and its forces are whole Himalayas of power marked by heady leaps of thought, ballistic missiles of aspiration, and veritable Sputniks of comprehension. This gives a new intensity and edge, a greater depth and wideness, to human life. No limit, really, to man's desire for empire. An insatiable hunger for power possesses the mind of man as it surveys the past and views the future. What if death itself could be overcome?

Its right to be immortal it reserved,
But built a wall against the siege of death
And threw a hook to clutch eternity.[61]

Yet the mind, a giant helper upto a point, degenerates soon into a serious liability. Logic itself proves often deceptive, and theorems can stifle the human soul. Preoccupied with the glamorous appearance, man tends to lose infinitudes of the soul within. "Dwarf lusts and brief desires" chain him to the earth-crust, and the mind too acquiesces in the fall:

> Absorbed in the little works of its prison-house
> It turned around the same unchanging points
> In the same circle of interest and desire,... [62]

Whatever the seeming achievements of the mental being, however impressive the march of civilisation, the crux of the human situation remains unsolved. A total emancipation is yet to arrive. Aswapati can sense in this Kingdom of the Little Life,

> ...no vast perspectives of the spirit,
> No swift invasions of unknown delight,
> No golden distances of wide release. [63]

V

'THE GODHEADS OF THE LITTLE LIFE'

Aswapati has seen clearly enough that all the Kingdoms in the Empire of the Little Life—even the most advanced in appearance —are encased in a giant ignorance. But as he peers closer into this empire, he is able to glimpse the godheads behind it:

> As when a search-light stabs the Night's blind breast
> And dwellings and trees and figures of men appear
> As if revealed to an eye in Nothingness,
> All lurking things were torn out of their veils
> And held up in his vision's sun-white blaze.[64]

These are the forces that urge, however obscurely or unconsciously, the 'little life' to strive for the higher and larger life; these are "the little deities of Time's nether act", "imps with wry limbs", "errant divinities trapped in Time's dust", in sum, "a trepidant and motley multitude". Fallen godheads these, who warp everything on earth:

> All models they corrupt, all measures cheat,
> Make knowledge a poison, virtue a pattern dull
> And lead the endless cycles of desire
> Through semblances of sad or happy chance
> To an inescapable fatality. [65]

All is perversion and defeat now; yet there lie concealed in them the seeds of ultimate purification and triumph. As yet conscious life seems to be at the mercy of these insidious promptings from the depths of the unconscious. This must go on till the wrong suggestions are superseded by right suggestions from the far home of Truth and "Infinity takes up the finite's acts". Only then will end this nightmare nether life that holds us in thrall.

What is this teasing paradox of Creation? The Spirit of its own accord wears the insignia of limitation and becomes inconscient Matter—"a body sleeping without sense or soul". There is at first "only an etheric Space"; then, through the processes of expansion and contraction, come touch and friction, force and energy:

> An ocean of electric Energy
> Formlessly formed its strange wave-particles
> Constructing by their dance this solid scheme,
> Its mightiness in the atom shut to rest;
> Masses were forged or feigned and visible shapes;
> Light flung the photon's swift revealing spark
> And showed, in the minuteness of its flash
> Imaged, this cosmos of apparent things. [66]

The play of 'blind' chance is controlled by the "fixed and immutable" laws of Nature. From this *ordered* material universe—the Kingdom of matter and energy—there wakes up at some auspicious moment "a dream of living"; thus life arrives on the cosmic scene. But life by its very nature is no static divinity, for it hides in its pulse "a consciousness with mute stifled beats of sense"; and in an agony of excitement and uncertainty it gropes for mind. The brute becomes man, equipped with the "delicate enginery" of mind. When man acts, he relies not on the instinct alone (as does the brute) but also on the play of thought's processes. From the marriage of matter and energy, first life, then mind, have ensued and now there are higher potentialities still:

> The illumined soul-ray fell on heart and flesh
> And touched with semblances of ideal light
> The stuff of which our earthly dreams are made.[67]

The unseen indwelling Spirit, the mighty Witness, sees all and facilitates further advance "towards the still greatness of a distant hour".

The play of mind on the material universe and life's realms is enterprising and exciting, but it cannot effectively 'control' events, and it cannot pluck the heart of the mystery of existence:

> This minute elaborate orchestrated life
> For ever plays its motiveless symphonies.
> The mind learns and knows not, turning its back to truth;
> It studies surface laws by surface thought,...[68]

The mind sees darkly, and gathers inconsequent crumbs of Truth in a rats-alley hunting-ground! But deep within "a puissance acts", there is a power working "concealed in the subliminal secrecies", and in the result "speech leaps, thought quivers, the heart vibrates, the will/ Answers and tissue and nerve obey the call".[69]

The surface mind is thus only a puppet; mental processes and creations are but shadows and hence hardly affect the essential quality of life or the ultimate destiny of the soul. Insect, ape and man, all share a similar fate. Man—even thinking man—spends his little hour in "little things", in the monotonous circle of love and jealousy and hate, of joy and heart-pain and strife. Convention and routine deaden our lives, or we seek an escape through "lust's hot glare" or "passion's crimson stain". All our endeavours—even those of Science the Giantess—leave our life unaltered, the same, the same as ever. Only religion is a sort of cure, though it is really a self-deception rather than a cure; what use religion's "unprovisioned cheques on the Beyond?"

However, Aswapati can also see that this spectacle of Mind-moulded, mind-directed life is no more than "a provisional scheme". There is a "deeper seeing from within", and the promise of a rich response from above. The present tale of error and ambiguity and failure must soon have its ending, and its sequel will speak of "muffled throbs of laughter's undertones" and paint the portrait of "a heart of bliss within a world of pain". There will be no chapters detailing life's little ironies, no inset elegies, no tragedies, no farces; with the greater Self informing the self within,

> All shall be captured by delight, transformed:
> In waves of undreamed ecstasy shall roll
> Our mind and life…
> The body's tissues thrill apotheosised,…
> Like a clay troll kneaded into a god
> New-made in the image of the eternal Guest,
> It shall be caught to the breast of a white Force
> And, flaming with the paradisal touch
> In a rose-fire of sweet spiritual grace,
> In the red passion of its infinite change,
> Quiver, awake, and shudder with ecstasy. [70]

This splendorous possibility is awaiting to be enacted, and "our hearts must inform with heavenly strength…and cleave the darkness with the mystic fire".[71]

Cheered by the promise of this possibility, Aswapati races yet further, from the Kingdoms of the Little Life to the Kingdoms of the Greater Life; the passage is through seas of darkness, and only his own spirit's inextinguishable flame guides him through the abysses and brings him safely to his next destination.

VI

'THE KINGDOMS AND GODHEADS OF THE GREATER LIFE'

From the "grey anarchy" of the 'lower vital' world, Aswapati now approaches the 'higher vital' world, a region ineffectual and purposeless still, where life see-saws between vain denial and dubious hope. It is a world of deceptive illuminations and spasmodic actions, of hopes unrealised and possibilities unfulfilled. Life goes round and round as it were, but goal there seemingly is none. Allurements come from every direction, only to be followed by discomfiture. All is "unsafe, miraculous and half-true".

As Aswapati travels further on from these outskirts, the sky clears, the earth smiles, and he reaches "the kingdom of the morning star". His eyes are lit up with a surer hope. From within well up the beginnings of a new authentic knowledge. Immortality glimmers in the distance, a beckoning star; love is a releasing force making for the heart's fullness and freedom; Truth flames forth in the Word, thrown up "from a chance tension of the soul". These first faint raptures naturally lead to "vaster hopes":

> A progress leap from sight to greater sight,
> A process march from form to ampler form,
> A caravan of the inexhaustible
> Formations of a boundless Thought and Force.[72]

Cannot eternity itself be caught in the net of time? Cannot the Spirit be coerced into matter? *Prakriti* or Nature is "an Energy of perpetual transience" and is endlessly resourceful, finding "new bodies for the Infinite and images of the Unimaginable." Nature dazzles us by her infinite variety and termless restlessness; she is a timeless actor playing her intriguing parts on a temporal stage. Although earth centered, the higher vital world is not altogether beyond the reach of intimations from above. On the contrary, this world dares to gaze beyond the "barriers of apparent fact", to trust "dream-mind and the soul", and even to hunt "spiritual verities":

> It feels a saviour touch, a ray divine:
> Beauty and good and truth its godheads are.[73]

It is a world where divers pulls meet, a meeting ground of demon, man and God, of hell, earth and heaven. It is a world of high exertion and limitless possibility; "its greatness is to seek and to create".

This genius to create, this Life-Force or creative urge, sleeps in matter, stirs in plant and insect, and manifests itself strongly in bird and animal. The push of evolution is a power that persists and presses on. Death itself is no end, but only a fresh beginning. Inertness is but a nap; the struggle, the striving, starts again and goes on, apparently for ever. There is, no doubt, the seeming grapple between *Prakriti* and *Purusha*:

> Although she is ever in him and he in her,
> As if unaware of the eternal tie,
> Her will is to shut God into her works
> And keep him as her cherished prisoner
> That never they may part again in Time.[74]

Prakriti keeps him in her close embrace; he may wrestle, but he may not get away! This is the mystic truth behind an affirmation like Hopkins': "The world is charged with the grandeur of God".[75] This mystic struggle and embrace is really the law of life and evolutionary advance. There are stumblings and set-backs, there are even naps and swoons, but the work is taken up again, and the assault and ascent are renewed once more.

The play of consciousness here in the higher vital world is lit by Truth, but does not contain or hold the Truth as a permanent condition; it is like the little room lit by the rays coming through the window, not the Sun, not his total realm. At best this life is "a first immigration into heavenliness", not a final occupation. Nevertheless, there are ardours and hectic strivings that are characteristic of this world. The hero is a recurrent emergent here. In him alas! good and evil intermingle, yet is he impressive in mould, whether his careerings end in defeat or success. King, Pope, Tyrant, all have their little hour of dominion, and then fade away. Power corrupts, absolute power often corrupts absolutely—"the harlot power that slays the soul".

The artist and poet are of an order apart and "catch the All-Beautiful's ray". Behind the scenes, subliminal powers inflate the hero, the seeming Superman, with incalculable energy, and unleash terrific love or hate till forest fires join and rage. But even when things promise most, there comes sudden discomfiture in the end: the paths of beauty, love, glory, lead but to the grave; the final reward of bliss and peace eludes. As Aswapati moves among these shapes and feels racked by riddles all round, he grows a riddle to himself. The mystery refuses to be cleared, except through the fabrication of fresh mysteries; the question, the questioner, and the answer are riddles, riddles all.

Following the track of the Life-Force's march, Aswapati presently comes to,

> ...a high release from pettier cares,
> A mightier image of desire and hope,
> A vaster formula, a greater scene. [76]

Higher still and higher, onward and forever onward, Nature circles above, aiming "at a target kept invisible". Here the atmosphere is ethereal rather than dense—more and more ethereal with the flight into the higher regions. Aswapati sees Nature's variegated strivings, the colours have a blinding dazzle, but the white radiance of Truth can nowhere be seen. Is Truth playing hide and seek? There are strange attractions, random recognitions, sudden thrills of glory; every corner, every crevice in Nature has hidden intensities of beauty and joy:

> In her green wildernesses and lurking depths,
> In her thickets of joy where danger clasps delight,

He glimpsed the hidden wings of her songster hopes,
A glimmer of blue and gold and scarlet fire.[77]

Aswapati is fascinated by it all and moves freely amidst the "live symbols" of Nature's occult power; and her manifold—if as yet flawed —magnificence casts a profound spell upon him. Some 'clue' there certainly must be that can guide the seeker through her labyrinthine ways of passion and power; but the clue, the "interpreting word", is lacking still. Nature at this height strikes Aswapati as "a fugitive paradise":

Brief are her snatches of felicity
That touch the surface, then escape or die:...[78]

Even so, in spite of all these marks of circumscription, life at this level is surely worth all the toil and the pain, the spasm and the ache.

On the other hand, this medial half-hearted felicity cannot content *Prakriti*, and she cannot long abide here. Her cardinal aspiration to bring the heavens down and charge the body with the soul's delight cannot accept defeat as a permanent condition; neither is she able to force the pace of rounded fulfilment. "A sense of limit haunts her masteries", but she will not give up her "beat of action" and "cry of search". Is all existence no more than, "a vain necessity's act...A play without denouement or idea,/A hunger march of lives without a goal?"[79] But hope whispers that another play is possible, that a divine comedy shall fill the stage; and faith and doubt wrangle, the yea and the nay glare at each other, and the issue is yet to be concluded. True enough it is that the present error, defeat, pain, the reign of death, the empire of futility, must be exceeded; but for the time being,

All seems in vain, yet endless is the game.
Impassive turns the ever-circling Wheel,
Life has no issue, death brings no release.[80]

VII

'THE DESCENT INTO NIGHT'

Aswapati, having reached this dead end, this cactus end of final frustration in Life's efforts at self-transcendence, is anxious to locate the cause of it all, and so he dons the mantle of giant courage, peers into the "viewless Vast", and sees,

> ...a grey carved mask of Night
> Watching the birth of all created things. [81]

He has plunged into an immitigable abyss and recognises therein the sources of misrule, which are really perversions of the sources of order above. Power, presence, light, love—all are here, but only in a twisted and perverted shape. The subtle serpent Ignorance can spew out "a perverse sweetness, heaven-born malefice". Life and love are sicklied over with the baleful coating of sin and fatality, and happiness is doomed to play a losing game of cards with pain, and progress becomes "a purveyor of Death" and lust chases away love, the spurious overwhelms the genuine, and unutterably bleak is "the wasteland of life's descent to Night". And behind this evil empire of misrule there is "a dark Unseen...its breath is a subtle poison". This is the author of the whole book of evil, and he has his own army of slaves to carry out his behests. As Aswapati sees the handiwork of evil—the spectacle of men maimed, suffering, men pitifully helpless—he is aghast; and all the more so because he also sees that the wretched victims do not, and indeed cannot, even recognise "the authors of their fall". Moving farther yet, Aswapati arrives at,

> ...a no-man's land of evil air,
> A crowded neighbourhood without one home,
> A borderland between the world and hell. [82]

This is the world of the false, the misleading, the self-deceiving, the transient, the slippery, the sardonic, the sinister. The Fiend himself wears the sceptre here, but he poses as an angel bright, quotes scripture facilely, and traps his victims in nets woven by their own good intentions. He is armed with sinister powers, and he can turn logic, law, light, letters into instruments of doom. The battle between evil and good is waged here as if it can have no ending; only death is certain, avoid it how we may.

In these cities of ancient ignorance, there is clash perpetual between warring groups. Men are driven by their egos and false propensities, and man proves wolf to man—*homo homini lupus*! Hypocrisy assumes Himalayan proportions, and people pose the "worst iniquities on equity's base". In the name of religion, too, shoreless are the struggles that are engineered; but while religion of a sort flourishes, true spiritual seeking is discountenanced. Tyrannies a hundred oppress and slay, and a unity is reared upon force and fraud. A perilous route, this, barring Aswapati's way; too fatally easy it is to slip, to be lost. But Aswapati, armed by prayer and the Name, crosses the murky no-man's-land, though only to confront, "a greater darkness…a worse reign,/If worse can be where all is evil's extreme." [83]

As in the circles in Dante's *Inferno*, beneath Horror's depths are lower circles of deepening Horror. Now Aswapati is in the land of the unashamedly vicious, the licentious and the lost—the "fell dun suburbs of the cities of dream-life". What orgiastic harlotry, what criminal concupiscence! Lust is traded as "a decorative art":

> Impure, sadistic, with grimacing mouths,
> Grey foul inventions gruesome and macabre
> Came televisioned from the gulfs of Night. [84]

Here are the night-clubs, opium dens, and miscalled palaces of pleasure; Dionysian riot, left-hand orgies, and other repulsive practices make "a ritual anguish" that consecrates death; and a new false philosophy theorises evil's rights and glories "in the shimmering rot of decadence".

Nor men nor rational creatures are these; rather are they "a race possessed". They have trampled the humane in the mud and set up the reign of 'Big Brother' Evil Unlimited. Called variously Nazi, Fascist, Party, these inhuman sadists impose a "grim totalitarian reign":

> All on one plan was shaped and standardised
> Under a dark dictatorship's breathless weight. [85]

And the patriot and the demagogue! How they seem to fly skyward borne upon the wings of eloquence, yet how base and inhuman in their motivation and action, ready for even the "lowest reptile's crawl"! A dog is obeyed in office, and the more the dog snarls, the more implicitly is it obeyed! Big Brother, who is demon and goblin and ghoul, yet passes for titan, hero, god, and ordains,

> The huge laughter of a giant cruelty
> And fierce glad deeds of ogre violence...
> Armed with the aegis of tyrannic Power,
> Signing the edicts of her dreadful rule
> And using blood and torture as a seal,
> Darkness proclaimed her slogans to the world. [86]

There struts Orwellian 'double-think' wedded to 'double-talk'; and where is Truth? And what is still more astonishing is that people actually glory in their swinishness and slavery:

> Flaunting its cross of servitude like a crown,
> It clung to its dismal harsh autonomy.
> A bull-throat bellowed with its brazen tongue;
> Its hard and shameless clamour filling Space
> And threatening all who dared to listen to truth
> Claimed the monopoly of the battered ear;
> A deafened acquiescence gave its vote,
> And braggart dogmas shouted in the night... [87]

Aswapati the "lone discoverer" sees it all, and manages to wade through it without actually contaminating himself. For a time he is threatened by the reigning blasphemies and darkness, he feels the invasion of the thickening Night, he scents the claim of the Abyss for his own soul. But he survives the onslaught; peace and safety return; the mighty Godhead in him awakes to face "the pain and danger of the world", and he meets "with his bare spirit naked Hell".

VIII

'THE WORLD OF FALSEHOOD, THE MOTHER OF EVIL, AND THE SONS OF DARKNESS'

The nether-most circle in Hell; the hidden heart of Night. Aswapati has gravitated to the bottom, and sees revealed there "the endless terrible Inane", the zero begetter of the worlds. All is dark, hideous, false, and vile; perverse Thought, priestess-sorceress,

> In darkling aisles with evil eyes for lamps
> And fatal voices chanting from the apse,
> In strange infernal dim basilicas
> Intoning the magic of the unholy Word,
> The ominous profound Initiate
> Performed the ritual of her Mysteries. [88]

Like the figure of Satan chewing a human skull in Inferno's ultimate circle, here is a horrid shape too, squatting on Death, and swallowing "all things born". "No worse, there is none". [89]

When in the beginning inconscient Matter was about to be kindled with life and the journey of evolution was about to commence, a shadow fell across, being cast by "the grey python Night". Life's move had thus been countered and criss-crossed ere ever it even got into its stride. This shadow

> ...falsified the primal cosmic Will
> And bound to struggle and dread vicissitudes
> The long slow process of the patient Power. [90]

Working against the Mother of Light, this Mother of Evil "with a grey distorted silhouette in the Night" strove to thwart the steady climb of the soul and pull it to the depths if she could. This primal struggle goes on, in changing climes with changing vicissitudes; and still the Mother of Darkness "prowls around each light" and tries to slay in the cradle "the divine Child". She is verily "a cowled fifth-columnist" who converts the climber of the worlds to defeatism and death!

Like the Mother, so her sons: "terrible agencies", they are "offspring of the gulfs" and "haters of light" who "load the dice of Doom with wizard lies". They have usurped all holy places, all cells of life, all nerves of joy:

> Armoured, protected by their lethal masks,
> As in a studio of creative Death
> The giant sons of Darkness sit and plan
> The drama of the earth, their tragic stage. [91]

This is the Hell Aswapati traverses on his way to Heaven. Hoping to gauge the whole malignant forces of Hell, its presiding Mother Evil, her sons, Aswapati takes a close view of them all, "challenging the darkness with his luminous soul". What deserts of joylessness, what infinitudes of pain! No peace, no ease; only pain and tears. The soul, caught in the spider's web of ignorance, worships the pitiless Power. Science and technology fashion iniquitous edifices of woe and engines of summary massacre and liquidation. And blasphemy of blasphemies! the murderers brazenly take the name of God and "make him an accomplice of their crimes".

In Hell's deepest hole, while numbed and awed he stands, Aswapati still seeks the cause—the clue—"the root and cause of Hell" and the clue to Night's "dreadful heart". Nay more, he is ready to drink the poison to know its taste. By a feat of forged identity he sees through its secret essence, and infers that behind it, behind even quintessential Hell, is a cosmic Will:

> Torn were the formats of the primal Night
> And shattered the stereotypes of Ignorance. [92]

When this sudden blaze of realisation flashes before him, Aswapati feels a whole load removed; like a house of cards crashes down Hell's "huge abrupt facade"; Night opens, and vanishes "like a gulf of dream". Verily, verily, the reign of Night would be over soon; what Aswapati has seen in a "vision splendid" must come to be. There pours "a wide intimate and blissful Dawn", and Aswapati shakes off the grim memories of the nightmare death-in-life he has left behind.

IX

'THE PARADISE OF THE LIFE-GODS'

Like a man returned to life, Aswapati luxuriates in the "great felicitous Day" that now warms him up and intoxicates him with the "wine of God". Here life is in league with light and love; it beats "a jewel-rhythm of the laughter of God" and lies "on the breast of love".[93] Aswapati can now move with light dancing steps, on plain or ridge or hillside, or look over "dreaming cities of Gandharva kings". He can visit "shining Edens of the vital gods" and watch Beauty, Peace, Love, Strength, Desire, Pleasure and Dream play their truly appropriate roles. All here is under God's sway; pain changes to joy, the commonplace to the miraculous. Such is this "Paradise of perfect heart and sense".

Aswapati too feels profoundly affected by the blissful climate of the place. His body acquires a new glow; earth-nature changes; he becomes a comrade of Heaven. A bliss overwhelms him, a fiery felicity possesses his soul.

X

'THE KINGDOMS AND GODHEADS OF THE LITTLE MIND'

The Life-Gods' paradisal felicity is complete and final; there is no further progress, nor any possible regress. This "breath of hundred hued felicity" renews eternally, and flawless happiness forever prevails. This is the Life-Heavens, whose inhabitants cherish their happiness on the mid-way peaks of ascent, nor wish to mount to the ultimate heights. Not so Aswapati. He still must respond to "a greater adventure's call" and scale the climb to Timelessness. Be the hazard what it may, Aswapati must march on, and stop not till the goal is reached.

First he meets "a silver-grey expanse where Day and Night had wedded and were one". This is the territory where the obscured animal being dimly awakes into its basic sensory perceptions. The insect crawl is no end but the beginning of glorious things to come; the roads of frailty converge to triumphant strength; and the tunnels of infectious obscurity remotely point to sunrise splendours and seas of light. As yet it is but an ambiguous terrain:

A coalition of uncertainties
There exercised uneasy government
On a ground reserved for doubt and reasoned guess,
A rendezvous of Knowledge with Ignorance. [94]

Next Aswapati notices a higher slope in this steep ascent "where dawn-sheen gamboled with the native dusk". The region of twilight recedes, and morning beckons the Traveller of the Worlds:

He came into a realm of early Light
And the regency of a half-risen sun. [95]

Here mind in its first hazy manifestations emerges as a principle of consciousness and starts its snail-like operations; then it acquires a certain puissance and self-confidence, studies matter's constitution, and deduces Nature's laws; and in course of time Mind waxes into "a master Magician of measure and device". Man's "prototypal deft intelligence" structures the marvels of theoretical and inventive science and fabricates audacious systems of equivalence and association. The *maya* of the material and sensory universe yields its secrets one by one:

A bodiless energy put on Matter's robe;...
And the invisible appeared as shape
And the impalpable was felt as mass:...
Idea was disguised in a body's artistry,
And by a strange atomic law's mystique
A frame was made in which the sense could put
Its symbol picture of the universe. [96]

Although all this load of knowledge has some value, man is still unable to ford or canter across the stream of the last Ignorance that divides us from integral Truth. The million bits of truth isolated or analysed in the laboratories do not complete the sum; there is an exasperating insufficiency in even the most ambitious of mental operations.

In her tireless strivings to pluck the heart of the mystery, Mind has three divers deputies—three loyal serfs—to advance her cause and promote her work. The first of these is,

A pigmy Thought...
A technician admirable, a thinker crude,
A riveter of Life to habit's grooves,
Obedient to gross Matter's tyranny,... [97]

It is the perfect servant, but lacks adventure and initiative; weights and measures it can handle with competence, but it shies away from the subtler engines of the mind. It can foot the well-trodden path, but turns away from trackless jungles and strange seas of thought. Although content thus to feed on "scraps of life and Matter's bones in its kennel of objective certitude", even this pigmy figure plays an allotted role in the cosmic play.

The second of Mind's deputies is "a rash Intelligence" with its thousand shapes and numerous names:

It licked at knowledge with a smoky tongue.
A whirlpool sucking in an empty air,
It based on vacancy stupendous claims,
In Nothingness born to Nothingness returned,

Yet all the time unwittingly it drove
Towards the hidden Something that is All. [98]

It makes sudden, strange, startling guesses, achieves "wild-ass" feats of speculation and generalisation, and makes "flash-images of half-seen verities". Like the pigmy, this hunchback too—albeit he is rash and his findings are tentative—nurses "a portion of infinity's strength".

The last and greatest of Mind's henchmen is Reason, "the squat godhead artisan...The strongest, wisest of the troll-like Three."[99] It is the philosophic schematising power that seeks to "reduce to rules the mystic world"; although not quite knowing yet, she "ferrets out Nature's process, substance cause" and hopes to force "a pattern of eternal fixity". In her characteristic attitudes, in the sum of her achievements, she seems a wonder, and the mother of many civilisations. Abstract thought makes impressive conquests, and Reason, with an insatiable hunger, makes further conquests still:

For the world seen she weaves a world conceived:
She spins in stiff but unsubstantial lines
Her gossamer word-webs of abstract thought,
Her segment systems of the Infinite,
Her theodicies and cosmogonic charts
And myths by which she explains the inexplicable...
Her sciences precise and absolute...
The vast encyclopaedia of her thoughts;
An algebra of her mathematics' signs... [100]

Breathtaking though these achievements are, Reason's manifold toil is in the last analysis but "an inconclusive play"; what is gained today is lost or superseded tomorrow. Science, having made absolute claims for a while, now wisely acknowledges her limitations:

But now is lost her ancient sovereign claim
To rule mind's high realm in her absolute right,
Bind thought with logic's forged infallible chain
Or see truth nude in a bright abstract haze. [101]

Science or philosophy, politics or ethics, Reason-erected edifices have unsure foundations, and cannot stand the shocks of adverse circumstance. What a stupendous ado for achieving "a million purposes with purpose none!"

> Ideals, ethics, systems had no base
> And soon collapsed or without sanction lived;
> All grew a chaos, a heave and clash and strife...
> All reeled into a world of Kali's dance. [102]

Can mere meaningless chaos be the final meaning of the universe? No; some other power must there surely be that can render Mind's handiwork far from futile:

> Then science and reason careless of the soul
> Could iron out a tranquil uniform world, ...
> A reasonable animal make of man
> And a symmetrical fabric of his life. [103]

But this too is no consummation to be wished, for who would care to stifle the promptings of the soul and make the human body a perfect machine? There is no room for despair, however; "many-visaged is the cosmic Soul" and "a greater Mind may see a greater Truth". Either this way is open, or all is a total defeat.

The hazy twilight of Instinct and Sensory Perception; the dawn of Mind, and her minions, Thought, Intelligence and Reason; what next? Aswapati reaches now "the bright kingdoms of the rising Sun" where "all is a birth into a power of light". The mere Mind's laborious constructions are but "interim reports"; the final reports are still a-drafting, they are still to come. Mind's knowledge has to be followed by a "greater Gnosis". Aswapati marks two new powers over-shadowing the "dwarfish trinity" and perched in a "high breathless stratosphere". These two "sun-gaze Daemons" are "a huge high-winged Life-Thought" and "a pure Thought-Mind"; these powers hold the key to the higher Gnosis; these are the godheads of the Kingdoms of the Greater Mind.

XI

'THE KINGDOMS AND GODHEADS OF THE GREATER MIND'

Racing beyond the "circles of mortal mind" Aswapati heads towards "the far spiritual light". It is actually a glorious escape into freedom, for mortal mind, albeit it lords over its petty realms, is after all a prison. It may be that man's book of origins is in blissful Heaven, but his embroilment in Matter has been to his utter discomfiture:

> Ourselves are citizens of that mother State,
> Adventurers, we have colonized Matter's night.
> But now our rights are barred, our passports void;
> We live self-exiled from our heavenlier home.[104]

Aswapati is determined to revisit his native place, and so he makes the supreme effort:

> On meditation's mounting edge of trance
> Great stairs of thought climbed up to unborn heights
> Where Time's last ridges touch eternity's skies
> And Nature speaks to the spirit's absolute.[105]

First to meet Aswapati is "a triple realm of ordered thought", which is reached by "a triple flight", itself but "a small beginning of immense ascent". Even as Dante speaks of the descending circles of Hell and the ascending slopes of Purgatory, here in *Savitri* Sri Aurobindo views the cosmos symbolically as a descending and an ascending stair of worlds, the descent leading to the Abyss and the ascent to the Heights. A segment of the ascent comprises the passage from the limited human Mind to the all-knowing and all-powerful Supermind. In the chapter entitled 'The Ascent towards Supermind' in *The Life Divine* Sri Aurobindo writes:

> ...the scrutiny of a given line of ascent may be expected to throw light on the principle of all ascending possibilities; such a

> scrutiny of one line is all that can be attempted. This line is, as all must be, governed by the natural configuration of the stair of ascent: there are in it many steps, for it is an incessant gradation and there is no gap anywhere; but, from the point of view of the ascent of consciousness from our mind upwards through a rising series of dynamic powers by which it can sublimate itself, the gradation can be resolved into a stairway of four main ascents, each with its high level of fulfilment. These gradations may be summarily described as a series of sublimations of the consciousness through Higher Mind, Illumined Mind and Intuition into Overmind and beyond it; there is a succession of self-transmutations at the summit of which lies the Supermind or Divine Gnosis.[106]

Whereas these gradations are described in vivid psychological terms in *The Life Divine*, in *Savitri* the gradations become so many distinct worlds—abstractions give place to imaginative constructions—and nobly articulate philosophical prose becomes the sovereign poetry of the Spirit. It is not the translation of one mode into another, but a veritable transmutation.

Aswapati starts the immense ascent. The first of the triple realms of ordered thought is "close and kin" to the world of man. The deities of this realm are not indifferent to human aspirations and actually "shape our greater thinking's roads". This world may almost be called a "world-kindergarten of young souls", where the alphabet of the higher knowledge is laboriously learnt and the first theorems of the geometry of the cosmic body are mastered. Not Heaven, not quite earth, this is a transitionary rest-place, inhabited by powers and presences who maintain a fruitful commerce with the human world. Thanks to them, the elementary laws of causality are deduced, matter's movements are conned, and knowledge is "built from the cells of inference into a fixed body flasque and perishable". The observance of new facts leads to new formulations of the laws, and so,

> A cage for the Infinite's great-eyed seraphim Thoughts
> Was closed with a criss-cross of world-laws for bars

And hedged into a curt horizon's arc
The irised vision of the Ineffable. [107]

Second among the thought-realms is the world of "a subtle archangel race", associated powers endowed with a keener, a more integral, vision into the truth of things:

A light of liberating knowledge shone
Across the gulfs of silence in their eyes;...
High architects of possibility
And engineers of the impossible,
Mathematicians of the infinitudes
And theoricians of unknowable truths,... [108]

This gifted race of imaginative thinkers are adepts in hypothesis, speculation and bold generalisation; they can reduce to an algebraic formula or an equation in Tensor Calculus the mysterious and manifold workings in four-dimensional Space-Time; and they can psycho-analyse the Cosmic-self itself! These are the symbol Einsteins, Plancks, Rutherfords and Freuds who draw Necessity's logarithmic tables and derive "the calculus of Destiny". Their massive insight—and their monumental effrontery!

All was coerced by number, name and form;
Nothing was left untold, incalculable.
Yet was their wisdom circled with a nought:... [109]

Third and highest among the thought-realms, to be reached in "a sublimer and more daring soar", is the habitation of the "sovereign Kings of Thought". Whereas in the first of the three realms of ordered thought, consciousness is "close and kin" to the human consciousness, here in the highest of the three realms, consciousness is more close and kin to the divine than to the human consciousness; all creatures here have a clear sense of infallible direction towards Truth; and they even dare to translate the unknown unthinkable into "a stripped imperative of conceptual phrase/Architectonic and inevitable."[110] They are the infallible seers, who are also the revealers through inspired utterance of the cosmic truths that they have seen:

> A single law simplessed the cosmic theme,
> Compressing Nature into a formula;
> Their titan labour made all knowledge one,
> A mental algebra of the Spirit's ways,
> An abstract of the living Divinity.
> Here the mind's wisdom stopped; it felt complete;...[111]

While these bright gods of Thought are engaged in the pursuit of the ultimate Truth, while they scheme and plan to snare and clasp her, she too—she the Power of Truth or *Para Shakti*—makes at last the appropriate response. As one knocks with persistent imaginative attention, one finds that the door opens at last; as one seeks without intermission, one finds what one is seeking for; and if one asks, the answer is given unto him. As the seers, the laureates of the Spirit, strain to see and hymn the splendours of what they see, the response comes from Above. The culminating human call is answered, *Para Shakti* responds, and man the seer and thinker finds wondrous vistas of new possibilities opening before him:

> A new beginning flowers in word and laugh,
> A new charm brings back the old extreme delight:...
> She has lowered her heights to the stature of our souls
> And dazzled our lids with her celestial gaze...[112]

Even so but a portion of the Infinite arrives and is recognised in the world of man; tying Truth down in human categories, we really crib and cabin it almost out of recognition:

> Thus is it even with the seer and sage;
> For still the human limits the divine:...[113]

The proper thing would be, not to imprison her in our thought, but to leap out of the prison-house, and effect a total surrender to her:

> Then the Unmanifest reflects his form
> In the still mind as in a living glass;

The timeless Ray descends into our hearts
And we are rapt into eternity.[114]

XII

'THE HEAVENS OF THE IDEAL'

The tireless traveller of the worlds, Aswapati continues the ascent, looking out for new worlds still:

At each pace of the journey marvellous
A new degree of wonder and of bliss,
A new rung formed in Being's mighty stair,
A great wide step trembling with jewelled fire.[115]

Beyond the triple realm of ordered thought are the "heavens of the ideal Mind.../The lovely kingdoms of the deathless Rose".[116] Such an inspired poem, mantric in its efficacy, as Sri Aurobindo's *Rose of God* is uncannily appropriate to this region of the deathless Rose, where at the feet of God unfolds the mystic bud, and the spiritual aspirant has his first real taste of bliss, light, power, life and love:

All the high gods who hid their visages
From the soiled passionate ritual of our hopes,
Reveal their names and their undying powers.
A fiery stillness wakes the slumbering cells,
A passion of the flesh becoming spirit,...[117]

While one end of the effulgent stair leads to the regions of the deathless Rose, the other end leads to "the mighty kingdoms of the deathless Flame". The Rose is the symbol of bliss, while the Flame is the symbol of knowledge. Realisation could come both as the bliss of Brahman and as the knowledge of Brahman. In his poem *Moon of the Two Hemispheres*, Sri Aurobindo writes, using not the imagery of ascent but the imagery of the boat making for its port:

A gold moon-ship sails or drifts ever
In our spirit's skies and halts never, blue-keeled,

And it throws its white-blue fire on this grey field,
Night's dragon loop,—speeding,
The illumined star-thought sloops leading
To the Dawn, their harbour home, to the Light unsealed,
To the sun-face Infinite, the Untimed revealed. [118]

The Flame, on the other hand,

...rises through the mortal's hemisphere,
Till borne by runners of the Day and Dusk
It enters the occult eternal Light
And clambers whitening to the invisible Throne. [119]

If the Rose guides the aspirant through world after coloured and ecstatic world towards "some far unseen epiphany", the Flame likewise guides him through "a pale-sapphire ether of God-mind/ Towards some gold Infinite's apocalypse." [120]

Aswapati is rather at home in both the kingdoms of the Ideal—the worlds of the Rose and the Flame.

They offered to the Traveller at their gates
A quenchless flame or an unfading flower,
Emblem of a high kingdom's privilege. [121]

But he realises that even in these deathless kingdoms there is but the reign of partial—though intense—light; he therefore passes on to a "diviner sphere" where the Flame and the Rose are in perfect partnership:

There, joined in a common greatness, light and bliss,
All high and beautiful and desirable powers
Forgetting their difference and their separate reign
Become a single multitudinous whole. [122]

XIII

'IN THE SELF OF MIND'

It is as though Aswapati has passed the last camp and has finally touched Everest:

> At last there came a bare indifferent sky
> Where Silence listened to the cosmic Voice,...
> He stood on a wide arc of summit Space
> Alone with an enormous Self of Mind. [123]

There are evidently no more heights to conquer, no more worlds to traverse; Aswapati has reached the centre of Silence, "the mystic birthplace of the soul". Is this the end, the very last lap of his quest?

> The great perturbed inquirer lost his task;
> Nothing was asked nor wanted any more.
> There he could stay, the Self, the Silence won:
> His soul had peace, it knew the cosmic Whole. [124]

This, however, is no more than a temporary swoon in nirvana; "suddenly a luminous finger" falls on the great variety of terrestrial things, the earth-consciousness returns, and doubt infects everything. Aswapati cannot wholly get away from the memory of the limitations of man's life on earth. He remembers with a sting of shame the failure of man's efforts at thought and certainty:

> The magic hut of built-up certitudes
> Made out of glittering dust and bright moonshine
> In which it shrines its image of the Real,
> Collapsed into the Nescience whence it rose. [125]

The total Silence is no answer to the total burden of human wail and woe. Aswapati therefore feels that,

> A greater Spirit than the Self of Mind
> Must answer to the questioning of his soul.[126]

Yet where is he to look for the answer? Above, all is "blank and still";

around, an immense vacancy and silence; below, deep down below, only "the ocean surge of Life/Along the coasts of mortal Ignorance".[127] Is *this* the final Truth? Is the meaning of the cosmos no more than the balance of the opposing hemispheres of silence above, strife below, or of light above, darkness below?

XIV

'THE WORLD-SOUL'

To the anxiously seeking eyes of Aswapati there now appears, "in a far-shimmering background of Mind-Space a glowing mouth…a luminous shaft…a recluse-gate…a veiled retreat…a tunnel of the depths of God."[128] This is a way out, this is an escape from the icy stare of immaculate Silence!

> As one drawn to his lost spiritual home…
> Into a passage dim and tremulous
> That clasped him in from day and night's pursuit,
> He travelled led by a mysterious sound. [129]

He is lured on and on by murmurs, voices and harmonies untranslatable—reminiscent of the "jingling silver laugh of anklet bells" or,

> …a vast forest's hymn,
> The solemn reminder of a temple gong,
> A bee-croon honey-drunk in summer isles
> Ardent with ecstasy in a slumbrous noon,
> Or the far anthem of a pilgrim sea. [130]

He reaches at last "a wondrous bodiless realm"; it is earth's perfect antidote, with the "intimacy of God" everywhere. It is the utter region of the World-Soul. One treads there on soul-ground, one contacts soul-stuff, one rises in soul-space, one experiences soul-joy. Here "in voiceless internatal trance" club together the souls that have emancipated themselves from the chain of birth and death; or they await "the adventure of new life". It is clear to Aswapati that he has penetrated to creation's centre where the wandering spirit finds,

> ...the silence of its starting-point
> In the formless force and the still fixity
> And brooding passion of the world of Soul. [131]

By sure instinct he passes on,

> Along a road of pure interior light,
> Alone between tremendous Presences,
> Under the watching eyes of nameless Gods,...
> To the source of all things human and divine. [132]

Here he beholds *Purusha-Prakriti*, the deathless Two-in-One,

> A single being in two bodies clasped,
> A diarchy of two united souls,
> Seated absorbed in deep creative joy;... [133]

And behind them stands "the sole omnipotent Goddess ever-veiled", whose mask is the making of the world and whose footfalls are the rages of the ages. Aswapati folds his hands in prayer, and to him is vouchsafed a sudden half-glimpse of "the ravishing enigma of her eyes". He is now finally overwhelmed by her "implacable light and bliss", and he is like an atom of her illimitable self, a drop of the ocean of her ecstasy:

> Drunk with a deep golden spiritual wine,
> He cast from the rent stillness of his soul
> A cry of adoration and desire
> And the surrender of his boundless mind
> And the self-giving of his silent heart.
> He fell down at her feet unconscious, prone. [134]

XV

'THE KINGDOMS OF THE GREATER KNOWLEDGE'

Returning to consciousness "after a measureless moment of the soul", Aswapati knows that here once and for all has "closed the finite's crawl to the Infinite". This is an experience without parallel, and Aswapati feels new-made; renewed, purified, strengthened:

> Absolved from the ligaments of death and sleep
> He rode the lightning seas of cosmic Mind
> And crossed the ocean of original sound;...[135]

He gains new insights into the heavens above and the abyss below, and he grows in the "wisdom of the timeless Child". One more effort at self-transcendence, and all that he has aspired for himself are now finally his; he is heir to primal Energy and overwhelming Light; he reads the book of the Overmind and he tingles with the rapture of the Oversoul:

> A borderer of the empire of the Sun,
> Attuned to the supernal harmonies,
> He linked creation to the Eternal's sphere.
> His finite parts approached their absolutes,
> His actions framed the movements of the Gods,
> His will took up the reins of cosmic Force.[136]

And that is the end of Aswapati's ascent as a typical representative of the race. He has realised all for himself, and he has seen the Possibility open to the race. He has reached after endless trials and heroic persistence the shining tablelands of the Kingdom of the Greater Knowledge. He has been thrilled by the mighty currents in the "kingdom of the Spirit's power and light", and his inviews of Reality and outviews of Possibility have coalesced into a clear and ardent hope for the future of man and of the earth.

SECTION C

'THE BOOK OF THE DIVINE MOTHER'

I

'THE PURSUIT OF THE UNKNOWABLE'

The whole adventure of Evolution, the long weary climb of man himself up the steps of civilisation and culture, the castles of achievement and the inns of tranquillity on the way, all have made Aswapati what he is—the spearhead of the advance of the human race, humanity's worthiest representative and leader. Through yoga he has perfected himself, and it has helped him to gather in himself all the potentialities of the evolutionary adventure and make an ascent to the highest possible heights. He has surveyed the past, present and future—not in space and time alone, but also, and more particularly, beyond space and time. He has journeyed in the occult worlds of Night, Twilight, and Day, and he has traversed the heady stairs of Descent and Ascent. He is greatly enriched by all this experience, and he learns to aspire endlessly, to press on and on, to resist successfully the attacks of Falsehood and Ignorance.

But Aswapati is dissatisfied still. Whatever the fruits of yogic aspiration and striving, they affect the *yogin*, but not the world as a whole. Terrestrial life remains what it has always been. The badges of human imperfection retain their shape and colour and character. A Presence, a Glory is lacking, "like Love when the Beloved's face is gone". There is indeed a tantalising quality about the Essence, the Cause, the Truth; from a distance it lures the searcher, but when he approaches it, it retreats and flies. Aswapati must seek out again—he will not accept defeat. The dim Possibility alone is not enough; it must be realised here on earth. The Power that alone can bring about this transformation must be sought out, and the way should be opened for the descent of the Power and the change of earth nature into supernature.

Aswapati will now make a third yogic climb into the realms above and seek out the ultimate Power and plead for its descent into this world so that the desired transformation may be brought about. For a time the ascent is made "invincibly...without pause"; but presently he is confronted by "a tremendous choice". The horizon of known forms ends, the cloud-capped palaces of Nescience collapse without a trace:

> In an abysmal lapse of all things built
> Transcending every perishable support
> And joining at last its mighty origin,
> The separate self must melt or be reborn
> Into a Truth beyond the mind's appeal. [137]

Aswapati sees extending before him a universe that defies every attempt at comprehension:

> Only a formless Form of self was left,
> A tenuous ghost of something that had been,
> The last experience of a lapsing wave
> Before it sinks into a bourneless sea,—...[138]

But at last Something responds to Aswapati's passionate call; nor form nor motion nor word, it has nor mind nor heart nor passion; only a Being "formless, featureless and mute...uncreating, uncreated and unborn"...

> A silent Cause occult, impenetrable,—
> Infinite, eternal, unthinkable, alone. [139]

Aswapati has cantered across the manifested worlds and has reached the threshold of the White Radiance, the throne of the transcendent Divine; he is before the great Unknowable who faces him "with its dumb tremendous calm".

II

'THE ADORATION OF THE DIVINE MOTHER'

It is a tremendous moment for Aswapati. Terrestrial trappings fall from him, human vestiges vanish; separative identity is ended, the drop has been swallowed up by the ocean! Is this, then, the end? Not to *be*—the soul lost in the "boundless silence of the Self". For Aswapati himself, such is no doubt a consummation devoutly to be wished. But he is more than the individual, Aswapati. He is also a king, and he is the spearhead of aspiring and evolving humanity; he is the trustee of the earth's and humanity's future. An individual salvation, a personal leap into "a glad divine abyss" cannot redeem the earth nor hew pathways to humanity's advance. The bliss of nirvana is but the bliss of the Everlasting Nay.

> But where is the Lover's everlasting Yes,
> And immortality in the secret heart,
> The voice that chants to the creator Fire,
> The symbolled OM, the great assenting Word,
> The bridge between the rapture and the calm,
> The passion and the beauty of the Bride,
> The chamber where the glorious enemies kiss,
> The smile that saves, the golden peak of things? [140]

But Silence is not death; an absolute power sleeps therein, and when it is awakened, the Nay can turn into the Everlasting Yea. Aswapati cannot lose himself in nirvana; he must 'beyond' it, or penetrate it, till the great Yea is awakened to grant him his and the earth's and humanity's innermost heart's and soul's desire.

As he stands poised on the edge of being, desperately resisting and denying the finality of nirvana, his faith is answered and an auspicious Presence draws close to him and, like a mother, clasps him and Nature and the world to her breast. She is the All-Beautiful Mother of all godheads and all strengths, she is the mediatrix between earth and Heaven. Aswapati is lifted out of himself, cleansed of all dross, and finds new doors of perception. He sees for the first time, he hears, he feels, he knows with an utter immediacy and completeness. The knowledge invades and possesses him, strength streams into him, joy thrills him. The Divine Mother is the Arts and Sciences all:

> The spirit's alchemist energy is hers;
> She is the golden bridge, the wonderful fire…
> Above, the boundless hushed beatitudes,
> Below, the wonder of the embrace divine. [141]

Aswapati is overpowered as well as renewed; it is the end that makes the real beginning. He will surrender to the Mother in absolute trust, and she will fill him with her own strength and purpose:

> Only he longed to draw her presence and power
> Into his heart and mind and breathing frame;
> Only he yearned to call for ever down
> Her healing touch of love and truth and joy
> Into the darkness of the suffering world. [142]

III

'THE HOUSE OF THE SPIRIT AND THE NEW CREATION'

Intent on achieving the conditions that will make possible world-transformation and a new creation, Aswapati retreats to the stillness of the soul and sits,

> …like an incarnate hope
> Motionless on a pedestal of prayer. [143]

He will not lose his links with the world, not even with the Inconscience; the Inconscient is infinite too and cannot be mocked! Not an escape but a total embrace, not an ignoration but a total comprehension of all matter and all life, is the way to the goal he has set before himself. From self-knowledge radiates world-knowledge, and the infinitesimal becomes the infinite:

> In this tremendous universality
> Not only his soul-nature and mind-sense
> Included every soul and mind in his,
> But even the life of flesh and nerve was changed
> And grew one flesh and nerve with all that lives;...
> His universal sympathy upbore,
> Immense like ocean, the creation's load...[144]

In him are centred the world's strivings and hopes; he incarnates for the nonce the world's pathways to Possibility; he stands "fulfilled on the world's highest line". Beyond sense and feeling, beyond word and thought, comprehending everything but also transcending everything, carrying a world's plea but also implying the inevitable assent, Aswapati is now actor and witness, he is the child of time admitted to "the sessions of Infinity". Aswapati's culminating ascent and patient vigil amidst the desolate solitudes of the heights coerce the descent and the response. It is as though he has received a fresh accession of strength and a new extension of vision. He clearly catches glimpses of the great Possibility of world transformation:

> There was no sob of suffering anywhere;
> Experience ran from point to point of joy:
> Bliss was the pure undying truth of things...
> In these new worlds projected he became
> A portion of the universal gaze,
> A station of the all-inhabiting light,
> A ripple on a single sea of peace.[145]

He sees too "a hierarchy of lucent planes"—a hierarchy, not an anarchy, of lucent (not opaque) realms. The contours of limitation we see here on earth are not found there:

> The Powers that here betray our hearts and err,
> Were there sovereign in truth, perfect in joy,

Masters in a creation without flaw,
Possessors of their own infinitude...
The will obeyed the thought, the act the will.
There was a harmony woven twixt soul and soul...
A mystery drama of divine delight,
A living poem of world-ecstasy,
A kakemono of significant forms,... [146]

It is the vision of our heart's ultimate desire, it is the glimpse of the 'never-never-never realm' of absolute perfection, it is "Reality's summer-house on the beaches of the sea of Infinity".

There are the "two vast negations", of course—'the Materialist Denial' and 'the Refusal of the Ascetic', as Sri Aurobindo calls them in *The Life Divine*. It is these negations that hinder the total marriage of matter and spirit and the emergence here of a new creation. But the negations shall be themselves denied:

A new creation from the old shall rise,
A Knowledge inarticulate find speech,
Beauty suppressed burst into paradise bloom,
Pleasure and pain dive into absolute bliss. [147]

Himself emancipated, Aswapati is nevertheless the bearer of the burden of the world's desire that climbs up to him "from the striving planes"; he is two beings now, "one wide and free above,/One struggling, bound, intense, its portion here".[148] He is the witness to the splendour above, he is also the voice of supplication from below. Defying the denials, he articulates earth's prayer to the Unknown, and listens for the answering footsteps,

...for the fiat of the Word
That comes through the still self from the Supreme. [149]

IV

'THE VISION AND THE BOON'

The stage now is his own heart, the auditorium the "listening spaces of the soul". Aswapati looks inward, he thrills at the sacred stir and approach; mind, members, life, are "merged in ecstasy" and partake beatitude. "Flame-pure, ethereal-tressed a mighty Face" appears, the lips quiver, the words come. Aswapati is the elect, the transfigured, but he is asked to leave the Inconscient alone:

> How shalt thou speak for men whose hearts are dumb,
> Make purblind earth the soul's seer-vision's home
> Or lighten the burden of the senseless globe?...
> Awake not the immeasurable descent,
> Speak not my secret name to hostile Time;
> Man is too weak to bear the Infinite's weight. [150]

Death must be unconquered still on earth, and the dramas played in the theatre of Time must still diet on suffering and pain. It is man's merit that he is awake, that he has memory and desire, that he cannot help aspiring "to change the cosmic dream". But the law of Chance and Death cannot be altered; man is condemned yet to be no more than "a link between the demigod and the beast"; he must veer between the pulls of darkness and light, and play endlessly this inconclusive game. But the wheels of the evolutionary advance, though they grind slowly or by fits and starts, grind also with a complete inevitability, and man is the base on which the citadels of the seeming impossible are to be reared in the future. Aswapati is to hope and persevere, not force the pace:

> Traveller upon the bare eternal heights,
> Tread still the difficult and dateless path
> Joining the cycles with its austere curve
> Measured for man by the initiate Gods...
> Ask not the imperfect fruit, the partial prize.

Only one boon, to greaten thy spirit, demand;
Only one joy, to raise thy kind, desire…
All things shall change in God's transfiguring hour.[151]

Having seen what he has seen, having glimpsed the great crests of future Possibility, must Aswapati still return to *this* bank empty-handed, hugging only the phantom of Hope and donning only the armour of Patience? A cry is wrung from Aswapati:

How shall I rest content with mortal days
And the dull measure of terrestrial things,
I who have seen behind the cosmic mask
The glory and the beauty of thy face? [152]

What use were waiting, when "all we have done is ever still to do", when humanity is apparently doomed to follow the circuit of folly and failure? How long this compromise between the beast and God? As the beast has been exceeded by man, shall not man in turn be superseded by a greater than man, the Superman?

This high divine successor surely shall come
Behind man's inefficient mortal pace,
Behind his vain labour, sweat and blood and tears:…
Inheritor of the toil of human time,
He shall take on him the burden of the gods;… [153]

"He shall"—but when, oh when! The earth has waited long, and man has waited long; the Mother can remain indifferent no longer, and leave things to the slow process of change. The sterile plant of hope must put forth an immediate bud of promise so that the rich fruit may not be long withheld. Aswapati will not miss this golden moment and miss the promise of a hastened Dawn. Aswapati's winged words fly up to the Presence with their load of anguished memory and hope, of urgent prayer and entreaty:

O Wisdom-Splendour, Mother of the universe,
Creatrix, the Eternal's artist Bride,
Linger not long…

Let thy infinity in one body live,
All-Knowledge wrap one mind in seas of light,
All-Love throb single in one human heart...
Pack with the eternal might one human hour
And with one gesture change all future time.[154]

Aswapati has articulated his and the world's paramount desire and has sought the boon of an imminent divine advent. Let the Mother herself come down as a human being to lead the struggle against the Darkness and establish the reign of Light, Love and Immortality. Let it be no purblind groping after far horizons which, as one approaches them faster and faster, only fly further and further; let it rather be a purposeful forging ahead, a bold storming of the fortress of Nescience, under the leadership of a choice superior spirit. The Divine Mother now gives her wide consenting voice to expectant Aswapati:

O strong forerunner, I have heard thy cry.
One shall descend and break the iron Law,
Change Nature's doom by the lone spirit's power...
Beauty shall walk celestial on the earth,
Delight shall sleep in the cloud-net of her hair
And in her body as on his homing tree
Immortal Love shall beat his glorious wings...
She shall bear Wisdom in her voiceless bosom,
Strength shall be with her like a conqueror's sword
And from her eyes the Eternal's bliss shall gaze.
A seed shall be sown in Death's tremendous hour,
A branch of heaven transplant to human soil;
Nature shall overleap her mortal step;
Fate shall be changed by an unchanging will.[155]

The words cease, and the splendour fades away; only the echoes of the promise fill the chambers of the soul and make new cadences that are untranslatable. Eternity recedes, and Time's slow tread is heard. Aswapati, having gained his heart's immaculate desire, returns to the familiar ways of the world. But it is to be no vain repetition of the old routine; he is sustained now by the vision splendid and the Promise nectarean. It is the lord of a spiritual empire who has imposed his mastery on the occult realms of the World Stair that now returns to where he started from and resumes,

> ...his mighty rounds
> In the scant field of the ambiguous globe.[156]

SAVITRI'S STORY

SECTION A

'THE BOOK OF BIRTH AND QUEST'

I

'THE BIRTH AND CHILDHOOD OF THE FLAME'

There are two backgrounds to the central drama played in *Savitri*. There is the cosmic background, sketched already in Books II and III—'The Book of the Traveller of the Worlds' and 'The Book of the Divine Mother', and there is the human background, to be sketched now in Book IV, 'The Book of Savitri's Birth and Quest'. The wider cosmic background includes the smaller human background, for they are both centred in Savitri. Aswapati's Yoga articulates the earth's cry for perfection, and in answer, the Power behind the cosmos promises the advent of Savitri. Aswapati's aspirations on behalf of evolving humanity are to be realised by Savitri, though only after a struggle. The struggle and the victory are the hard core of the drama of *Savitri*, the rest is epic scaffolding. The outer scaffolding being concluded, Sri Aurobindo now turns to the nearer scaffolding, that is, Savitri's earlier story upto the dawn of the fateful day in her and in the world's history. This recital takes four Books, made up of sixteen cantos. It is only when this spell of retrospective narration is over that the drama can be continued from the point where it has been left at the end of Book I, canto 2.

Revolving earth participates in the cycle of the seasons. The sea of inconscience beats against the shores of infinity. Life appears obscurely, appears and disappears and reappears. The seasons pass, the seasons return. What is the far-off event towards which all creation is striving?

> Amid the ambiguous stillness of the stars
> She moved towards some undisclosed event
> And her rhythm measured the long whirl of Time. [157]

The seasons are turns in the rhythm, and mark "the symbol pageant of the changing year". First summer, with its violent noons and torrid light, "and the blue seal of a great burnished sky", follows the season of rain-tide, the sky is overcast with clouds, the furrowed earth receives the torrents, and heaven's waters trail and dribble through the drowned land. The dry soil is muddied and miry, earth assumes a dull-grey look, till "a last massive deluge" clears up the mess and leaves everything in "lulled repose". It is the creative mating of the sky and the earth, the secret fashioning of the cosmic purpose.

> A calmness neared as of the approach of God,
> A light of musing trance lit soil and sky
> And an identity and ecstasy
> Filled meditation's solitary heart.
> A dream loitered in the dumb mind of Space,
> Time opened its chambers of felicity,
> An exaltation entered and a hope:... [158]

As the days and months pass, as "three thoughtful seasons" scan their pregnant hours, there is the expectancy of a flame, a mighty birth to come. Summer has given place to autumn, which in turn is followed by winter: the season of mellow fruitfulness is followed by dew-time conservation, and the "tranquil beauty of the waning year":

> Then Spring, an ardent lover, leaped through leaves
> And caught the earth-bride in his eager clasp;
> His advent was a fire of irised hues,
> His arms were a circle of the arrival of joy. [159]

Million-hued, joy blossoms forth, and to live is very ecstasy; all sights, all voices, breathe new charm; colours fuse into patterns of delight, while cries coalesce into litanies, and all Nature is at beauty's festival.

Spring always signals the "arrival of joy", but a special and unique joy is Aswapati's when, in answer to his yearning and the earth's, "a mediating ray" touches the human vessel and lights a new lamp. There is verily "a consanguinity of earth and heaven", for ever since the earth-plasm first tingled with life, heaven is invading earth and pressing "perfection on life's stumbling powers". But although relapses are easy and success eludes, the strivings continue without intermission and heaven drives the earth to new attempts at reaching infinitude. At the culmination of many such adventures in transcendence there is this new descent invoked by the pressure of Aswapati's Yoga—Savitri is conceived, Savitri is born. An immaculate event in this symbol spring of humanity's reviving year, the child is "as yet a prophecy only and a hint"; but she is more, much more, when new dawns fill her with beauty and purpose:

> Even in her childish movements could be felt
> The nearness of a light still kept from earth,...
> As needing nothing but its own rapt flight
> Her nature dwelt in a strong separate air
> Like a strange bird with large rich-coloured breast
> That sojourns on a secret fruited bough,

Lost in the emerald glory of the woods
Or flies above divine unreachable tops.[160]

Savitri's childhood and girlhood are a wonder apart, for while she is apparently at home in the world of Nature and man, she is also not of it, she is ruled by an occult godhead, and it is as though,

Invisibly protected from our sense
The Dryad lives drenched in a deeper ray
And feels another air of storms and calms
And quivers inwardly with mystic rain.[161]

The traditional stories of "Krishna Lila" reveal the boy who was also God, the innocence that was also Wisdom, the baby-tenderness that was also sovereign Power. Likewise, in the life of the child and girl Savitri, a tenuous line separates the human from the divine:

As from the soil sprang glory of branch and flower,
As from the animal's life rose thinking man,
A new epiphany appeared in her.
A mind of light, a life of rhythmic force,
A body instinct with hidden divinity
Prepared an image of the coming god;... [162]

As the years add to her strength of limb and grace of form, as the movements of her heart gather the world into her and endear her to all, even so her 'solitary greatness' only grows and grows, a warrior will paces "in her city of strength/Inviolate, guarding Truth's diamond throne". [163]

Sri Aurobindo's description of the birth and childhood of Savitri is far from conventional. The legend and the symbol intertwine and contribute to their mutual enrichment. The magnificent account of the burst of rain-tide, the rumble of thunder and the dazzle of lightning, the "emissary javelins" and the "surge and hiss and onset of huge rain", the assault of the sky on the recumbent earth, the downpour and drip, the fullness and the exhaustion, the contentment and the lulled repose, all suggestively lead to the promised miraculous event of Savitri's conception and her birth, "three thoughtful seasons" later, in the season of spring. The cosmic and terrestrial planes meet in an intimate embrace, and out of the flux and the tension, the passion and the creative will, is born the child Savitri who shall be the redeemer, the saviour. Of the child Lucy, William Wordsworth writes:

> Three years she grew in sun and shower,
> Then Nature said, 'A lovelier flower
> On earth was never sown;
> This Child I to myself will take...'

The occult powers behind the phenomena of Nature lend Savitri their graces and their strengths, as Nature moulds Lucy; but Savitri draws to herself other powers too, from the home and base of all:

> An invisible sunlight ran within her veins
> And flooded her brain with heavenly brilliances
> That woke a wider sight than earth could know.[164]

She is the dream made real, "an image made of heaven's transparent light", a "perfect whole", harmonious, immense and various; a "golden bridge" spanning earth and heaven.

II

'THE GROWTH OF THE FLAME'

Vyasa is succinctness itself when he records in the *Mahabharata*: "And, in course of time, the girl (Savitri) attained maidenhood". Just that. But Sri Aurobindo is nothing if not elaborate, richly yet relevantly elaborate. The child grows into the girl, and the girl becomes a young woman. A common enough occurrence though always compact of wonder and romance; how much more so when the girl is Savitri!

Savitri is a king's daughter. Her father Aswapati rules over the land of Madra, as rich and variegated in its landscape as in its spiritual 'inscape', the home of beauty and grace, of reverie and trance.

An ideal background for the fostering of the "incarnate Flame" that is Savitri:

> Over her watched millennial influences
> And the deep godheads of a grandiose past
> Looked on her and saw the future's godheads come
> As if this magnet drew their powers unseen. [165]

The more immediate influences, however, are the usual educative and human forces that help to foster the growth of a child in a properly adjusted society. Beauty in art and Nature, "the harmony of a rich culture's tones", the discipline of ethics and philosophy, the climb of the mind to eagle heights, the leaps of thought "crossing the mystic seas of the Beyond", all play their part in Savitri's mental and spiritual evolution. Sculpture and painting, music and architecture, dance and poetry, the many arts and crafts, these are pressed into service too, and Savitri masters them, and is moulded by them. Nor are the intellectual disciplines and knowledges ignored—astronomy, mathematics and physics that make a "theorized diagram of mind and life". Yet Savitri thirsts for something vaster still, for the knowledge that exceeds the knowledges, for the "art and wisdom of the Gods". Something of this obscurely stirs within her;

> ...waiting as yet for form,
> It asked for objects around which to grow
> And natures strong to bear without recoil
> The splendour of her native royalty,... [166]

She still needs the cause and field of action, the human media that can both receive and give and thus create "a transcendent action's sphere".

It is but natural that growing Savitri should turn to human companionship and camaraderie—even love, perhaps, the love of universal sisterhood. She sees others as "her soul's reflections, complements, counterparts", which are bound to her own spirit "by ties divine". Cannot she clasp in one immense embrace the whole body of created things? But her friends and companions miss the main intent of her life or are put out by the fierce glare of her all consuming love:

> Only a few responded to her call:
> Still fewer felt the screened divinity...[167]

She is their leader more than a friend, she outpaces them, and when nearest to them she is yet "divine and far". Varied is the stream of humanity that passes her by—some are aloof and admire her, some approach her with desire and recoil in discomfiture, and some others still stand troubled and tantalised in the extreme,

> Inapt to meet divinity so close,
> Intolerant of a Force they could not house.[168]

Although passing her days in this world and among these hearts, Savitri feels unengaged yet in the secret infinities of her heart and soul; none strikes a responsive chord within, and nowhere she finds "her partner of high tasks". Meantime the news of her rare beauty and power runs "murmuring on the lips of men/Exalted and sweet like an inspired verse".[169] But neither homage nor fame lessens her solitariness; like a goddess in a crowded temple, she is worshipped marvelously, but none dares to claim her; she must live amidst them awhile yet until "her hour of fate" projects before her, her God to claim and be claimed.

III

'THE CALL TO THE QUEST'

In the splendour of her radiant beauty, Savitri strikes her beholders as a being verily divine; and so men are content to worship, and are afraid to ask her hand in marriage. Such is the simple statement in the old legendary narrative. Vyasa adds further that king Aswapati, finding that there are no suitors for Savitri, becomes sad in consequence. He accordingly asks her to look for herself and choose a husband who may be worthy of her. This essential situation is retained by

Sri Aurobindo, though he elaborates and embellishes it so as to fill the canvas of the vast symbol drama that is superimposed on the simple legendary one.

While Savitri dwells "apart in herself" though circling humanity with her love and comprehending with, "her spirit's large and free delight...the ardent-hued magnificent lives of animal and bird and flower and tree",[170] a day dawns that is like other dawns, yet burdened with a special destiny; a trembling expectancy fills the air, a lyric *coil* cries "among the leaves"; and King Aswapati's awakened ear catches the accents of earth's "wordless hymn to the Ineffable" and the answering word that leaps from "some far sky of thought". The word of accusation and exhortation, heard so often before, is heard again. Why *would* man tread this dolorous way of ignorance and misery when the way of knowledge and happiness is there before him?

> O petty adventurers in an infinite world
> And prisoners of a dwarf humanity,
> How long will you tread the circling tracks of mind
> Around your little self and petty things? [171]

The lesser tasks engage us, the greater remain unattempted, unachieved. Mortal mind obscures these greater tasks and the veils must needs be pierced and broken through. Earth is potentially the kin-soil of heaven, and deserves to be cultivated as such. Invisible immortal visitants flame past our doors, but we do not recognise them, nor align ourselves with them. The trapped divinity seeks release in vain. The race of seers, the sages and the poets, have exhorted us in vain. The great illusion has us still in thrall, and we wriggle helplessly, plan purposelessly, and fail.

As the stern voice of admonition and compassion is stilled at last, there advances towards Aswapati, "like a shining answer from the gods", his darling daughter, Savitri. It is a preordained concatenation:

> There came the gift of a revealing hour:...
> A deathless meaning filled her mortal limbs;
> As in a golden vase's poignant line

They seemed to carry the rhythmic sob of bliss
Of earth's mute adoration towards heaven
Released in beauty's cry of living form
Towards the perfection of eternal things.[172]

It is his child still, he sees the familiar face and limbs, he meets the eyes lighted up with love, but he now sees them as the vessel of the immortal spirit, as Yasoda sees Krishna when he opens his mouth and reveals all the worlds to her. Savitri is no mere girl, but the "traveller of eternity"; she sojourns amidst ordinary humanity, yet is also "armed for the splendid hazard" of her life; but even she cannot abide alone any longer "missalled in aureate virginity". She shall now go out into the world and choose the Lord of her life:

Depart where love and destiny call your charm.
Venture through the deep world to find thy mate...
The lyrist of thy soul's most intimate chords
Who shall give voice to what in thee is mute...
Ascend from Nature to divinity's heights;
Face the high gods, crowned with felicity,
Then meet a greater god, thy self beyond Time.[173]

As Savitri receives the full impact of these words, it is as though the mantra, slowly sinking in the *yogin*'s ear, starts rhythmic strains and induces "an ecstasy and an immortal change"; a "greatness in her life" is sown, the seed of the great ecstasy and change that are to come. Savitri spends the day and night in a hushed fullness of anticipation, and when another day dawns, she has already left her father's roof, and the palace wakes "to its own emptiness".

IV

'THE QUEST'

From the shelter of her parents' home and city, Savitri loses herself in the wide world's unchartered ways, and feels dazzled by the unfolding panorama of "new brilliant scenes" and divers soil and country, clans and peoples. She is a part of all she meets, the very stars and winds are her dear comrades, and she feels sometimes as though she is but tracing "again a journey often made". She sees and remembers, or she remembers and sees, and from her silent heights she can peer through the dim play of appearance. She sees multi-foliate Nature and million-hued humanity, and winds her way through the still untravelled world:

> Her carven chariot with its fretted wheels
> Threaded through clamorous marts and sentinel towers
> Past figured gates and high dream-sculptured fronts
> And gardens hung in the sapphire of the skies,
> Pillared assembly halls with armoured guards,...[174]

Not populous far-famed cities only but the humbler haunts of common folk also draw Savitri's attention and affectionate gaze. The virgin silences of unfrequented hills and valleys have a deep purpose of their own for it is there the great Creatrix nurses "her symbol mysteries" and guards for "her pure-eyed sacraments":

> The valley clefts between her breasts of joy,
> Her mountain altars for the fires of dawn
> And nuptial beaches where the ocean couched
> And the huge chanting of her prophet woods.[175]

Deep in the woods' recesses are the hermitages of the wise, and Savitri visits them too and studies the lives of the "strong king-sages" and their "young grave disciples". They are not as other men, but live "immaculate in tranquil heights of self"; and their ministry makes their neophytes "comrades of the cosmic urge,/No longer chained to their small separate selves".[176] They are masters of knowledge, and "vessels of the cosmic Force"; they are pacifiers and harmonisers, and they are the healers of the "hard and wounded world". And when they lisp in numbers, they sing "Infinity's names and deathless powers/In metres that reflect the moving worlds".[177] Active or passive, in speech or in silence, in creation or in contemplation, these wise children of the forest help the world in its toils and guard and extend the immaculate treasures of the spirit.

As Savitri glides in and out of these hermitages and haunts of the wise, her sensibilities are quickened still further and she feels "the kinship of eternal calm". Yet her quest keeps her moving on and on, for she is yet to find what she has set out to seek. She calls the Powers to her help, and hopes that she may not be "overwhelmed by the immensity" of the world stretching before her. Still Nature lures her on, still she wanders, gazes, communes; the crickets' cry rings in her ears, the serpentine road seems an endless coil; the desert sands are bleak, the jungle voices are eerie; yet she will persevere in her quest, however hard the earth and torridly oppressive the sky:

> The months had fed the passion of the sun
> And now his burning breath assailed the soil.
> The tiger heats prowled through the fainting earth;
> All was licked up as by a lolling tongue.
> The spring winds failed; the sky was set like bronze.[178]

SECTION B

'THE BOOK OF LOVE'

I

'THE DESTINED MEETING PLACE'

The "destined spot and hour", however, draw close. Naught happens but has its time and setting in the preordained cosmic play. Savitri now approaches a region,

> ...of soft and delicate air
> That seemed a sanctuary of youth and joy,
> A highland world of free and green delight
> Where spring and summer lay together and strove
> In indolent and amicable debate,
> Inarmed, disputing with laughter who should rule.[179]

Sri Aurobindo's description of the 'other Eden', this 'demi-Paradise', recalls Milton's description of Paradise before the Fall. Man, bird and beast are at peace with themselves and with circumambient Nature. Sri Aurobindo's fancy takes wings and snaps a scene of almost other-world felicity:

> Pale waters ran like glimmering threads of pearl.
> A sigh was straying among happy leaves;
> Cool-perfumed with slow pleasure-burdened feet
> Faint stumbling breezes faltered among flowers.
> The white crane stood, a vivid motionless streak,
> Peacock and parrot jeweled soil and tree,
> The dove's soft moan enriched the enamoured air
> And fire-winged wild-drakes swam in silvery pools.
> Earth couched alone with her great lover Heaven,
> Uncovered to her consort's azure eye...[180]

A space sanctified, a meeting-place of earth and heaven, a home for the profession of love and beauty, a primeval realm for the reign of peace, a retreat for solitude and fresh creation,

> This was the scene which the ambiguous Mother
> Had chosen for her brief felicitous hour;...[181]

Here love will confront Savitri, and her quest—so long pursued and so often renewed—will end in the glory of the recognition and acceptance of love.

II

'SATYAVAN'

As Savitri's "high carven car" winds its way through the wilderness on this day of predestination, she spies beyond the road deep recesses and groves and even catches the accents of speech:

> Sweet like desires enamoured and unseen,
> Cry answering to low insistent cry.[182]

A "single path, shot thin and arrowlike" seems to lead into the half-hidden bowers of peace, and while following it, suddenly he appears,

> ...against the forest verge
> Inset twixt green relief and golden ray.
> As if a weapon of the living Light,
> Erect and lofty like a spear of God
> His figure led the splendour of the morn.[183]

He is like "a wide daybreak of the gods", his body—albeit a youthful *rishi*'s—is "a lover's and a king's". Destiny had sent him here to be the "foster-child of beauty and solitude", and he has grown in strength of limb and transparent lucidity of soul, mastering all knowledge and finding repose in the Spirit.

This day of all days, Satyavan has—as if out to keep an appointment—strayed from his customary paths and gravitated towards the "forest's flowering verge", and there the vision of beauty, the divine shock of love, overwhelms him. At first Savitri from her car gazes vaguely about her, drinking in the loveliness of the place, and seeing him too, though not with particular intent; but presently her vision settles on him, the magic recognition takes place, and all is changed. Is he the genius of the spot? He looks "a king of life outlined in delicate air".[184] But the mere thinking faculty soon abdicates its function, waves of sudden ecstasy beat upon her, she is caught in a "mystic tumult from her depths", she is smitten by the arrows of pain and desire, the birth-pangs of a great new emotion throw her into convulsion, and at last she flings open the doors of her soul to this splendorous Sun. Their eyes meet, and the great alchemy works:

> Then trembling with the mystic shock her heart
> Moved in her breast and cried out like a bird
> Who hears his mate upon a neighbouring bough.[185]

The reins of the horses are drawn instantaneously back, the chariot stands "like an arrested wind"; and Satyavan, now alerted into attention,

> ...looked out from his soul's doors
> And felt the enchantment of her liquid voice
> Fill his youth's purple ambiance and endured
> The haunting miracle of a perfect face.[186]

Is this a new divinity undreamt of before? Satyavan misses his moorings and flounders "as in fire"; he is lost, another has seized him entire; even in the mere "sight's embrace", infinity merges with infinity. As dazed Satyavan dares Savitri's eyes:

> He met in her regard his future's gaze,
> A promise and a presence and a fire,
> Saw an embodiment of aeonic dreams,...[187]

No chance or new meeting is this, though it seems such to be; nor aliens nor strangers are they, but soulmates since the beginning of things, and now awakening into a new recognition of each other by the roseate dawn of love.

Love is a spiraling phenomenon, its base is on earth and earthy, its crown is in the highest heavens; its power has a uniform potency, though the effects may differ at different points of the spiral. At the lower reaches, there are not wanting debasing and corrupting influences that cheapen and poison love. But in its essential movement and in its proper field, "Love is a glory from eternity's sphere". None is really dead to love, but each waits "like an unopened flower" for the destined moment of unfolding. Love is the "child-god" who variously accomplishes the blaze of transfigurement in which man and woman run into mutual recognition, and each exclaims:

> Behold the one
> For whom my life has waited long unfilled,
> Behold the sudden sovereign of my days.[188]

There is marvellous communion between heart and heart, limb and limb, and all the world seems to be charged with the beauty of heaven. Such a moment has come to Satyavan and Savitri:

> Attracted as in heaven star by star,
> They wondered at each other and rejoiced
> And wove affinity in a silent gaze.
> A moment passed that was eternity's ray,
> An hour began, the matrix of new Time.[189]

III

'SATYAVAN AND SAVITRI'

There is recognition in the depths of their being, joy wells up, yet they strive for understanding speech. There is resistance from "the screen of the external sense", the inner sight is impeded, the right words are slow in coming. Satyavan first comes out of the trance of fascination and apostrophises her as one might a goddess who has swum across one's view:

Whence hast thou dawned filling my spirit's days,
Brighter than summer, brighter than my flowers,
Into the lonely borders of my life,
O Sunlight moulded like a golden maid?[190]

Not unused to the denizens of the upper air, Satyavan has in the past heard the "centaur's wizard song", glimpsed the *apsaras* in their abandon, and "beheld the princes of the Sun"; has she come too from "the Thunderer's worlds?" Perhaps she will condescend to abide with mortals:

If our time-vexed affections thou canst feel,
Earth's ease of simple things can satisfy,
If thy glance can dwell content on earthly soil,
And this celestial summary of delight,
Thy golden body, dally with fatigue
Oppressing with its grace our terrain, while
The frail sweet passing taste of earthly food
Delays thee and the torrent's leaping wine,
Descend. Let thy journey cease, come down to us.[191]

His father's hermitage is near, where "bare, simple is the sylvan hermit-life"; there she can find a "resting chamber" fit for her.

Savitri, shaking herself free from the magic web of his echoing voice, tells her name—"I am Savitri, Princess of Madra"—and asks in turn for his, and why he is content to abide in the forest's inaccessible solitudes. He tells his story too; he is Satyavan, the Shalwa King Dyumatsena's son—but a king no more, for he has lost eyesight and kingdom both:

Outcast from empire of the outer light,
Lost to the comradeship of seeing men,
He sojourns in two solitudes, within
And in the solemn rustle of the woods.[192]

And so has Satyavan been led to cultivate "the frankness of the primal earth", with the sunlight's companionship in day-time, and "the moonbeam's silver ecstasy" shaping his sleep at night. Nature's ministry has been gentle and unfailing, and has given him intimations vast and profound; kingfisher, swan, pranked butterfly, peacock, spotted deer, these and other "high beauty's visitants" have found ways of reaching to his soul. Above all he says,

> I carved my vision out of wood and stone;
> I caught the echoes of a word supreme
> And metred the rhythm-beats of infinity
> And listened through music for the eternal Voice.[193]

He has seen fragments of humanity, the Self obscured beyond recognition, each living "in himself and for himself alone"; and he has "sat with the forest sages in their trance" and pierced the veil of the many to reach the presence of the One. Yet matter's stubborn resistance to change has defeated him, he has failed to convert the Inconscience, and Death and the Void are giant spectres still. If only Savitri would share Satyavan's life, could they not with their joint efforts succeed where singly he had failed?

But Savitri would like Satyavan to continue speaking—it is music to her ears—till her spirit's intimations arm her 'mortal mind' with the power to see and the will to accept. And Satyavan's heart melts in "many-coloured waves of speech" and floods her with the joy of growing recognition. Satyavan describes his ardours and longings, his strivings and realisations; he has roamed in dark caverns with thought for his lantern; he has made a deep study of logic and semantics, ethics and metaphysics; he has seen through matter's atomic universe, its "secret laws and sorceries"; he has explored aesthetics, and sought in beauty and art the clue to the still elusive ultimate Truth; yet one or the other has always failed him, the hither or the thither shore. But Savitri's very appearance is like a cure for all Satyavan's earlier frustrations. From his heart's depths comes the cry:

A strange new world swims to me in thy gaze
Approaching like a star from unknown heavens;
A cry of spheres comes with thee and a song
Of flaming gods…
Come nearer to me from thy car of light
On this green sward disdaining not our soil…
O my bright beauty's princess Savitri,
By my delight and thy own joy compelled
Enter my life, thy chamber and thy shrine.[194]

"I know that thou and only thou art he," says Savitri as she steps down from her car "with a soft and faltering haste". Then follows a passage of great sensuous beauty touched also by the accents of the purer poetry of the soul. The woman whose whole response has been awakened offering her love and herself to the man who has kindled this fire of ardour and adoration in her, is the archetype of the world's most thrilling and most moving romantic poetry. There is a traditional ritual about this sacrificial offering which is the basis of life's perennial resurrection. In India from times immemorial it is the girl who advances, bashfully yet bravely, with garland in hand, and so does Savitri here:

A candid garland set with simple forms
Her rapid fingers taught a flower song,
The stanzaed movement of a marriage hymn.
Profound in perfume and immersed in hue
They mixed their yearning's coloured signs and made
The bloom of their purity and passion one.
A sacrament of joy in treasuring palms
She brought, flower-symbol of her offered life,…
She bowed and touched his feet with
worshipping hands;…[195]

Satyavan humbly bends to receive her and gather her into an embrace, and Savitri feels "her being flow into him as in waves/A river pours into a mighty sea".[196] The river has found the sea, the mortal has wakened into Eternity. This is the phoenix hour, the time of their ineffable union. They are married already in the eyes of Heaven, and the symbol rites take their own course:

> On the high glowing cupola of the day
> Fate tied a knot with morning's halo threads
> While by the ministry of an auspice-hour
> Heart-bound before the sun, their marriage fire,
> The wedding of the eternal Lord and Spouse
> Took place again on earth in human forms:...[197]

The priest-wind chants the mantras, the leaves hymn the "choral whisperings", and "one human moment was eternal made".

Now Satyavan leads Savitri to their future home, and calm and content possess her heart. But before she can rest in this felicity she needs must return to Madra and tell Aswapati the choice she has made. But she will return, nor ever again agree to part from Satyavan. So saying she mounts her car once more, and speeds "swift-reined, swift-hearted" towards her parental home; but in the "still lucidities of sight's inner world" she is with Satyavan still in his hermit thatch behind the nave of forest trees.

SECTION C

'THE BOOK OF FATE'

I

'THE WORD OF FATE'

In the old legendary story, when Savitri returns to her father, she finds the Sage Narad with him. When she says she has chosen Satyavan as her consort, Narad ejaculates that it is a wrong decision: not because Satyavan is not worthy in every way, but because he is fated to die in a year's time. Aswapati asks her to choose again, but Savitri says that she can but choose once. Narad now advises the king to allow the marriage to take place.

This raises a number of questions. What is predestination? If fixed fate is a fact, of what use is free will? What is fate, after all? Is there really no armour against fate? If all is predestination what is left of man's individuality?

Again, in the old story, Savitri not only defies fate but changes its course. Fear of death will not make her give up Satyavan, but there is more in it than the emotional constancy of love. There is stern resolve as well. And there is some secret source of strength that feeds this resolve and makes her victory possible.

In his epic, Sri Aurobindo gives the key place to this act of will on Savitri's part. It is a positive act of commitment to a chosen course, come what may. She will be no thistledown of fate. She will not be deflected from her chosen path by these advancing intimations of predestination.

In this tense psychological drama as it is unfolded in 'The Book of Fate' by Sri Aurobindo, four characters participate: King Aswapati, his queen, Sage Narad and Savitri herself. The queen is just human, and hence sees the problem of love and marriage and fate and death and widowhood in the ordinary way of the world. She would take the line of least resistance. Avoid, if possible, the decree of fate; or raise her voice against the rank injustice of it all. Aswapati is the enlightened man, the seer-king, and hence he sees the problem in a wider perspective. Narad the divine-seer can see even further into the future than the king.

But while all three can only talk of what is in their minds, or prevent hasty speech from uttering itself, it is Savitri alone who has to decide: hers is the call to action: she is the protagonist of the play here. Sri Aurobindo accordingly presents these four—the queen, the king, the sage and Savitri—as an ascending order of consciousness, from the mental to the supramental. Savitri needs no advice from Narad nor any encouragement or consolation from her parents. Her decision is made: she knows her way, and she knows that she must go her own way alone. It is the other three who engage in this drama of question and answer, doubt and assurance, and clarify the developing psychological action.

There is one other point, too, to be remembered. In Sri Aurobindo's epic, there is a double significance to every action. If the date of Satyavan's death is pre-determined, so is the common plight ofhumanity also pre-determined. Man is a prey to desire, incapacity and death. He can whimper, he can wail, but he cannot change his destiny. Fate holds him in complete thrall: *It* cannot be affected by tears or through prayer. Savitri's decision has thus a special significance in the symbolic action. She is going to redeem, not her husband alone, but humanity also at the same time. Hers, then, is verily a redeemer's role in the action of the poem. Sri Aurobindo therefore puts into Narad's mouth words that have a special relevance to these two problems: the problem of fate and the role of the redeemer in human affairs.

Before we turn to the poem, it would be instructive to refer to Sri Aurobindo's own views on these subjects as outlined in his more formal writings. In the Indian view, 'fate' and 'karma' are inter-related: "We ourselves are our own fate through our actions, but the fate created by us binds us…Still, we are creating our fate for the future even while undergoing old fate from the past in the present. That gives a meaning to our will and action and does not, as European critics wrongly believe, constitute a rigid and sterilizing fatalism. But again, our will and action can often annul or modify even the past Karma…"[198]

The cosmos is not a mere machine, all a Law and an unalterable Process; there is a Spirit behind it all, which is the Process as well as the Power that regulates it. "The destiny which binds our physical being", writes Sri Aurobindo, "binds it so long or in so far as a greater law does not intervene. Action belongs to the physical part of us, it is the physical outcome of our being; but behind our surface is a freer life power, a freer mind power which has another energy and can create another destiny and bring it in to modify the primary plan, and when the soul and self emerges, when we become consciously spiritual beings, that change can cancel or wholly remodel the graph of our physical fate."[199] The so-called finality of fate is thus not quite so final, after all. Fixed fate doesn't rule out free will. The perversity of the outer ego is not the source of this will; on the other hand, there is a deeper centre and it is from there the true self wills and achieves:

> But the Will within, exceeding the moments of Time, knows all these, and the action of Nature in us is an attempt, we might say, to work out under the difficult conditions of a natural and egoistic ignorance what is foreseen in full supramental light by the inner Will and Knowledge.[200]

When fate seems to bar one's path, there is one recourse possible: appeal to spiritual force. All is possible then. The law itself may be exceeded, and predestination held at bay or even effectively turned back:

> …as soon as one enters the path of spiritual life, this old predetermined destiny begins to recede. There comes in a new

> factor, the Divine Grace, the help of a higher Divine Force other than the force of Karma, which can lift the *sadhak* beyond the present possibilities of his nature. One's spiritual destiny is then the divine election which ensures the future.[201]

Savitri is herself the manifestation of the Divine Grace, and it—becomes her duty—the law of *her* nature—to defy fate and fight the battle for Satyavan and for mankind. She is the avatar, the world-redeemer, and hers is the responsibility to realise, to establish:

> ...something essential and radical needed for the terrestrial evolution which is the evolution of the embodied spirit through successive stages towards the Divine.[202]

To return to the poem: in the first canto of 'The Book of Fate' we are back in the Madra kingdom. Savitri hasn't arrived in her father's palace yet, but towards this home of the royal seer, Aswapati, the divine seer, Narad, descends from the clouds:

> In silent bounds bordering the mortal's plane
> Crossing a wide expanse of brilliant peace
> Narad the heavenly sage from Paradise
> Came chanting through the large and lustrous air.[203]

Narad is Heaven's minstrel and messenger in one, but he can jumble his functions well so that his deeper purposes cannot at once be seen. What brings him from the spaces of heaven to "these rooms of a see-saw game of death and life?" As he wings and sings his way to Aswapati's abode, the seer rapidly reads as from an open book the secrets of life; the cosmic panorama unrolls before him, he passes from mind to the realm of material things; and what he sees, what he reads, he tunes to immortal song. As he gazes at the terrestrial play, his mood changes, his voice quivers with pathos and pity, and he chants the still sad music of humanity. He sings of the beginnings, "how stars were made and life began"; he sings of dumb matter and its veiled self, "its blind unerring occult mystery"; he sings the saga of darkness yearning towards the Light, of death aspiring to immortality; of man and the blossoming of his mind and the throb of his soul and the ache of his brooding Love; and also of his future and his destined rise to the godhead:

> He sang of the glory and marvel still to be born,
> Of Godhead throwing off at last its veil,
> Of bodies made divine and life made bliss,
> Immortal sweetness clasping immortal might,...[204]

As he steps into Aswapati's palace, Narad's face wears "a beautiful mask of antique joy", and the king and queen give him a royal welcome, and for an hour he feasts their ears with his "measured chant" bespeaking the tale of human joys and woes:

> He sang to them of the lotus-heart of love
> With all its thousand luminous buds of truth,...
> And one day it shall hear a blissful voice
> And in the garden of the Spouse shall bloom
> When she is seized by her discovered lord.[205]

Even as Narad sings of this transfiguring marvel, the miracle of the bud of the human heart's sudden efflorescence under the warmth of Love, there appears Savitri herself before them as if in quick fulfilment of the sage's prophetic song. Narad himself is taken aback, but as he flings on her "his vast immortal look", knowledge streams into him, and there is nothing that he cannot see. Yet he holds back this shaft of foreknowledge but rather gives vent to his seeming sense of wonder and glorious surmise. Who is this marvel, the flame-born, the beauty-arrayed? Can the halo of love bring about such a wondrous sea-change and cast a miracle-light on a human frame? Narad is so touched with ecstasy that he cries out to her:

> From what green glimmer of glades
> Retreating into dewy silences
> Or half-seen verge of waters moon-betrayed
> Bringst thou this glory of enchanted eyes?...
> Reveal, O winged with light, whence thou hast flown

> Hastening bright-hued through the green tangled earth,
> Thy body rhythmical with the spring-bird's call.[206]

Narad has travelled oft in the realms of this earth and the other earths; but this vision is like no other he has seen. Here is spring poised towards summer, here is morning making towards the noon, here girlhood glows into womanhood, and here is earth's hope straining towards fruition. Narad's sudden immortal gaze has seized the truth behind the layers of appearance, he knows Savitri's high destiny on earth, he knows too how her path will be strewn with difficulty and danger. Although he has striven to rein back knowledge, the words escape him all the same:

> O thou who hast come to this great perilous world
> Now only seen through the splendour of thy dreams,
> Where hardly love and beauty can live safe,
> Thyself a being dangerously great,...
> As high, as happy might thy waking be!
> If for all time doom could be left to sleep![207]

The dreaming—and the waking; and the shadow of doom in between, this is what Narad sees, and the word is almost spoken. The dream is vivid, being decked in golden hues. Savitri has been to an enchanted grove, she has drunk a joy from no earthly cup, her soul has "answered to a Word unknown". The "ravishing flutes of heaven" are still echoing in the secret chambers of her heart. The "thrill of a remembered clasp" burns into her still. But can reality rise to the expectation of the splendour of her dreams? Is the world of reality safe enough for love and beauty to live in peace? Isn't doom always round the corner, as it were!

Narad has spoken one word too many; he checks himself too late. Aswapati has "marked the dubious close" and inferred behind the words a sinister hint, but he covers up his anxiety with tact and asks the sage rather to bless his child, who is his treasure and his sole hope and only heir:

Behold her, singer with the prescient gaze,
And let thy blessing chant that this fair child
Shall pour the nectar of a sorrowless life
Around her from her lucid heart of love,
Heal with her bliss the tired breast of earth
And cast like a happy snare felicity.[208]

What can Narad say, knowing as he does that "words are vain and Fate is lord"? Assuming, therefore, a mere human curiosity, he asks about the "mission" from which Savitri has returned with "Paradise made visible in her eyes". Aswapati turns to Savitri, and she gives the answer in a few chosen words sufficient to the occasion:

I have obeyed my heart, I have heard its call.
On the borders of a dreaming wilderness
Mid Shalwa's giant hills and brooding woods
In his thatched hermitage Dyumatsena dwells,
Blind, exiled, outcast, once a mighty king.
The son of Dyumatsena, Satyavan,
I have met on the wild forest's lonely verge.
My father, I have chosen. This is done.[209]

All are astonished, all sit silent "for a space". A "heavy shadow" floats before his inner vision, but Aswapati sees also a pursuing light; all may yet be well. He tells his daughter that she has chosen well:

If this is all, then all is surely well;
If there is more, then all can still be well.[210]

When Narad is about to warn Savitri, Aswapati stays the "dangerous word" and tells him that not to know the future is best:

Impose not on the mortal's tremulous breast
The dire ordeal that foreknowledge brings;...[211]

Narad takes the hint and is silent, but the queen's fears are thoroughly roused by the oblique speeches of the sage and the king. The former mentioned "doom"—then quickly withdrew into himself. The king has spoken darkly too—spoken as if some future danger threatened Savitri.

She therefore roundly questions the sage. On the face of it, Savitri's choice is unexceptionable. But, perhaps, Narad can scent something. What is it? What shadow lies sprawled across their future wedded life? And so she concludes with the entreaty:

> Or if crouches unseen a panther doom,
> If wings of Evil brood above that house,
> Then also speak, that we may turn aside
> And rescue our lives from hazard of wayside doom
> And chance entanglement of an alien fate.[212]

But Narad merely answers, elaborating the king's prudential exhortation:

> A future knowledge is an added pain,
> A torturing burden and a fruitless light
> On the enormous scene that Fate has built.[213]

The sages know that fate is inexorable; why, then, should mortals—frail as they are—burden themselves with this sure foreknowledge and thus agonisingly anticipate the preordained event? Why should the eyes of the mind be clouded by a future foreknown, for that can only destroy even the little flavour there is yet in life! So potent a power is fate that the very words a man speaks are already numbered in 'The Book of Fate'. Narad's words go home, as arrows released by an expert archer unerringly find their target. Although Narad has doled out but vague ominous generalities, this the queen now knows without a doubt: some dark danger lies in wait for her beloved daughter if she marries Satyavan. The dignified queen now yields place to the agitated mother who gives way to uncontrollable grief and begins reviling the law that makes it possible for the fairest lilies to fester or fade away so soon. The Shalwa boy himself, Satyavan, now seems a thing of evil to the queen:

> Perhaps he came an enemy from her past
> Armed with a hidden force of ancient wrongs,
> Himself unknowing, and seized her unknown.[214]

In her frantic mood, this accusation becomes a certainty:

> Old cruelties come back unrecognized,
> The gods make use of our forgotten deeds.[215]

Tossed about thus in the play of the gods, our lives, one and all of them, are an endless tragic sequence. But the gods do not know this; they are not human, hence they have no pity. We are not the bloodless, eternally young (or everlastingly mature) gods, who can create passion, play havoc with human lives, themselves remaining unmoved by anything, love or hate:

> An ancient tale of woe can move us still,
> We keep the ache of breasts that breathe no more,
> We are shaken by the sight of human pain,
> And share the miseries that others feel.[216]

It is the very nature of man to be moved by the miseries of others, and rush forth to the aid of the sufferer; thus has it been always with the compassionate queen of Aswapati. But now on her, on her whose heart had often gone out to her beloved subjects, on herself is this calamity cast:

> Even a stranger's anguish rends my heart,
> And this, O Narad, is my well-loved child.[217]

Now that she has come to know of some misfortune to this beloved daughter of hers, it is better to know the worst that is to be; for otherwise she will be dreading it everywhere and all the time; in the very steps of Savitri she may have to read the book of her fear Therefore she wants to know what it is about so that afterwards, if it is indeed an irredeemable fate, she can at least wait for the event with stoic forbearance.

Now Narad realises that she ought to be told the truth, for it would be no use trying to hide this fatal secret from the queen, thereby torturing a mother's heart. He also hopes to steel and strengthen the will of Savitri to face the coming ordeal. He begins by saying that Satyavan is the best of men, in whom,

> ...soul and Nature, equal Presences,
> Balance and fuse in a wide harmony.[218]

He is made on earth, of heaven. In him the godhead resides, but not for long:

> Heaven's greatness came, but was too great to stay.
> Twelve swift-winged months are given to him and her;
> This day returning Satyavan must die.[219]

Thus has Narad communicated the terrible word of doom. But the queen, in her disturbed ignorant state, in vain tries to clutch at any straw that may be available and save the joyful spring-time of her dear daughter. She hopes to order fate to change her certain course; rejecting "the grace and the mockery" of the gods, she asks Savitri to go forth into the world again and choose for herself another bridegroom that would live long happily with her, and quite forget Satyavan. But vain is the remedy, Savitri is sure of her steps and her resolution holds:

> Once my heart chose and chooses not again...
> Death's grip can break our bodies, not our souls;
> If death take him, I too know how to die.[220]

Savitri, born by the grace of the divine Mother, full of "untrembling virgin fire", will she yield the ground to the foe without struggling against the injustice? No, she was not born to die; neither will it be Satyavan's fate. Savitri will not allow blind fate to cut the cords of love that bind her to Satyavan and the ties that bind both to this world. They are born to plan and achieve the raising of the mortal's life to the Life Divine. They will not yield to mortality. Savitri denies death and affirms life:

> I am stronger than death and greater than my fate;
> My love shall outlast the world, doom falls from me
> Helpless against my immortality.
> Fate's law may change, but not my spirit's will".[221]

And now comes a very curious passage. Like *Rishi* Jabali in the *Ramayana*, the queen, who has hitherto led a life of devotion and love, now driven by her despair, preaches to her daughter the philosophy of Hedonism. She assures Savitri that all talk of love, pledge, troth and devotion are meaningless. What is most important is a life lived in the full current of joy and pleasure. In this ever-changing world, can we forever cling to a set of unchanging laws and moral codes?

> Here on this mutable and ignorant earth
> Who is the lover and who is the friend? [222]

Savitri's talk of love and pledge are meaningless, for essentially she and Satyavan are strangers. Once Savitri loses sight of Satyavan's physical body, she loses him forever. The physical remains of the Shalwa prince will be distributed between the five elements, which will again fashion forth another man who will love and live and die again, having a soul lodged within him for some time. The queen feels that the physical beings are like shirts after all, worn for a time, and then cast away.

Thus our souls come to this earth time and again, take residence in a physical object for some time, and then part forever:

> But for our souls, upon the wheel of God
> For ever turning, they arrive and go,
> Married and sundered in the magic round
> Of the great Dancer of the boundless dance.[223]

Will not her dear daughter Savitri realise what it is to set such a high store upon these lofty ideals, when all the time she knows that human life is too short and our cup of joy never even half-full? It is for that reason man has been given the faculty to choose for himself a reasonably happy life within the prescribed limits of this all too short life. He has been given the power of reason, and with that he must carefully avoid the pitfalls as far as possible, and seek the wine of joy when and where he can find it. Man is between the titan and the animal. The former cares not for his destiny, and with all brute force and belief in his own power rushes towards his destiny with eyes open, so that in this mad onrush he would be able to climb upto and above the divine; the animal has no thinking power at all, and with blind eyes it meets its destiny.

But man can hew for himself the middle path; he need not unnecessarily thrust himself before the gaze of wide-eyed fury, nor need he receive his fate unknowingly. He can think, and decide on the best course; with wary eyes he can choose for himself the golden path that will lead him to happiness. The queen warns Savitri not to rely on any platonic or aesthetic love to console her in her trial. Her human love for Satyavan will be no match against the relentlessness of fate: only when Savitri is able to merge with the One completely can she realise the unity of humanity and be happy therein. But for such consciousness she is too young; the gods have been kind enough to warn her of her fate, and it would be better to follow a different course of action and thus avoid the impact of the foretold calamity.

But Savitri has decided; the specious reasoning falls flat and she replies:

> My strength is not the Titan's; it is God's.[224]

Hers is not the love merely of a beautiful face; it is rather a true marriage of minds at the first dawn of spiritual sight. She has found her true lord and lover; she has found true reality,

> Beyond my body in another's being…[225]

No, no, Savitri will not bend; she has found her haven. A renewed fill of joy and strength has enriched her since her meeting the Shalwa prince:

> If for a year, that year is all my life.
> And yet I know this is not all my fate
> Only to live and love awhile and die.
> For I know now why my spirit came on earth
> And who I am and who he is I love.
> I have looked at him from my immortal Self,

I have seen God smile at me in Satyavan;
I have seen the Eternal in a human face.[226]

II

'THE WAY OF FATE AND THE PROBLEM OF PAIN'

Sage Narad has unveiled Savitri's future; a future that is death. But Savitri, undaunted, has accepted the challenge, and instead of changing her path, has decided to travel on the same road, although fraught with seeming annihilation. And she has uttered the word of fate that she believes more in her own immortal destiny than in the blind workings of a mechanical God. The king and the *rishi* sit quiet looking straight into the "eyes of Fate", not willing to disturb the workings of Providence. But Savitri's mother will not so easily be silenced. Although she is the queen, yet is she a human mother also who cannot bear ill luck to befall her child. Aswapati's queen decides to arraign Destiny itself. In this turbulent condition of mind, she loses all balance; her mind that had hitherto won for itself a place on the higher planes of living now descends into the vital plane where ordinary human passions rage and rule. To her now earthly mind, the workings of destiny come as an unnatural shock. In her throat rises the desperate cry of all humanity that groans under the load of a freakish destiny.

Mankind is essentially ignorant of the cause that produces the effect of human pain. Forced into a tragic condition man cries out why there should be all this grief and pain. Savitri's mother too questions the sage:

By what pitiless adverse Necessity
Or what cold freak of a Creator's will,
By what random accident or governed Chance
That shaped a rule out of fortuitous steps,
Made destiny from an hour's emotion, came

Into the unreadable mystery of Time
The direr mystery of grief and pain?[227]

Why should there be these perversions, these tumours and cankers in this world which should essentially be a beautiful creation of God? Did God make his handiwork successfully, and did some demon come afterwards to wreck its harmony? Something must have gone wrong with creation even from the beginning:

A fatal seed was sown in life's false start
When evil twinned with good on earthly soil.[228]

With the sowing of this dragon seed, there,

...first appeared the malady of mind,
Its pang of thought, its quest for the aim of life.[229]

Man had eaten the forbidden fruit, alas! No more for him the life in blessed ignorance and unfeeling matter; the free and simple ways, the guileless frankness, are lost forever. The birth of 'mind' has ushered in the vicious circle of evil and pain. Heaven has breathed into him reason, mind, intellect and imagination. The rose of man has bloomed in its fullness. But in this very rose of humanity the canker of tragedy finds a place and reduces the human flower to nought.

A grisly company of maladies
Come, licensed lodgers, into man's bodily house,
Purveyors of death and torturers of life.[230]

And the result?

Life is a marvel missed, an art gone wry;...[231]

God's gift of this bright and pleasant world to man is itself darkened by a shadow overhanging it. All Nature is ambivalent; there is a good, bright side, and withal, a bad and cloudy side too.

Error is the comrade of our mortal thought
And falsehood lurks in the deep bosom of truth,
Sin poisons with its vivid flowers of joy
Or leaves a red scar burnt across the soul;

Virtue is a grey bondage and a gaol.
At every step is laid for us a snare.[232]

Torn and frustrated at the very beginning of our benevolent thoughts and honest actions, we espy in this world only a wreckage before and a desert after:

A growing register of calamities
Is the past's account, the future's book of Fate.[233]

Not satisfied with fate's wreckage, man also contrives miseries of his own doing. He commits countless blasphemies and unthinkable follies and brings retribution upon himself. And drunk with Faustus-like success he invades the secret chambers of Nature and commits again sacrilege of various kinds:

His science is an artificer of doom;
He ransacks earth for means to harm his kind;
He slays his happiness and others' good.[234]

These researches of man will bring him no good, for he has lost the Godhead's seal that alone could make his science holy and fruitful. Instead, his science is pursued for selfish ends and brings him only doom and death. But in spite of the heavy budget of dooms, he has not grown any wiser; still he takes the same path of tragedy and falls headlong into the same pit of Hell. Centuries of bitter lessons have not made him take the path of Dharma. He has remained what he ever was; still does he fight and war for selfish ends, and bedews Mother Earth with innocent blood. Not only does he go in search of the Devil's tools, but he also destroys the good in the world. Some wise men create something beautiful, but there are others to destroy the work:

War making nought the sweet smiling calm of life,
Battle and rapine, ruin and massacre
Are still the fierce pastimes of man's warring tribes;
An idiot hour destroys what centuries made,
His wanton rage or frenzied hate lays low

The beauty and greatness by his genius wrought
And the mighty output of a nation's toil. [235]

Thus man unmakes God's beautiful and kindly creation and "wallows in his self-made misery". What is this life on earth, made miserable by ruthless fools? Is it not merely "an episode in a meaningless tale?" It has been said that we have come here from a heavenly source, and that in us is lodged the heavenly Life-spark. It has also been said that the ultimate goal of our life is to return to our harbour-home, that golden source of the Life Divine. If that were so, if we are of Heaven and are to return there again, where is the need for this strange savage interlude of the earth? Why should we be made to pass through this aimless futile drama of pain, terror, rapine and death? The queen's mind is indeed a whirl of questions. Why, why this tragedy of a world signifying nothing? Is all the world, is all life, a mere illusion? In the end, the tragedy that threatens Savitri turns her mother almost into a nihilist.

Perhaps the soul we feel is only a dream,
Eternal self a fiction sensed in trance. [236]

The queen is a woman, and being also a mother, she has come to a stage when the higher thinking powers have been numbed by the shadow of a doom. Now it behoves Narad to guide the sorely afflicted queen out of the labyrinth of her ignorance. So the eternal seer begins:

Was then the sun a dream because there is night?
Hidden in the mortal's heart the Eternal lives:... [237]

It is the cloud of unknowing that prompts us to deny the light of the world and the spirit. The sun does not cease to exist during the night. Even so, the presence of tragedy does not exclude the reality of the Eternal spirit that abides in our inmost heart. Our own ignorance veils the light *within* us, even from ourselves. Because of this ignorance in mankind pain was born, for pain naturally follows ignorance. And it is also true that one cannot attain joy without first undergoing pain. But for the throes of labour, there would be no birth. Even in the beginning of things, "by pain Life stirred in the subliminal deep"; so does pain through shock and difficulty push mankind to the heights:

> Pain is the hammer of the Gods to break
> A dead resistance in the mortal's heart,
> His slow inertia as of living stone. [238]

The image of the Superman is hewn out of the earthy mortal by inflicting on him the pain of death. Unless we are tested and tempered by failures, we would rest quite Oblomov-like in a trance of success and miss the chance of self-transcendence, for it is when we are struck by tragedy that we wish to transcend to the higher states:

> If the heart were not forced to want and weep,
> His soul would have lain down content, at ease,
> And never thought to exceed the human start
> And never learned to climb towards the Sun.[239]

Hence the Divine Mother cries out for yet bigger and acuter trials for mankind, so that out of the tremendous labour and pain a greater creation may come into being. Vain are the deluded cries of mortals like the queen against the pain inflicted by Providence:

> Pain is the hand of Nature sculpturing men
> To greatness: an inspired labour chisels
> With heavenly cruelty an unwilling mould. [240]

In every mortal resides the divine spark; it is to be fanned into a divine flame. The greater the pain the mortal undergoes, the sooner will it assume its real glow. Of course it is all very easily said, but actually the cosmic pain and the cosmic evolution implicit in the process are indescribable. It is on those who are selected to undergo this cosmic suffering, it is on those who wish to save this world, that the mantle of thorns unerringly falls. They are the persons who have to undergo this cosmic pain. As examples Narad (or Sri Aurobindo) projects before us the vision of Christ and the vision of Shiva. There is Christ who has "drunk the bitter cup" and who "has signed salvation's testament with his blood":

It is finished, the dread mysterious sacrifice,
Offered by God's martyred body for the world;
Gethsemane and Calvary are his lot,
He carries the cross on which man's soul is nailed;
His escort is the curses of the crowd;
Insult and jeer are his right's acknowledgement;
Two thieves slain with him mock his mighty death.
He has trod with bleeding brow the Saviour's way.
He who has found his identity with God
Pays with the body's death his soul's vast light.
His knowledge immortal triumphs by his death. [241]

It is clear that Narad here wants to prepare Savitri's mind and strengthen her will by describing the tribulations of the world-redeemers. She herself is one; Narad tells her how Christ and Shiva did their tasks unflinchingly, undaunted by death or poison. Mankind has its ills and pains; no human being is exempt from them. But the tortures that a saviour of mankind has to undergo are tremendous and have epic dimensions. The pertinent question would of course be: Why should a saviour be subjected to these mortal tribulations? But even a saviour must know what afflicts mankind before he could prescribe the necessary cure:

Exempt and unafflicted by earth's fate,
How shall he cure the ills he never felt? [242]

Therefore Christ had to undergo the jeers of the lewd people and had to be nailed on the cross. It is for the same purpose Shiva had to drink the poison from the sea. To save mankind, God dons a mortalgarb, undergoes human suffering and ultimately even 'dies' to give birth to a brave new world. The saviour's situation is terrible indeed. The very people whom he has sought to save turn against him, mock at him, and do their best to wreck his hard-wrought handiwork. This is because there is a dark spot in man's own mind that continuously instigates the lower instincts in him, and drags him to Hell. Hence, however often the great saviours come to this earth, they in the end succeed in saving only a few. So, first of all, a "larger light" must come and clear man's heart of the dark spots, and hand him over as a clear plate for God to write thereon the Song Celestial of Eternal Life. The ordinary mind of man must give way to a "supramental plane of mind" where everything is pure white, and nothing sullies its white radiance. Till that is done,

> ...till the evil is slain in its own home
> And Light invades the world's inconscient base
> And perished has the adversary Force,
> He still must labour on, his work half done. [243]

The world-redeemer, the divine soul, stands steadfast in this tremendous task, and is neither tired nor daunted by failures and difficulties. His will is of steel, his determination of iron. In spite of the barriers and troubles,

> In the dreadful passages, the fatal paths,
> Invulnerable his soul, his heart unslain,
> He lives through the opposition of earth's Powers
> And Nature's ambushes and the world's attacks. [244]

This saviour who has understood the ways of the world and the workings of fate, the gnostic being, undergoes the darkest of earth's terrors, the acutest of the world's pains and the deepest of human sufferings, so that he may bring to the dark world—even to the dark world—the Light Divine:

> He must enter the eternity of Night
> And know God's darkness as he knows his Sun.
> For this he must go down into the pit,
> For this he must invade the dolorous Vasts. [245]

Having passed through this dark night of the soul, the gnostic being would emerge into the Eternal Light.

> The superconscient beam shall touch men's eyes
> And the truth-conscious world come down to earth

Invading Matter with the Spirit's ray,
Awaking its silence to immortal thoughts,
Awaking the dumb heart to the living Word.
This mortal life shall house Eternity's bliss,
The body's self taste immortality.
Then shall the world-redeemer's task be done. [246]

After this lucid account of man's spiritual becoming, Narad turns to the immediate problem and warns the queen not to meddle with the decree of Providence. Any attempt to assume a greater cunning, and try to change the course of destiny, would bring the fate that befalls the titans. The path of the titans is self-destructive. By denying God's sovereignty the titan brings retribution on his own head. The queen will be well advised not to tempt Providence. But if she will bear her yoke patiently by strengthening her will, all will yet turn out well.

Thy spirit's strength shall make thee one with God,
Thy agony shall change to ecstasy,
Indifference deepen into infinity's calm
And joy laugh nude on the peaks of the Absolute. [247]

While trying to explain to the queen the birth of pain in this world, Narad tells her a short parable. The spirit of mankind was originally perfection itself. But the spirit was not content to rest in its perfect state. It wished to see what the world was like. In this adventure it descended into the lower levels and travelled through the vital planes. In this original descent was the fall that brought pain in its wake. As a result the inner splendour was veiled from its casket, man. The forbidden fruit had been plucked and eaten. So the pain of knowledge came and, with it, this half-seen, little understood, undefined world:

Thus came, born from a blind tremendous choice,
This great perplexed and discontented world,
This haunt of Ignorance, this home of Pain:

> There are pitched desire's tents, grief's headquarters.
> A vast disguise conceals the Eternal's bliss. [248]

Pain is now quite natural to mankind, and a world-redeemer like Savitri has to carry her own tremendous load of pain and affliction.

The king now questions the sage whether there is any power in man to save himself, or is he merely ruled by an external spirit. He had heard, on her birth, that such an inner power had descended with Savitri. Is not this inner power equal to the task of facing the threatened fate? Can she not save herself from pain through the exercise of this power? In answer, Narad tells the king that the Superior Divine rejects the prayers of unthinking mankind forunbroken joy on the mortal plane. It is true that Savitri is born with an imprisoned splendour:

> A greatness in thy daughter's soul resides
> That can transform herself and all around [249]

But even she, the daughter of Aswapati, "must cross on stones of suffering to its goal". Man's mental machine is limited in its scope, and cannot perceive the integral truth and the self that lurks behind the law of the universe. The limited vision of man sees only a lifeless law in the workings of the universe and thus misses the fact that the spirit of man works along with the wisdom and spirit of the Universe. For Savitri's future, the external spirit, God, has pronounced its decree. Now it remains for the internal spark to burst into a flame. But it is not for Narad to say what exactly is going to happen:

> It is decreed and Satyavan must die;
> The hour is fixed, chosen the fatal stroke.
> What else shall be is written in her soul [250]

Fate's decree is not altogether final; "Man can accept his fate, he can refuse". And if man is thwarted once, he can always rise again and again to fulfil his real destiny. The true seeker after Truth will not be frightened even by the dread alarm of fate. So if Savitri's destiny is to achieve ultimate victory, she will never waver in her quest for the Life Divine. Even if trouble and pain lie before her, she will not fail to advance. Hence the king need entertain no doubts regarding her future, and try to change the course of her destiny. And neither Aswapati nor his queen should try to separate the young lovers because of the encircling doom. The present situation is all for the best:

> In vain thou mournst that Satyavan must die;
> His death is a beginning of greater life,
> Death is the spirit's opportunity.
> A vast intention has brought two souls close
> And love and death conspire towards one great end. [251]

Narad further tells the queen to leave the course of destiny to its own fulfilment. Nor need she think that Savitri is too frail and weak to be the agent of the world's redemption:

> Sometimes one life is charged with earth's destiny,
> It cries not for succour from the time-bound powers.
> Alone she is equal to her mighty task. [252]

Soon will a day come when, armed by her own will, she will be facing alone a mighty power. But in her loneliness she will find her strength:

> The great are strongest when they stand alone.
> A God-given might of being is their force,
> A ray from self's solitude of light the guide; [253]

thus armed and strengthened, Savitri will have to face the day,

> ...when she must stand unhelped
> On a dangerous brink of the world's doom and hers,
> Carrying the world's future on her lonely breast,
> Carrying the human hope in a heart left sole
> To conquer or fail on a last desperate verge,...
> Must cross alone a perilous bridge in Time
> And reach an apex of world-destiny
> Where all is won or all is lost for man. [254]

In that hour neither the queen nor anybody else can help her, "alone she must conquer or alone must fall". The queen would do better to stand back and leave Savitri to work out mankind's destiny:

> Think not to intercede with the hidden Will,
> Intrude not twixt her spirit and its force
> But leave her to her mighty self and Fate. [255]

Having done his appointed task of enlightening the queen and strengthening Savitri's will, Narad now vanishes from the human scene. But even after he has gone, even after the holy seer has merged with the skies, the listening souls on earth, the king, the queen and Savitri, hear a golden song of hope from the eternal heavens:

> A high and far imperishable voice
> Chanted the anthem of eternal love. [256]

SECTION D

'THE BOOK OF YOGA'

I

'THE JOY OF UNION; THE ORDEAL OF THE FOREKNOWLEDGE OF DEATH AND THE HEART'S GRIEF'

'Fixt fate: Free will' is the seeming paradox at the heart of existence. Man has freedom of choice, but once the choice has been made, he cannot control the consequences. As we sow, so shall we reap. Is even the act of choice no real choice at all but an item of unalterable predestination? Is, then, 'free will' itself a delusion?

> Man's hopes and longings build the journeying wheels
> That bear the body of his destiny
> And lead his blind will towards an unknown goal.
> His fate within him shapes his acts and rules;
> Its face and form already are born in him,
> Its parentage is in his secret soul:...
> Nature and Fate compel his free-will's choice.[257]

Free will is a misnomer, then; yet this too is not the whole truth about the matter. The wages of sin, we know, is death; but Grace has limitless powers. By definition the Almighty is all-mighty; nothing is impossible for him. From the human end things may seem unalterable; but from the divine end? And where exactly do we draw the line that separates the human from the divine? Man ordinarily is a slave of circumstance, a pitiable victim of fate, a creature subject to the curbs of death, desire and incapacity. But humanity can range from the level of the near-inconscient to the dizzy heights of the superconscient—from the beast to the god. Thus it appears that to the adamantine law of fate there *can* be exceptions:

> But greater spirits this balance can reverse
> And make the soul the artist of its fate. [258]

Savitri's resolution to keep faith with Satyavan in defiance of Sage Narad's premonitory forecast of the coming events is no mere exercise in willfulness but rather the measure of her own strength which, if put to the supreme test, may very well bend "the long cosmic curve" itself. But this consciousness of the indwelling power doesn't blot out the human Savitri, the creature of trembling sensibility, who has made a willing and total surrender of herself to Satyavan.

Leaving her parental home a second time, Savitri speeds back to rejoin Satyavan. It is a sharp fundamental passage from the palace with its "tinged mosaic of the crystal floors" to the bare hermitage in the bosom of the forest. But affection and infinite consideration await her here, and so she commences in the wild woods her married life with Satyavan. This solitude strikes her for a time as the sweetest society:

> There was a chanting in the casual wind,
> There was a glory in the least sunbeam;
> Night was a chrysoprase on velvet cloth,
> A nestling darkness or a moonlit deep;
> Day was a purple pageant and a hymn,
> A wave of the laughter of light from morn to eve. [259]

Can love with its divine accent and 'sex' with its human base ever fuse into the 'holy' wedded state? Before their 'fall', did Adam and Eve experience what C.S. Lewis has called 'paradisal sexuality'? John Keats could not imagine any mingling of 'goatish winnyish lustful love with the abstract adoration of the deity'. But nothing is impossible to the "greater spirits" who are called into being to enact the higher synthesis. The first realisations of the wedded life of Savitri and Satyavan are of this order:

> A fusing of the joys of earth and heaven,
> A tremulous blaze of nuptial rapture passed,

A rushing of two spirits to be one,
A burning of two bodies in one flame...[260]

The woman at no time is less than woman merely because she is also potentially divine.

It is doubtless an intolerable situation for Savitri. She alone has the foreknowledge which Narad has communicated to her; Satyavan, his revered parents, the other inmates of the hermitage, all are spared the knowledge that continually lacerates her. She cannot share her pain, she musn't even give the remotest hint of it. Can she at least try to *forget*? She tries desperately, she tries to lose herself in love's divine frenzy:

Vainly she fled into abysms of bliss
From her pursuing foresight of the end.
The more she plunged into love that anguish grew;
Her deepest grief from sweetest gulfs arose.
Remembrance was a poignant pang, she felt
Each day a golden leaf torn cruelly out
From her too slender book of love and joy.[261]

Vain is her attempt—vain are all her attempts—to escape the pain in her heart that is like her own inseparable shadow. Her life with Satyavan, although it is the very image of love's complete fulfilment, is for her now more and more a mask. Nor love's maddening excesses nor the minutiae of an ardent housewife's round of duties are an effective cure for the wound in her heart that she cannot bare to others, not even to her soul's mate, dear Satyavan. She brings more and more concentration into her routine movements, achieving thereby,

A oneness with earth's glowing robe of light,
A lifting up of common acts by love.[262]

From her actions flow peace and joy to others, and to her too, because others are happy; yet the void within remains, the space of the allotted year contracts, the tread of remorseless Time approaches. In a new frenzy of alarm she rushes to Satyavan's arms again:

Intolerant of the poverty of Time
Her passion catching at the fugitive hours
Willed the expense of centuries in one day
Of prodigal love and the surf of ecstasy;... [263]

Has Satyavan no hint of this hell that is hidden in her heart? Doesn't love give him a sixth window of sense to see the spectre she fain would hide? She will not tell him, she cannot tell him, yet he knows, however obscurely, that something, somewhere, somehow is wrong:

Satyavan sometimes half understood,
Or felt at least with the uncertain answer
Of our thought-blinded hearts the unuttered need,
The unplumbed abyss of her deep passionate want. [264]

But the barrier of reticence remains. For his part, he readily, eagerly, gives her as much of his time as he can—still rushing to her from the forest after hewing wood or from attendance on his sightless father.

Retired to the still secrecy of her heart, Savitri ponders whether, when the trial is upon her at last, she must not immolate herself and follow Satyavan "into the sweet or terrible Beyond". What would happen, then, to "those sad parents", Satyavan's mother and blind father? Who will "help the empty remnant of their day"? Nay more: the burden of the whole world's pain presses on Savitri, for in her own pain she recognises the world's as well. She is now like,

...a dumb priest with hidden gods
Unappeased by the wordless offering of her days,
Lifting to them her sorrow like frankincense,
Her life the altar, herself the sacrifice. [265]

The sole year of permitted bliss now draws to a close. Like a jungle crouching in silence, Savitri waits in sombre expectancy.

II

'THE PARABLE OF THE SEARCH FOR THE SOUL'

Her nights are sleepless, for still she hears and sees "the dumb tread of Time and the approach of ever-nearing Fate". Then one night she is startled by a mighty voice invading her mortal life; she is jerked into a trance and becomes "a stone of God lit by an amethyst soul". What use Savitri—"O spirit, O immortal energy"!—coming to "this dumb deathbound earth" if it was merely to nurse a hopeless grief in a helpless heart? Not passive sufferance but positive action is expected of her:

> Arise, O soul, and vanquish Time and Death.

Still in her tranced state, Savitri replies: How can she strive when she has neither the strength nor the will to fight? Feeble are her chances of success, feeble the chances of the ignorant race of man responding to the "saviour Light" from above. "Is there a God whom any cry can move?" Isn't he careless of mankind, their dolour and their defeat?

> What need have I, what need has Satyavan
> To avoid the black-meshed net, the dismal door,
> Or call a mightier Light into life's closed room,
> A greater Law into man's little world? [266]

For her own problem there surely is cure enough; she can follow Satyavan to the far off bourne and there "lie inarmed breast upon breast...forgetting eternity's call, forgetting God". Almost a drowsy and petulant reply, hardly worthy of Savitri; the voice therefore admonishes her: "Is this enough, O spirit?" She has come down with a mightier intent, and it will not do to shrink from the task:

> Cam'st thou not down to open the doors of Fate,
> The iron doors that seemed for ever closed,

> And lead man to Truth's wide and golden road
> That runs through finite things to eternity? [267]

The petulant human rebel is silenced, and another power, the creator spirit within her, makes a reply. Savitri is ready for action as a vessel of the immortal Spirit; when she knows what she has to do, she will readily strive to do it. The voice answers:

> Find out thy soul, recover thy hid self,
> In silence seek God's meaning in thy depths,
> Then mortal nature change to the divine. [268]

Human thought and human sense can be barriers checkmating the passage of the soul to the Soul; casting away everything, everything has to be gained; and by this means Savitri will be able to invoke the force of the Supreme and conquer Death.

The voice is withdrawn, and Savitri finds herself sitting "rigid in her gold motionless pose" by sleeping Satyavan's side. The sky lours, thunder rumbles, rain hisses; but Savitri sits impassive still in self-absorbed concentration. She will look into herself, she will go in quest of her soul (as earlier she had gone in quest of her spouse), and she will not turn back till she sights and claims her hidden self.

Her first series of insights disclose to her, "the cosmic past, the crypt-seed and the mystic origins,/The shadowy beginnings of world fate". It is a vivid and breathless pageantry—from the cosmic whirl of atomic space, the appearance of huddled masses of matter, the emergence of 'life' in algae, plant and tree, in insect, bird and beast, to the ultimate flowering of 'mind' in man:

> Mind nascent laboured out a mutable form,
> It built a mobile house on shifting sands,
> A floating isle upon a bottomless sea. [269]

Restless and enterprising, Mind has made conquests of all sorts and organised the "thousandfold commerce of the world". Sometimes probing below, sometimes gazing above, Mind has extended its inquiries into the lower as well as the higher regions of consciousness, nether Hell as also high Heaven. Mind has its handmaidens—fancy, imagination—and they annex vast territories of experience for man to lord over. In apprehension like a god, yet man can also solicit the dark and devalue himself:

> Man's house of life holds not the gods alone:
> There are occult Shadows, there are tenebrous Powers,
> Inhabitants of life's ominous nether rooms,
> A shadowy world's stupendous denizens...
> The Titan and the Fury and the Djinn
> Lie bound in the subconscient's cavern pit
> And the Beast grovels in his antre den... [270]

They are best kept caged and cribbed in the chambers of the underground, for once you start negotiating with them, they seize you body and soul, pervert all instruments, press their advantages without mercy, and deluge man's world with blood and terror:

> The terrible Angel smites at every door:
> An awful laughter mocks at the world's pain
> And massacre and torture grin at Heaven:... [271]

Man has propensities both towards good and evil; to give evil full and free play is to turn God's purposes upside down, for,

> It imitates the Godhead it denies,
> Puts on his figure and assumes his face.
> A Manichean creator and destroyer,
> This can abolish man, annul his world. [272]

Thus man finds himself at the crossroads where meet opposing paths that show the way either to the world of the blessed or to the condemned wastes of hell. Man has a past and future, and the narrow isthmus of the present is his playground of trial and striving. While his mind is his helper, he cannot wholly depend upon it; mind too can mislead, unawares sometimes, and sometimes deliberately. There are other forces, however, to redress the balance, at times also to tilt it to dangerous consequence:

> A portion of us lives in present Time,
> A secret mass in dim inconscience gropes;
> Out of the inconscient and subliminal
> Arisen, we live in mind's uncertain light
> And strive to know and master a dubious world
> Whose purpose and meaning are hidden from our sight.[273]

But this is no more than a first report or preliminary finding; deeper meanings, clearer purposes, emerge on a closer look at the human drama that is being played on the cosmic stage. Not out of a "blind Nature-Force" has life emerged, and then mind; the sea of inconscience carries the potencies of life, mind, and any powers that may be above mind, though all as yet held in suspension as it were. What is 'involved', nascent or held in suspense comes out when the time is ripe, and so the evolutionary march begins and continues.

There is a law that controls, yet transcends, the wide ranges of consciousness, from inert matter to man and the future superman. It may be that man has his "prone obscure beginnings" in the jungle ape; but he has not ceased to grow, he has not ceased to hanker after good and beauty and God, and he has been moving "in a white lucent air of dreams". The setbacks have been many, the frustrations numberless, but pioneering man has moved breast-forward, flirted with the omniscient, and made vague approaches to omnipotence:

> Thus man in his little house made of earth's dust
> Grew towards an unseen heaven of thought and dream
> Looking into the vast vistas of his mind
> On a small globe dotting infinity.
> At last climbing a long and narrow stair
> He stood alone on the high roof of things
> And saw the light of a spiritual sun. [274]

As Savitri sees these vistas pass before her, the realisation comes to her that the mighty Mother has made her,

> ...the centre of a wide-drawn scheme,...
> To mould humanity into God's own shape

And lead this great blind struggling world to light
Or a new world discover or create. [275]

But for this to be accomplished, the heavenly psyche hidden in Savitri should come out into the open and "liberate the god imprisoned in the visionless mortal man".

III

'THE ENTRY INTO THE INNER COUNTRIES'

Savitri's problem is to penetrate appearance and reach the reality about herself. This is a spiritual quest leading to a spiritual end. The nature of the quest, the stages in the progress, and the configuration of the goal, all must defy description in everyday language, which is no more than one of the functions or manifestations of the appearance. Hence the poet is obliged to resort to a parable and to the language of symbols. The 'parable' of Savitri's search for her soul spans across several cantos, and symbol regions with their contours, laws and inhabitants are passed in review, and Savitri is shown as making her progress through the 'inner countries', even as, in Book II, Aswapati is shown as careering through the occult worlds in the cosmos.

Right at the commencement of her quest, a voice tells Savitri that her aim should be to "help man to grow into the God",not to achieve her own salvation alone; in other words, the sorrow and darkness threatening her life with Satyavan, being symptomatic of the present human destiny, should be tracked to their source, struggled with and mastered finally.

As Savitri approaches the 'inner countries', she is confronted by an ebony gate barring her passage. From within comes the porter's "formidable voice" of forthright warning to Savitri. Although this serpent-guardian and its attendant hounds, trolls, gnomes and goblins raise hideous rout, Savitri forces the gate open and enters, unconcerned and unaffected, the inner worlds. Who is this forbidding portress? Who are her attendants? Always, when one starts on a new adventure, a nameless fear and its progeny of hesitations and vague premonitions seem to bar the way. One needs courage and resolution to withstand these sullen initial impediments that try to prevent the first step being taken. However, they have no effective power to throw back; they can frighten, and if their bluff is called, they are really powerless.

The occult inner continents follow one after another; these are the new fields of Savitri's cognitive experience. There is, first, the world of 'subtle matter', analogous to the world Aswapati (as described in Book II, canto 2) passes through—analogous but not identical, for no two spiritual quests are exactly the same. This dense region "of subtle Matter packed"—a sort of no-man's land between the dusk of subconscience and the first streaks of life—leads presently to,

> ...a form of things,
> A start of finiteness, a world of sense: [276]

This sense-driven life is without order, without direction, without meaning; as with ignorant masses clashing in the dark, there is motion without aim, or striving without positive result. Such must be the fate of all endeavours when "the sense's instinct (is) void of soul/Or when the soul sleeps hidden void of power".

Savitri, guided by "the saviour Name", edges round this chaotic world of "disordered impulses", the kingdom of little life, and enters the kingdom of greater life, "a giant head of Life ungoverned by mind or soul". The Life-Force itself rages here in its elemental vastness; it is no tenuous trickle, but verily "a spate, a torrent of the speed of Life" breaking "like a wind-lashed driven mob of waves/Racing on a pale floor of summer sand". Blind but fierce, aimless but irresistible, the heady current of this unleashed force achieves marvellous results through inadvertence:

> Out of the nether unseen deeps it tore
> Its lure and magic of disordered bliss,

Into earth-light poured its maze of tangled charm
And heady draught of Nature's primitive joy
And the fire and mystery of forbidden delight
Drunk from the world-libido's bottomless well,
And the honey-sweet poison-wine of lust and death,
But dreamed a vintage of glory of life's gods,
And felt as celestial rapture's golden sting. [277]

This is the world of primitive heroism, compact of great striving and impressive results; fighters, daring explorers, uncalculating hedonists, restless dreamers, magicians, lovers, haters, fill this world. There is the clash of violent opposing furies, there are alternations between fear and joy, ecstasy and despair. But, whatever its particular tinge, life in this region is everywhere intense; and speech has a downrightness, and song "its ictus of infallibility". Yet all this marvel and splendour has no sure base on Truth, but are reared on shifting sands compounded of half-truths and gross-errors. Total perversion is possible and sometimes reigns unabashed:

Here in Life's nether realms all contraries meet;
Truth stares and does her works with bandaged eyes
And Ignorance is Wisdom's patron here:
Those galloping hooves in their enthusiast speed
Could bear to a dangerous intermediate zone
Where Death walks wearing a robe of deathless Life. [278]

Here too lies "the valley of the wandering Gleam", a self-created self-perpetuating nightmare death-in-life. Savitri withstands the terror and the lure, the passion and the pain, and steadily journeys forward to 'fresh woods and pastures new'.

The next region is "a brilliant ordered Space", fed and fostered by reason. The impetuous Life-Force is held in leash by reason. The passage has thus been from a Dionysian to an Apollonian world. Yet control too can be carried too far. Fleeing from the riot of exuberance, one can canter into the utter formality of death:

> The ages' wisdom, shrivelled to scholiast lines,
> Shrank patterned into a copy-book device. [279]

It is, no doubt, a balanced reign, but also a cabinned reign; there is no room or scope for the play of imagination, for daring leaps of thought, for the unrestrained climb of the spirit. It is like the cloistered virtue of "a highbred maiden with chaste eyes/Forbidden to walk unveiled the public ways". There is a mean self-sufficiency, a petty perfection here that effectively rules out "rhythms too high or vast", the play of high ideas, and the sovereign richness and variety of life in the Spirit. In this "quiet country of fixed mind", an authoritative spokesman accosts Savitri and assures her that this is truly "the home of cosmic certainty" where all is "docketed and tied"; thought's apotheosis has fashioned this realm; here reign order and safety, clarity and peace. But Savitri is ill at ease in this cold small world, "this ordered knowledge of apparent things"; she cannot abide here, she must seek her soul elsewhere. Her decision surprises, and even offends, some of the self satisfied inhabitants of this place, while one, wiser and sadder than the rest, murmurs:

> Is there one left who seeks for a Beyond?
> Can still the path be found, opened the gate? [280]

Undaunted, unwearied, Savitri passes on till she arrives at a place thronged by a crowd of, "brilliant, fire-footed, sunlight-eyed... messengers from our subliminal greatnesses,/Guests from the cavern of the secret soul". Savitri is attracted by these "strange goddesses with deep-pooled magical eyes", and she would like to live with them and share the light of their life, but first she will pursue her quest for the discovery of her secret innermost soul. Surely, these bright creatures will help her in her quest. How may I, she asks,

> ...find the birthplace of the occult Fire
> And the deep mansion of my secret soul... [281]

The amazing answer comes:

> O Savitri, from thy hidden soul we come...
> O human copy and disguise of God

> Who seekst the deity thou keepest hid
> And livest by the Truth thou hast not known,
> Follow the world's winding highway to its source.
> There in the silence few have ever reached,
> Thou shalt see the Fire burning on the bare stone
> And the deep cavern of thy secret soul. [282]

Inaccessible to—not negotiable by—any but "rare wounded pilgrim-feet", the great winding road now bears the tread of Savitri's feet, and "a few bright forms" emerge from unknown depths and look at her "with calm immortal eyes":

> There was no sound to break the brooding hush;
> One felt the silent nearness of the soul. [283]

IV

'THE TRIPLE SOUL-FORCES'

Savitri's single-minded quest has now brought her almost to the threshold of her inmost, her secret soul. She is met, one by one, by the soul's triple forces, each embodied as a mother spirit, as a Madonna. First the Madonna of suffering, Mother of sorrows and grief divine; next, the Madonna of might, Mother of works and force; and last, the Madonna of light, Mother of joy and peace. Each claims to be Savitri's soul, and each is partly right; but Savitri cannot, she will not, accept these partial identifications. She will not stop till the full splendour of self-discovery overwhelms her.

First to meet Savitri during the "passion of the first ascent" is a woman in "a pale lustrous robe", seated on "a rugged and ragged soil", with "a sharp and wounding stone" pressed against her feet. She is as it were the incarnation of the world's pain. From the anxious moment of birth to the "dolorous end of life", it is a tale of striving and failure, sorrow and pain; and the Mother's compassion goes out to man as he thus lies stretched on the cross:

> Accepting the universe as her body of woe,
> The Mother of the seven sorrows bore
> The seven stabs that pierced her bleeding heart:
> The beauty of sadness lingered on her face,
> Her eyes were dim with the ancient stain of tears. [284]

"I am thy secret soul", she tells Savitri, "I am woman, nurse and slave and beaten beast/…I am the spirit in a world of pain". [285] In the course of her long sad impassioned speech, she gives an account of her unique preoccupation with human suffering and her round of painstaking works to tend the lowly, the miserable, the nearly lost. However seemingly hopeless the human lot, however apparently unavailing the appeals to Heaven, she has neither denied nor lost hope of deliverance. When she concludes her speech, however, there explodes a cry from below, the voice of the Man of Sorrows, breathing exasperation and despair, a job in his burning passion of defeat:

> I am he
> Who is nailed on the wide cross of the universe;
> To enjoy my agony God built the earth,
> My passion he has made his drama's theme.
> He has sent me naked into his bitter world
> And beaten me with his rods of grief and pain… [286]

And so on, a mixture of defiance and impatience, assertion and negation, Titan and man. Savitri, having heard both the Madonna and the Man of Sorrows, answers with serene understanding; the Madonna is indeed a "portion" that Savitri's soul has put forth "to bear the unbearable sorrow of the world"; because of her, the wretched can somehow bear their wretchedness and hope against hope for a dawn of deliverance. Savitri promises to return to the Madonna with an accession of strength that will enable them to abolish cruelty and misery forever from the earth. But, in the meantime, Savitri must continue her quest.

Next to meet Savitri on her upward route is a woman in "gold and purple sheen, /Armed with the trident and the thunderbolt"; her feet on a lion's back, her eyes emitting fire, her head ringed with a halo of lightnings; it is the Mother of Might, and she tells Savitri:

I am Durga, goddess of the proud and strong,
And Lakshmi, queen of the fair and fortunate;
I wear the face of Kali when I kill,
I trample the corpses of the demon hordes...
I rend man's narrow and successful life
And force his sorrowful eyes to gaze at the sun
That he may die to earth and live in his soul. [287]

While Durga-Lakshmi claims that she alone is Savitri's secret soul, there comes a "warped echo" from below, from "the dwarf Titan, the deformed chained god" that is man the master of knowledge and power, the *asuric* man; he is the man that has mastered Nature and would one day supersede God; he would smash the atom, canalise cosmic energy, "expunge a nation or abolish a race". Savitri, having heard them both, admits that while knowledge and power are necessary, without wisdom they cannot achieve much. Savitri promises to return to the Madonna of might with an accession of light that will enable them together to abolish fear and weakness and hatred forever from the heart of man. In the meantime, Savitri will continue her quest.

Savitri meets last the Mother of joy and peace. The Madonna of light stands revealed on a piece of clear and crystalline ground; sun-bright her face, moon-bright her feet, nectarean her smile; she too claims in captivating musical speech to be Savitri's secret soul:

I have come down to the wounded desolate earth
To heal her pangs and lull her heart to rest
And lay her head upon the Mother's lap
That she may dream of God and know his peace
And draw the harmony of higher spheres
Into the rhythm of earth's rude troubled days. [288]

She buoys up man with dreams and visions, with ideals and aspirations; freedom, valour, justice, resignation, thought, wisdom, beauty, truth, good, all are but godheads of the human soul; against the pressure of the ignorance, man struggles to raise himself to the level of the gods, and the Madonna arms him with the necessary faith and perseverance:

> I bring meanwhile the gods upon the earth;
> I bring back hope to the despairing heart;
> I give peace to the humble and the great,
> And shed my grace on the foolish and the wise.
> I shall save earth, if earth consents to be saved. [289]

Once again, as the Madonna's voice ceases, there comes up another cry, "a warped echo naked and shuddering" from the mental Man, man the apologist and would-be practitioner of pure reason:

> The finite he has made his central field,
> Its plan dissects, masters its processes,…
> His knowledge scans bright pebbles on the shore
> Of the huge ocean of his ignorance. [290]

Hasn't the sum of the giant endeavours of mere mental man petered out into nothing? No wonder "a cosmic pathos" trembles through the moan of the "all-discovering Thought of man", man the natural scientist and philosopher. He makes a melancholy song about his achievements, for, while all battles are won, the campaign itself is invariably lost:

> The tree of evolution I have sketched,
> Each branch and twig and leaf in its own place,
> In the embryo tracked the history of forms,
> And the genealogy framed of all that lives.
> I have detected plasm and cell and gene,
> The protozoa traced, man's ancestors,
> The humble originals from whom he rose;
> I know how he was born and how he dies:
> Only what end he serves I know not yet
> Or if there is aim at all or any end

Or push of rich creative purposeful joy
In the wide works of the terrestrial power. [291]

Matter has been explored, and mind too; the sciences are multiplying, and the techniques of analysis or organisation are getting to be more and more subtle and complicated; yet the central mystery of creation remains, and man doesn't yet know how to pluck the heart of the mystery. Is the phenomenal world but the play of the magic of *Maya*? Is there a realm of absolutes? But mind-centred man cannot achieve transcendence; he is content—he must be content—to stew in the juice of his own mental concoction:

Human I am, human let me remain
Till in the Inconscient I fall dumb and sleep. [292]

He will not seek escape from his feeling of futility by positing the existence of a God who can care for humanity. For the third time, having heard thesis and antithesis, the Madonna and the Man of Sorrows, Savitri acknowledges her kinship with the Madonna, and promises to return to her with an accession of strength from him, and that will be the time when,

...the holy marriage be achieved,
Then shall the divine family be born.
There shall be light and peace in all the worlds. [293]

Now she must pass on, for her quest is not ended yet.

V

'THE FINDING OF THE SOUL'

Leaving the three Madonnas behind, Savitri presses on her quest to the "soul's mystic cave" and first steps into "a night of God" where the familiar powers of the world-knowledge, wisdom, truth—are held in a screened solution in the reigning holy hush and dark:

In a simple purity of emptiness

> Her mind knelt down before the unknowable.
> All was abolished save her naked self
> And the prostrate yearning of her surrendered heart: [294]

It is somewhat like the mixing and merging of a drop with the ocean,

> A night of person in a bare outline
> Crossing a fathomless impersonal Night,... [295]

Presently this general immobility gives place to a new stir of life, the blossoming of "a rose of splendour on a tree of dreams"; the "night of God" changes to day, the air is sweet, the sky is lustrous, and the "mystic cavern...of her secret soul" stands revealed:

> And a holy stillness held that voiceless space.
> An awful dimness wrapped the great rock-doors
> Carved in the massive stone of Matter's trance. [296]

Two golden serpents round the lintel, an eagle with massive wings above, doves at the cornices; inside the court, as in a South Indian temple, sculptured gods snapping moments in the cosmic play; on the walls, pictures conveying the "hieratic message of the climbing planes": the whole a parable of the "extension of the self of God/... And his passion and his birth and life and death/And his return to immortality".[297] Savitri seizes the meaning of it all, not through ratiocination, but by her soul's identity with each symbol which is also an order of reality:

> A sealed identity within her woke;
> She knew herself the Beloved of the Supreme:... [298]

She is Mother, Brahma's word, Shiva's spouse, Krishna's Radha; and, indeed, she is the 'Adorer and Adored self-lost and one". Savitri now comes to the last chamber where she espies the formless fount of her "straying force", and passing beyond it through a tunnel to a house of flame and light, there she meets her secret soul:

> Here in this chamber of flame and light they met;
> They looked upon each other, knew themselves,

The secret deity and its human part,
The calm immortal and the struggling soul.
Then with a magic transformation's speed
They rushed into each other and grew one. [299]

The long night's journey into day is over; Savitri has explored the inner countries of the spirit, much as a modern visitor to one of the big temples in South India might explore concentric courts, the *prākārās*, the numerous shrines within, the statues of the minor gods and goddesses and the *bhaktas* and the god-intoxicated, the paintings on the walls and the sculptured pillars and walls reproducing scenes from epic and *purana*, the cosmic play and the *tāndav* dance, and moving from sacred enclosure to another enclosure, always moving within, observing the *vāhanās*, being enraptured by the ritual, the swaying of the lights and the chanting of hymns, dazzled by the bejewelled gold-shaped outer manifestations of the deity and his consort, and penetrating at long last to the ultimate sanctum, the innermost home of the deity, and receiving the ineffable impact of the 'mystical tremendum', the blaze of the total truth that blinds, the shower of the Grace that cleanses; Savitri has at last seen and grown into her secret Soul. She is now back in the world of man, the same yet different; she is filled with the glory and power of God, and all in her have undergone a "high celestial change"; and henceforth her every act will be "an act of god". Head, brows, throat, heart, navel, all coiled petals of the unfolding bud of this lotus flame have received the impress of new divinity, and in the apparently human mould of Savitri "a first perfection's stage is reached at last":

There is won a new proximity to the skies,
A first betrothal of the Earth to Heaven,
A deep concordat between Truth and Life:
A camp of God is pitched in human time. [300]

VI

'NIRVANA AND THE DISCOVERY OF THE ALL-NEGATING ABSOLUTE'

Even the self-finding of her secret soul and the joy, power and peace that well up in her as a result are but the first decisive stage in Savitri's Yoga. Two more trials, two more realisations, await her. She is yet to be shocked into—or seized of—the realisation that her sovereign secret soul has really a cosmic compenetration and comprehension, and also that it is at the same time supracosmic, beyond space and time, beyond all imaginable beyonds. Her secret soul is infinity, it is all infinities; lost in the transcendent, it is lost, and is still functioning here in phenomenal space-time; of the secret soul it can indeed be said, infinity minus infinity is infinity still.

After her first realisation, her life with Satyavan is a round of serene fulfilment:

> And Savitri's life was glad, fulfilled like earth's;
> She had found herself, she knew her being's aim.
> Although her kingdom of marvellous change within
> Remained unspoken in her secret breast,
> All that lived round her felt its magic's charm:...
> Even the smallest meanest work became
> A sweet or glad and glorious sacrament,
> An offering to the self of the great world
> Or a service to the One in each and all. [301]

She sees Satyavan now, not as one condemned, but as the gate of a rich new possibility; they are together always in "love's unseen atmosphere, /Inseparable like earth and sky". It is the sun's hour of meridian glory before the slowly approaching threat of "abysmal Night".

Then one day, at the very moment of sweet fulfilment, she is suddenly invaded by a nameless new force. An utter void seems to seize and swallow her "and end the fable of the joy of life"; it is a black infinity stretched across the space of a dark eternity; it is superlative emptiness, it is the zero of all zeros, it is the ultimate Nihil. This all negating featureless spectre taunts Savitri that she is but hugging the illusion of her secret soul's sovereign identity:

> I have created all, all I devour;
> I am Death and the dark terrible Mother of life,
> I am Kali black and naked in the world,
> I am Maya and the universe is my cheat. [302]

For a while Savitri is drained of all her strength, but presently another voice comes from the heights, the squadrons of light decisively vacating the aggression of dark. But the voice also reminds Savitri that the task that lies ahead of her is of cosmic, rather than of a limited, significance; to be effective at that level, she should share the world's multitudinous pain and achieve a cosmic consciousness, know herself,

> ...older than the birth of Time,
> Creation an incident in its consciousness,
> Arcturus and Belphegor grains of fire
> Circling in a corner of its boundless self,
> The world's destruction a small transient storm
> In the calm infinity it has become. [303]

Savitri should for a time "banish all thought...and be God's void"; in the absolute condition of silence of the mind so created she will see the true origins of things and also the shape of the desired transfiguration of earth into heaven, human life into the Life Divine.

Archimedes is said to have remarked that he could lift the earth with a lever if only he could himself be detached from the earth and find a place outside to stand on. Our efforts to observe and understand the operations of the cosmos are frustrated because we are ourselves intimately implicated in it. In the strictly material world, one cannot be both within and without, the observed and the observer; in the realms of the spirit, however, nothing is impossible. Savitri stands back,

...detached and calm,
A witness of the drama of herself,
A student of her own interior scene [304]

and "watches the passion and the toil of life" and hears "in the crowded thoroughfares of mind/The unceasing tread and passage of her thoughts". It is as though she is looking beneath the polished surface of a delicate instrument, and scrutinising the wires, the springs, the complicated machinery. She sees the processes of sensory and vital activity, the surges of passion, the frenzied agitation of the nerves, the grapple of opposing forces; but more particularly her gaze pursues the "birth of thought". Does thought take shape in the brain? Does it issue from the subtle body? Does it come from outside, from somewhere in the unmapped cosmos? Does it well up from the heart or does it crystallise in the soul? As she views the field of thought and ponders over thought's variety, life grows "marvellous with transfiguring hope":

Thoughts, glistening Angels, stood behind the brain
In flashing armour, folding hands of prayer,
And poured heaven's rays into the earthly form.
Imaginations flamed up from her breast,
Unearthly beauty, touches of surpassing joy
And plans of miracle, dreams of delight:... [305]

It is as though each part of her body has thoughts appropriate to it, and carries its yearnings to the point of complete expression. But average humanity cannot achieve such quick or perfect translation of yearning or impulse into thought or idea. What's opaque to others is transparent to Savitri, and thus she sees clearly the happenings in the spirit's house:

Eyes looked through crevices in the invisible wall
And through the secrecy of the unseen doors
There came into mind's little frontal room
Thoughts that enlarged our limited human range,

> Lifted the ideal's half-quenched or sinking torch
> Or peered through the finite at the infinite. [306]

With an expansive range of consciousness, Savitri receives thought-intimations from far and near, from the dim inconscient as well as the overhead planes:

> Thoughts leaped down from a superconscient field
> Like eagles swooping from a viewless peak,
> Thoughts gleamed up from the screened
> subliminal depths
> Like golden fishes from a hidden sea. [307]

And beholding these varied "births of thought", Savitri realises that the human mind itself is but a small machine that quickly wears out, whereas,

> The word, the form, the charm, the glory and grace
> Are missioned sparks from a stupendous Fire;... [308]

The receiving, transmitting mind but defaces or corrupts the purity of the original thought, and thereby often becomes the vehicle of error and ignorance.

Savitri now rises out of her human mind to escape its law of limitation and force of perversion, and from a vantage height dedicates her "sovereign will...to God's timeless calm". Her mind itself is calm, as if a dynamo has ceased to work, and it is this condition that "men call quietude and prize as peace". Presently, mental activity is not only stilled but wholly ceases; the body is like a stone, although still excluding "eternity's hush", for now and then a stray thought, like a leaf floating from afar, falls on the surface of the immense calm and recoils, receiving no response. Soon these too cease, and all is "immobile, self-rapt, timeless, solitary". In this absolute hush of her mind,

> Emotion slept deep down in the still heart
> Or lay buried in a cemetery of peace:... [309]

There is the utter collapse of thought, but her body sees and moves and speaks, always to the right purpose though without a specific mental push; she is no more a particular individual, she is a vessel of the Supreme; there is "no frame of things, no figure of soul", but delivered from the tyranny of the dualities, Savitri now shares the "Superconscient's high retreat". Yet a giant doubt assails her: Has she come to the very end of things, only waiting for annihilation's final act, or can she hope for an affirmation that can annul annihilation itself? Can the all-negating Absolute and the all-Delight of Existence, in other words Nihil and *ananda*, be themselves reconciled?

VII

'ROSE OF GOD'[310]

Meantime Savitri lives her routine in the forest, gracious to all, striking them as being no different from what she has always been. She is "the same perfect Savitri", apt in speech and action, although inhabiting a total silence of mind. The power behind her life is "the miraculous Nihil…a cipher of God". It is a trance, a somnambulistic play of life, not the life that we know; yet nothing is wrongly done or said, whether she is with Satyavan or with "the sages of the woods"; sometimes, indeed, her mouth becomes the channel of "ineffable truths", and the sages marvel at her,

> …for she seemed to know
> What they had only glimpsed at times afar.[311]

She is seemingly a plastic instrument in the hands both of inconscient Nature and the superconscient mystery. Her being's scope seems to spread more and more into widening circles of infinity, "a world without form or feature or circumstance,/…no ground, no wall, no roof of thought."[312]

Sitting thus by sleeping Satyavan, a voice not hers begins to stir, and suddenly the world of unreality ceases to be. No, no, negation is not the ultimate truth; omnipresent Reality is other and more than the Nihil, more than "a cipher of vastness in unreal Thought"; Savitri sees that omnipresent Reality is her own self and the self of all:

> …it was Timelessness and Time,
> It was the Bliss of formlessness and form.
> It was all Love and the one Beloved's arms,
> It was sight and thought in one all-seeing Mind,
> It was joy of Being on the peaks of God. [313]

Savitri sees "the world as living God", and she is herself both a single being and all beings, "their bodies her many bodies kin to her":

> Out of the infinitudes all came to her,
> Into the infinitudes sentient she spread,
> Infinity was her own natural home…
> The distant constellations wheeled round her;
> Earth saw her born, all worlds were her colonies,
> The greater worlds of life and mind were hers;…
> She was the single self of all these selves,…
> She burned in the passion and splendour of the rose,
> She was the red heart of the passion-flower,
> The dream-white of the lotus in its pool….
> She was the godhead hid in the heart of man,
> She was the climbing of his soul to God. [314]

Savitri is the link between man and God, time and Eternity, existence and Transcendence.

THE STRUGGLE AND THE VICTORY

Then came, at a predetermined moment,
a moment in time and of time,
A moment not out of time, but in time, in what
we call history: transecting, bisecting the world
of time, a moment in time but not like a moment of time,
A moment in time but time was made through that moment:
for without the meaning there is no time,
and that moment of time gave the meaning.

T.S. ELIOT

SECTION A

'THE BOOK OF DEATH'

I

THE TWO MISSING CANTOS

In the two opening cantos of *Savitri*, the action of the epic begins, as in Western epics like the *Iliad* and *Paradise Lost*, at a critical point, even the most critical; the action plunges *in medias res*, into the middle of things: it is the dawn of the day when Satyavan is fated to die according to Sage Narad's reading of the future. After the first two cantos that constitute the exordium, there comes a long, long spell of retrospective narration, sketching the personal and cosmic backgrounds to the central action. This has taken thirty-eight cantos in all out of the forty-nine that now make the poem, or a little over 600 pages out of the total 814 in the definitive one-volume edition of the poem.[1]

Book VIII, entitled 'The Book of Death', is to continue in strict time-sequence the story as begun in the first two cantos of Book I. But of the three projected cantos of Book VIII, only canto 3 seems actually to have been completed by Sri Aurobindo from an earlier version and rewritten at places.[2] The reference to the *trirāttra* (three-night) fast in the original *Mahabharata* has already been transformed by Sri Aurobindo into the vast dimensions of 'The Book of Yoga', which describes Savitri's realisations of her secret self, of cosmic consciousness, and, finally, of supracosmic or transcendent consciousness.

The events of the fateful day from dawn to evening are compressed into a few pregnant verses in the *Mahabharata*, and nothing that is material is omitted in canto 3. Thus it is difficult to speculate as to how Sri Aurobindo had planned to fill the spaces of the proposed cantos 1 and 2, for canto 3 itself forms a natural continuation of the story impressively begun in Book I, cantos 1 and 2. Probably Sri Aurobindo had tentatively divided Book VIII into three cantos, hoping to enlarge the scope of the present canto 3 so as to split it meaningfully into three cantos and give Book VIII an ampler base and a richer substance. However, taking the poem as it is, the supposed gap in Book VIII, though it intrigues us a little and introduces a possible element of incompleteness, doesn't vitally affect our comprehension of the epic action or really impair the striking unity of the whole. Once we concentrate on the foreground action, that is to say, once we shift our gaze from antecedents and backgrounds to the centre of the stage, the drama involving Savitri and Satyavan on the appointed day—the drama proceeds from dawn to evening, from evening to night, from night to twilight, and from twilight to day.

II

'DEATH IN THE FOREST'

On the great day when the issue is to be joined, the dawn finds Savitri awake earlier than Satyavan, recapitulating the events of the year just about to end:

> The whole year in a swift and eddying race
> Of memories swept through her and fled away
> Into the irrecoverable past.[3]

This is clearly an earlier draft of the poem, not fully brought in tune with the new inspiration. The opening canto itself, after describing 'The Symbol Dawn', refers to Savitri awaking among the forest tribes and hastening "to join the brilliant Summoner's chant", and the second canto states that "twelve passionate months led in a day of fate"; thus Book VIII almost harks back to Book I, mentions the same details though from a rather lesser height of poetic inspiration, before continuing the story. In the present version we have the bare bones of the *Mahabharata* story transformed into the flesh and blood of a spacious narrative poem like *Urvasie* and *Love and Death* of Sri Aurobindo's Baroda period; what is lacking in Book VIII is the epic amplitude, the luminous extravagant richness, the cosmic overtones and the more or less consistent overhead inspiration behind the rest of the poem.

After a moment of silent prayer before the image of the Goddess Durga, Savitri approaches 'the pale queen mother', asks her permission to accompany her son, Satyavan, to the forest. During her year's life with Satyavan, Savitri hasn't once explored the silences of the great forest with him, and might she not this day go with him and satisfy her longing? The queen-mother readily consents, and so "the doomed husband and the woman" go out with linked hands "into that solemn world". Satyavan shows her,

> ...all the forest's riches, flowers
> Innumerable of every odour and hue
> And soft thick clinging creepers red and green
> And strange rich-plumaged birds,... [4]

As he points out the things he has loved, his dumb forest play-fellows and companions of many a livelong day, she listens deeply, but inly she has other thoughts, love despairing, anguish attentive at every step, thinking that this might prove to be Satyavan's last spoken word:

> Her life was now in seconds, not in hours,
> And every moment she economised
> Like a pale merchant leaned above his store,
> The miser of his poor remaining gold. [5]

Now Satyavan wields his axe, felling branches, and singing, "high snatches of a sage's chant/That pealed of conquered death and demon slain"; these and his interspersed words of endearment are manna to Savitri who seizes them "like a pantheress.../And carried them into her cavern heart." But this day Satyavan quickly tires, he wields the axe with diminishing force, and soon "the great Woodsman hewed at him and his labour ceased"; Satyavan sways a little and cries out to Savitri:

> Such agony rends me as the tree must feel
> When it is sundered and must lose its life.
> Awhile let me lay my head upon thy lap
> And guard me with thy hands from evil fate:
> Perhaps because thou touchest, death may pass. [6]

They sit beneath a kingly trunk, and Satyavan stretches himself with his head on her lap:

> All grief and fear were dead within her now
> And a great calm had fallen. [7]

As she intently observes his face, "his sweet familiar hue" changes into "a tarnished greyness", his eyes grow dim, and after one last poignant clinging cry, his eyes close, his head falls limp in the very act of a despairing final kiss. And already she smells the presence there of something "vast and dire",

> ...a silent shade immense
> Chilling the noon with darkness for its back.
> An awful hush had fallen upon the place:
> There was no cry of birds, no voice of beasts.
> A terror and an anguish filled the world,
> As if annihilation's mystery
> Had taken a sensible form...
> She knew that visible Death was standing there
> And Satyavan had passed from her embrace.[8]

SECTION B

'THE BOOK OF ETERNAL NIGHT'

I

'TOWARDS THE BLACK VOID'

Left alone in the "huge wood", with Satyavan's limp head on her bosom, she ignores the dread presence of the dark god and clasps to her the mute lifeless form of her dead lover and husband. She is a woman, and must feel her loss like a woman. But she is also Savitri, and of a sudden she stands revealed to herself, the human veil being torn;

> A new sight comes,…
> Immortal yearnings without name leap down,
> Large quiverings of godhead seeking run
> And weave upon a puissant field of calm
> A high and lonely ecstasy of will. [9]

She heaves to great heights of puissance and perceives near her a "slow embodiment of the aeonic will", a cosmic mightiness assuming a symbol form. On the eve of the tremendous struggle that is to commence, this "thousand-petalled home of Power and light", invulnerable to the shafts of time, omnipotent, "enters the mystic lotus" in Savitri's head and becomes the "doer of her works and fountain of her words". [10]

Savitri is thus ready for the mighty hour and its momentous fray. The pain, the grief, the fear are gone; her mind is still; "now all her acts sprang from a godhead's calm." She gently lays Satyavan's head on the ground and rises to meet the "dreadful god", but not before one more look at the prone dead lover. Then, "like a tree recovering from a wind", she raises her eyes:

> Something stood there, unearthly, sombre, grand,
> A limitless denial of all being

That wore the terror and wonder of a shape.
In its appalling eyes the tenebrous Form
Bore the deep pity of destroying gods;
A sorrowful irony curved the dreadful lips
That speak the word of doom...
His shape was nothingness made real, his limbs
Were monuments of transience and beneath
Brows of unwearying calm large godlike lids
Silent beheld the writhing serpent, life. [11]

As the two, Woman and Death, face each other unflinchingly, the sad formidable voice of worldly wisdom cries to Savitri to let go her invisible grasp of Satyavan, to weep for a while as is proper, and then to forget, as is human nature. She relaxes her hold, but otherwise listens not to the voice, but stands "gathered in lonely strength",

Like one who drops his mantle for a race
And waits the signal, motionlessly swift. [12]

Death too leans down, as if to draw out Satyavan; and "another luminous Satyavan" arises, starting up from the prone corpse and stands between the mortal woman and the God. Who will finally claim him? The issue is undecided:

...two spirits strove;
Silence battled with silence, vast with vast. [13]

Now Satyavan moves forward, as if irresistibly pushed; behind him, Death; and Savitri last, her mortal pace equal with the God's; intent and wordless thus she follows Satyavan's steps "into the perilous silences beyond".

They move on in single line for a while, still close to earth's familiar smell, "its sweetness and its greenness and delight", till they reach some unfamiliar "boundary's intangible bar", and she feels that *they* might escape and disappear. Her "violent spirit" therefore soars at Satyavan, leaving her own mortal body on the forest soil; she is no mere Savitri but an ocean surge of will, saving her treasured Satyavan "from the collapse of space". And so they keep step again in these new symbol realms of weird grass, weird treeless plains, weird roads running phantasmal between sombre pillared rocks and brooding gates. Turning round, Death now cries out to shadowing Savitri not to persist in a "vehement trespass" into forbidden worlds. But Savitri answers not:

> Her high nude soul,
> Stripped of the girdle of mortality,
> Against fixed destiny and the grooves of law
> Stood up in its sheer will a primal force...
> A columned shaft of fire and light she rose. [14]

II

'THE JOURNEY IN ETERNAL NIGHT AND THE VOICE OF THE DARKNESS'

Arrived at length at the "chill dreadful edge of night", all three pause in vague expectancy:

> Heaven leaned towards them like a cloudy brow
> Of menace through the dim and voiceless hush. [15]

Now daring all, Savitri first affronts the abyss and foots, "the ruthless eyeless waste" and grapples with the "mystery of terror's boundlessness". A realm of sinister Nought, "clotted cipher", this Death's dark kingdom is a place where:

> Mind could not think, breath could not breathe, the soul
> Could not remember or feel itself; it seemed
> A hollow gulf of sterile emptiness,
> A zero oblivious of the sum it closed,
> An abnegation of the Maker's joy... [16]

Into these grim shadows Savitri darts and vanishes, although there is "no course, no path, no end or goal", amidst "a blindness of extinguished souls". Yet at the last extremity of this "corpse of life", a faint gleam slowly begins to assert itself, and hope itself palely approaches; and still the gleam grows brighter, the hope stronger; Death suffers a firm repulsion, and Savitri's soul exceeds the grasp of pain and gropes towards joy. And once more, out of the silence and the dark, the tread and form of Satyavan assert themselves to her consciousness.

But Death's iron-hearted voice yet warns her against any further trespass into the eternal Night, though, as earlier, she answers him not, replying on the "undying fountains of her life". Once more the dire god tries speech, this time mingling sternness with sugary appeasement. Why seek to bring Satyavan back to life? Why prolong the earthly tale of "incurable unrest?" What use playing any longer the God's game of laughter and tears? Human life is but thwarted purposing, courage being met by defeat, wisdom being mocked by Death, and knowledge being fenced with ignorance? Yet Death will extend reluctant appreciation to Savitri —the strength of her great love deserves no less—and will grant her gifts to soothe her "wounded life". While not acknowledging Death's sovereignty, while indeed calling him variously "huge mask", "black lie" and "grim jest", while also disclaiming any desire to play the meek applicant, Savitri nevertheless responds to Death's offer thus:

> First I demand whatever Satyavan,
> My husband, waking in the forest's charm
> Out of his long pure childhood's lonely dreams,
> Desired and had not for his beautiful life.
> Give, if thou must, or, if thou canst, refuse. [17]

Death grants the boon, even as she demands it, with little apparent grace; Satyavan's father, Dyumatsena will get his kingdom and eyesight again, for these had long been in Satyavan's thoughts. Now at least must Savitri retire, not violate further the laws of life and death.

As Savitri has made it no bargain, she firmly stands her ground, and declines to be cowed into brazen retreat. She too is immortal, though caged in apparent mortality; she can therefore afford to dare the "stone eyes of Law and Fate", and she will retrace her steps only when Satyavan too can measure with her "earth's flowering spaces". Death's irritation rises to fever pitch and he mounts a new dialectical offensive, as ferocious as the rush of the sea's waves towards a swimmer. Death has created all things, created them only to destroy them; he has made the worlds his net, "each joy in a mesh"; he has dealt out sin with one hand and punishment with the other; to flee from him is vain, for his "tireless Wrath/Hell cannot slake nor heaven's mercy assuage". This too fails to frighten Savitri, who bravely meets his negations with her own affirmations. The God of destruction is not the God she knows or acknowledges; hers is rather the God of Will and Love:

> Love's golden wings have power to fan thy void:
> The eyes of love gaze starlike through death's night,
> The feet of love tread naked hardest worlds.
> He labours in the depths, exults on the heights;
> He shall remake thy universe, O Death. [18]

And so they travel on in sepulchral silence for a while, for Death is speechless for the space of "a deep and perilous pause", now he speaks again, and in a more insinuating tone. Cannot Savitri see that earth-life with Satyavan can be no more than,

> The brilliant idol of a fugitive hour...
> A thin dance of fireflies speeding through the night,
> A sparkling ferment in life's sunlit mire? [19]

Death only lasts, Death is the vast, Death is alone the only God; Savitri's supposed immortal self itself is but "a shadowy icon" of Death's infinite; and formless itself, Death has assumed form, face and voice only because Savitri has come out to struggle with him. In the one final home of Death everlasting, there is neither Satyavan nor Savitri, and "no Savitri/Claims from brief life her bribe of joy". If she must, let Savitri play with her own soul's illusive immortality; let her leave Satyavan alone. This deceptive speech strikes sudden fire in Savitri who says simply:

> O Death, who reasonest, I reason not,
> Reason that scans and breaks, but cannot build
> Or builds in vain because she doubts her work.
> I am, I love, I see, I act, I will. [20]

Discomfited, yet Death tries one more dialectical stunt, affirming the need for "knowing", but Savitri replies that there will be time for knowing when she has loved forever; in fact, knowledge best comes through love:

> I know that knowledge is a vast embrace:
> I know that every being is myself,
> In every heart is hidden the myriad One.
> I know the calm Transcendent bears the world,
> The veiled Inhabitant, the silent Lord:
> I feel his secret act, his intimate fire;
> I hear the murmur of the cosmic Voice.
> I know my coming was a wave from God. [21]

Death is once more silenced, and stands a shadow figure "girt with the terrors of his secret sword". Now they resume their march, and Savitri travels,

> ...through the dumb unhoping vasts.
> Around her rolled the shuddering waste of gloom,...
> Through the long fading night by her compelled,
> Gliding half-seen on their unearthly path,
> Phantasmal in the dimness moved the three. [22]

SECTION C

'THE BOOK OF THE DOUBLE TWILIGHT'

Already, in Book IX, while the dramatic situation derives from the *Mahabharata* original, the dialectic in which Savitri and Death (Yama) engage begins increasingly to assume a distinctly Aurobindonian hue and cast. In Vyasa's epic, Savitri is the pure wife whose deathless love for her husband moves Yama—who is also Dharma Raja or Lord of Righteousness—to compassion as well as admiration, till at last he readily grants her the final boon of Satyavan's return to life. Essentially, Savitri is the silent and worthy suppliant, while Yama is the gracious and righteous giver

In the Aurobindonian conception, on the other hand, Death (the name 'Yama' is scarcely mentioned) is the static God of ignorance, illusion and destruction, while Savitri is both humanity evolving into divinity and the transcendent divine itself, in other words, a more prepotent power than Death, who has taken a human form, not to destroy or be destroyed, but to fulfil a mission and help the Divine's secret purposes to be fulfilled. From the very beginning almost, Savitri refuses to be cowed down by Death's terrible aspect and imperious attitudes, refuses to be deviated from her set purpose, refuses to be patronised.

This challenge to his assumed, and so long unquestioned, omnipotence is a new experience for Death, and he is unsure of the moves he should make to frighten or cajole Savitri into acquiescence. His seemingly gracious offer of a boon is accepted by her as though he has but irresistibly complied with her demand. His threats have cut no ice with her, his loud affirmations have been met by her own, not a whit less categorical, nor less instinct with self-assurance and consciousness of power, than his own. Savitri has not got her Satyavan back, nor has Death succeeded in making her drop her demand and go back to her home on the earth. It is the perfect stalemate.

Savitri, being more than the 'legend' that it is in the *Mahabharata* and, in Sri Aurobindo's conception, a 'symbol' besides, the human and the symbolic figures, worlds and actions, generally run parallel; but sometimes either the legend or the symbol monopolises the foreground, though the other too is not ignored altogether. The 'action' comprises a single day: dawn to another dawn, quickly passing over morning, noon and afternoon (these are rapidly slurred over in the legendary action described in Book VIII), but lingering over evening, dusk, night and twilight, and ushering in the new dawn of everlasting day. Books IX, X, XI speak of 'Eternal Night', 'Double Twilight' and 'Everlasting Day', the juxtaposition of adjective and substantive in each case suggestive of the dual significance of the action, the legendary and the symbolic.

Sri Aurobindo has remarked that "the central conception of the *Veda* is the conquest of the Truth out of the darkness of Ignorance and by the conquest of the Truth also of Immortality".[23] *Savitri* too is a symbolic scripture when viewed from one angle, and its characters stand out both as persons and as powers, and the esoteric meaning is not less, but perhaps more important than the surface meaning. Death seizes Truth (Satyavan), Darkness swallows up Light; Ignorance has brought about the collapse of Knowledge. Who is Savitri, that she should resist Ignorance, Darkness and Death, and finally recover Light, which is Truth-being or Satyavan?

Savitri partly harks back to the Sun God who is addressed in a Vedic hymn "as the source of divine knowledge and the creator of the inner worlds", [24] and partly to the infinite Mother, Aditi, also with hoary Vedic associations; and above all to the creative inspiration behind Savitri in Sri Aurobindo's own metaphysics as outlined in *The Life Divine* and his dynamic psychology as set forth in *The Synthesis of Yoga*. Much of this comes to a head in Book X or 'The Book of the Double Twilight'. In the four cantos of this mass of verse sustained at a consistently high level of poetic inspiration, the dialectical issue between Death and Savitri is joined once again, all arts are tried, thesis is countered by antithesis, the soap-bubble of casuistry is pricked to nothingness, false lures are firmly rejected, challenges are triumphantly accepted; Savitri attempts dialectical persuasion, and fails; when all fails, she assumes her *visvarūpa* or cosmic form, which at long last proves to Death that his game is over, and he retreats into the shadows from which he had come earlier. Savitri has her Satyavan again.

I

'THE DREAM TWILIGHT OF THE IDEAL'

For a time all three, Savitri, Death and Satyavan's spirit, move in a region that is a 'house of void' making for a Nowhere in this land of Nought. If a beam of light anywhere appears at all, even that seems a ghostly unreal thing. Has she been mistaken, after all? Her present discomfiture seems like expiation for the pride of her assumption that, although made of dust, she can be "a living fire of God". Is she to be chastised for her sense of immortality? Is corruption greater than incorruption? That cannot be. The fact is, the superconscient is in a trance of sleep in the inconscience of matter:

> Death is a stair, a door, a stumbling stride
> The soul must take to cross from birth to birth,
> A grey defeat pregnant with victory,
> A whip to lash us towards our deathless state...
> Night is not our beginning nor our end;
> She is the dark Mother in whose womb we have hid
> Safe from too swift a waking to world-pain. [25]

Now comes a golden fire to burn out the heart of Night; there is the faintest stir of light and consciousness; and "intolerant darkness" pales and slowly draws apart. Night reluctantly gives place to twilight.

The description of twilight is one of the great passages in *Savitri*, almost comparable to the evocation of the Symbol Dawn in the opening canto. The touches are at once physical and supra-physical, and the lines have—if one may say so—the distinct ring of 'overhead' poetry:

> There is a morning Twilight of the gods;
> Miraculous from sleep their forms arise
> And God's long nights are justified by dawn.
> There breaks a passion and splendour of new birth
> And hue-winged visions stray across the lids,
> The dreaming deities look beyond the seen
> And fashion in their thoughts the ideal worlds
> Sprung from a limitless moment of desire
> That once had lodged in some abysmal heart.
> Passed was the heaviness of the eyeless dark
> And all the sorrow of the night was dead:...[26]

Savitri is surprised into joy by this decisive change in the prospect; all is strangely, vaguely, intangibly fascinating. Sri Aurobindo repeats the word 'vague' like a soothing caress, a drowsy incantation:

> Vague fields were there, vague pastures gleamed, vague trees,
> Vague scenes dim-hearted in a drifting haze;
> Vague cattle white roamed glimmering through the mist;
> Vague spirits wandered with a bodiless cry,
> Vague melodies touched the soul and fled pursued
> Into harmonious distances unseized;...[27]

Kaleidoscopic, ever-changing like ever-new formations of clouds, forever playing games that never end, forever holding out hopes that gaily defy realisation, this is a brittle bright world:

> Here vision fled back from the sight alarmed,
> And sound sought refuge from the ear's surprise,
> And all experience was a hasty joy.[28]

Savitri walks half-enraptured the spaces of this attractive unreal world, "besieged, by the illusion of a mystic space" feasted by the sight "of wonder Satyavan before her". Not Death himself is able quite to darken this lustrous world:

The sombre Shadow sullen, implacable
Made beauty and laughter more imperative;...
Pain grew a trembling undertone of bliss
And transience immortality's floating hem,
A moment's robe in which she looked more fair,
Its antithesis sharpening her divinity. [29]

II

'THE GOSPEL OF DEATH AND THE VANITY OF THE IDEAL'

The gossamer evanescence of this twilight world tempts Death to try his wiles once more. See this unsubstantial pageant, he tells Savitri ingratiatingly; this is the source of her idealistic dreams and cravings, mere ethereal stuff as dreams are made on—no more, no more!

The ideal dwells not in heaven, nor on the earth,
A bright delirium of man's ardour of hope
Drunk with the wine of its own fantasy. [30]

And love, is there such a thing as love? Flesh calls to flesh no doubt, and lust calls itself love! Death grows subtly rhetorical, as if pitying the human lot and man's capacity for self-deception:

O human mind, vainly thou torturest
An hour's delight to stretch through infinity's
Long void and fill its formless, passionless gulfs,
Persuading the insensible Abyss
To lend eternity to perishing things,
And trickst the fragile movements of thy heart
With thy spirit's feint of immortality. [31]

Love has a miry origin and can never rise to the spiritual heights which the resourceful human mind creates in the air. Ideals, however alluring they may be, when they are sought to be translated into actuality, become of the earth, earthy. If there be God indeed, he too is not of the earth; why should he care to entangle himself in the stupidities of the earth? There have been avatars, messiahs, founders of great faiths and what have they achieved in the end?

> Vain was the sage's thought, the prophet's voice;
> In vain is seen the shining upward Way.
> Earth lies unchanged beneath the circling sun;... [32]

Why must Savitri harp upon love! Is it any more than the flesh hungering, the nerves burning, the mind dreaming, the heart fluttering? With casuistry worthy of Milton's Belial or Comus, Death tries to wear down Savitri's wall of resistance to the invasion of falsehood. Ah yes, love's momentary thrill seems "a golden bridge across the roar of the years"; but, alas! spent soon, all too soon. The honey that turns to bane, the heaven that leaves hell behind! Even had Satyavan not died, would love for him have suffered no change? Love dies a thousand deaths—"a word, a moment's act can slay the god". Worse than the death of love is love's inevitable decay:

> A dull indifference replaces fire
> Or an endearing habit imitates love:
> An outward and uneasy union lasts
> Or the routine of a life's compromise:...
> Two strive, constant associates without joy,
> Two egos straining in a single leash,
> Two minds divided by their jarring thoughts,
> Two spirits disjoined, forever separate.
> Thus is the ideal falsified in man's world:
> Trivial or sombre, disillusion comes,... [33]

Better than such humiliating decay is the total death of love—or of the lover. Death thus has saved Savitri from love's decay and has saved Satyavan, too, from a like fate. Savitri should "chastise" her heart with this knowledge and be reconciled to her lot, forgetting "the joy and the struggle and the pain".

Savitri has no difficulty in exposing the hollowness of Death's fabric of specious reasoning. She tells him straight: love has come to her from God, and such love is heavenly, partaking not of the corruptions of the flesh and heart. Besides, all love, even the most flawed, provokes "a whisper of divinity". Nor is ideal love unrealisable on earth. Hasn't there been a Lord of Brindavan:

> One who came love and lover and beloved
> Eternal, built himself a wondrous field
> And wove the measures of a marvellous dance....? [34]

Satyavan and she had loved each other since the beginning of things; their love will never change, for only one heart beats within her breast, "and one god sits there throned".

Although one attempt has misfired, Death accepts no defeat but tries again. Cannot Savitri yet realise that her thoughts are mere hallucination? Vain, all vain is her "longing to build heaven on earth". Matter is the only ultimate reality; soul itself is but "a brief flower by the gardener Mind" created on "Matter's terrain plot". In self-deception lies no safety. What boots it to camouflage the reality of matter with dazzling dream-fabrics of resourceful Mind? Death is the universe's sovereign ruler, and it is, thanks to him, that nothingness has taken 'form':

> I formed earth's beauty out of atom and gas,
> And built from chemic plasm the living man.
> Then Thought came in and spoiled the harmonious world:
> Matter began to hope and think and feel,
> Tissue and nerve bore joy and agony. [35]

Death would perhaps like Savitri to believe that Mind is an aberration, the source of much disaffection, the illusory father of lies and dreams and sighs. What presumption! "Born from a gas, a plasm, a sperm, a gene", yet to assume the god, affect his powers, and wish to divinise earth! There is no true wisdom because all human knowledge is error's make; and human love is but "a posturer on earth-stage/Who imitates with verse a faery dance". Children of the dust must return to the dust, leaving not a rack behind; such is the adamantine law. Death concludes with the appeal compounded of derision and seeming solicitude:

> How shall the will-o'-the-wisp become a star?
> The Ideal is a malady of thy mind,
> A bright delirium of thy speech and thought,
> A strange wine of beauty lifting thee to false sight...
> O soul misled by the splendour of thy thoughts,
> O earthly creature with thy dream of heaven,
> Obey, resigned and still, the earthly law...[36]

III

'THE DEBATE OF LOVE AND DEATH'

Again Death's laboured plea misfires. Sophist, beguiler, perverter of truth, Death has tried to veil the Real with his own dark semblance. He has called Truth to vindicate his lie; his is the truth that slays, not like Savitri's, the truth that saves. Isn't Death aware of the true nature of the evolutionary race? In inert Matter itself lay God in a self-wrought swoon:

> The Timeless took its ground in emptiness
> And drew the figure of a universe,
> That the spirit might adventure into Time
> And wrestle with adamant Necessity
> And the soul pursue a cosmic pilgrimage.[37]

It has been a marvellous tale of inner urge and the throwing up of life in matter, and of mind in life; like the plant from the seed, like the flower from the tree, like the fruit from the flower, new powers have emerged, and more are to come. From the windows of the mind can be espied the dim figure of the coming superman, the demi-god.

Shall we blame man for nurturing these visions, visions that shall certainly prove true:

> Motionless, voiceless in foreseeing depths,
> He stands awake in Supernature's light
> And sees a glory of arisen wings
> And sees the vast descending might of God. [38]

Death alas! is purblindly looking on an "unfinished world" and condemning it entire and denying God. "How shall the child already be the man?" Death seems to ignore "the occult spiritual miracle":

> Our imperfection towards perfection toils,
> The body is the chrysalis of a soul:... [39]

Proof of God's existence! There is glory in the glimmering moon, and glory in the purple sky; there is greatness in the wheeling stars, and beauty in tree and flower; and "the blue sea's chant, the rivulet's wandering voice/Are murmurs falling from the Eternal's harp".[40] The world is crammed in every rift and crevice with the glory of God!

Doubtless there are "brutal masks" and "evil acts", but these only contribute to the variety and complexity of God's "passion-play",

> A play and yet no play but the deep scheme
> Of a transcendent Wisdom... [41]

The wrangle of the dualities, the merging and mingling of a thousand aspects in one central unity, the "tangle-dance of passionate contraries /Locking like lovers in a forbidden embrace", all blunder and struggle "towards the one Divine". Perversion of both mind and heart is possible:

> A crooked maze they made of thinking mind,
> They suffered a metamorphosis of the heart,
> Admitting bacchant revellers from the Night
> Into its sanctuary of delights,
> As in a Dionysian masquerade. [42]

But the possibility of perversion doesn't destroy the reality of the pure condition. Knowledge *does* grow from more to more; Philosophy "climbs up Thought's cloud-bank peaks" and "Science tears out Nature's occult power"; Thought is turned skyward, it is turned inward; the visionary projects lightning flashes, the mystic has marvellous insights. Savitri reminds Death that he has only taken advantage of the exigencies of God's "passion-play" to establish his own dark reign on earth. The Light is heavily obscured, the divine Inhabitant is thickly veiled, and the "eyes of the creatrix Bliss are closed". Joy is held a sin:

> A puritan God made pleasure a poisonous fruit,
> Or red drug in the market-place of Death,
> And sin the child of Nature's ecstasy. [43]

Nevertheless it is folly to believe that, not *Ananda* or Bliss, but pain is at the root of things. World-Delight is the basically operative field of force in which we live. Nature talks the language of beauty and essays the epic of joy. Nay more:

> Even in this labour and dolour of Ignorance,
> On the hard perilous ground of difficult earth,
> In spite of death and evil circumstance
> A will to live persists, a joy to be. [44]

Joy is a universal urge, it explores all being and sounds all experience, it seeks self-expression in art, poetry, action, thought. Still to be unsatisfied, still to race towards the heights, is the malady of man; there arise in due course immortal strivings in him, his soul "cries for the clasp of God," –

> And Love that was once an animal's desire,
> Then a sweet madness in the rapturous heart,
> An ardent comradeship in the happy mind,
> Becomes a wide spiritual yearning's space. [45]

Savitri concludes by maintaining that love like hers for Satyavan is centred in God, and if she claims from Death "the living Satyavan", it is only "for his work and mine, our sacred charge":

For I, the woman, am the force of God,
He the Eternal's delegate soul in man. [46]

But Death by way of answer can only say that Savitri is cheating herself with "splendid Thoughts" that are the progeny of the "glorious charlatan Mind". Her words are no more than "large murmurs in a mystic dream". Man is a two-legged naked worm in which it is futile to "see a face and form divine". But Savitri is unruffled and firmly answers:

Yes, I am human. Yet shall man by me,
Since in humanity waits his hour the God,
Trample thee down to reach the immortal heights,
Transcending grief and pain and fate and death.
Yes, my humanity is a mask of God:
He dwells in me, the mover of my acts,
Turning the great wheel of his cosmic work.
I am the living body of his light,...
In me are the Nameless and the secret Name.[47]

Once more Death sends out the cry that Spirit and Matter, being eternal foes, cannot be reconciled; either man dies in his body to live in the Spirit or dies in the Spirit to inhabit his body; he, Death, is the only God.

Savitri retorts: My heart's strength can carry the world's burden of grief, nor falter in its task. Death: "Art thou indeed so strong, O heart, O soul, so free?.../show me thy strength..."[48] He will grant her what she wants on earth, except only Satyavan. But she hedges; Death may give her what it pleases him; her own claim (not 'request' but 'claim') is for Satyavan alone. Death, being not easily put out, tells Savitri that she can return to the earth and become the mother of daughters as beautiful as herself and also of "hero sons", implying that she might marry again. Savitri spurns these gifts with the words: "Earth cannot flower if lonely I return". At last she sternly snubs him for his mocking irony which can never succeed in deflecting her from her chosen path. Hers are no "twilight thoughts" liable to be twisted out of recognition; she knows her mind, she sees her path clearly before her; she will yet be the eternal bride of Satyavan, the eternal bridegroom. Even Death, as he listens to Savitri,

> As if by secret ecstasy assailed,
> Shuddered in silence... [49]

Thus is the war of words waged between the "great opponents". Nothing decided yet, the stalemate defying resolution, they continue their march through the symbol realms of the "double twilight":

> The mortal led, the god and spirit obeyed
> And she behind was leader of their march
> And they in front were followers of her will. [50]

IV

'THE DREAM TWILIGHT OF THE EARTHLY REAL'

Death has tried, by referring to the dream twilight of the ideal, to convince Savitri that the 'real' on earth, being only derived from the shadowy twilight ideal, is of no consequence. He has been unable to convince her, for she knows in her heart of hearts that all derive from the ultimate fount of the Supreme, not from the mediate ambiguous realms. The poisoned darts of irony, the honeyed phrases of appreciation, the offers of bounty on earth, the barrage of specious logic, all have failed to shake Savitri from her resolve not to return to the earth unless Satyavan goes with her also.

Now Death tries yet another ruse. The twilight of the ideal having failed, he advances the twilight of the earthly real to support his argument. They come to a downward slope where the "dim-heart marvel of the ideal" is lost:

> Thought fell towards lower levels; hard and tense
> It passioned for some crude reality...
> A straining taut and dire besieged her heart;

Heavy her sense grew with a dangerous load,
And sadder, greater sounds were in her ears,... [51]

As in a glass vaguely and dimly, here Savitri sees reflected the rattle and hurry and drive of the actual world of man, the perverse translation of the ideal world she had earlier seen. It is a variable phantasmagoria of baffled human hopes, of false constructions of Titan, of miserable crawlings of the worm, of "scripts of vanishing creeds", of the endless emergence and disappearance of "ideals, systems, sciences, poems, crafts":

The rolling cycles passed and came again,
Brought the same toils and the same barren end,
Forms ever new and ever old, the long
Appalling revolutions of the world. [52]

Thinking that he has now the right background to reinforce his argument, Death asks Savitri to mark the "symbol realm" before her, "its motion parable of human life", signifying "man's incurable malady of hope". Presently he waxes eloquent and draws a graphic picture of the futile frenzy of the human lot on the earth:

These polities, architectures of man's brain
That, bricked with evil and good, wall in man's spirit
And, fissured houses, palace at once and jail,
Rot while they reign and crumble before they crash;
These revolutions, demon or drunken god,
Convulsing the wounded body of mankind
Only to paint in new colours an old face;
These wars, carnage triumphant, ruin gone mad,
The work of centuries vanishing in an hour,
The blood of the vanquished and the victor's crown
Which men to be born must pay for with their pain,
The hero's face divine on satyr's limbs,
The demon's grandeur mixed with the demigod's,
The glory and the beasthood and the shame;

Why is it all, the labour and the din,
The transient joys, the timeless sea of tears,...
The aimless journey that can never pause,
The waking toil, the incoherent sleep,... [53]

Mind is no honest broker, he falsifies and renders only "gold coin with bright alloy"; not God, but the empty name of God, is hers; and if God there be, somewhere or other, he is indifferent to, "the animal's agony and the fate of man". If Savitri desires to reach the God she believes in, she must first die to herself, and make of Death "the gate of immortality".

Death the "sophist God" is himself the great perverter, making the less seem the greater reason, calling "Light to blind Truth's eyes". Savitri tries sweet reasonableness with a view to making this dark itself suffer the kindling of light. "The world is a spiritual paradox", she tells impervious immitigable Death,

A symbol of what can never be symbolised,
A language mispronounced, misspelt, yet true. [54]

To limit from present appearances the utmost term of all future possibility is not right. There is a trend, a movement, a direction in the world's affairs that means and suggests a lot. Didn't the elemental Void put forth the first stirrings of creation?

If from a bodiless Force Matter was born,
If life could climb in the unconscious tree,
Its green delight break into emerald leaves
And its laughter of beauty blossom in the flower,
If sense could wake in tissue, nerve and cell,
And Thought seize the grey matter of the brain,
And soul peep from its secrecy through the flesh,
How shall the nameless Light not leap on men,
And unknown powers emerge from Nature's sleep? [55]

The blind atheist body may deny knowledge of God, but why should "the sage deny the Light, the seer his soul?"

Death, even Death, begins obscurely to feel the results of this sustained assault on his fortress of dark strength. The edge of his intolerance is blunted a little, and "his form of dread" seems to thaw and to admit "our transient effort at eternity". He adopts a seemingly more deferential tone and cunningly suggests that, although she may be mighty herself and filled with the Goddess Durga, she should not make the "unfit souls" of the earth her field of action, lest they should receive more hurt than gain:

> Touch not the seated lines, the ancient laws,
> Respect the calm of great established things. [56]

But Savitri is quick to detect the hidden paw behind the velvet speech and pointedly asks him:

> What is the calm thou vauntst, O Law, O Death?
> Is it not the dull-visioned tread inert
> Of monstrous energies chained in a stark round
> Soulless and stone-eyed with mechanic dreams? [57]

Dull fixity is not the eternal law; Savitri will strive to change terrestrial life or perish in the attempt. Death innocently asks why should the "noble and immortal will" bother about petty terrestrial affairs and change the field of his action from the courts of heaven to the deserts of the earth? Savitri has her answer ready:

> Easy the heavens were to build for God.
> Earth was his difficult matter, earth the glory... [58]

Between the static perfection of heaven and its gods and the dynamic evolving destiny of earth and its inhabitants, there is a vast difference; and it is earth and man that really engage the creative soul of God and offer a fruitful field for his *lila* or ecstatic passion-play.

Death now changes his tactics, for flattery too has failed. Assuming the mask of childlike innocence and curiosity he asks Savitri what exactly this Truth is and who can find her form:

> Show me the body of the living Truth
> Or draw for me the outline of her face

> That I too may obey and worship her.
> Then will I give thee back thy Satyavan. [59]

Savitri ignores the challenge implied in Death's speech and contents herself with an exposition—a *Gita*, shall we say—of God's secret purposes. Death is a god too, a power of no mean significance, but still no more than a shadow of the Real. A collapse of mere logic should precede our attempts to apprehend Truth as god himself. He defies reason, and is himself:

> Universal, he is all, – transcendent, none.
> To man's righteousness this is his cosmic crime,
> Almighty beyond good and evil to dwell
> Leaving the good to their fate in a wicked world
> And evil to reign in this enormous scene. [60]

But the human drama is no tale told by an idiot, though such it seems to be to purblind impatient man. "There is a purpose in each stumble and fall;" and the chaos of a million discords only prefigures the dancing stars to come. Man has had a chequered history, but the tale is not ended:

> Out of this tangle of intellect and sense,
> Out of the narrow scope of finite thought
> At last he wakes into spiritual mind;... [61]

There have been already the god-intoxicated climbers of the Himalayas of the Spirit, who have reached radiant altitudes, and glimpsed the far splendours of the "house of Truth". There have been laureates of the Spirit who have uttered the revelatory word,

> a mighty and inspiring Voice,
> Enters Truth's inmost cabin of privacy
> And tears away the veil from God and life. [62]

The image of humanity's future hope is installed in the heart of the seer-spirit who is also striving for the advent:

> A cosmic vision, a spiritual sense
> Feels all the Infinite lodged in finite form

And seen through a quivering ecstasy of light
Discovers the bright face of the Bodiless,
In the truth of a moment, in the moment's soul
Can sip the honey-wine of Eternity. [63]

But if Death wants to see Truth's glorious face, who can oblige him? Human speech can only present a shadow of the Truth. If, however, Death touches Truth indeed, he would "grow suddenly wise and cease to be!"

For the last time Death speaks to Savitri. Half tauntingly but also half in earnest, Death asks :

Who then art thou hiding in human guise?
Thy voice carries the sound of infinity,
Knowledge is with thee, Truth speaks through thy words;
The light of things beyond shines in thy eyes.
But where is thy strength to conquer Time and Death? [64]

And Death repeats his challenge that she should reveal her power or at least show that the Mighty Mother is with her. As Krishna assumes his *viśvarūpa* or cosmic form in the *Gita* in response to Arjuna's imperative request, Savitri too now permits her whole greatness to invade and possess her:

A mighty transformation came on her.
A halo of the indwelling Deity,
The Immortal's lustre that had lit her face
And tented its radiance in her body's house,
Overflowing made the air a luminous sea.
In a flaming moment of apocalypse
The Incarnation thrust aside its veil. [65]

She seems a "little figure in infinity", yet seems the "Eternal's very house"; her forehead has the lustre of Omniscience, her eyes blaze like stars; she is the marvel Eternity moulded into shape. The words too stir in the lotus of her heart and a Voice of ineffable sweetness and power breaks the awful silence of the hour:

Release the soul of the world called Satyavan
Freed from thy clutch of pain and ignorance
That he may stand master of life and fate,
Man's representative in the house of God,
The mate of Wisdom and the spouse of Light,
The eternal bridegroom of the eternal bride. [66]

Death can hardly credit what he sees or comprehend what he hears; this is beyond all imaginings, all reckonings. Silent she stands, but her force invades him; resistance is useless; his darkness pales before her blaze, his limbs feel hypnotised by the power of her spoken word of command. What remains? He makes a despairing appeal to his associates:

He called to Night but she fell shuddering back,
He called to Hell but sullenly it retired:
He turned to the Inconscient for support,
From which he was born, his vast sustaining self;
It drew him back towards boundless vacancy…
His body was eaten by light, his spirit devoured.
At last he knew defeat inevitable…
Afar he fled…
In the dream twilight of that symbol world
The dire universal Shadow disappeared
Vanishing into the Void from which it came…
And Satyavan and Savitri were alone. [67]

But neither stirs yet, for between them there rises "a mute invisible and translucent wall". They await "the unknown inscrutable Will".

SECTION D

'THE BOOK OF EVERLASTING DAY'

I

'THE ETERNAL DAY'

The great Savitri-Yama dialectic has spanned the ineluctable spaces of Eternal Night and the Double Twilight, and with the withdrawal of the shadow, twilight gives place to day—the symbol realm of Everlasting Day—and Savitri and Satyavan are alone though still with the nameless veil, the translucent wall, between them. Death's thesis and Savitri's antithesis have rung in our ears and echoed through the corridors of the symbol worlds of night and twilight. With Death's retreat, can it be said that Savitri's antithesis has decisively and finally vanquished Death's thesis? This would be too crude an end to the cosmic debate. A synthesis is called for, a harmony that involves both thesis and antithesis, both a changed Yama and a subdued Savitri. The poetic projection of the synthesis is the subject of 'The Book of Everlasting Day.'

When night flees, when twilight lifts, then is the time for day's unfolding. What is this Eternal Day like? Paradisal must be its colour and texture and tone and rhythm. Sri Aurobindo invades this invisible realm and in trying to snap its extravagance of paradisal beauty achieves one of the greatest flights of poetic imagination on record. Light, power, beauty, harmony, truth-consciousness, bliss, are some of the features of paradise as conceived by man, but the picturing of the realm itself is seldom attempted and hardly ever satisfies. Sri Aurobindo, however, makes us see with Savitri's eyes, share her sense of wonderment and exultation and her own awakened sense of voyaging through beautiful seas of light and felicity. These are "worlds of deathless bliss", a marvellous sun looks down upon them; here is "perfection's home", surrounded by God's "everlasting day".

Savitri quivers "with eternity's touch" and her soul stands "close to the founts of the infinite". Here she sees 'immortal clarities of form", since twilight and night are no more and all is awake to the splendour of the sun:

> Arisen beneath a triple mystic heaven
> The seven immortal earths were seen, sublime:
> Homes of the blest released from death and sleep
> Where grief can never come nor any pang… [68]

Earth-nature seems changed, the very air seems "an ocean of felicity", the lowliest of earths seems a heaven now. All Nature hymns the glory of the ordainer of order. Rivers taking their origin on hills and flowing to the sea, when translated into their divine archetypes, become a celestial choir:

> A chanting crowd from mountain bosoms slipped
> Past branches fragrant with a sigh of flowers
> Hurrying through sweetnesses with revel leaps;
> The murmurous rivers of felicity
> Divinely rippled honey-voiced desires,
> Mingling their sister eddies of delight,
> Then, widening to a pace of calm-lipped muse,
> Down many-glimmered estuaries of dream
> Went whispering into lakes of liquid peace. [69]

The inhabitants of this realm enjoy an unending happiness, and neighbouring realms are peopled by "eternity's luminous tribes" Colour, shape, word, rhythm, all fuse into perfection. Variety and harmony, richness and sufficiency, impulse and law, all achieve a splendid co-existence. In this community of spirits, one wanders in the wind, another broods on leaf or stone, and from others rise "unfathomed, inexpressible, chantings":

> In those far-lapsing symphonies she could hear,
> Breaking through enhancements of the ravished sense,
> The lyric voyage of a divine soul

Mid spume and laughter tempting with its prow
The charm of innocent Circean isles,
Adventures without danger beautiful
In lands where siren Wonder sings its lures
From rhythmic rocks in ever-foaming seas. [70]

Savitri feels feasted in her senses and her soul, and it is a marvel to her that things limited or imperfect or maimed or causing satiety on earth should, in this other kingdom, be flawless, whole, and of perennial relish. The heart is a "torch lit from infinity", the limbs are "trembling densities of soul". But Savitri realises that there are even nobler worlds, opening beyond the large sapphire gates:

Endless aspired the climbing of those heavens;
Realm upon realm received her soaring view. [71]

On the crown of a glorious ascent where the finite mates with the infinite, she beholds great forms of deities, *apsara* goddesses, heaven's cupbearers, magician builders, wind-haired Gandharvas, and also our great ancestors, high seers and poets. At the last point of vision,

Beyond what tongue can utter or mind dream,
Worlds of an infinite reach crowned Nature's stir. [72]

Here all is a "potent and lucid joy"; here time dwells with Eternity as one; and here immense felicity joins rapt repose.

When the first dizziness of this impact of paradisal beauty and bliss wears off, Savitri looks about herself and sees a familiar yet strange being who is the "living knot and source" of all the worlds:

One whom her soul had faced as Death and Night
A sum of all sweetness gathered into his limbs
And blinded her heart to the beauty of the suns.
Transfigured was the formidable shape. [73]

The Dark has become exceeding Light, the dread aspect is now sweet, the sombre cowl is replaced by the "godhead's lurking love". He seems a God carrying all godheads "in his grandiose limbs", with the "fourfold being" for his crown. He is first, Virat the architect, Will working through Matter and creating the visible world. He is second, Hiranyagarbha, thinker and dreamer and the creator of the invisible worlds of possibility, "the Angel of mysterious ecstasies". The third spirit, the hidden cause of the other two, is "a mass of superconscience closed in light,/Creator of things in his all-knowing sleep/...the centre of the circle of God. [74] Fourth and last is the 'brooding bliss of the Infinite,/Its omniscient and omnipotent repose,/Its immobile silence absolute and alone." [75] Crowned by this "fourfold being", the transfigured God meets Savitri's gaze, and "Soul sees Soul in equality and understanding". [76]

II

'THE SOUL'S CHOICE'

Savitri has successfully withstood the blandishments and temptations of the Dark God. An even subtler trial awaits her now. A voice rises as it were from her heart. The voice of "inviolable Ecstasy", she is the "beauty of the unveiled Ray", and death itself is the "tunnel" she drives through life to reach her "unseen distances of bliss". Heaven and Earth have an intimate kinship:

> Heaven in its rapture dreams of perfect earth,
> Earth in its sorrow dreams of perfect heaven. [77]

Savitri and Satyavan can "serve the dual law" now only distantly glimpsed, and serve the earth and its inhabitants; but if they would rather leave the earth to its fate and achieve their own permanent felicity, now is the time to ascend into the "blissful home". Earth's desire is but an "ambiguous myth"; Savitri and Satyavan might as well rise to their own immortality. Savitri at once rejects this promise to her of personal salvation:

> I climb not to thy everlasting Day,
> Even as I have shunned thy eternal Night...
> Earth is the chosen place of mightiest souls;

Earth is the heroic spirit's battlefield,
The forge where the Archmason shapes his works.
Thy servitudes on earth are greater, King,
Than all the glorious liberties of heaven. [78]

She cannot solace herself in heaven when earth is full of suffering men. With Satyavan by her side, she will be able to give battle to the world's woe, lift man's soul to God, and bring immortality to the earth.

A fresh doubt is posed before Savitri. Is it ever possible that the basic distinction between earth and heaven can be annulled? With average humanity preoccupied with the routine cares of the earth, a general emancipation is out of question:

Heaven's call is rare, rarer the heart that heeds;
The doors of light are sealed to common mind,
And earth's needs nail to earth the human mass… [79]

Not merely ascent is difficult, relapse and descent are far easier and quicker; no wonder the human mass is content to lay waste their lives merely eating and spending. It is easy to say that existential limitations should be transcended; but how? It is easier said than done. How is man to borrow the Omniscient's eyes? Or the Omnipotent's force? Savitri's compassionate heart does great credit to her, but she is foredoomed to failure if she is going to make the earth the stage of her action:

Leave to its imperfect light the earthly race:
All shall be done by the long act of Time. [80]

Let Savitri consent to breaking into eternity "her mortal mould", receive Satyavan into her boundlessness, and ignore the world and its intolerable budget of woes. But Savitri refuses to be tempted with the promise of solitary bliss for herself and Satyavan. She says simply:

To bring God down to the world on earth we came,
To change the earthly life to life divine. [81]

She will not sacrifice earth to "happier worlds". Wasn't it God who made the earth and planted in it the seed for perfection? God has made earth, and earth must bring down her God. Savitri has actually "felt a secret spirit stir in things/Carrying the body of the growing God", and hence earth's climb to its own eternity is certain.

Realising at last that Savitri's purpose holds despite the doubts posed and the difficulties prophesied, the god tells her that while he appreciates the strength of her vision and will and voice—because these have had their origin in him—he must warn her about "the tardy process of the pace of Time"; a quick transformation of human and earth-nature is not to be thought of and she should guard against daring "too soon the adventure of the Light". But he will not raise impediments of his own any further:

> As I have taken from thee my load of night
> And taken from thee my twilight's doubts and dreams,
> So now I take my light of utter Day.
> These are my symbol kingdoms but not here
> Can the great choice be made that fixes the fate
> Or uttered the sanction of the Voice supreme.
> Arise upon a ladder of greater worlds
> To the infinity where no world can be. [82]

But the double-faced god, one side dark and the other bright, who is the master of the magic that makes the worlds, is himself no more than a mediate power, and his worlds of night, twilight and day too are only mediating links between the Spirit above and Matter below. If Savitri is determined indeed to deliver humanity from its thrall of incapacity, misery and death, she should ascend into her timeless self, "choose destiny's curve and stamp thy will on Time". With these valedictory words, the god withdraws, and with him the "heaven-worlds" too vanish in "spiritual light". And Savitri lives fulfilled in "an ineffable world", experiencing a rapture, a virgin unity,

> Housing a multitudinous embrace
> To marry all in God's immense delight,

Bearing the eternity of every spirit,
Bearing the burden of universal love,
A wonderful mother of unnumbered souls. [83]

In her condition of superlative receptiveness, "a crypt and sanctuary of brooding light/...the last recess of things beyond" now opens before her, and she listen again, and catches the accents of another voice. This is the very last test, although it is repeated four times. Savitri is asked to choose between life on earth and,

An immense extinction in eternity,
A point that disappears in the infinite, –... [84]

The woman's heart replies: Thy peace, thy oneness, thy energy, thy joy of the embrace, O Lord:

Thy magic flowing waters of deep love,
Thy sweetness give to me for earth and men. [85]

Not for herself, or for Satyavan and herself, but "for earth and men". Four times the choice is given, and four times Savitri elects earth-life and shared sorrow to easy escape into the "negative eternity" of extinction in the infinite. She will need all heaven's powers, but earth will be the area of her action. She cannot forget the cry of a million creatures, nor ignore the "dreadful whirlings of the world"; she must go back to the earth with Satyavan and start building the house divine there.

III

'THE SUPREME CONSUMMATION'

The Supreme's blissful word comes at last:

My will is thine, what thou hast chosen I choose.
All thou hast asked I give to earth and men. [86]

Thesis and antithesis have been clashing through the symbol worlds of night, twilight and day, and even in the highest realms of the

Supreme; the possibility of any true ideals being quarried out of the crude hard rocks of the Inconscience has been questioned, and the possibility of earthly realisations being permanent has been doubted; the advisability of leaving the earth and mankind to their fate and achieving a personal salvation either through the enjoyment of the bliss of heaven or through total extinction in nirvana has also been persuasively and almost peremptorily canvassed. Savitri has stood her ground without flinching in the least. Now the supreme tells her that hers is the right choice, *nay* his own choice in her! This is the synthesis towards which the dialectic has been moving all along. The tests have led to right self-knowledge, to the awakening of the requisite will, to the organisation of the right means to achieve the right purpose. The word comes again:

> Because thou hast chosen to share earth's struggle and fate
> And leaned in pity over earth-bound men
> And turned aside to help and yearned to save,
> I bind by thy heart's passion thy heart to mine
> And lay my splendid yoke upon thy soul...
> O Sun-Word, thou shalt raise the earth-soul to Light
> And bring down God into the lives of men;... [87]
>
> Descend to life with him thy heart desires.
> O Satyavan, O luminous Savitri,
> I sent you forth of old beneath the stars,
> A dual power of God in an ignorant world,
> In a hedged creation shut from limitless self,
> Bringing down God to the insentient globe,
> Lifting earth-beings to immortality. [88]

It is a speech of about 500 lines, and many of the ideas already elaborated in earlier cantos are here gathered up into a comprehensive and significant whole. The intention from the very beginning had been that Savitri and Sayavan should be God's dual power—Savitri the force and Satyavan the soul—operating on earth to divinise it; between them they are to give the right turn to human life and point to "the souls of men the routes to God". When favourable conditions have been created by the dual power,

> The superman shall wake in mortal man
> And manifest the hidden demigod
> Or grow into the God-Light and God-Force
> Revealing the secret deity in the cave. [89]

All shall then change, a magic order will displace the "mechanic universe", and "the superman shall reign as king of life,/Make earth almost the mate and peer of heaven." [90] As a "high crown of all", there will result "the end of Death, the death of Ignorance". Matter's world will itself be transformed, for "Matter shall reveal the Spirit's face". Nature too will be transfigured, "a divine force shall flow through tissue and cell" and every feeling will become a "celestial thrill":

> Thus shall the earth open to divinity
> And common natures feel the wide uplift,
> Illumine common acts with the Spirit's ray
> And meet the deity in common things.
> Nature shall live to manifest secret God,
> The Spirit shall take up the human play,
> This earthly life become the life divine. [91]

The subtle music ceases at the conclusion of the great ambrosial revelation, and presently, "through unseen worlds and bottomless spaces forced", Savitri's soul sinks down to the earth, drawing with her, "like a flower hidden in the heart of spring", dear Satyavan's soul as well. As they career towards the earth,

> Invisible heavens in a thronging flight
> Soared past... Then all the blind
> And near attraction of the earth compelled
> Fearful rapidities of downward bliss. [92]

Their return is earth's moment of destiny; "a crimson seed of God's felicity" is lodged on earth:

> A power leaned down, a happiness found its home.
> Over wide earth brooded the infinite bliss. [93]

SECTION E

'EPILOGUE: THE RETURN TO EARTH'

Savitri now awakes from out of the "abysmal trance" of her spirit; she espies the "green-clad branches" above, and peering through an "emerald lattice-window of leaves" notes the thinning day and the evening's peace. Satyavan's living body is by her side, and all her being rejoices in enfolding his:

> Supine in musing bliss she lay awhile
> Given to the wonder of a waking trance. [94]

But Satyavan is still asleep, "like an infant spirit unaware", reclining on her breast; presently awake, he finds her eyes waiting for his, he feels her hands, and embracing her and vaguely recollecting strange impossible happenings, he says incredulously;

> Whence hast thou brought me captive back, love-chained,...
> For surely I have travelled in strange worlds
> By thee companioned, a pursuing spirit,
> Together we have disdained the gates of night.
> I have turned away from the celestials' joy
> And heaven's insufficient without thee. [95]

Besides, he asks her: Where is that formidable shape that rose against us? Was it all a dream? She answers with utter sufficiency:

> Our parting was the dream;
> We are together, we live, O Satyavan. [96]

All is as before excepting that they have "left Death's night behind" and their souls have been "illumined by the light of symbol worlds". Satyavan marks a "high change" in Savitri. Always adorable, a golden bride, now she seems "too high and great/For mortal worship". Her answer, however, comes softly:

> All now is changed, yet all is still the same.

Lo, we have looked upon the face of God,
Our life has opened with divinity. [97]

Grief is now dead, and they are to seek out the bliss in the heart of all the days to come. Yet joy is vouchsafed to them, not for themselves alone, but to be shared with all:

To lead man's soul towards truth and God we are born,
To draw the chequered scheme of mortal life
Into some semblance of the Immortal's plan,
To shape it closer to an image of God,
A little nearer to the Idea divine. [98]

Now hand in hand they leave the forest spot and direct their steps to their "sylvan home"; late afternoon shades off to evening, and soon day and night lean "to each other's arms". They are met on the way by a press of people :

...unknown faces, thronged
With gold fringed headdress, gold-broidered robes,
Glittering of ornaments, fluttering of hems,... [99]

headed by King Dyumatsena, "no more/Blind, faltering-limbed", and his queen. Dyumatsena gives the glad news of a kingdom's return and the restoration of eyesight, but he also gently chides Satyavan and Savitri for being so late. Satyavan merely answers, pointing at Savitri:

Lay all on her; she is the cause of all...
Behold, at noon leaving this house of clay
I wandered in far-off eternities,
Yet still, a captive in her golden hands,
I tread your little hillock called green earth
And in the moments of your transient sun
Live glad among the busy works of men. [100]

The company is amazed, the elders cast inquiring looks on Savitri, and feel that she is lit by a vast new revelation. But Savitri, veiling her transcendent light, merely replies:

Awakened to the meaning of my heart
That to feel love and oneness is to live
And this the magic of our golden change,
Is all the truth I know or seek, O sage. [101]

Now, with linked hands, Savitri and Satyavan return triumphant hearing "a marriage march and nuptial hymn" to their new home. And with the moon palely filling the skies a silver peace reigns over the earth, and Night—

She brooded through her stillness on a thought
Deep-guarded by her mystic folds of light,
And in her bosom nursed a greater dawn. [102]

PART III

SAVITRI: SIGNIFICANCES

And thou reachest, O Savitri,
to the three shining worlds of heaven;
and thou art made manifest
by the rays of the Sun;
and thou encirclest the Night
upon either side;
and thou becomest the Lord of Love
by the law of thy actions, O God.

Rig Veda

THE 'LEGEND' AND THE 'SYMBOL'

The face of Truth
is hidden
by a brilliant golden lid;
that do thou remove,
O fostering Sun,
for the Law of the Truth,
for sight.

O sole Seer, O Ordainer,
marshal thy rays,
draw them together;
let me see the Lustre,
thy most blessed form of all.

Isha Upanishad

I

INTRODUCTION

It was on 15 August 1946, when Sri Aurobindo was seventy-four, that the opening canto of *Savitri* was first published.[1] The title-page carried *Savitri* in bold green lettering, followed by the subtitle, in smaller type, *A Legend and A Symbol.* For some years previously, there had been references in private talks and even in print[2] to this poem, this enormous 'work in progress', and the emphasis was on the 'legend' as well as on the 'symbol'. As further instalments of *Savitri* appeared more or less regularly once a quarter, the small anxious—almost impatient—public tried to grasp the unfolding dual significance of the poem. The present definitive edition (1954), however, omits the subtitle, not because it is not deemed appropriate any more, but perhaps because the 'symbolic' character of the poem, being obvious, needs no particular emphasis even on the title-page. *Savitri* remains a 'legend' and a 'symbol', for so Sri Aurobindo wrought it throughout.

For the 'legend', Sri Aurobindo went to the *Mahabharata*. In the *Vana Parva* (The Book of the Forest), *Rishi* Markhandeya tells many stories to Prince Yudhishtira, partly to instruct him and largely to console him. One of the tales so narrated covers the story of Rama, his exile, the abduction of his wife, Sita, by Ravana, the expedition against the demon-king, and the final rescue of Sita—all this is also the subject of Valmiki's great epic, the *Ramayana*. Even as Rama had been able to triumph over his tribulations ultimately, Yudhishtira too should be able, notwithstanding his present plight, to get back to his own.

But Yudhishtira is still scalded by the memory of the outrage on his wife Draupadi, following the disastrous game of dice. He therefore asks Markhandeya whether he has seen or heard of Draupadi's peer, in her chastity and strength. In reply, Markhandeya tells the story of Savitri and her *pātivrata māhātmya*, which may be explained as the 'glorious efficacy of wifely chastity'.

The efficacy of virgin purity is the theme of many a story, for example Milton's *Comus*; but a wife's chastity and utter devotion to her husband (even when he doesn't deserve such devotion) are qualities apart and unique, and the Hindu has believed that they can work wonders, even arrest Nature's normal process (as in the story of Nalayani who could prevent the sun from rising), and achieve the impossible. In the Greek story of Admetus and Alcestis (the theme of Euripides' *Alcestis*), the wife dies so that the husband may live. Although Admetus' father and mother both decline to die in his place, his wife Alcestis agrees to make the sacrifice.

Yet Alcestis is no Savitri, and Admetus no Satyavan. Alcestis is a simple woman who accepts death as a duty, while Admetus is merely petulant and egoistic. It is Heracles who sets upon Thanatos (the messenger from Hades) and rescues Alcestis and restores her to her husband. Alcestis is a passive character, heroic in her own silent way, who is willing to make the supreme sacrifice for the sake of her husband and children.

But Savitri's role is essentially dynamic; she braves Fate and fights Death, she saves her husband and redeems his and her father's families. The *Savitri upakhyana* or episode in the *Mahabharata* is the most dearly cherished of such stories; indeed it is more than a mere story, for Savitri to this day is deeply imbedded in the Hindu woman's consciousness as the pure virgin awaiting her future husband or as the pure wife, warding off with the armour of her chastity, all evil and danger from her husband.

II

THE LEGEND

In the *Mahabharata*, the Savitri story is told in the course of seven cantos (291 to 297 in the *Vana Parva*). Aswapati, the King of the Madra, is pious, virtuous, high-souled, a good giver, the protector of his people, and therefore the well-beloved. But he is sorrow-stricken, being old and childless. For eighteen years he undergoes austerities, daily offering a hundred thousand oblations to the fire to the accompaniment of mantras in honour of the Goddess Savitri, who appears at last in her resplendent form and promises that a daughter of great beauty (*kanyā tejasvinī*) will be soon born to him.

Returning to his duties as a king, he lives as righteously as before, and his eldest wife bears in due course a daughter, who, being the gift of the Goddess Savitri, is also now named Savitri. She grows in beauty worthy of a goddess, and the child becomes a maiden; but her eyes are like lotus-pools, incandescent in their splendour, and hold at a distance all would-be suitors. On a certain auspicious day, having fasted and taken her bath and offered prayers to the gods, Savitri approaches her father, touches his feet in reverence, offers flowers, and stands silent and expectant by his side.[3] Her god-like bloom of beauty (*deva-rūpinīm*) takes away his breath, yet saddens him, for none asks him for her hand. He tells her simply: "Seek a husband and choose for yourself". There is no bandying of idle words, and Savitri starts on her quest accompanied by wise and elderly counsellors.

When the *rishi* continues the tale in the next canto, there is a leap over time, a break in the sequence and we find Aswapati seated with Sage Narad engaged in conversation; and now Savitri, having visited all ashrams and holy bathing places, returns to her father's court with her counsellors, and pays her respects to the sage and the king. Is she not married yet, asks Narad, and Aswapati, in answer, directs Savitri to speak. She first describes the misfortunes of Dyumatsena, the Shalwa King, who had lost his sight in old age, and so lost his kingdom as well, for it was seized by an enemy neighbour; Dyumatsena had been thus driven to take refuge in the forest with his wife and infant son. Savitri concludes by saying that this son, Satyavan, born in the city but grown to manhood in the ashram (*tapovana*), is alone worthy to be her lord and husband.

Narad, taken aback, describes the choice as a great wrong (*mahat pāpam*), but also refers to Satyavan in eulogistic terms; he is verily what his name implies, the truthful; handsome as great Vivasvan, Brihaspati's compeer in his mind, Indra's equal in prowess, long suffering as the Earth (Vasudeva); generous in giving, respectful to teachers, noble as Yayati, fair as the moon; another Asvin in form and dignity of bearing; gentle, self-controlled, steadfast, modest, free from envy, and entirely righteous. Pressed by Aswapati to name Satyavan's faults (*doṣān*), if any, Narad answers succinctly: "One fault, and one only; his race run, Satyavan will die a year hence."

The king is shocked, and urges Savitri to choose again, but she answers with firm resolve: "There are things that are done but once; be he long-lived or short-lived, be he endowed with or bereft of virtues, I have chosen, and cannot choose again; seized by the mind, presented in speech, it remains only to be translated into deed." It is one of the supremely incandescent utterances of all time. Narad, the divine sage, is himself overpowered by her defiant resolution, and promptly advises the king to act according to Savitri's desires. All shall be well yet. The king proceeds with the preparations for his daughter's marriage.

After the tense drama of the second canto, the third is on a more subdued key. The king completes the wedding preparations and taking his daughter, the priests and others with him, he sets out on an auspicious day for Dyumatsena's ashram. After fraternal exchanges, Aswapati explains the object of his visit and requests the hermit-king to accept Savitri as his daughter-in-law. Dyumatsena wonders whether Aswapati's daughter, used to comfort, will be able to put up with the rigours of ashram life in a forest, but Aswapati reassures him and importunes him to accept Savitri as Satyavan's wife. Forest life can have no terrors for Savitri, because she knows full well that happiness and misery are impermanent. Dyumatsena now reveals that he had himself desired this alliance, although, because of his circumstances, he had not moved in the matter. The marriage is now performed, and leaving with Savitri a worthy retinue, Aswapati returns to his homeland.

Satyavan and Savitri are mutually happy in having secured their heart's desire. She now puts by all her ornaments and rich clothes, and lives the bare pure life of a dedicated hermitress. Her many virtues, her serviceable acts and her gentle subdued behaviour please one and all. She ministers to her mother-in-law's wants, and wins her affection; with her restrained speech and worshipful aspect, she wins her father-in-law's delighted approbation. She wins her husband's entire trust and affection with her honied words, her skill in works, her modesty, and her loving ministrations in private. Yet, as time passes by, day and night Savitri keeps in mind the fateful word spoken by Narad, and she can have no inner peace.

In the fourth canto, the tale moves towards the preordained crisis foretold by Narad. When hardly four days are to go before the threatened danger to Satyavan's life, Savitri, still carrying in her sole bosom the burden of this fate, resolves to undertake the *tri-rāttra* vow, fasting, praying and standing night and day. She stills Dyumatsena's fears and anxieties on her behalf and assures him that she will be able to carry out her vow. When the third night of the vow spends itself out, Savitri reminds herself 'Today then is *that* day', pours a libation to the flaming fire, completes her morning rites, and bows down in due order before all the elders in the forest and receives their benediction that she may never suffer widowhood. Filled with the answering assent in her heart, she stands rapt in contemplation, poised on expectancy. Her parents-in-law now ask her to take food without further delay, but she says she will do so only at sundown.

Just then Satyavan starts for the forest with his axe, and Savitri asks him to take her with him, as she cannot bear to be parted from him. As he remonstrates, she tells him that the fast hasn't exhausted her, and therefore he should not forbid her. He gives in, but asks her to take his parents' permission first. Savitri accordingly approaches them and says: "My husband is starting to go to the forest for the sake of his elders' sacrificial fire (*agnihotra*); I musn't therefore stand in his way. But let me go with him, for separation today is unbearable to me. Besides, for almost a year I haven't gone out, and I am eager to see the blossoming woods." This being her first request to her parents-in-law, Dyumatsena gives her leave to go with Satyavan. And so, with apparent joy though with a heavy heart, Savitri accompanies Satyavan, admiring the multifoliate woods echoing with the peacock's cries. His gestures and sweet words of explanation receive all her attention, but as she remembers Narad's words, he strikes her as one already dead; yet she follows him close, although her heart is breaking under the strain, and she silently awaits the fated hour.

Now opens the fifth canto. Satyavan first gathers fruits, then starts chopping wood; in the act of felling a branch, he suddenly perspires profusely, he is overcome by fatigue and his head begins to ache. He wearily comes to his beloved wife, who is intently observing him all the time, and confesses to a splitting headache and a desire to sleep. She makes him sit by her side, and lays his head on her lap. The very day, the very hour and minute foretold by Narad is upon her, she thinks. And already she sees before her a clear-skinned bright-robed figure, handsome and majestic, a diadem on his head, a noose in his hand; altogether terrifying is his aspect.

She rises, having first gently shifted her husband's head to rest on the ground, and salutes him reverentially though with an agitated heart and asks this form divine what his business is. He is Yama, he says, and he has come to carry off Satyavan, as his days on earth are over; and he has come himself, as befitting so worthy and virtuous a person as Satyavan. So saying Yama draws forth from Satyavan's body his life (*prana)*, which is the measure of a thumb, and so the body becomes untenanted, lustreless, inert and unsightly. As Yama now walks away in a southerly direction, Savitri too follows him, her heart overwhelmed by sorrow.

Now begins the great debate between fixt fate and the power of Love, the law of adamantine Necessity and the variant play of Freedom; Yama at first asks Savitri to retrace her steps and perform her husband's funeral rites. She says that wherever her husband goes or is taken, there she must follow him; whatever the hazard. Having walked seven paces with Yama already, she can claim the privilege of friendly converse with him. Actually she seems to talk in conundrums. Of the four 'classic' stages of human life (*vāsa* or *brahmacarya*, dharma or *gṛihastha*; *vānaprastha*; and *sannyāsa*; that is, studentship, married life, hermit-life, and life as a wandering ascetic), Savitri and Satyavan have been living the second, which properly lived, can assurely lead to realisation as the others. Her whole point is that Yama, who is also Dharma, should permit Savitri and Satyavan to continue their dharma or *gṛihastha* mode of life and not separate them. [4]

Yama is pleased, and asks her to choose a boon, only the life of Satyavan excepted. Savitri asks for the restoration of eyesight to her father-in-law, and this is granted. But she is not to be shaken off still, and she speaks insinuatingly to Yama, pleading and almost preaching. A second boon he grants, and a third; she desires that her father-in-law may regain his kingdom, and that her father, Aswapati, may have a hundred sons of his own. Pressed now to return, Savitri says again that her place is with her husband wherever he may be, and adds fair and flattering speech, which invokes the grant of a fourth boon. "May a hundred sons be born to me and Satyavan", she says naively, and Yama grants this boon as well and begs her to return.

But she tarries still, and speaks more sweetly and wisely than ever before extolling the efficacy of the good and the righteous, so much so Yama concedes her a final incomparable boon. Savitri tells him simply that unless Satyavan's life is restored, the earlier boon of a hundred sons to them will be incapable of accomplishment; let Satyavan live again, for she cannot live without him. Yama is entangled in the web of his varied boons, and he realises that Savitri is right. He releases Satyavan's life, blesses her heartily, and disappears. Savitri, her love's labour won, returns to the place in the forest where she had earlier left her husband's listless body.

Sitting once more on the ground, Savitri lifts Satyavan's head and places it on her lap. He regains consciousness, views her face with lingering affection like one just come home after a long sojourn abroad, and says; "I seem to have slept long, you should have awakened me; but where is that dark person that tried to take me away?" "A long time indeed you've slept, my lord", answers Savitri, "and Yama has departed, and all is well. The night is far gone, and you may rise if you are able." As they get up, he recapitulates aloud the happenings of the day—how he came with her to gather fruits, how he felt a pain in his head as he chopped wood, how unable to stand he slept on her lap, how in the darkness he saw the effulgent figure. What did it all mean? Has he been merely dreaming?

But Savitri tells him that they should first return to the ashram, it being late already, and she will tell him everything in the morning. The fearful denizens of the jungle are abroad and are making fearful noises. Satyavan wonders whether, since all is utterly dark, they can find their way back to the hermitage. Savitri, however, sees a withered burnt tree still showing flickers of flame as the wind blows upon it—the aftermath of a forest conflagration; she will therefore light some faggots, and if Satyavan is still weak, they can spend the night in the forest, and when the woods are visible in the morning they can start for the hermitage. But Satyavan assures her he is all right now, and besides his parents would be anxious. He is their only crutch, and deprived of him they cannot live even an instant. Often in the past, in their excessive solicitude, they had chided him for being late in homecoming, however little he might have tarried. Surely they would be racked by anxiety today. His blind old father and his old distraught mother would be asking everybody about Satyavan. The thought of his parents' plight, the result of his own tardiness and untimely sleep, overpowers Satyavan, and he weeps bitterly.

Savitri wipes away the tears from Satyavan's eyes, and articulates the prayer that her husband and her parents-in-law may come to no harm, and all may be well with them and prove auspicious to them; she has ever been truthful, compassionate and regular in her religious observances, and by the power of the truth of her life she wishes that all may be well. Satyavan is less self-possessed than Savitri, and is a prey to fears, and says he cannot live himself, should anything happen to his parents. But Savitri's head is as clear as her heart is whole. She hangs the pot of fruits from the branch of a tree, for it may be fetched later on, and she carries the axe herself; then with his arm on her left shoulder and her own right arm round his waist, giving him every support, she gently leads him on. Satyavan presently finds that his feet know the path very well by force of habit, and so they recognise landmarks like clusters of trees, and walk in rapid strides towards the hermitage.

In canto six, we move to the hermitage. Yama's first boon has already brought about the restoration of Dyumatsena's eyesight. With his wife he searches for Satyavan in the hermitages, the rivers, the woods and the lakes; they are almost maniacal in their grief. The brahmins of the place now try to console them and reassure them, and bring them back to their own hermitage. But Dyumatsena and his wife recall Satyavan's childhood doings, and off and on piteous cries escape them regarding the fate of the young couple. One by one the elderly brahmins—Suvarchas, Gautama, Bharadvaja, Dalbhya, Mandavya, Dhaumya—tell the aged parents that since Savitri is chaste and well behaved, as she has completed her vow, as she has no marks that indicate possible widowhood, as Satyavan himself is rich in virtues and his strength of limbs indicates long life, and as, besides, all the omens are auspicious, there surely is no danger to Satyavan's life.

These words help to steady Dyumatsena's mind, and a little while hence, Savitri with her husband joins them, and there is general rejoicing. They all sit down, and the forest-dwellers ask Satyavan out of curiosity how he happened to return so late, causing his parents so much anxiety. Satyavan truthfully refers to his headache while felling the branch of a tree, his deep sleep, and the consequent delay, but as this leaves unexplained Dyumatsena's regaining his eyesight, Gautama turns to Savitri and asks her to tell the truth if it can be told. Now Savtiri reveals all the circumstances—Narad's prophecy, her vow, her accompanying Satyavan to the woods, Yama's coming, her truthful speeches, the five boons, and the happy ending of it all. The ascetics praise her with one voice, take leave of Dyumatsena and Satyavan, and go to their respective abodes.

The last canto is a brief one and may be called, after Thomas Hardy, 'aftercourses' or, more appropriately, 'fulfilment'. In the morning, even as the ascetics are talking to Dyumatsena about Savitri, there come to the hermitage the people of Shalwa with the news that the usurper has been slain by his minister, the troops have dispersed, and the people want their beloved king back in their midst. This is Yama's second boon fulfilling itself. The people are more delighted still when they find that their king has recovered his sight and is in magnificent health. Dyumatsena, his queen, his son and his daughter-in-law presently take leave of the ascetics and are taken in a chariot to his kingdom where he is anointed king again, and Satyavan becomes the heir apparent. The other boons too fulfil themselves: Aswapati becomes in due course the father of a hundred sons, and so are Satyavan and Savitri too blessed with progeny.

Rishi Markhandeya concludes his narrative thus: 'Even thus did Savitri redeem from peril and raise to high fortune herself, her father and mother, her father-in-law and mother-in-law, as also the whole race of her husband (*bharthuḥ kulam*)'.

III

'THE WONDERFUL POEM'

Such is the *Mahabharata* 'legend'. No summary or paraphrase, no attempt at translation, can do adequate justice to the bareness and strength and utter self-sufficiency of the original. Not a word is wasted, and as one reads the poem one feels that what needs to be said has been said; one accepts the story as something primordial and permanently significant like the Sun itself. There are other 'episodes'—the Nala and the Sakuntala, for example—in the *Mahabharata* that have also won the affections of many generations of men, but the Savitri stands apart even among them, verily a star. "The 'story of Savitri' is the gem of the whole poem", wrote Alfred Wallace,[5] "and I cannot recall anything in poetry more beautiful, or any higher teaching as to the sanctity of love and marriage. We have really not advanced one step beyond this old-world people in our ethical standards."

Savitri is presented by the ancient poet as beauty, truth, goodness, and, above all, power incarnate. She is the gift of the Goddess Savitri and the fruit of eighteen years' severe austerities. She is so beautiful that like the Sun itself she keeps at a distance would-be wooers. She doesn't speak an untrue word even in small matters. She radiates goodness as a matter of course, and all benefit by it. But *shakti* or power is what makes Savitri unique among the heroines of legend and history. It is characteristic of her that she never weeps. Satyavan weeps aloud thinking of his parents, Dyumatsena weeps thinking of his son; Savitri does not weep—not when Narad speaks the cruel words, not when Satyavan dies, nor when, after coming back to life, he breaks down at the thought of his parents. Neither is it callousness, indifference, or want of feeling; rather is it the measure of her stern purpose, her poised readiness to face any eventuality whatsoever, her tranquil consciousness of her own strength.

Toru Dutt, the marvellous Bengali girl who mastered two 'alien' languages like English and French and wrote with distinction in both, felt attracted to the Savitri story and translated it into English verse. The daughter of a Christian convert, yet she felt drawn to this Hindu story (as also to another great Hindu heroine, Sita). "The chief thing in Savitri's life which attracted the vehement soul of Toru", writes S.V. Mukerjea, "was that she could not but have been the child of a society of freedom." [6] A society where purdah, male domination and child marriages are the governing factors could certainly not have evolved such a heroine as Savitri. Yet it would be wrong to call Savitri an Amazon, a vague Indian Penthesilea. For there is a quality in Savitri—her flaming love for Satyavan—that gathers up and gives edge to her other qualities, her beauty, truthfulness, goodness and power. She is the eternal feminine coming from the home of the Absolute, not the conventional feminine—the fair sex, the weaker sex, made out of one of the ribs of Man!

If Savitri never weeps, neither does she ever beg or play the pathetic suppliant. When Narad's terrible warning is uttered and Aswapati asks her to choose again, she doesn't plead with them to be permitted to marry Satyavan; she merely says that once only can her heart be given away. It is Narad who changes his mind and persuades Aswapati to give her in marriage to Satyavan. Neither divine sage nor terrestrial king is able to resist her simple steely resolution. She takes the decision to undertake the *tri-rāttra* vow herself; her father-in-law later merely acquiesces in her decision. Hers is the decision not to touch food even on the fourth day till nightfall; hers too is the decision to accompany her husband on the fatal day to the woods. "I'm determined to go with you, please don't forbid me", she tells Satyavan; even her request to her parents-in-law is couched in such terms that there can be only one answer.

When the anticipated blow comes at last and life is extinct in Satyavan and Yama stands in front of her, her self-possession doesn't leave her, she is Savitri still. There is just a hint of defiance (not meant as such, though) in her question: Who are you, and what is it you want to do? When Yama carries away Satyavan's life (*prana*), she follows her husband, and every time speaks only when spoken to by Yama; there is no pleading or entreaty in her voice or aspect; she speaks fairly and truly and wisely, and increasingly Yama is put on the defensive. Yama is also Dharma; the Lord of Death is also—should be also—the Lord of Righteousness. This is the whole point of her gentle, seemingly sententious, speeches. She doesn't ask, it is Yama who offers one boon after another; and she takes them as they come, thinks first of her parents-in-law, then of her own parents, and last only of herself and Satyavan. Yama almost feels instructed more and more, feels awakened to his true role as Dharma, and so it is with relief that he releases Satyavan's life and takes leave of Savitri. As Winternitz remarks,...in the whole of the *Mahabharata* the idea prevails that Yama, the god of death, is one with Dharma, the personification of Law. But nowhere is the identification of the King of the realm of death with the lord of law and justice expressed so beautifully as in the most magnificent of all brahmanical poems which the epic has preserved, the wonderful poem of faithful Savitri. [7]

Savitri is thus throughout dignified, masterful and independent without for a second lacking in real womanliness or respect for elders or reverence for tradition. Winternitz is right when he says that Savitri "recalls more the women of heroic poetry, such as Draupadi, Kunti and Vidula, than the brahmanical ideal of woman",[8] though it is doubtful whether even these, great as is their capacity to suffer and sacrifice, measure upto Savitri's incandescent purity of motive and action. If Savitri transcends the brahmanical ideal of woman because throughout she acts as a being essentially free, electrically free, from considerations other than the imperatives of Dharma, she transcends no less the merely heroic or even tragic ideal of woman, because she is never racked by a sense of guilt, she is never uncertain of herself, she is involved in no 'inner struggle'; on the other hand, her sense of direction is uncanny, the way she gets ready for the event shows how well she can time her actions, and her words, gestures and general strategy and particular tactics are those of an infallible General, a self-poised self-sustained Woman of Destiny. She is the darling daughter, the loving girl-wife, the solicitous daughter-in-law, no doubt; she forgets none of the duties of a daughter, of a wife, or of a daughter-in-law. Yet, even as she is ideally these, she also transcends them, and is also the protectress, the benefactress, of her father's and her husband's families as well.

The Savitri story takes up about 700 lines in the original Sanskrit, but the quality of the poetry is pure molten gold. To quote Winternitz again, "Only a great poet was capable of placing this noble female character before us so that we seem to see her before our eyes. Only a true poet could have described in such a touching and elevating manner the victory of love and constancy, of virtue and wisdom, over destiny and death, without even for an instant falling into the tone of the dry preacher of morality."[9]

The scenes, the characters, and the tremendous action in which they are both intimately implicated, all literally tingle with life. No theme can be more 'romantic', for it is a story of love at first sight, love defying destiny, love victorious over death; yet no theme could have been rendered with more 'classic' restraint and poise, or more immaculate 'Apollonian' grace. The poet waves his wand, and we see the king engaged in the self-absorbed concentration of *tapas* invoking the blessings of the Goddess Savitri; the poet waves his wand, and the scene where Savitri's resolution gets the better of Narad and Aswapati leaps before our eyes; again the poet waves his wand, and the forest, its groves, its pools, its rivers, the *agnihotra* sacrifices, the elected silences are upon us, and we are a part of them; or we watch the deathless scene of the retreat of Death; or we admire Savitri's attention to detail when she hangs the pot of fruits from the branch of a tree and carries the axe herself, lest Satyavan should be encumbered with it; or we watch with a rush of tenderness and a feeling of personal relief and joy the reunited couple, his left arm on her shoulder, her right arm around his waist, returning in 'the dark that is light enough' to their hermitage.

The Savitri story inevitably challenges comparison with the much longer Nala story, which also finds a place in the *Vana Parva* of the *Mahabharata*. Nala is more of a tragic hero, and Damayanti more of a long-suffering heroine, than Satyavan or Savitri. Damayanti is a heroine wholly without blemish, and Nala himself is more sinned against than sinning; it is the dark God who engineers most of the mischief. Humanity could almost raise the plaint, "As flies to wanton boys are we to the gods!" The Savitri story is reared on quite other foundations. Man here is master of his fate; Woman is *shakti*, the redeemer, the transvaluer of values, the subduer of destiny. Comparing the two stories Sri Aurobindo writes:

> The *Nala*...has the delicate and unusual romantic grace of a young and severe classic who has permitted himself to go a-maying in the fields of romance. There is a remote charm of restraint in the midst of abandon, of vigilance in the play of fancy which is passing sweet and strange. The *Savitri* is a maturer and nobler work, perfect and restrained in detail, but it has still some glow of the same youth and grace over it. [10]

Idea and word, character and action, background, atmosphere, the psychological tension, the drama in Death's dream kingdom, all crystallise into a radiant and sparkling unity.

Although *Savitri* can be read simply as a poem, since there is nowhere any obtrusive religious or ethical stress, still the story of Savitri has in the course of the ages come to be invested with a primal religious significance that transcends all regional, sectarian or racial considerations. Savitri remains the heroine of legend to lovers of poetry, but she is also to the Hindus, to Hindu women especially, a very personal goddess, and to this day girls and wives perform the *Savitri-vrata* to ensure a happy married life for themselves. Rama is the hero of the *Ramayana*, but he is also the prince who became God to millions of devoted Hindus; Krishna is the protagonist of the *Bhagavata* and Arjuna's friend and charioteer in the *Mahabharata*, but he is the Lord of Brindavan too, the *bhagavan* who indites the *Gita*, to his numberless devotees. Likewise, Savitri is the goddess of virgin purity and married fruitfulness, of goodness and truth and faithfulness and strength. She is not formally worshipped as other deities are, but she has her rosy sanctuary in the untrodden regions of Hindu women's minds and hearts, and she reigns there forever.

IV

THE TALE AND THE EPIC: A COMPARATIVE ANALYSIS

It is this poem in seven cantos, making a total of about 700 lines in the original Sanskrit, that Sri Aurobindo has expanded and transformed into a modern English epic in twelve Books, of forty-nine cantos, spread over nearly 24,000 lines. What is omitted in the original is supplied by Sri Aurobindo in luxuriant detail (for example, the details of Savitri's 'quest' and the first meeting of Savitri and Satyavan); what is seminal or vaguely implied is elaborated with almost overwhelming effect (for example, Aswapati's Yoga and Savitri's Yoga); and what is seemingly a personal victory is invested with the overtones and undertones of spiritual significance so as to chime with the current psychological idiom and gain a sure access to men's souls.

A comparative tabular analysis of the action of the *Upakhyana* and of the epic may prove rewarding, and is therefore attempted below:

	Vyasa's *Upakhyana (Tale)*	**Sri Aurobindo's *Mahākāvya (Epic)***
Canto 1.	Aswapati's eighteen-year long austerities; the Goddess Savitri's promise of the birth of a daughter.	Book I, Cantos 3-5; Book II, Cantos 1-15; and Book III, Cantos 1-4: all these describe Aswapati's yoga, the Vision of the Divine Mother and the promise that, "One shall descend and break the iron Law."

Canto 1.	Birth of Savitri, her girlhood, and her being sent by her father in quest of a husband.	Book IV, Cantos 1-4; Savitri's birth, her girlhood, and her starting out on her quest.
	(Not covered in Vyasa's tale).	Book V, Cantos 1-3: 'The Book of Love'. Savitri meets Satyavan, and they recognise, each in the other, the destined soulmate.
Canto 2.	Aswapati with Narad; Savitri's return from her quest; Narad's warning, Savitri's resolution, and Narad's acquiescence; preparations for the marriage.	Book VI, Cantos 1-2: The Book of Fate. Aswapati, his queen, Narad and Savitri; Narad's foreknowledge, the queen's defiance, Savitri's resolution, and Narad's speech on the way of Fate and the problem of Pain.
Canto 3.	Marriage of Savitri and Satyavan in Dyumatsena's ashram; Aswapati's return to his own Kingdom.	Book VII, Canto 1: Savitri returns to Satyavan's hermitage to begin her wedded life.
Canto 4.	Approach of the fateful day: Savitri begins the three-nights' vow and, at its conclusion, still fasting, she goes with Satyavan to the forest, with inward expectancy of peril.	Book VII, Cantos 1-8; Book I, Cantos 1-2; and Book VIII, Canto 3 (pp. 561-564): Savitri's Yoga, the 'symbol dawn', the issue to be faced; Savitri goes with Satyavan to the forest on the fatal morning.
Canto 5.	Satyavan gathers fruits and fells branches; his headache; he rests with his head on Savitri's lap, and falls asleep.	Book VIII, Canto 3: 'Death in the Forest' (pp. 564-566)
	Yama's arrival, his taking away Satayavan's *prana*; Savitri follows her husband; Yama grants five boons, and finally releases Satyavan.	Book IX, Cantos 1-2; Book X, Cantos 1-4; and Book XI, Canto 1: Death (Yama) appears, and walks away with Satyavan's *prana*; Savitri's 'symbolic struggle' with Night, Twilight and Everlasting Day; victory for Savitri.

	Savitri returns to Satyavan; he wakes up; his anxiety about his parents; arm in arm, the young couple return to the ashram finding their way through the darkness.	Book XII, 'Epilogue' (pp. 715-724).
Canto 6.	Dyumatsena recovers his eyesight; the parents' anxiety; the return of Satyavan and Savitri, and the latter's explanation.	Book XII, 'Epilogue' (pp. 721-724) As Savitri and Satyavan return, they are met by Dyumatsena who has already recovered his eyesight and crown.
Canto 7.	In the morning, the people of Shalwa come in deputation and offer the crown to Dyumatsena. Return to Shalwa and coronation. All five boons granted by Yama are fulfilled in due course.	Part of this is anticipated in Book XII (Epilogue), and the rest is implied, and is to be taken for granted.

It will be seen that although the modern epic in English is about thirty-five times as long as the ancient *Upakhyana* in Sanskrit, although they are separated by two or three millennia of historic time, yet they are grounded on more or less that same base and seem to rise and stand in the same solitary grandeur against the contemporary literary landscape. The main lines of the human story remain unaltered, in spite of the successive revisions or recasts of the epic in Sri Aurobindo's hands. There are minor differences: neither Aswapati's wife nor Dyumatsena's is given speaking parts in the original poem; Aswapati in Sri Aurobindo's poem doesn't follow his daughter to her husband's place but merely sends her away, acquiescing in her decision; many of the details in cantos 3, 5, 6 and 7 in the poem have no parallels in the epic. To an even greater extent than in the short *Upakhyana*, the massive epic concentrates on the principal character, Savitri.

V

NEW DIMENSIONS

While the changes in the formal human story are few, there are, however, elaborations, psychological explorations, profound spiritual intimations, which are grafted on the original so as to give the epic impressive new dimensions quite beyond the scope of the *Upakhyana*. On the other hand, it will be seen, mighty though the overarching Banyan that is the epic, its seed—no bigger than an atom—is still in the old bardic poem. The bare bones of the original are Aswapati's eighteen-year long austerities followed by the birth of Savitri, the challenge of fate when Savitri marries Satyavan, Savitri's three-nights' fasting and austerities, and Savitri triumphing over Yama and fate and reclaiming 'lost' Satyavan and redeeming her parents' and parents-in-law's family fortunes.

Sri Aurobindo's epic retains these cardinal features but packs them with enormous fresh significance. Eighteen years' austerities? Only for the birth of a child? What symbol worlds, spiritual realms, psychic regions might Aswapati not have traversed in the course of his austerities? Musn't he have grown in understanding, musn't even his original aspiration have suffered a progressive sea-change with the widening of the horizons of his understanding? The ancient poet has referred to the Goddess Savitri, and the goddess herself speaks on behalf of 'Grandfather' Brahman. Children, of course, could unquestioningly grasp these extra-terrestrial situations; but the adult rational mind, emptied of imagination, shakes its head.

Sri Aurobindo accordingly explores in the epic the nature of Aswapati's Yoga, presents its various stages, maps out the worlds travelled, the depths sounded, the heights scaled. Not every poet could do this. The experiences described are supra-normal; and besides the inspiration of the Vedas and the Upanishads, Sri Aurobindo has also had to draw very largely upon his own Yogic experiences. A few verses in the original poem became a "small passage" in the early drafts of

Sri Aurobindo's epic; and, ultimately, this "small passage" came to be replaced by a whole Book, in fifteen cantos.[11] In fact, Aswapati's Yoga and the promise of the Goddess Savitri, which take about ten lines in the *Mahabharata*, occupy almost half of Sri Aurobindo's entire epic, which means more than a thousand-fold expansion!

The second key event is Narad first uttering a grave warning against Savitri's marrying Satyavan, and, later, after hearing Savitri, actively advising Aswapati to allow Savitri to have her own way. Even in the original, the situation is not lacking in an elemental self-sufficiency. Savitri was the sort of person that neither sage nor king could stand against; they yielded, because such was the power of her personality. But Sri Aurobindo explains and elaborates. Savitri's quest is described by Vyasa in the three stanzas at the end of the first canto, and it is only from the retrospective narration that we learn about her meeting and falling in love with Satyavan. But Sri Aurobindo lingers with affection on the meeting, and tries to probe behind the minds of Aswapati, Narad and Savitri in the tense scene described with shining succinctness by Vyasa in the second canto. It is also worth recapitulating that the very last additions Sri Aurobindo made were in the long speech of Narad, towards the close of Book VI, canto 2.[12] It is therefore evident that Sri Aurobindo attached particular significance to this climactic scene in the epic, and kept returning to it again and again, and could give it the finishing touch only a few days before he passed away.

There is, then, the *tri-rāttra* vow—fasting, standing day and night, offering libation to the fire, saluting the elders. These are the objective hints regarding Savitri's austerities, even as the reference to the eighteen-year duration of Aswapati's austerities was an indication of their temporal extension. But *tapas*, yoga, prayer have their true measure in subjective, rather than objective terms; one has to look *within*, enter the "inner countries", lose (and find) oneself in the infinitudes of the Spirit. Faced with a great danger, how does one forge a spiritual armour in self-defence and in defence of the world? How does one tear asunder veil after veil of deceptive appearance and penetrate to the core, the hidden source, the still centre of Reality? Surely it was no simple business of fasting and physical endurance; these were but the outward signs of a profound inner quest, a prolonged inner struggle, capped by an accession of knowledge and power.

As with Aswapati's Yoga, Sri Aurobindo turns the searchlight of revelation to the purposes and processes of Savitri's Yoga also; the earlier cantos describing Aswapati careering through the "worlds" are now seen to be complementary to the five cantos in Book VII ('The Book of Yoga') which describes Savitri's quest for her soul, her entry into the "inner countries", and her ultimate finding of her true soul and the Soul. Here, too, the pregnant hint contained in a couple of stanzas in the original undergoes an impressive elaboration, a meaningful exploration of hidden realms of consciousness, a confrontation of apocalyptic visions, all with their source of inspiration in Vedas and Upanishads and with ample corroboration from Sri Aurobindo's and his spiritual collaborator, the Mother's own yogic strivings and realisations. No wonder this part of the epic spans over about 125 pages, or nearly 4,000 lines.

Finally, and most important of all—for the rest are but a preparation, a leading to it—is the scene, a scene probably without a parallel in all literature, where Savitri faces alone Yama that is Dharma as well, and follows him as he carries away Satyavan's life, and compels the law of predestination itself to yield ground and submit to the imperatives of Savitri's love for her husband. Vyasa has treated this part of the story with more subtlety and elaboration than the earlier parts, for it covers about one-fourth of the whole poem. What, exactly, is the writ of Fate? Are we to take it to mean something unalterably predetermined? Thus Omar Khayyam (or Fitzgerald) says:

> The Moving Finger writes; and having writ,
> Moves on: nor all thy Piety nor Wit
> Shall lure it back to cancel half a Line,
> Nor all thy Tears wash out a Word of it.

If Yama is the executant of this law of predestination, how is he Dharma also at the same time?

In the old legend, Savitri pits her strength—the strength of her purity and chastity, the strength that she has acquired through the fulfilment of the vow, and the strength that envelops her on account of her elders' blessings—against this stern adamantine law of predestination. Her speeches to Yama are a strange mixture of naivety and subtlety and even a little ambiguity. There is no pleading, there is no fight or defiance; Savitri and Yama are both on their best behaviour, exchanging civilities and disarmingly polite expressions. "I'm pleased with your words...you speak words that please my mind...your word is life-giving as water to a thirsty man...I have never heard such delightful speech as yours...I respect you because you speak so agreeably, righteously, and laden with significance": such are Yama's reactions, and boon follows boon, culminating in the release of Satyavan himself. Savitri too claims to have done no more than praising the god (Yama) with "true speech" (*Satyena vacasā*).

But when one looks beneath the surface, it is clear that what really happens is this: Savitri effects a transformation in Yama himself; the static God of Death is made to look inward and realise the dynamic God of Dharma that is veiled within. If Savitri can thus change the course of predestination, if she can compel change in the God of Death, she must be more than the woman and wife that she is in appearance, and the struggle is not for a single life alone, not for progeny alone, but also for a profounder, a basically revolutionary reason.

The individual, personal problem must be capable of relation to a wider, cosmic context. The characters should be both persons and symbols, individuals no less than elemental powers involved in the cosmic play. Sri Aurobindo has therefore elaborated this deathless scene too in accordance with the possibilities opened by his own conception of Aswapati's and Savitri's Yoga. Three whole Books—'The Book of Eternal Night', 'The Book of the Double Twilight' and 'The Book of Everlasting Day'—taking up a total of over 150 pages, are devoted by Sri Aurobindo to this unearthly scene where Savitri comes to clash with alien or seductive powers and succeeds finally in asserting the claims of life, light, and joy.

It would thus be not far wrong if we concluded that what Sri Aurobindo has tried to accomplish in his epic is largely to work out in poetical terms the possibilities already implied or inherent in the legendary story. Aswapati asks for a child; Savitri is born; and while trying to redeem Satyavan, her husband, she brings happiness to all (*sarvam*)—herself, her father, her mother and all her husband's family.

Re-reading the old bardic tale from a fresh angle, Sri Aurobindo invests Aswapati's *tapas* with a vaster significance; it is a growth in self-knowledge and world-knowledge, it brings him face to face with earth's fetters and the prison-house of man's ignorance; and, at last, the fruit he seeks from his *tapas* is the solution of no personal problem or the answering of no personal need, but the sundering of earth's fetters, the shattering of man's prison-house. At the culminating point of his yogic realisation, Aswapati incarnates all the world's agony of desire and thereby "compels" Savitri's birth.

In the Aurobindonian conception, then, Savitri is not merely the gift of the Goddess Savitri, she is her incarnation as well. The divine-human quality of Savitri is basic to Sri Aurobindo's scheme, and colours the whole rich vast canvas of the epic. Like Aswapati and Savitri, Satyavan and Yama too, are seized in a larger context and enveloped in varied layers of significance. The characters become more than characters, more even than 'round' characters; now they are persons, now they are gods or god-like figures, and now they are verily occult forces or symbol regions or powers. The bardic 'legend' thus becomes a yogic 'symbol', without however ceasing to be a legend, or even a romance.

An American poet and critic writes (though in a different if similar context): "I take it that a long poem, a narrative poem, must be about something. A narrative without plot would be as intolerable as a narrative with plot only. The symbol must be a thing before it becomes its meaning."[13] The "thing" here is simply the old bardic story that has triumphantly stood the test of time, and lives as vividly today in the Hindu racial memory as in the early days of its currency. There is no doubt a seeming dilution, an "unconscionable" elaboration, even perhaps a little complication, in the Aurobindonian version; but it cannot be denied that the main hard lines of the old story—the contours of the "thing"—remain. What, then, is the 'symbol', the 'meaning' of the supposed action?

In one of his explanatory letters Sri Aurobindo wrote: "The whole of *Savitri* is, according to the title of the poem, a legend that is a symbol and this opening canto is, it may be said, a key beginning and announcement."[14] With particular reference to this canto, he wrote in the course of another letter: "I am not writing a scientific treatise, I am selecting certain ideas and impressions to form a symbol of a partial and temporary darkness of the soul and Nature which seems to a temporary feeling of that which is caught in the Night as if it were universal and eternal."[15] Again, in yet another letter: "Savitri is represented in the poem as an incarnation of the Divine Mother." [16] Like Homer and Milton, Sri Aurobindo also plunges *in medias res* in the opening canto; exclusive of the sections devoted to necessary retrospective narration, the main action of the epic comprises but a single day, and the opening canto describes the dawn of "the day when Satyavan must die". Being intended as "a key beginning and announcement", this canto vividly, impressionistically, projects the "symbol dawn", and thereby anticipates the "greater dawn" referred to in the last line of the epic. In the issue between Night and Day, Darkness and Light, Dawn obviously forms the link, the mediator, the passage; and Savitri the "incarnation of the Divine Mother" is here the mediator, the vanquisher of Night and redeemer of Day.[17]

VI

LEGENDS AND MYTHS

It should be remembered that myths, legends and symbols shade into one another and they are the creations of man, especially poetic man, awake, alert, inquiring and responsive. A.E. (George Russell) wisely says:

> The myths were born
> Out of the spirit of man and drew their meaning
> From that unplumbed profundity...
> ...Yet from fleeting voices
> And visionary lights a meaning came
> That made myth contemporary. And those
> Who read may find titans and king within
> Themselves. [18]

The notion that myths, legends, symbols belong to the childhood of the human race, that humanity in its supposed present adulthood has no use for them, dies hard. But nothing can be further from the truth. George Santayana rightly points out that, "a good mythology cannot be produced without much culture and intelligence. Stupidity is not poetical...A developed mythology shows that man has taken a deep and active interest both in the world and in himself, and has tried to link the two, and interpret the one by the other. Myth is therefore a natural prologue to philosophy, since the love of ideas is the root of both." [19]

But the text doesn't invalidate the prologue; it is often the prologue that offers the real key to the text. A myth like the legendary story of Savitri redeeming Satyavan from the clutches of Yama or of angered Rudra reducing Kama the God of love to a handful of ashes is, in its own sovereign right, an utter rendering of reality, "an ideal interpretation in which the phenomena are digested and transmuted into human energy, into imaginative tissue",[20] bearing the same relation to dialectical discourse or philosophical statement as a tragedy by Aeschylus bears to an exposition by Socrates.[21] Max Muller asserted that, "There is mythology now as there was in the time of Homer, only we do not perceive it, because we ourselves live in the very shadow of it, and because we all shrink from the full meridian light of truth."[22] Modern writers like Joyce, Eliot, Gide and Camus have felt the need for myths appropriate to our times, and Herbert Read categorically observes:

> ...the farther science penetrates into the mystery of life, the more it reverts to a mythological world. I refer more particularly to the science of the individual psyche, where all science culminates; for we know nothing unless we know ourselves. And the more we learn about ourselves by the objective methods of observation and analysis, the more we realise that our knowledge is already crystallised in the ancient myths...Myths that were dead are now alive again, and it may be that in the course of time all the old gods and heroes, that for centuries peopled and pacified the minds of men, will return and resume their symbolic functions.[23]

It may be that with too many people talking far too often on far too many inessential or superficial things the edges of myths tend to get blunted, the sharp scent of their meaning to be generally diffused if not wholly lost, the shock of recognition to be tamed beyond notice, but Ernest Cassirer finds even in this an advantage, for, under the altered conditions of "civilised existence" today "word and mythic image... have become a light, bright ether in which the spirit can move without let or hindrance."[24]

Myths, then, and legendary stories based upon them, have a connotative richness, an endless capacity for extension in significance, and an unbelievable capacity for survival even in a scientific and technological age, perhaps more so now than at other times. The mind returns to the myths, and their bank balance of meaning seems to run no danger of exhaustion. Eliot's recent plays are an attempt to recapture the meaning of the Eumenides, the Alcestis, the Ion and Oedipus Coloneus in a contemporary context; Jean Anouilh has likewise sought inspiration in the legendary or mythical stories of Antigone, Medea and Eurydice; other dramatists too—Andre Gide, Jean Giradoux, Jean-Paul Sartre, John Cocteau, Eugene O'Neill, Tennessee Williams, Jack Richardson—have found the ancient Greek myths susceptible to transplantation on the soil of our uncertain, agonised, tortuous modern consciousness.

Dr Richards is thus right in describing the 'saner and greater' mythologies as, "The utterance of the whole soul of man and, as such, inexhaustible to meditation...Through such mythologies our will is collected, our powers unified, our growth controlled... Without his mythogies man is only a cruel animal without a soul—for a soul is a central part of his governing mythology—he is a congeries of possibilities without order and without aim."[25] Seminal myths are sources of knowledge, not scientific or experimental knowledge but the knowledge that comes from a renewal of experience,[26] and without such knowledge man is but a mass of blind energies.

While myths may no doubt be read literally (and perhaps dismissed), or interpreted allegorically as a poetic shorthand for the physical sciences attempting "an expression in imaginative terms of the goings-on of the universe", there are more rewarding approaches still, namely the moral and psychological and the analogical and symbolical. The 'moral' and 'psychological' approach attempts to find in myths what John Masefield has called (though in a Shakespearian context) lessons in "deportment on life's scaffold", looking at mythology as though it is but "an exteriorisation of events in the psyche".[27] The analogical-symbolic approach is really the true spiritual approach, the way of seeking the straight and narrow gate that opens to the "interior countries" and the blissful home of ultimate Reality.

VII

THE VEDIC STOREHOUSE OF MYTH

India's (and the world's) most ancient literature, the Veda luxuriates in myths and legends; there are gods, energies, primal forces, assaults, sacrifices, victories; and scholars have tried to interpret this ancient body of poetry from various angles—philological, ritualistic, naturalistic, allegorical, ethical, symbolical. In his important study, *The Secret of the Veda*, Sri Aurobindo has tackled the problem afresh and his main conclusions are these:

> The hypothesis I propose is that the Rig-Veda is itself the one considerable document that remains to us from the early period of human thought of which the historic Eleusinian and Orphic mysteries were the failing remnants when the spiritual and psychological knowledge of the race was concealed, for reasons now difficult to determine, in a veil of concrete and material figures and symbols which protected the sense from the profane and revealed it to the initiated...Hence they favoured the existence of an outer worship, effective but imperfect, for the profane, an inner discipline for the initiate, and clothed their language in words and images which had, equally, a spiritual sense for the elect, a concrete sense for the mass of ordinary worshippers... [28]

> The central conception of the Veda is the conquest of the Truth out of the darkness of Ignorance and by the conquest of the Truth the conquest also of Immortality... [29]

> Knowledge itself was a traveling and a reaching, or a finding and a winning; the revelation came only at the end, the light was the prize of a final victory. [30]

The Vedic myths, then, and the legends in which they are enshrined, have as a general rule both an exoteric sense and an esoteric significance; central to the Vedic scheme is the conception of the struggle between Darkness and Light, and the ultimate conquest of Light, which is Truth, which is also Immortality; and the conquest involves a travelling, a pursuit, a reaching, a winning. The celebrated chant in the *Brihadaranyaka*—

> Lead me from the unreal to the real!
> Lead me from darkness to light!
> Lead me from death to immortality!

splendorously crystallises this inner spiritual drama of conflict, pursuit and victory. Yet it is not always possible, it is not always wise, for average humanity to plunge straight into the conflict; the full blaze of the Truth may sometimes have a blinding effect; and therefore some preparation, initiation, is called for. The myth-making power could be such a mediator/initiator. In *Savitri* describing 'The Kingdoms and Godheads of the Little Mind', Sri Aurobindo writes:

> Thus worked the Power upon the growing world;
> Its subtle craft withheld the full-orbed blaze,
> Cherished the soul's childhood and on fictions fed
> Far richer in their sweet and nectarous sap
> Nourishing its immature divinity
> Than the staple or dry straw or Reason's tilth,
> Its heaped fodder of innumerable facts,
> Plebian fare on which today we thrive. [31]

Knowledge of the divine life, spiritual knowledge, is best insinuated through myths and the key symbols that constitute them rather than through logic or philosophy. "Only a mythology", says Berdyaev, "which conceives of the divine celestial life as a celestial history and as a drama of love and freedom unfolding itself between God and His other self, which He loves and for whose reciprocal love He thirsts, and only an admission of God's longing for His other self, can provide a solution of celestial history and, through it, of the destinies of both man and the world."[32] There is, for example, the symbol of the Hound of Heaven, which Francis Thompson has turned into a wonderful poem. In the *Rig Veda*, there are references to Sarama and the Sarameya, her two dogs; some pursuit is implied and the 'quarry' is hunted down at last. But what is the esoteric meaning? The object of the pursuit is to reach the wideness of the cows; and the cow is really the symbol of the divine reality. Thus the symbolism of Sarama and her dogs really conveys the idea of the true nature of a spiritual quest:

> Whether Sarama figures as the fair-footed goddess speeding on the path or the heavenly hound, mother of these wide-ranging guardians of the path, the idea is the same, a power of the Truth that seeks and discovers, that finds by a divine faculty of insight the hidden Light and the denied Immortality. But it is to this seeking and finding that her function is limited. [33]

Such symbols, then, are the heart and soul of the myths, which are themselves the heart and soul of the great legends that treasure the deepest memories of the human race. Seemingly irrational and unscientific, myths and symbols are attempts to open the gateways of Reality, and if a philosopher like Plato himself made pregnant use of them, it was because he realised that it is, "the only type of language in which the world of 'becoming' can be expressed at all." [34]

VIII

'SYMBOLS'

We come at long last to a consideration of 'symbols'. The word 'symbol' like many other words ('love' for example), has suffered from promiscuous use. There are symbols, and symbols, and symbols. There are algebraic symbols, which seem to be mere abstractions; but they too are pointers towards the real. There are election symbols, a hut for one party, a pair of yoked bullocks for another, the hammer and scythe for a third, and so on. Colours, singly or in combination or in lines and patterns, have a symbolic value too, as in national flags.

And words, language itself, can be symbolic. Bernard Stambler describes a symbol as, "a tool, a device for expressing a difficult, complex, or even ineffable concept in concrete and even pictorial terms."[35] For example, T.S. Eliot has made use of the symbol of the 'Waste Land' to convey with over-powering effect the sense of the bleakness, ugliness and sterility of contemporary urban civilisation. Likewise, Albert Camus has exploited the symbol of the plague to expose the political and other evils that raged in German-occupied France, though the immediate situation of the plague-infested city is not lost sight of either.

The essential thing to remember, however, is that the symbol is not just an arbitrary equation; there must be something of a natural relation, an inevitability, in the equation between the symbol and the thing it is meant to symbolise. As Jolande Jacobi says,

> A symbol is never entirely abstract, but always in some way 'incarnated'. For this reason even the most abstract relationships, situations, or ideas of archetypal nature are visualised by the psyche as specific forms, figures, images, objects, etc…It was this image-making power of the human psyche which, for example, cast the archetype of the 'conflict between light and darkness, or good and evil' into the forms of the hero's fight with the dragon…or translated the 'idea of death and rebirth' into representable episodes in the life of a hero, or into the symbol of the labyrinth…[36]

There are, of course, two terms to every symbol, and these are equated; on the one side there is the visible image or sign (the Sun, the Hound of Heaven, the Cross, the Swastika, the quincunx), and on the other side the idea or force that the image or sign is meant to signify. "The condition for the valid use of symbolic language is", writes W. T. Stace, "that both terms should be in some sense present to the mind…It is not necessary that the meaning of the symbolic language, or symbolizandum, should be *clearly* before the mind. It may be only dimly and faintly apprehended in the borderlands of consciousness, or perhaps in the sub-conscious…But clearly or dimly, the symbolizandum must be apprehended for the language to have any meaning."[37] If it is immediately and perfectly understandable, the symbol is superfluous; if it cannot be understood at all, or if an arbitrary meaning has to be imposed on it, the symbol fails to achieve its purpose. In a legitimate efficacious symbol, "there is concealment and yet revelation: hence, therefore, by silence and speech acting together, comes a double significance."[38] It is simply the process of groping one's way from the twilight to the dusky regions, from the more known to the less known. And the process can almost be endless. When the passage from Ignorance to Truth is symbolised as the passage from Darkness to Light, it is not merely that such a similitude just occurred to some people in the past and found general currency; it means also, and more basically, that such a way of putting things is natural, it is inherent in the very nature of things, and indeed there is no other way in which the right distinctions can be made and fixed in the consciousness, to be a part of it forever.[39]

The symbol, it would appear then, is a natural starting-point of a journey of discovery and realisation; the starting point, the face set towards the goal, the ardour of the journey (or the chase), all are somehow implied in the symbol. To quote Jacobi again, "symbols present an objective, visible meaning behind which an invisible, profounder meaning is hidden"; the invisible is crystallised into the visible symbol, which as it were 'contains' the invisible infinite; or, in Goethe's words (as quoted by Jacobi), "symbolism transforms the phenomenon into idea and the idea into image; in the image the idea remains infinitely effective and unattainable and even when expressed in all languages remains inexpressible."[40]

As in the best poetry, more is meant than meets the ear, as with the best paintings, more is meant than meets the eye, it is as though one is looking into a deep pool or the tranquil blue sky. A mystic symbol like 'AUM', a dramatic symbol like the Lord himself driving Arjuna's chariot through the embattled hosts on the field of Kurukshetra, a religious symbol like the Cross, a hunting symbol like the Hound of Heaven pursuing the frightened sinner, a dialectical symbol like Savitri vanquishing Yama, are all vivid and vague at once, vivid and therefore fixed in the mind, vague and therefore intriguing and hence compelling a drawing on or tapping of "a stored experience and a vestigial wisdom."[41]

Traditional symbolism, although with its roots in antiquity, is never rigid; had it been so, it should have gone atrophied or died long ago. There is a dynamism in all living symbols, they always (though in each age, perhaps, a little differently) take the mind from the narrow to the more wide regions, from the surface play to the deeper reality, and hence Gai Eaton is right in affirming that, "traditional symbolism is never a closed system, for its terms are fluid and susceptible of different applications, but it is always precise."[42]

IX

SAVITRI IN THE VEDA

"Always precise", that is to say, precise in its denotation; but the connotation may vary from age to age, even from person to person. For instance, there can be no denotative ambiguity about Darkness and Light, but the area or depth or intensity of the meaning we invest them with may vary. When they become the symbols of ignorance and knowledge, the sense is precise enough, yet there may be layers and layers of significance which in one quick view we cannot hope to exhaust. Now Light itself is too abstract, and hence we may wisely choose to equate the Sun with Light, and sunrise with the gradual unfoldment of light. "The sun with its powerful rays, its warmth and light, its life-giving qualities", writes Wilbur Marshall Urban, "becomes a natural symbol for the creating and eliciting power. Moreover, the contrasts bound up with it, light and darkness, power and weakness, life and death, spirit and matter, good and evil, become a natural vehicle for the expression and embodiment of moral and other value contrasts as they develop in the life of man."[43] Energy, creativity, life, power, knowledge, enjoyment may come naturally to be associated with light, or the sun; and it would be also natural to represent the gradualism of sunrise as "a parallel to the awakening of consciousness",[44] with any number of gradations. For example, the ancient Hindus imagined that each phase of sunrise was presided over by an appropriate deity: the Aswins first, then Usha (or Dawn) in her three forms, the grey, the bright, and the resplendent, and finally, the Sun with his five phases.[45]

In the Vedic system of linked equivalences, the Sun is sometimes referred to as *savitar*, which is a name for the God Indra also; *Savitri* is feminine, whereas *savitar* is masculine, and means a mother or a cow; and a cow, again, can mean a ray of truth, and 'lost cows' may mean 'hidden truths'; and *savitri* means a ray of light and also the Gayatri mantra. By sleight of hand as it were, the poet can shift from one sense to another, or imply two or more at one and the same time. Thus Sri Aurobindo could not have chosen a richer, a more many-sided, or a profounder symbol than Savitri—the name, the person, the power—at once to unify and fill the immense epic canvas of his great poem.

There is, further, the double conception of the Surya Savitri and the Bhaga Savitri, who are themselves aspects of Surya, the Sun; for the Sun is, not only Truth, but also Light; he is the creator (Surya Savitri), the fosterer or increaser (Pushan), and the enjoyer (Bhaga Savitri). Like reflections of light on a sheet of trembling water, meanings merge and separate and mingle again in some of these ancient Riks:

> And thou art powerful for every creation; and thou becomest the Increaser, O God, by thy movings; and thou illuminest utterly all this world of becomings.[46]

> Today, O divine Producer, send forth on us fruitful felicity; dismiss what belongs to the evil dream.[47]

Surya Savitri, creator and increaser, and Bhaga Savitri, receiver and enjoyer, come into a natural relation or partnership; from the unmanifest come the "seven delights", thanks to Surya Savitri, and Bhaga Savitri prevents their misuse and induces "fruitful felicity", or creative enjoyment:

> Surya Savitri, who is Bhaga, stands between the Infinite and the created worlds within us and without... When in us each creation of the active *Ananda*, the *prajāvat saubhagam*, comes thus out of the unmanifest, received and heard rightly of the knowledge in the faultless rhythm of things, then is our creation that of Bhaga Savitri, and all the births of that creation, our children, our offspring, *prajā*, *apatyam*, are things of the delight, *viśva vāmāni*.[48]

Nay more: Savitri the creator, Surya Savitri, is not only Bhaga, but also three other divinities: Varuna, Mitra and Aryaman. Surya and Savitri are themselves a unity in difference, the passive and the active (rather like light and heat); Surya the light of Reality, which is *satyam ṛitam bṛihat*—or the truth, the right and the vast—and Savitri its dynamic or creative aspect, are inseparably linked, being but the reverse and obverse of the same ultimate Truth. But Savitri is also the power to approach from the human end, and this is the reason why the Gayatri mantra, the holiest and most celebrated verse in the Veda,[49] is addressed to Savitri and is besides referred to as the Savitri mantra as well. As the creator-spirit (*sanctus spiritus*), Savitri is invoked to inspire and charge with his power and presence the thoughts of his worshippers.

It is Savitri who makes the human body the home of the affiliated deities—Varuna, Mitra, Aryaman and Bhaga—who signify graces and powers and functions of their own. Varuna is the power of the indefinable Infinite, from which is derived everything else; less distinct than the other gods because he is the manifestation of omniscience, and being everywhere, present and active, his particular presence and activity are apt to be blurred or little noticed. Mitra, on the other hand, is more to the foreground; he is beauty and grace, he is builder and harmoniser, he is embracer and container. And Varuna and Mitra are complementary to each other. The third deity, Aryaman, is the patient executant, the traveller of the worlds of striving, the pathfinder who hews his way through the jungles of resistance and difficulty, and takes us in his wake to the threshold of the luminous sanctuary where the journey ends and the blissful enjoyment of Bhaga awaits us:

> The goal of the path is the divine beatitude, the illimitable joy of the Truth, of the infinity of our being. Bhaga is the godhead who brings this joy and supreme felicity into the human consciousness; he is the divine enjoyer in man...Bhaga is Savitri the Creator, he who brings forth from the unmanifest Divine the truth of a divine universe, dispelling from us the evil dream of this lower consciousness in which we falter amidst a confused tangle of truth and falsehood, strength and weakness, joy and suffering...Thus is the divine creation of the fourfold Savitri founded on Varuna, combined and guided by Mitra, achieved by Aryaman, enjoyed in Bhaga: Aditi the infinite Mother realises herself in the human being by the birth and works of her glorious children. [50]

Although at first the references to the various, the numerous, divinities of Vedic mythology may tend to confuse, a closer scrutiny will reveal a sparkling system of psychological correspondences, imposing thereby a significant unity in difference on the whole. The clue to the puzzle is that "each god contains in himself all the others, but remains still himself in his peculiar function."[51] Naming the different limbs of the body doesn't destroy the unity of the whole; each limb has its character and function, yet the whole is somehow more than the sum of the parts; and the Vedic deities bear the same relation of Reality that the limbs bear to the human body:

> The Vedic deities are names, powers, personalities of the universal Godhead and they represent each some essential puissance of the Divine Being. They manifest the cosmos and are manifest in it. Children of Light, Sons of the Infinite, they recognise in the soul of man their brother and ally and desire to help and increase him by themselves increasing in him so as to possess his world with

> their light, strength and beauty. The Gods call man to a divine companionship and alliance... To the Vedic seers they (the Gods) are living realities; the vicissitudes of the human soul represent a cosmic struggle not merely of principles and tendencies but of the cosmic Powers which support and embody them... On the world-stage and in the individual soul the same real drama with the same personages is enacted.[52]

The key-sentence is the last: the same drama is played, with the same actors, both on the world-stage and in the theatre of the individual soul. The macrocosm *is* the microcosm; infinity is reflected, is summed up, in a grain of sand. The cosmic drama is also the human drama; *Savitri* the cosmic symbol is also the human legend.

A drama, whether cosmic or human, or cosmic as well as human, implies a conflict—a conflict clinched by the tragedy of defeat or the fulfilment of victory. One term of the conflict is the Sun, in his double aspect of light and heat, knowledge and power, an "all-illumining Light" and an "all-creative Truth", the body of Surya and the force of Savitri. The other term of the conflict is—shall we say?—Death, in his double aspect of Darkness and Ignorance, Falsehood and Nescience. But, then, how did the conflict start in the first instance? This is really the central mystery of phenomenal existence, and taking his cue from the Vedic revelatory hints Sri Aurobindo attempts the following explanation of the origins of the cosmic conflict:

> This antinomy between the Light and the Darkness, the Truth and the Falsehood has its roots in an original cosmic antinomy between the illumined Infinite and the darkened finite consciousness. Aditi the infinite, the undivided, is the mother of the Gods, Diti or Danu, the division, the separative consciousness the mother of the Titans; therefore the gods in man move towards light, infinity and unity, the Titans dwell in their cave of the darkness and issue from it only to break up, make discordant, wounded, limited his knowledge, will, strength, joy and being.[53]

In Sri Aurobindo's poem, the two aspects of the first term are incarnated as Satyavan and Savitri: the all-illuminating light and the all-creative truth, light's being and its truth-becoming. The second term, of course, is Yama or Death, not the Yama that is both Death and Dharma, but the Yama that is Death and Falsehood and Ignorance and all the scheming, deluding, baffling Titans who obstruct the passage to Bhaga or Felicity. The two terms thus become three: Satyavan, self-luminous, passively right and purposive; Savitri, a flame of energy, actively creative and truth-becoming; and Death, active, false, destructive. The drama turns out to be a trial of strength between Savitri and Death for the redemption of Satyavan, who is for a time the lost Sun, but presently re-emerges in all his splendour in the company of Savitri, while the shades of Night and Death retreat and disappear.

The essence of the Vedic drama of imprisonment, struggle and release is that Aditi the infinite consciousness is, "espoused and held by the lower creative power which works through the limited mind and body", but is ultimately, "delivered from this subjection by the force of the divine or illumined Mind born of her in the mentality of man".[54] But in Sri Aurobindo's handling of the theme, there is an even greater wideness and totality of comprehension than any simple statement of the Vedic conception or of even the Aurobindonian worldview would suggest. Being poetry, and especially symbolic mystical poetry, *Savitri* is richer in its overtones and more massive in its comprehension than any merely intellectual formulations.

X

ALLEGORICAL INTERPRETATIONS OF THE LEGEND

The *Mahabharata* version has, no doubt, provoked divers allegorical interpretations. There is the simple, obvious, and in its own way satisfactory view that it is an allegory of Love triumphant over Death. A more ingenious view has been offered by Narayan Aiyangar:

> To say that there was but a swoon and that the fancies of a zealous and imaginative wife were portrayed as real truths, would be doing but poor justice to the ancient Vedantic poet of the Purana. I would take Satyavan, meaning 'he who has Satyam', one of the well known names of Brahman, to be the enlightened soul of a knower. He at first plays with the horses, the senses; but finding out by experience that the pleasures they give are insipid and unreal, he converts them into lifeless pictures. His father is probably the personification of Kama, Desire, having at first for his fulfilment the *dyumat*, shining, *sena*, troop, of the phenomenal forms or objects of the selfish world. In their pursuit he is at last worsted by stronger selfish men and finds himself to be really poor and blind, not having yet realised the all loving Self…So in the wilderness of samsara, he repents and cries: When will I see Light?…In this state he has his own enlightened self as the son of support. That son is self-sacrifice, as he devotes his life to support by hard manual labour his poor parents. So, the sacred Gayatri alias Savitri, the personification of Brahma-vidya, the heroine of disinterested love, elects him as the only fit husband for her. Her father Aswapati, the lord of horses, may be taken to signify one who has subdued the senses…Wedded to her, Satyavan lays down his life in the service of his distressed parents and thus completes his self-sacrifice. [55]

This brings fulfilment to Dyumatsena, for he gets his eyesight back and can *see* his real son, his *atman*, raised by Yama-Dharma-Raja to immortality. The same writer has also given a phenomenal interpretation of the legend: Satyavan is the moon wedded to Rohini, daughter of the Sun or Savitar; the star helps the moon through his winter and rough *samsāric* weather; on the new moon day, Satyavan (the moon) dies on the lap of Savitri (Rohini), "not far from Yama, the regent of the asterism Bharani"; and Satyavan's resurrection is merely "the elevated state of the moon as the regent of Mrigasirsas, so near the Rohini."[56]

Such interpretations are more fanciful than otherwise. The old legend is very clear on two points: Satyavan first dies, and there is then—after an interval—a resurrection. Yama being also Dharma feels compelled by the impact of Savitri's personality to grant a renewal of Satyavan's life. The gods are gods, after all, and they can amend inexorable fate itself. And men and women, too, could rise to—or be accorded—a divine status: Pururavas exceeded the human bounds, *Rishi* Vishvamitra's austerities enabled him to work wonders, including the creation of a new heaven, and Savitri was also able to effect a "change of heart" in Yama and obtain her heart's desire. The gods and men do verily belong to one world, and they do come together sometimes, and out of their partnership great things do happen. Such was the faith of the ancients, and it must have been sustained by their own unique experiences. Even a modern writer like Henry Miller asserts:

> I say the whole world, fanning out in every direction from this spot, was once alive in a way that no man ever dreamed of. I say there were gods who roamed everywhere, men like us in form and substance, but free, electrically free. [57]

There is thus no need to impose on the original legendary story of Savitri and Satyavan any elaborate or ingenious interpretation. The death and the resurrection are both meant to be accepted unquestioningly. The esoteric meaning, which in no way cancels the validity of the human story, is equally clear, since the very names of characters carry, to people familiar with the Veda, symbolic meanings impossible to miss. The bardic story is explicit that Satyavan was so named because both his parents were given to speaking the truth; Savitri was so named because she was the gift of the Goddess Savitri. Satyavan had another name too, Chitrasva, he who has beautiful horses, because as a child he apparently loved horses and made clay-horses and also drew pictures of horses. Satyavan, the possessor of the higher Truth, has "espoused" and is in a way held by the "lower creative power which works through the limited mind and body"; this is 'bondage', and the wages of such bondage is death. But Satyavan is himself espoused by Savitri, Surya Savitri the Creator, and he is ultimately "delivered from this subjection by the force of the divine or illumined Mind", a power that can break the bars of the cage, purify what is impure, raise what is low, divinise what is human.

XI

SYMBOLISM IN *SAVITRI*

While Sri Aurobindo found the bardic story a piece of pure and austere sublimity, he felt that it could be rendered anew in the current idiom of our century in the light of his own spiritual quests, struggles and fulfilments. His basic thesis is that Felicity, if it is to come, must come *here*, here on earth, and even when the soul is undivorced from the body. If the many human instruments, mind, soul, emotions, works, could be god-inspired and god-directed, so could the body itself be. Mere asceticism is vain; inflicting on the body all sorts of punishment cannot lead to any easy escape. The body too is the house of the Spirit, and the body could be made to deserve that honour. An integral transformation of all the elements that make man is indeed the whole aim of the evolutionary adventure. Sri Aurobindo saw this—almost experienced it—as a distinct possibility and as a near probability. In *The Life Divine* he wrote:

> Life and the body would be no longer tyrannous masters demanding nine-tenths of their satisfaction, but means and powers for the expression of the spirit. At the same time, since the matter and the body are accepted, the control and the right use of physical things would be a part of the realised life of the spirit in the manifestation in earth-nature. [58]

"The matter and the body are *accepted*", accepted and made fit instruments for housing the divine; this is no turning away from life, seeking felicity in a remote *Vaikuntha* or Paradise in a vague hereafter, but seeking it *here* and *now*.

Sri Aurobindo affirmed, indeed, that an integral transformation, a divinisation, of human nature and earth-nature is a thing "decreed and inevitable".[59] He even laid down the main lines of this progressive transformation in his treatise, *The Synthesis of Yoga* and hinted at the nature of the final change:

> The integral liberation comes when this passion for release, *mumkṣutwa*, founded on distaste or *vairāgya*, is itself transcended; the soul is then liberated both from attachment to the lower action of nature and from all repugnance to the cosmic action of the Divine. This liberation gets its completeness when the spiritual gnosis can act with a supramental knowledge and reception of the action of Nature and a supramental luminous will in initiation. The gnosis discovers the spiritual sense in Nature, God in things, the soul of good in all things that have the contrary appearance. The liberation of the Nature becomes one with the liberation of the spirit, and there is founded in the integral freedom the integral perfection. [60]

Adam and Eve, in their state of innocence, inhabited and filled with their unblemished joy an earthly Paradise; and such paradisal felicity certainly didn't exclude the pleasures of the body. A return to such paradisal felicity, an establishment *here* of the life divine, must mean the breaking of the seals of our present human imperfection—namely, false desire, the corroding feeling of failure and incapacity, the dread of unavoidable death.

Are we asking for the impossible? Is it more prudent to accept our present limitations? Is it foolhardy to take up arms against this seeming sea of the impossible? But such false prudence can be a "deadly sin", says Abercrombie:

> For this refuseth faith in the unknown powers
> Within man's nature…

> Narrows desire into the scope of thought.
> But it is written in the heart of man,
> Thou shalt no larger be than thy desire…
> But send desire often forth to scan
> The immense night which is thy greater soul;
> Knowing the possible, see thou try beyond it
> Into impossible things, unlikely ends;
> And thou shalt find thy knowledgeable desire
> Grow large as all the regions of thy soul,
> Whose firmament doth cover the whole of Being,
> And of created purpose reach the ends. [61]

Prudence tells Savitri that Satyavan, being fated to die within a year, is no suitable husband for her; prudence tells her, again, that irresistible fate is not to be checkmated. Yet she sets herself against Fate; the impossible becomes possible; the lie becomes the truth. Sri Aurobindo too refused, as a Yogi, as a philosopher and as a poet, "to recognise the physical breaking-up as an inescapable destiny".[62] It was an earthly paradise, a human divinity, that seemed to him the goal of the whole evolutionary process.

In Sri Aurobindo's epic, as in the old bardic legend, Savitri strives by herself, but not for herself alone. In the legend, along with Satyavan regaining his life, Dyumatsena regains his eyesight and kingdom, and Aswapati has the promise of a hundred sons; in the epic, Satyavan's returning to life means all these, and also the inauguration of a new age in man's and earth's history. Savitri and Satyavan are the "first-born of a new supernal race"; they are the Supreme's dual power—she the Force, he the Soul—set in the world to refashion human nature and earth-nature. The promise is given:

> Mortality's bond-slaves shall unloose their bonds,
> Mere men into spiritual beings grow
> And see awake the dumb divinity. [63]

This is more than a personal or individual victory, more even than the recovery of a kingdom or the promise of increase and prosperity; this is a revolutionary change, this is a total victory. In Savitri are exemplified the powers and personalities of the Vedic Varuna, Mitra, Aryaman and Bhaga; and it is her adamantine purpose, arduous preparation, and inflexibly vigilant struggle in the dark spaces of Night, the quick-sands of Twilight, and the blinding regions of utter Day that help her to, "bring down into this world of obscurity and falsehood and death and suffering Truth and Light and Life divine and the immortal's *Ananda*". [64]

XII

THE SYMBOLISM OF THE 'SACRIFICE'

Since there is this tremendous extension in significance as regards the victory, it has to be matched by a proportionate elaboration and heightening of the antecedents and preparations as well; and this is the reason why the Books covering Aswapati's Yoga, Savitri's Yoga, and Savitri's struggle with Death seem to occupy so much space. The seeds of all these are in the original, but Sri Aurobindo has planted them on rich soil and given them what seems almost like extravagant nurture.

Aswapati's Yoga is in the main cast in the form of a journey through the Worlds; Savitri's is likewise a penetration into the "Inner Countries"; and even the struggle between Savitri and Death has for its objective reference a movement, a pursuit, a progress, an ultimate destination. The common feature is the movement, the journey, the progression, for without these, and the continual sacrifice they involve, there can be no gain, no conquest, no spiritual victory. One has to sacrifice everything, one has to die almost, if one is to gain new life, the life everlasting; and the journey—be it ascent, exploration or penetration—is also a battle, for the traveller is opposed by the hostile powers of evil and falsehood, and no sooner a victory is gained than another issue is joined, and one has to fight again, and conquer again.

If Aswapati's Yoga or Savitri's Yoga is described at what appears at first sight unconscionable length, the reason is that each of them is the epic of a soul in its immortal ascent to the peaks or ineffable journey to the centre.

The Veda often talks of the triple divine worlds, the triple lower worlds, and a link-world, and there are, of course, further gradations, for "each world is divisible into several provinces according to different arrangements and self-orderings of its creative light of consciousness"; and although man but inhabits the material Earth and is apparently cooped up there, he is also a creature of infinite possibility, and "even into the solar worlds of the Truth he can rise, enter the portals of the Superconscient, cross the threshold of the Supreme...This human ascension is possible because every being really holds in himself all that his outward vision perceives as if external to him." [65] But it is possible only if man thirsts to break the bonds of his limited earth-life. The same gods who have structured the cosmic stair of the ascending worlds are also anxious, "to build up the same series of ordered states and ascending degrees in man's consciousness from the mortal condition to the crowning immortality."[66] The microcosm *is*—at least potentially—the macrocosm. But man's continual self-offering is called for if he is to make these ascents and conquests; one must be ready to lose one's soul if one is eager to save it; one must be ready to die if one is anxious to live:

> The image of this sacrifice is sometimes that of a journey or voyage; for it travels, it ascends; it has a goal—the vastness, the true existence, the light, the felicity...It has to climb, led by the flaming strength of the divine Will, from plateau to plateau as of a mountain, it has to cross as in a ship the waters of existence, traverse its rivers, overcome their deep pits and rapid currents; its aim is to arrive at the far-off ocean of light and infinity.[67]

The sacrifice, in the visible or physical sense, involves *agnihotra,* and Agni is, "at once the flame on the altar and the priest of the oblation. When man, awakened from his night, wills to offer his inner and outer activities to the gods of a truer and higher existence and so to arise out of mortality into the far-off immortality, his goal and his desire, it is this flame of upward aspiring Force and Will that he must kindle; into this fire he must cast the sacrifice."[68] Aswapati's austerities extend over a period of eighteen years and in the end the Goddess Savitri arises from the *agnihotra* oblation; Dyumatsena's name itself signifies a flame-like or Agni-like brightness, and it is to gather twigs for his *agnihotra* offering that Satyavan goes to the woods on the fateful day. Agni is the fusion of Light and Power, and also the mediator between man and his gods; Agni is a god who is invoked to come with the other gods; and Agni is also the conveyor from earth to the upper regions. In one of the Hymns to Agni, the god is directly invoked as the leader of the journey to guide the evolving soul through its successive births on its ascending planes of existence ("the march of my sacrifices"), to bear it "over every difficult crossing", and to be "the fosterer of our embodyings".[69]

Dyumatsena as well as Aswapati offer *agnihotra* oblations, and for much the same reason; they are really awakening the light and force of the indwelling God so as to grow in Truth-consciousness and labour towards the peaks of Realisation. Savitri on the other hand, being a woman, doesn't offer regular *agnihotra* oblations; her three-nights' *vrata* or vow ending with an oblation to the fire on the fatal morning has, however, the same essential purpose. She concentrates on a voyage of self-discovery; in self-absorbed meditation she explores the "inner countries" of the mind and soul; and she too grows in Truth-consciousness and reaches at last the plenitudes of its power. The dynamics of the movement are the same, whether it is an ascent as with Aswapati's Yoga or an inner movement as with Savitri's.

Aswapati literally means Lord of Horses. In the Veda, the horse and the cow are repeatedly referred to; as material possessions they are doubtless of considerable value, especially to a rural community; but they also represent "a concealed and imprisoned wealth which has to be uncovered and released by a divine puissance".[70] As tell-tale symbols, the horse and the cow stand for Force and Light, life-energy and soul-quality. Aswapati is accordingly equated in Sri Aurobindo's epic with "the symbol of the aspiring soul of man as manifested in life on earth".[71] But Aswapati the "Traveller of the Worlds", the climber towards the far Himalayas of the Spirit, rather recalls the Vedic Aswins, the twin horse-riders, who are inseparably together, inviolably youthful, irresistibly swift-moving. In one of his hymns, *Rishi* Vamadeva invokes the Aswins as follows:

> Full of honey upward rise the delight; upward horses and cars in the wide-shinings of the Dawn and they roll aside the veil of darkness that encompassed on every side and they extend the lower world into a shining form like that of the luminous heaven.
>
> Drink of the honey with your honey-drinking mouths, for the honey yoke your car beloved. With the honey you gladden the movement and its paths; full of honey, O Aswins, is the skin that you bear.
>
> Full of the honey are the swans that bear you, golden-winged, waking with the Dawn, and they come not to hurt, they rain forth the waters, they are full of rapture and touch that which holds the Rapture…[72]

The Aswins, blissful riders to the seas of delight, now ride horses and presently change to swans; they are honey-drenched, honey-hoarding, honey-dripping; their car is undecaying, and they travel over all the worlds towards the goals of enjoyment. Commenting on this wonderful hymn, Sri Aurobindo writes:

> The Aswins…are born or manifested from Heaven…their movement pervades all the worlds, the effect of their action ranges from the body through the vital being and the thought to the superconscient Truth…They are therefore *Nāsatyā*, lords of the movement, leaders of the journey or voyage…

> 'In the wide shinings of the Dawn' they rise...Our conscious existence is a hill (*adri*) with many successive levels and elevations, *sānūni*; the cave of the subconscient is below; we climb upwards towards the godhead of the Truth and Bliss where are the seats of Immortality...
>
> By this upward movement of the chariot of the Aswins with its burden of uplifted and transformed satisfactions the veil of Night that encompasses the worlds of being in us is rolled away. All these worlds, mind, life, body, are opened to the rays of the Sun of Truth.[73]

Such is the marvellous effect of the upward movement of the Aswins, who really embody the Vedic dualism of Light and Power, the Cow and the Horse. But *Rishi* Vamedava, by the force of his aspiration, himself rises also with the ascent of the Aswins: "by the action of the Aswins man's progress towards the beatitude becomes itself beatific; all his travail and struggle and labour grows full of a divine delight."[74] By now, however, the horses change into the Swans, the animal into the bird, thereby symbolising, "the soul liberated and upsoaring...winging upwards towards the heights of our being, winging widely with a free flight, no longer involved in the ordinary limited movement or labouring gallop of the Life-energy, the Horse, the *Aśva*."[75]

It will thus be seen that *Aśva*, *Aświn*, *Aswapati* form a linked sequence of symbols with very rich Vedic associations, and Sri Aurobindo has poetically exploited them to the full in the light of his own spiritual experiences. Likewise, in writing Book VII (The Book of Yoga), describing Savitri's "entry into the Inner Countries", he has drawn both on his own and on his great collaborator, the Mother's spiritual experiences and realisations. A symbol, after all, is a crystallised equivalent to a unit or pattern of experience, meant to give clarity and simplicity and directness to an otherwise complex, subtle and wide-ranging experience.

To Indians, at any rate, Savitri and Satyavan, Aswapati and the Aswins, the *Asva* and the *Hamsa*, are immediately suggestive symbols, and Sri Aurobindo has therefore built his epic on these and with these; as we are whirled about, we may grow dizzy and confused at times, but we are firmly seated in the saddle, and we cannot flounder or miss our sense of direction. Granted the validity and the utter appropriateness and adequancy of the main symbol of Light struggling with Darkness and finally overcoming it, the other related symbols fall into their place, for, "as the Symbol is ramified, Symbols within Symbols will arise, many of these secondary Symbols with no direct bearing upon the patterns of experience behind the key Symbol."[76]

Sometimes even these secondary symbols—for example, the Man of Sorrows, the Madonna of Suffering and the Mother of Might, are easily self-explanatory; but elsewhere—as when Sri Aurobindo refers to the "white-fire dragon bird of endless bliss" or, some ten lines later, to "one"[77]—we are free to draw surmises relevant to the context, the bird, perhaps, is the Bird of Bliss or *ananda*, or the Bird of Fire described by Sri Aurobindo in the poem of that title,[78] and "one" is presumably the Master of Evolution.[79] The central symbol is the main thing; once it has been seized in an act of imaginative identification, the rest—the proliferating subsidiary or supporting symbols—will fall into their right places and serve only to enrich the main symbol, and this is largely our experience when we read Sri Aurobindo's *Savitri*.

'OVERHEAD' POETRY AND *SAVITRI*

The lost music returns: a few bring it,
Verse like the straining of pointed waves shoreward:
The stress of the blades, the cradle of the slack between,
Some rising, some falling, the whole
Tumult order and beauty, but above all
The power and the heartbeat and male music of our being.

Brewster Ghiselin

I

THE PROBLEM

What is 'overhead' poetry? What are the 'overhead' planes of consciousness? How does 'overhead aesthesis' function in the poet no less than the responsive reader or *sahṛdaya*? What are the filiations between 'overhead' and 'mystic' poetry? To what extent can the best of Sri Aurobindo's poetry, especially *Savitri*, be legitimately described as 'overhead' poetry, at least as a first taste, a sure promise, of the future fully manifest 'overhead' poetry?

These questions are easier asked than answered. Whether wooed by an admirer or provoked by a critic, Sri Aurobindo himself found them no easy questions to answer:

> …these are exactly the subjects on which it is difficult to write with any precision or satisfy the intellect's demand for clear and positive statement…I am afraid I have to say what Arnold said about the grand style; it has to be felt and cannot be explained or accounted for…it is doubtful whether any such mentally constructed definition could be always applicable.[1]

Nevertheless, the hints he has scattered through his writings (including the letters), the categories he has enunciated, the examples he has cited from his own poetry or culled from the world's poetry, are still our surest guide in these matters. In other words, Sri Aurobindo remains his own best commentator and interpreter, and it is not surprising that it should be so. It is but a truism to say that his life comprised many dimensions, his thought branched out in many directions, and even his poetry burst into a multifoliate richness of beauty and splendour of meaning; but all had a still centre, a nodal point, which was the sustaining source of the inspiration, the unfailing key to all the mystery. Once this point of leverage is reached, the movements will baffle us less, and we shall be in a better position to understand Sri Aurobindo's thought and appreciate his poetry.

Of very few thinkers and poets can it be said, as it can be of Sri Aurobindo, that their most characteristic thought and poetry are an expression of their own unique spiritual experiences and realisations. As was pointed out in the first chapter, during the days of his 'silent Yoga' at Pondicherry, Sri Aurobindo had certain climactic experiences and realisations which seemed to indicate, in clear enough terms, the lines of the future development of man, of human nature generally, and earth-nature. Man would become superman, not a Shavian superman, not a Nietzschean superman, for those would be merely vital or mental projections, but a spiritually evolved superman, with the 'supermind' for his crown; human nature would undergo a like sea-change, and the earth itself, and all Nature would also feel the results of this fundamental change in the nature and powers of man. When man changes, his institutions—political, social, economic—and his arts—poetry, music, painting—will also change significantly, and in their sum and integral fusion will mark the establishment of the Life Divine on the earth.

Such was Sri Aurobindo's dream and vision of the future, which he explained in philosophical and psychological (or theoretical and practical) terms in the two immense but complementary treatises, *The Life Divine* and *The Synthesis of Yoga*. The political, sociological and aesthetic implications of the change from a mentalised to a supramentalised humanity were studied in *The Ideal of Human Unity*, *The Human Cycle* and *The Future Poetry*. In these five treatises Sri Aurobindo made his spiritual experiences transcend their personal or narrow limits and fill an ordered all-inclusive context so as to form a total body of coherent knowledge. The 'traditional' or 'scriptural' foundations of this new evolutionary leap were explored by a fresh study of the Veda, the Upanishads and the *Gita*, and the results were given out as translation, commentary and interpretation in works like *The Secret of the Veda* and *Essays on the Gita*. And, all the time, in the Sri Aurobindo Ashram at Pondicherry, this supramental yoga was also in action, operating with Sri Aurobindo himself and the Mother for the central inspiration and the source of all-round simultaneous control.

But one thing more was possible: a vivid picture of the world-transforming drama in terms of poetry. *What knows; what does; what is:* of this progression, *The Life Divine*, *The Synthesis of Yoga* and *Savitri* would be the verbal expressions. *Savitri* thus became the final explanation and justification of all Sri Aurobindo's life and work. "It is in fact for myself I have written it," he said once,[2] and this fact should not be lost sight of when we discuss *Savitri*. Nor is this peculiar to this particular poem or poet, for, as L.A.G. Strong points out:

> Poetry *is* difficult, ultimately, and the study of it has no end, because it is a highly organised and complex art, in which some of the greatest minds have tried to record, *for themselves*, and in the only form possible for them, their thoughts, their feelings, their flashes of revelation, about the universe. Nobody but a fool would expect to understand, without training and effort, the book in which a master mind has endeavoured to make new knowledge available to his readers. What of the book written for the master mind only, in a form (poetry) which uses no logic but its own, and extends in its urgency the very boundaries of thought and language? Of course, the ordinary student takes years and years to catch up on such thoughts and make them his own. That is one reason why so many great poets are not understood by their contemporaries.[3]

Although these lines were written over twenty-five years ago and in a very different context, they seem to be wonderfully appropriate to

Savitri as well. The Aurobindonian world is a completely self-poised self-explanatory world. While the synoptic centre is the dialectic of transformation from Mind to Supermind passing the intermediate stages of Higher Mind, Illumined Mind, Intuition and Overmind, while it is from here the divers rays radiate to the circumference of the Aurobindonian world, it is also true that, since it is a properly integrated world, one may start from any point—the philosophy, the yoga, the poetry, or what you please—keep on extending the area of coverage or plumbing the depth of understanding, till ultimately the whole world has been grasped in an odyssey of comprehension. [4]

II

THE OVERHEAD PLANES OF CONSCIOUSNESS

At the present stage of the evolutionary advance, man has a body, certain vital instincts and passions, and a directing and controlling mind. Mental man is a great improvement on the mere animal, but he is also a prey to various dissatisfactions. What is the reason? Sri Aurobindo's diagnosis is pointed and clear: the mind of man, a helper in many ways, a gleaner of bits of truth and partial fragments of knowledge, is nevertheless rooted in a basic Ignorance, functions from behind a veil that separates it from the source of the Truth-consciousness, and hence commits error upon error and piles up misery upon misery. As Sri Aurobindo writes in *The Synthesis of Yoga*:

> ...the mind in the ignorance lives in the moment and moves from hour to hour like a traveller who sees only what is near and visible around his immediate standpoint and remembers imperfectly what he has passed through before, but all in front beyond his immediate view is the unseen and unknown of which he has yet to have experience. [5]

It is a purblind vision, the vision of a man who strives to find his bearings in darkness; a walled-up agonised vision, vaguely apprehensive of everything and everybody. The mental man has no sense of community or communion, he is as it were by himself and for himself. Mind the efficient servant upto a point is also a weakening and defeating power, a power that divorces us from our environ -ment and even the ultimate sources of our strength. This is because, to quote Sri Aurobindo again, the mind has lost,

> ...the truth of indivisibility of Time, the indivisibility of Force and Substance. It has lost sight even of the obvious fact that all minds are one Mind taking many standpoints, all lives one Life developing many currents of activity, all body and form one substance of Force and Consciousness concentrating into many apparent stabilities of force and consciousness; but in truth all these stabilities are really only a constant whorl of movement repeating a form while it modifies it... [6]

How is this "lost Sun" to be recovered? How is the Ignorance to be superceded? The transition has to be effected, from the Mind, through the Overmind, to the Supermind. On the other hand, Sri Aurobindo warns us in unambiguous terms that, "the supramental change is difficult, distant, an ultimate stage; it must be regarded as the end of a far-off vista." [7] Figuratively it may be said that there is but a veil, a gulf, between the mental and the supramental levels of life, between Nature and Super-Nature. Rending of the veil, bridging the gulf—these too are only mentalised constructions. The real change is spiritual, not physical, and while figures of speech are convenient, they can also seriously mislead us.

While the Ignorance no doubt envelops us as a thick veil (to relapse into simile again), its reign is by no means absolute. There are transparent patches through which light trickles in. Messiahs have been our beacon lights. The ideal of the Fatherhood of God and the Brotherhood of Man has been repeatedly placed before us. Many a man and woman has transcended in the past the limiting ego and claimed the larger freedom of a more universal consciousness.

But these exceptions have nevertheless failed to effect a basic or total revolution in the mental consciousness. The mass of humanity has remained largely unaffected by the example of these great leaders of humanity. What Sri Aurobindo has called the 'lower' knowledge, in other words the knowledge of the apparent world gained through sensuous and mental processes, through the techniques of science, has to be matched—and more than matched—by the 'higher' knowledge, the knowledge of the truth of existence gained through an inner spiritual discipline. Although called, again for convenience, the 'lower' and the 'higher' knowledge, they are really but the reverse and the obverse of the same arc of integral knowledge:

> All knowledge is ultimately the knowledge of God, through himself, through Nature, through her works. Mankind has first to seek this knowledge through the external life; for until its mentality is sufficiently developed, spiritual knowledge is not really possible, and in proportion as it is developed, the possibilities of spiritual knowledge become richer and fuller. [8]

To cultivate the spiritual life is not to turn away from everyday life; it is not an escape from life but rather a steady confrontation of life and seeing it in its cosmic context. The little stream of life is seen lost in the ocean, the little bird of one's individuality is seen lost in the universality of the blue sky. The radical inner change, the profound spiritual transformation takes place when man the mental being aspires with his whole heart and soul to the 'higher' knowledge, and is seized and overwhelmed by it:

> The possession of the Infinite cannot come except by an ascent to those supramental planes, nor the knowledge of it except by an inert submission of Mind to the descending messages of the Truth-conscious Reality. [9]

Or, as the same process is described in the terms of yoga:

> There are two powers that alone can effect in their conjunction the great and difficult thing which is the aim of our endeavour, a

> fixed and unfailing aspiration that calls from below and a supreme Grace from above that answers. [10]

Ascent, descent, integration; aspiration, response, realisation: such are the classic terms of the Aurobindonian dialectic of spiritual evolution. Once spiritually awakened, mental man strives to exceed himself, and as he explores the ascending possibilities, he reaches stage after stage of the overhead—or above mind—consciousness: Higher Mind, Illumined Mind, Intuition, Overmind, and beyond it—"at the end of a far-off vista"—Supermind. Sri Aurobindo devotes several pages in *The Life Divine* [11] and the whole canto in *Savitri* entitled 'The Kingdoms and Godheads of the Greater Mind' to a vivid or luxuriously picturesque description of these spiritual resting-houses between Mind and Supermind. The advance, the progress, really implies an increasing capacity for comprehension, the emergence of a new power of direct vision, the play of puissant truth-consciousness and truth-effectuation:

> As the Higher Mind brings a greater consciousness into the being through the spiritual idea and its power of truth, so the Illumined Mind brings in a still greater consciousness through a Truth sight and Truth Light and its seeing and seizing power... [12]

> Intuition is always an edge or ray or outleap of a superior light; it is in us a projecting blade, edge or point of a far-off supermind light... [13]

Less analysis, more comprehension; less uncertainty and the confusing play of light and shade, more sureness and the luminous glow of a steady light; less division and isolation, more universality and the consciousness of unity: these are the symptoms of the higher thought and the illumined thought. But intuitive thought is like a momentary streak of lightning; an instantaneous flash, a sudden—an almost blinding—revelation; presently all is dark again, only the memory of the brilliant moment remains.

The next stage takes us still nearer the supramental level of consciousness:

> When the overmind descends, the predominance of the centralising ego-sense is entirely subordinated, lost in largeness of being and finally abolished; a wide cosmic perception and feeling of a boundless universal self and movement replaces it: many motions that were formerly ego-centric may still continue, but they occur as currents or ripples in the cosmic wideness. Thought, for the most part, no longer seems to originate individually in the body or the person but manifests from above or comes in upon the cosmic mind-waves... [14]

It is like a man drinking from a flowing stream, basking in the Sun's bright rays, or losing his thoughts in eternity; in other words, it is a basic change in the quality of his consciousness that enables him to be in the world but not of it, to think, speak and act but from "a vast cosmic instrumentation". This is the utmost change that man can hope for while still remaining man, for, "the overmind change is the final consummating movement of the dynamic spiritual transformation; it is the highest possible status dynamis of the spirit in the spiritual-mind plane." [15]

III

OVERHEAD AESTHESIS

Now all these overhead planes—Higher Mind, Illumined Mind, Intuition, Overmind—can influence, each to the measure of its distinctive or sovereign power, our various activities or preoccupations at the mental or the below-mental—the vital and the material planes. If the resistance from the lower powers—matter, life (or the vital), mind is formidable, as it often is, the influence of the higher powers, the result of a chance or temporary descent of one of them to the lower planes, will be negligible or evanescent. But where the aspiration has been strong enough and sustained enough, the descent will yield more fruitful and lasting results. This is particularly exemplified in the arts, and in poetry most of all. Now 'overhead' poetry is simply poetry that has been thus influenced, whether to a greater or a lesser extent, by the spiritual power of the Overmind or by the other overhead powers, Higher Mind, Illumined Mind or Intuition. The influence may be the result of the higher power acting in one of two ways:

> ...in one it touches the ordinary modes of mind and deepens, heightens, intensifies or exquisitely refines their action but without changing its modes or transforming its normal character; in the other it brings down into these normal modes something of itself, something supernormal, something which one at once feels to be extraordinary and suggestive of a superhuman level. [16].

The first way may be compared to a tutor making a few significant changes in a scholar's essay; the second is the essay of the scholar of yesterday who has completed his training and has himself mastered the art of writing. Thus the word "greater" is applied by Sri Aurobindo, "with the necessary qualifications, to the second way and its too rare poetic creation." [17] As regards the Overmind power itself and the divers intermediate powers and the manner in which they express themselves in poetry, what happens is that these overhead or essentially spiritual powers undergo translation in poetical terms; and since poetry involves the idea, the word, and the rhythm, these overhead powers too charge with new or universal significance any or all of them and the result is 'overhead' poetry:

> ...the Overmind thinks in a mass; its thought, feeling, vision is high or deep or wide or all these things together...it goes vast on its way to bring the divine riches, and it has a corresponding language and rhythm. The Higher Thought has a strong tread often with bare unsandaled feet and moves in a clear-cut light: a divine power, measure, dignity is its most frequent character. The outflow of the Illumined Mind comes in a flood brilliant with revealing words or a light of crowding images, sometimes surcharged with its burden of revelations, sometimes with a luminous sweep. The Intuition is usually a lightning flash showing

> up a single spot or plot of ground or scene with an entire and miraculous completeness of vision to the surprised ecstasy of the inner eye; its rhythm has a decisive inevitable sound which leaves nothing essential unheard, but very commonly is embodied in a single stroke.[18]

Such are the overhead planes and their characteristic powers, which are more or less spiritual in their origin and impulsion. When these powers engage themselves, partly or wholly, in the creation and communication of beauty, overhead aesthesis may be said to have come into play. 'Aesthesis' is normally viewed as the opposite of 'physis', for feelings, thoughts, the tremblings of one's sensibility are subjective whereas facts, actions, the vicissitudes of outer phenomena are objective. Aesthesis is the energising activity, artistic or poetic creation (and enjoyment) is the result:

> By aesthesis is meant a reaction of the consciousness, mental and vital and even bodily, which receives a certain element in things, something that can be called their taste, *Rasa*, which, passing through the mind or sense or both, awakes a vital enjoyment of the taste, *Bhoga*, and this can again awaken us, awaken even the soul in us to something yet deeper and more fundamental than mere pleasure and enjoyment, to some form of the spirit's delight of existence, *Ananda*.[19]

Rasa, *bhoga*, *ananda* are the three terms in the ascending scale of artistic (and especially poetic) activity, and aesthesis is the functioning of this trinity of powers. There is the *rasa*, the essential taste, of a word, its sound, its idea; the word may become the starting-point for a sequence of echoes and intimations that may have a global sweep; starting from almost anywhere, any word, any sound, any idea, a vivid sense of the cosmos may surge with overpowering effect, and it is as though one sees with new eyes, hears with new ears, and the surrender to this wonderful experience is the *bhoga* or enjoyment of it, and results in aesthetic delight or self-forgetful bliss (*ananda*).

Of course, such aesthesis, although ordinarily associated with art and poetry, really derives from the universal *ananda*, the cosmic ecstasy of the Dance of Shiva, "which multiplies the body of the God numberlessly to the view: it leaves that white existence precisely where and what it was, ever is and ever will be; its sole absolute object is the joy of the dancing." [20]

Viewed on this cosmic scale, "Delight is existence, Delight is the secret of creation, Delight is the root of birth, Delight is the cause of remaining in existence, Delight is the end of birth and that into which creation ceases." [21] Yet the ordinary mentality sees a great deal of pain, which is the reverse of delight, in everyday life; ugliness, hate, and misery seem to contest the ground with beauty, love and happiness, and one almost feels like generalising that all is *duhkkha* or *asukham*, all is double, double toil and trouble. Indeed, in our life in the Ignorance, between the extremes of the possibility of the pure *Ananda* at one end and the actuality of the reign of misery at the other end, there is a middle no-man's-land governed by, "a general tone of neutrality and indifference born from the universal insensibility into which the *Ananda* sinks in its dark negation in the Inconscient."[22]

It is alone the opening of the overhead planes, the play of the overhead powers, that can effect a cure for this indifference and restore the lost taste for the original *Ananda*. Behind the *Manomaya*, the divided limited agonised mental self, there is the *Anandamaya*, the vast ineffable Bliss-Self of which the former is only "a shadowy image and disturbed reflection".[23] As we penetrate behind the surface or appearance and touch the reality within, this world of *Anandamaya*, new values replace the values of our lower mental, vital or material consciousness, and our aesthesis too, "shares in this intensification of capacity…As it enters the Overhead planes the ordinary aesthesis turns into a pure delight and becomes capable of a high, a large or a deep abiding ecstasy." [24]

The ordinary mentality is so deadened by dull routine that it is insensitive alike to pleasure and pain except, perhaps, when it makes a direct or personal invasion, and even then it is no more than an instinctive animal reaction, sharp but brief, and untranslated into the higher levels, undistilled as *rasa*, unassimilated in terms of *bhoga*, uncrystallised as *ananda*. A proper aesthesis can turn the experience of pain itself into fine poetry, as in:

> She sat like Patience on a monument,
> Smiling at grief.[25]

And, besides, overhead aesthesis connotes, not merely greater intensity of experience, but also a greater integrality and universality in its approach and functioning. It is concerned, as all aesthesis is, with beauty, but it is no less concerned with truth, love, delight, power; overhead aesthesis is thus "an essential aesthesis…a fundamental and universal aesthesis", putting truth first, though not by any means ignoring beauty or the other aspects of the cosmic play. What this really means is that, when the overhead aesthesis actively functions, truth ceases to be anything abstract or formless, but is seen to tingle with a life and beauty of its own, and this vision of truth becomes "a splendid discovery, a rapturous revelation, a thing of beauty that is a joy forever"[26]; there truth is beauty, beauty truth; and there too dwells and from there "springs the mystery of the inevitable word, the supreme immortal rhythm, the absolute significance and the absolute utterance",[27] in short, the mantra.

IV

MYSTIC POETRY AND THE MANTRA

If overhead poetry is the high-ranging Himalayas, then the mantra is their ultimate peak, Everest itself. Rhythm, verbal form, thought-substance, thought's radiant soul-quality, all fuse in the mantra to produce the effect of an incantation. When a Vedic *rishi* articulates a mantra, it really surges with a potent inevitability from the depths of his soul, and presently sinks into the depths of the hearer's soul, leaping over or penetrating intervening barriers like the analytical intellect, the sensory faculties, the bodily sheaths. Sri Aurobindo himself describes the process thus:

> Its message enters stirring the blind brain
> And keeps in the dim ignorant cells its sound;
> The hearer understands a form of words
> And, musing on the index thought it holds,
> He strives to read it with the labouring mind,
> But finds bright hints, not the embodied truth:
> Then, falling silent in himself to know
> He meets the deeper listening of his soul:
> The Word repeats itself in rhythmic strains:
> Thought, vision, feeling, sense, the body's self
> Are seized unalterably and he endures
> An ecstasy and an immortal change;
> He feels a Wideness and becomes a Power,
> All knowledge rushes on him like a sea:
> Transmuted by the white spiritual ray
> He walks in naked heaven of joy and calm,
> Sees the God-face and hears transcendent speech... [28]

The mantra is actually a creative force emanating from the highest overhead level, charged with the rapturous and lustrous potencies of the spirit, and using as its native language "a revelatory, inspired, intuitive word limpid or subtly vibrant or densely packed with the glory of this ecstasy and lustre." [29]

While the overhead aesthesis has wide-ranging heights and depths for its action, the mantra has a much more restricted play, though when it does come into action its effect is unerring and long-lasting. The Vedic mantra has been called the *kamadhenu*, the divine cow; it is cloud-like, raining profusely; it is laden with metaphysical, psychical, and physical meanings. But when the mantra falls into the receptive ear, sinks into the awakened soul, apprehension turns to enjoyment, enjoyment to ecstasy, and ecstasy even to *samadhi* when, "in the language of psychoanalysis the ego returns to the primal rhythm."[30]

This really brings us to the region of mysticism and mystic poetry. While, of course, it is convenient to classify the mystical planes broadly as occult, psychic and spiritual;[31] while all these planes are equally beyond speculative reason, it is nevertheless the spiritual that is quintessentially the mystical mode of direct apprehension of Reality. 'Mysticism' could be derived, says Rufus M. Jones, from one of two German words: either from *mystizimus* "which stands for the cult of the supernatural, for theosophical pursuits, for a spiritualistic exploitation of psychical research", or from *mystik* "which stands for immediate experience of a divine-human intercourse and relationship."[32] Aswapati first explores the many occult worlds without, while Savitri explores the "inner countries" of her own psyche: but all mystical roads lead ultimately to the Divine. As Canon Overton puts it, "That we bear the image of God is the starting-point, one might almost say the postulate, of all Mysticism", and the goal is "the complete union of the soul with God". [33] And the Hindus have been described by Lin Yutang as "natural mystics," [34] for the aim of the spiritually awakened in India has always been to achieve the union of the *atman*, the individual soul, with the *Brahman*, the omnipresent Reality.

The double assumption of mysticism is that the universe *is* a cosmos, a macrocosm, and that it can be apprehended by man's awakened soul, the microcosm.[35] The thirst for self-transcendence, the reaching out of oneself to grasp a greater, the desire of the human moth for the Star of the spiritual firmament, these are recurrent phenomena in the world of man, particularly in the region inhabited by the 'van of humanity', the so-called mystics. Theirs is a supra-rational consciousness, in which,

> ...the knower, the knowledge and the known become one again...This quality of consciousness has been given many names —cosmic consciousness, the mystic vision, the unitive life, etc.— but it is certain that these refer to one and the same thing which

> in its fullness and permanence constitutes Enlightenment. It is the great returning home to God, with the God-like potentialities (which were there latent from the beginning in consciousness) now fully unfolded.[36]

All mystics need not be poets—at any rate poets who have actually written poetry—but all poets are perhaps also mystics in disguise (or without disguise), and at least the overhead aesthesis must partake of the mystical experience. Benjamin Kurtz is thus right when he observes:

> Is not mysticism of the essence of all deep aesthetic experience? If mysticism is a visioned conviction of a super-sensuous super-rational reality in which all things are somehow one without losing their disparateness, mysticism being thus a solution of the paradox of unity in variety, then each profound aesthetic moment is at least potentially mystical. For in that moment the mind is moved with a feeling of metaphysical identity of unlike things. [37]

Western thought generally gives to intuition the role that Sri Aurobindo gives to the several overhead powers, but that the primary inspiration behind poetry (and art) is supra-rational is universally conceded. Thus, Herbert Read says:

> All art originates in an act of intuition, or vision...The *process* of poetry consists firstly in maintaining this vision in its integrity, and secondly in expressing this vision in words...in the process of poetic composition words rise into the conscious minds as isolated objective 'things' with a definite equivalence in the poet's state of mental intensity. They are arranged or composed in a sequence or rhythm which is sustained until the mental state of tension in the poet is exhausted or released by this objective equivalence. [38]

The poet A.E. (George Russell) has acknowledged how words would rise from within like a water-lily from the bottom of a tarn: "The words often would rush swiftly from hidden depths of consciousness and be fashioned by an art with which the working brain had but little to do".[39] William S. Haas, again, makes the same point:

> All original and creative ideas occur in a shock-like inspiration. And this is regardless of whether they belong to the religious, the philosophical, the artistic or the scientific sphere. Their appearance resembles a sudden burst of light...The sensation of the individual is a feeling of being lifted above the regular flow of the psychological and intellectual stream. One touches for that illumined moment another realm. [40]

Arduous preparation of one or another sort may have preceded, and all the materials may be ready; yet the timing of the spark from heaven is always an unpredictable factor. Whenever the shock of recognition may come, it is certain to rock the whole being with the tremor of ecstasy; it is as though one is being seized and held by a prepotent superior power.

Generally speaking, all aesthetic experience is a kind of rebirth, "a making of oneself and of one's world, the self which was psyche being remade in the shape of consciousness, and the world, which was crude sensa, being remade in the shape of language, or sensa converted into imagery and charged with emotional significance".[41] The artist, the *kavi* (the poet), is truly a creator; he creates "new reality in a supra-rational, visional manner and presents it symbolically or metaphorically, as a microcosmic whole signifying a macrocosmic whole."[42] Intuition (taken as the short-hand for the overhead powers) may thus be accepted as the gateway to the divers realms of aesthetic experience.

It is not enough—perhaps it is not quite necessary—to be learned or clever or subtle; aesthesis is not the same thing as logic; what we call the 'magic' of poetry is merely this irrational onrush or surge of inspiration from uncharted regions. Not so much irrational as supra-rational or overmental, for these overhead powers function far otherwise than as the dark muddy powers of the subconscious and unconscious. These overhead powers (including Intuition) may light up, "various areas of experience, but when the intuitive mind is directed towards the things of God, intuition is called mystical intuition and the knowledge so possessed, mystical knowledge."[43] Aesthesis like this induces in the reader, the responsive *sahṛdaya*, an experience similar to the originating experience, thereby holding together in a trinitarian close embrace the *kavi*, the *anandamaya*, and the *sahṛdaya*.[44]

We have so far tried to see the filiations between 'overhead' poetry, mantric poetry, and mystic poetry. All 'overhead' poetry is not mystic poetry, neither is all mystic poetry necessarily mantric. At the top, at the very top, 'overhead' poetry is mantric as well as mystic. It is marked by the highest pitch of flight, the most radiant articulation, with the thought alive and rhythm irresistible, and all aglow with a soul-quality that gives the mantra a distinctly incantatory efficacy.

V

'OVERHEAD' POETRY

While describing Savitri's pilgrimaging in the "inner countries", Sri Aurobindo at one point snaps the scene where she confronts the throng of powers that are really the "messengers, the occult gods" who awake humanity to the beauty and truth of things:

> Into dim spiritual somnolence they break
> Or shed wide wonder on our waking self,
> Ideas that haunt us with their radiant tread,
> Dreams that are hints of unborn Reality,
> Strange goddesses with deep-pooled magical eyes,
> Strong wind-haired gods carrying harps of hope,
> Great moon-hued visions gliding through gold air,
> Aspiration's sun-dream head and star-carved limbs,
> Emotions making common hearts sublime.[45]

The nature of 'overhead' poetry cannot be more vividly brought out; all its immense range is suggested here, and the riot of its imagery well illustrates Middleton Murry's remark: "...the greatest mastery of imagery does not lie in the use, however beautiful and revealing, of isolated images, but in the harmonious total impression produced by a succession of subtly related images. In such cases the images appear to grow out of one another and to be fulfilling an independent life of their own."[46] Dreams, goddesses, gods, visions, aspirations, emotions, all leap to life, and are seen to be the powers behind 'overhead' poetry, powers that invade our ordinary life to possess and change it. Varied though these powers are, their common traits are Light and 'the mystic voice'.

Elsewhere Sri Aurobindo cites examples from world poetry of the overhead poignancy in thought, feeling, voice and rhythm:

Sunt lacrimae rerum; [47]

—Virgil

Insano indegno mistero delle cose
(The insane and ignoble mystery of things); [48]

—Leopardi

Absent thee from felicity awhile,
And in this harsh world draw thy breath in pain;

—Shakespeare

Voyaging though strange seas of thought, alone;

—Wordsworth

Anityam asukham lokam imām prāpya bhajasva mām
(Thou who hast come to this transient and unhappy
world, love and worship Me);

—*Gita*

Those thoughts that wander through eternity;

—Milton

Heaven's light forever shines, Earth's shadows fly;
Life, like a dome of many-coloured glass,
Stains the white radiance of Eternity,
Until Death tramples it to fragments;

—P.B. Shelley

And Paradise was opened in his face.

—John Dryden

These are what Sri Aurobindo has aptly described as "discoveries of an unexpected and absolute phrase",[49] and since phrase, thought, pitch, rhythm all fuse into a revelatory blaze in such lines, they defy the usual categories of analysis and criticism.

The sharp difference between the normal and the overhead aesthesis may be illustrated by citing two passages on the same subject, here is W.J. Turner—

They hunt, the velvet tigers in the jungle,
The spotted jungle full of shapeless patches—
Sometimes they're leaves, sometimes they're
hanging flowers,
Sometimes they're hot gold patches of the sun…[50]

which is a vivid enough and realistic enough description of the man-eaters in an Indian jungle; but here is William Blake—

Tyger! Tyger! burning bright
In the forests of the night,
What immortal hand or eye
Could frame thy fearful symmetry?—

and what a difference! This is the very incandescence of poetry truly wrought by a cosmic consciousness; we see the tiger poised in its terrible beauty, and dread and wonder strive for mastery; isn't he Rudra the fierce, or is he only the God's great creation? In quick short gasps the frenzy of fascination finds self-expression:

And what shoulder, and what art,
Could twist the sinews of thy heart?
And when thy heart began to beat,
What dread hand? and what dread feet?
What the hammer? What the chain?
In what furnace was thy brain?

What the anvil? What dread grasp
Dare its deadly terrors clasp?

The questions inevitably lead to the climactic "Did he who made the Lamb make thee?"—is Rudra the fierce also Shiva the serene and auspicious? The last lines but feebly echo the first; as in Thompson's *The Hound of Heaven*, here too the chase of discovery is over; the wheel has come full circle; the revelation is complete. Turner and Blake both write about the Tiger; but one is the creation of the vital or mental aesthesis, the other is a torrent of suggestion or an onrush of power from a higher plane.

Another example: here is Matthew Arnold on the prospect of death:

The air of heaven is soft,
And warm, and pleasant; but the grave is cold.
Heaven's air is better than the cold dead grave. [51]

This is good as far as it goes, but here is Shakespeare on the same theme, and now the illumination from above pours down in a flood:

Ay, but to die, and go we know not where;
To lie in cold obstruction, and to rot;
This sensible warm motion to become
A kneaded clod; and the delighted spirit
To bathe in fiery floods or to reside
In thrilling region of thick-ribbed ice;
To be imprison'd in the viewless winds
And blown with restless violence round about
The pendent world; or to be worse than worst
Of those that lawless and incertain thought
Imagine howling—'tis too horrible.
The weariest and most loathed worldly life
That age, ache, penury, and imprisonment,
Can lay on nature is a paradise
To what we fear of death. [52]

It is true Arnold is devising a dignified speech suitable for the legendary hero, Rustum, while Shakespeare has to write a speech appropriate to the mentality of an errant youth like Claudio; yet, while Arnold is almost flat, Shakespeare has given a glow even to Claudio's frenzied fear of death. It is easy to beg the question and say: Well, Shakespeare is, after all, the greater poet. But, then, how exactly has he touched these lines with greatness? Claudio's images are drawn from the vital and the physical, and yet they are passed through the fire and purified in the fountain and lifted up to a higher plane—say, that of the Higher Mind or the Illumined Mind—because, "there is something behind...which comes not primarily from the mind or the vital emotions or the physical seeing but from the cosmic self and its consciousness standing behind them all." [53] It is not only Claudio speaking but all frightened humanity recoiling helplessly at the very thought of the approach of the grim Spectre; it is limited life retreating tremblingly before Death. Arnold might have cited the passage as an example of the 'Grand Style' in Shakespeare; but its essential character is better suggested when we see it as an expression of the overhead aesthesis. To return to W. J. Turner again, when he writes—

> But the misery of the unsatisfied heart,
> The misery of the living life
> Whose flame is ever-renewed suffering— [54]

we see in it no more than the feeblest of feeble echoes of *Sunt lacrimae rerum* or *Anityam asukham lokam*; and when he writes—

> I gazed entranced upon his face
> Fairer than any flower—
> O shining Popocatapetl
> It was thy magic hour:
> The houses, people, traffic seemed
> Thin fading dreams by day,
> Chimborazo, Cotopaxi
> They had stolen my soul away— [55]

we have doubtless moments of excitement, the mind is quickened for the nonce by the *rasa* of the passage, but a second or third reading brings disappointment. It is here Keats scores magnificently:

> Charmed magic casements, opening on the foam,
> Of perilous seas, in faery lands forlorn— [56]

for one may read or repeat the lines to oneself any number of times, and yet not find them emptied of significance.

The overhead flight in poetry is, not unnaturally, seldom sustained over a passage of considerable length. It is generally a sudden blaze, a momentary swell. For even poets are but human beings and ordinarily function on the mental plane, although this plane itself is no uniform dry desert of reason but has its own sensuous arbours, delectable oases, and the towered castles of the imagination. It is interesting to watch the sudden rise in the tempo of a piece of poetry like Wallace Stevens' 'Negation':

> Hi! The creator too is blind,
> Struggling towards his harmonious whole,
> Rejecting intermediate parts,
> Horrors and falsities and wrongs;
> Incapable master of all force,
> Too vague idealist, overwhelmed
> By an afflatus that persists.
> For this, then, we endure brief lives,
> The evanescent symmetries—
> From that meticulous potter's thumb. [57]

After circling with slow deliberation at the middle height (nearer earth than sky), Stevens suddenly, skylark-wise, makes an ascent in the last two lines; a higher inspiration has seized and carried him, and we can merely gaze wonderingly at the phenomenon.

Isolated short passages or single lines of great beauty occur, of course, in modern American and English poetry, and it may not be far-fetched to recognise some kind of overhead inspiration in them. To cite a few almost at random:

Across my foundering deck shone
A beacon, an eternal beam; [58]

—Hopkins

A quartz contentment like a stone; [59]

—Emily Dickinson

Night is the beginning and the end
And in between the ends of distraction
Waits mute speculation; [60]

—Allen Tate

But there, where western glooms are gathering
The dark will end the dark...; [61]

—Edwin Arlington Robinson

I said to my soul, be still, and let the dark come upon you
Which shall be the darkness of God; [62]

—T.S. Eliot

Yet man's life is thought
And he, despite his terror, cannot cease
Ravening through century after century,
Ravening, raging and uprooting, that he may come
Into the desolation of reality;

—W.B. Yeats

The holy hush of ancient sacrifice. [63]

—Stevens

It is easy to dismiss some of the above lines at least as no more than verbal legerdemain; Tate, Robinson and Eliot, all three seem to make play with 'night' or 'dark'; Yeats seems to charge 'ravening' and 'desolation' with a certain violence; 'quartz' and 'stone' in Emily Dickinson and 'holy hush' in Wallace Stevens seem verbal tricks at first. Yet, in the particular contexts, when the words sink into the inward ear, the lines acquire a life and soul of their own, and, perhaps begging the question, we can only say that a higher inspiration has done its work.

The overhead powers are essentially, in their origin as also in their instrumentation, *spiritual* powers. A plant, an animal, a man, all share within limits the same life; yet man the mental being outsoars the others; and the man with an awakened soul outsoars average humanity insensitive to the intimations of the soul. The rhythmic word, too, "has a subtly sensible element, its sound value, a quite immaterial element, its significance or thought-value, and both of these again, its sound and its sense, have separately and together a soul value, a direct spiritual power, which is infinitely the most important thing about them."[64] It would appear that the poets in the passages or lines cited above have somehow managed to awake the "soul value", the "direct spiritual power", in the words brought together. An adroit balance of ideas and sounds may turn out lines that are in Lord Alfred Tennyson's words,

> Faultily faultless, icily regular, splendidly null,
> Dead perfection, no more. [65]

Andrea del Sarto, in Robert Browning's poem, concedes that although he may be a faultless painter himself, it is Raphael "pouring his soul" that is the real master; when Raphael paints "its soul is right". If one fights shy of the word 'soul', one might say with J.L. Lowes that words in poetry have more *connotation*, that they are charged with suggestion, whereas mere prose words have only *denotation*, a physical content. Actually, although all art and poetry may start from the physical and the vital, without the spiral of *dhwani* or suggestion culminating in this spiritual quality, they must pall more and more and go the way of all flesh, not enjoy the soul's immortality. Keats by calling the nightingale 'immortal Bird' and Shelley by calling the skylark 'blithe Spirit' have thrown a challenge to common sense. A bird is but a bird and must share the mortality of the world; how, then, can a bird either be a spirit or be immortal?

"There are people", Sri Aurobindo once wrote to a correspondent, "who thrill to Pope and find Keats and Shelley empty and misty... What the hell has 'a glowworm golden in a dell of dew' to do with the song of the skylark? But that simply means they like things that are intellectually clear and can't appreciate the imaginative connections which reveal what is deeper than the surface."[66] The bird is both bird and symbol, both body and soul, hence both mortal and immortal. The lie in the material world becomes the truth in the spiritual world, and it is the business of poetry, at least of poetry partaking of the overhead aesthesis, to insinuate, even to proclaim, this truth. Mr A.B. Purani has, in the course of a private conversation, drawn my attention to the fact that ancient Sanskrit literature recognised the distinction between the poetic creations of the mind and those of the overhead levels. The former were *laukika*, the latter, *ārṣa*; in the former, expression followed the poet's intention, while in the latter, the mantric utterances of the *rishi*s, meaning but limped behind the expression.[67]

In other words, the overhead inspiration is unpredictable, and comes without any antecedent mental activity; once the wonder of poetic expression has been spontaneously accomplished, the meddling intellect can, if it likes, try to anatomise the poetry. It would, perhaps, be wiser on the whole to surrender to the poem instead of dissecting it, for, when the *sahṛdaya* properly responds to the poem, he cannot fail to experience a feeling of freedom and joy. As Charles Morgan writes, "In a great style there is pressure behind the form. As you read, you are made aware of this pressure. You feel that all the heavens of reality are pressing upon the writer's mind; you look up, you imagine, and your own heavens open before you."[68] Longinus said simply that the 'sublime' was the 'echo of a great soul'; that it involved, at one end, elevation of language, and at the other end (the hearer's), 'transport'; and that, above all, the sublime pierces everything "like a lightning flash", a knock-out blow. Haas said "shock-like inspiration", " a sudden burst of light"; Sri Aurobindo's phrases, while describing Intuition, were "outleap of a superior light…a projecting blade"; and A.E. spoke of the sudden rising of a water-lily from the bottom of a tarn. Longinus' "transport" itself has been made to mean "religious mysticism" by Abbé Bremond and some sort of "ecstasy" by Arthur

Machen; but all are agreed that there is a supra-rational element in both the creation and the enjoyment of such 'great' or 'sublime' poetry, or poetry written in the 'grand style'.[69]

But the Aurobindonian theory of 'overhead' poetry is no question-begging phrase that these others are, for his theory is intimately linked up with his philosophy and his own yogic experiences and poetic experiments and achievements during the latter half of his life. His aesthetics chimes perfectly with his metaphysics and his psychology, and hence his theory of overhead aesthesis seems to come perhaps much nearer to an explanation of the mystery of poetic creation than almost any other theory that has been advanced hitherto. Being intimately related to his own integral view of Reality—Reality that is both Being and Becoming—the Aurobindonian theory of overhead aesthesis appears to have a sufficiency and inner logic of its own that is rather lacking in most other theories of poetry.

VI

OVERHEAD INFLUENCE IN SRI AUROBINDO'S POETRY

We shall now turn to Sri Aurobindo's own 'experiments' in the writing of overhead poetry. Mallarmé is reported to have told Dagas: "Poetry is not written with ideas, it is written with words."[70] But not mere words, not any words; words are variable and tantalising, they have looks, they have thought and sound values, and they have coils of significance; when coaxed into a particular order the current of rhythm flows through them, the *ordonnance* leaps to life, and the poetic line is, as it were, projected into eternity; "the secret chords of our being are awakened, we vibrate and thrill in response to its call… we listen to the unspoken, we gaze upon the unseen."[71] Rhythm is thus vitally important.

In his own poetic practice, Sri Aurobindo gave ample attention to rhythm and metre, and his metrical experiments were often doubled with his attempts to give expression to his mystical experiences, and the results have been astonishing. He no doubt attained an early mastery of the blank verse, as may be seen in his *Urvasie* and *Love and Death*, as also his plays—*Perseus the Deliverer*, *Vasavadutta*, *Rodogune* and *The Viziers of Bassora*. Presently he was attracted to the classical quantitative metres, notably the hexameter, and he was led in due course to develop his own theory of true quantity in English. Classical names like iamb, trochee, spondee, pyrric, anapaest, dactyl, not to mention the more unusual anti-bacchius, choriambus, ionic a majore and so on, signifying various combinations of long and short syllables, are often—now, perhaps, less often than before—used with regard to English verse also, even though there is no rigid system of longs and shorts in English as there is in ancient languages like Greek and Latin.[72]

The classicist in Sri Aurobindo was fascinated by the possibilities of quantitative verse in English and, while conceding that, "English quantitative metres cannot be as rigid as the metres of the ancient tongues", he nevertheless devised a workable system with certain rules: stressed syllables and syllables supported on a long vowel are to be treated as longs, while unstressed short vowel syllables unweighted with consonants are to be treated as shorts; with regard to many uncertain syllables the ear should decide whether they are to be treated as long or short; and, above all, free modulation should be permitted.[73] These rules really make one basic rule: "If we are to get a true theory of quantity, the ear must find it; it cannot be determined by mental fictions or by reading with the eye."[74] This is not the place to go into any great detail about the Aurobindonian theory of true quantity or even to discuss how far Sri Aurobindo has really succeeded in effecting a happy marriage between English verse and quantitative metres. The relevant point that is to be made here is that, in several of his later poems, Sri Aurobindo audaciously tried a two-fold experiment, namely 'overhead' poetry in quantitative verse.

The two poems in hexameters, *Ahana* in rhyme and *Ilion* the unfinished epic, are tour-de-forces. In *Ahana*, a philosophic poem in over 500 lines, as also in *Ilion*, running to about 5,000 lines, it is not to be expected that the pure overhead inspiration can be more than occasional. But there *are* passages in both that come like an "outleap of a superior light", a ray of cosmic consciousness, an intimation of the Infinite; and of the two long poems, *Ahana* is the more uniformly sustained, packed with high thought, luminous in many places and suffused throughout with the promised radiance of Ahana, the Dawn of God. Only a few lines can be given here as a sample:

> I shall sport with my dove from his highlands,
> Drinking her laughter of bliss like a god in my Grecian islands.
> Life in my limbs shall grow deathless, flesh with the
> God-glory tingle,
> Lustre of Paradise, light of the earth-ways marry and mingle.[75]

The *Ilion* is an epic after the manner of Homer, continuing the story of the siege of Troy from the point where *The Iliad* ends; but of the 5,000 lines of the epic that Sri Aurobindo left behind him, only the first 381 lines were cast in the final form and published in his lifetime. The quality of the hexameter, as well as the overhead sweep of cosmic comprehension can be illustrated by this truly Homeric simile, which has received the characteristic Aurobindonian stamp:

> Even as a star long extinguished whose light still travels
> the spaces,
> Seen in its form by men, but itself goes phantom-like fleeting
> Void and null and dark through the uncaring infinite vastness,
> So now he seemed to the sight that sees all things from the Real.[76]

Troy is already a doomed city; when Deiphobus hastens through the streets he is "a gleaming husk but empty", a corpse, although he doesn't know it; he is like the light of a star "long extinguished". Mr Sethna comments as follows on this simile: "It is a question whether in the entire range of similes there has been one so grandly apt and penetrating, so cosmic in its beauty and its glimpse of the supra-terrestrial."[77] Deiphobus appears "brilliant" to the men of Troy, but to the gods he is a dead man in a doomed city; the appearance belies the reality; the petty terrestrial drama is the echo of a voice hushed already. In one tremendous simile Deiphobus and Troy are presented both in Time and in Eternity. Behind man and his pigmy insignificance and inescapable mortality there looms, massive and sombre, the figure of ominous Doom. The verse, too, with its succession of five dactyls capped by a trochee—instead of the five dactyls followed by a spondee in Homer—has a majestic falling rhythm, while the range of modulations gives the verse a certain natural mobility and grace.

While the hexameter is in the main an epic measure and needs a corresponding amplitude for the language or rhythm to "rise to any great heights or reach out into revealing largenesses",[78] there are other classical metrical forms—about half a dozen of them at least—that Sri Aurobindo thinks can be suitably transplanted into English. Some of his short experiments on these lines are also among his very best. Here the rather novel rhythm and the distinct inspiration seem to fuse to high creative purpose and one feels almost that "a wide field to the large and opulent estate of English poetry" has been opened by Sri Aurobindo. Thus *Ocean Oneness* is in alcaics, *Trance of Waiting* is in elegiacs with rhyme in the pentameter, *Soul in the Ignorance* in dactylic tetrameter, and *The Lost Boat* in ionic a minore pentameter with an overflow of one short syllable. *Descent* in Sapphics is justly admired as being in, "the best of Pindar's style and Sappho's…coloured by a mystical experience of the 'overhead' type."[79] Here are two out of its seven marvellous stanzas:

> Swiftly, swiftly crossing the golden spaces
> Knowledge leaps, a torrent of rapid lightnings;
> Thoughts that left the Ineffables's flaming mansions,
> Blaze in my spirit…
>
> Mind and heart and body, one harp of being,
> Cry that anthem, finding the notes eternal,—
> Light and might and bliss and immortal wisdom
> Clasping forever. [80]

In *Ascent*, however, the human soul is exhorted to pass into the silence and presently to pass beyond the silence; here the movement is dactylic though there is no rigid metrical scheme:

> Outclimbing the summits of Nature,
> Transcending and uplifting the soul of the finite,
> Rise with the world in thy bosom
> O Word gathered into the heart of the Ineffable.[81]

What is probably the most astonishing of Sri Aurobindo's short poems, *Thought the Paraclete* is in modified hendeca-syllabics, remotely reminiscent of Catullus. In the Aurobindonian version, the ten syllables in the line are made up of a trochee, followed by a spondee, a dactyl, a trochee again, and a final long. The idea behind the poem is that, as human thought (which is man's mediator or paraclete between earth and the beyond) rises from the mental to the overhead planes, it becomes successively higher thought, illumined thought, intuitive thought, overmental thought, and so, ever climbing higher still and higher, vanishes into the transcendental. First, thought rises above the vital and mental planes:

> As some bright archangel in vision flies
> Plunged in dream-caught spirit immensities,
> Past the long green crests of the seas of life,
> Past the orange skies of the mystic mind
> Flew my thought self-lost in the vasts of God.[82]

An inspired opening: like an archangel winging homeward to God, *my* Thought raced beyond the *green seas* (the vital) and the *orange skies* (the mental horizons) and plunged into the *vasts of God* (the overhead planes of consciousness). The next movement covers the planes upto the Overmind:

> Sleepless wide great glimmering wings of wind
> Bore the gold-red seeking of feet that trod
> Space and Time's mute vanishing ends. The face
> Lustred, pale-blue-lined of the hippogriff,

Eremite, sole, daring the bournless ways,
Over world-bare summits of timeless being
Gleamed; the deep twilights of the world-abyss
Failed below. Sun-realms of supernal seeing,
Crimson-white mooned oceans of pauseless bliss
Drew its vague heart-yearning with voices sweet.

Through suggestive imagery and symbolism Sri Aurobindo has tried here to objectify what must, after all, defy such attempts. The key words —'wings of wind', 'gold-red', 'the face lustred…gleamed', 'sun-realms of supernal seeing'—make a chain of significant advance and indicate the flight through the worlds of Illumined Mind, Intuitive Mind, and Overmind. The hippogriff, the "fabulous griffin-like creature with body of horse",[83] naturally calls to our mind the Aswins of the Veda rising upward in the "wide-shinings of the Dawn"; and since the hippogriff is also a winged creature, it is seen affiliated to the *haṁsa,* the golden-winged swans that carry the Aswins to their goal of liberation and realisation. Sri Aurobindo has, however, conceded that, "these lines have not the vivid and forceful precision of the opening and the close and are less pressed home", though he has also maintained that, albeit rather vaguely, "the description is true, the epithets hit the reality and even the colours…are faithful to experience."[84] The third movement in the poem describes the climbing of the Everest of the Supermind and daring beyond it and disappearing in the transcendent:

Hungering, large-souled to surprise the unconned
Secrets white-fire-veiled of the last Beyond,
Crossing power-swept silences rapture-stunned,
Climbing high far ethers eternal-sunned,
Thought the great-winged wanderer paraclete
Disappeared slow-singing a flame-word rune.
Self was left, lone, limitless, nude, immune. [85]

The limited ego is dead, but the self is lost in the Self, zero has become infinity.

VII

SAVITRI: FIVE-FOLD AIM BEHIND ITS COMPOSITION

We come now, at long last, to *Savitri*. It is clear that Sri Aurobindo, in writing this colossal poem, had a five-fold aim. In the first place, he wished to write a modern epic, retelling the legendary story of Savitri with an epic amplitude and sweep. In the second place, he wished to write a poem that would at the same time be also a Manual of Yoga, embodying stairs and spirals of spiritual aspiration, involving trials and struggles, doubts and difficulties, but culminating in the summits and high-mountain lakes of spiritual victory and realisation; the poem was thus to comprise both the toil and the reward, the human effort to transcend humanity and the final blissful realisation, the manifestation, of the Divine. In the third place, *Savitri* was to be a cosmic epic, its human action symbolising the cosmic action, the visible terrestrial drama symbolising the total cosmic drama of the *lila* or ecstatic play of the Lord; this really meant translating into poetic terms the massive dialectic of *The Life Divine*. In the fourth place, Sri Aurobindo wished to make *Savitri*, a foretaste of the 'future poetry', the poetry of the overhead planes, the poetry that crystallises at auspicious moments into the mantra. Finally Sri Aurobindo wished to reproduce in *Savitri* something of the Valmikian, Upanishadic and Kalidasian verse movement; in other words, to evolve a blank verse movement that would strive to combine a Sanskritic clarity and purity with a Vedic manifoldness in meaning. It was to be a legend and a symbol, an experiment and an experience, a poetic philosophy and a yoga manual.

Sri Aurobindo's aims and hopes find candid expression in his correspondence:

> In the new form it will be a sort of poetic philosophy of the Spirit and of Life...[86]

> ...it expresses or tries to express a total and many-sided vision and experience of all the planes of being and their action upon each other. [87]
>
> *Savitri* is an experiment in mystic poetry, spiritual poetry cast into a symbolic figure...it is really a new attempt and cannot be hampered by old ideas of technique except when they are assimilable...' [88]
>
> I was not seeking for originality but for truth and the effective poetical expression of my vision...What I am trying to do everywhere in the poem is to express exactly something seen, something felt or experienced... [89]
>
> *Savitri* is the record of a seeing, of an experience which is not of the common kind and is often very far from what the general human mind sees and experiences...there must be a new extension of consciousness and aesthesis to appreciate a new kind of mystic poetry. Moreover if it is really new in kind, it may employ a new technique...new in some or many of its elements.[90]
>
> ...if I have not poetical genius, at least I can claim a sufficient, if not an infinite capacity for painstaking...for waiting and listening for the true inspiration and rejecting all that fell short of it... [91]
>
> But this (a spiritual vision such as that of the Vedantin arriving beyond the world towards the Ineffable) is not what *Savitri* has to say or rather it is only a small part of it and, even so, bound up with a cosmic vision and an acceptance of the world... [92]

The cardinal fact, then, is that Sri Aurobindo has *seen* something, experienced something, so vividly that, although many-splendoured, it is a living vision to him; this 'mystic' experience has comprised life and spirit, the world, the cosmos and the transcendent, and it is therefore a total, if also a many-sided, vision; the epic, *Savitri*, is an attempt both to retell an old story and to record in symbolic terms this experience, to project this vision, to interpret it in terms of philosophy; this being so unusual a theme and Sri Aurobindo's aim being so out of the ordinary, he has had, wherever necessary, to resort to new poetic techniques, and especially he has had to forge an overhead aesthesis as the main instrument of his poetic expression. He has had to wait and listen to the voice from above, the voice that can alone rightly interpret the beatific vision and find the right words and rhythm for its projection in a poetic form.

VIII

THE BASIS OF *SAVITRI*: SRI AUROBINDO'S YOGA

What was it that Sri Aurobindo *experienced*, what was it that he *saw*, what was the nature of the *realisations* that he later tried to record in prose and in verse? It is usual to call these yogic experiences. The word 'yoga' evidently comes from the same root as *jungo* in Latin, to unite; and the aim of yoga is to effect the union between the one (the individual) and the many (the All). This sense of union can come in many ways. It may come as an experience of intimate partnership, father-son or lover-beloved relationship; it may come as the experience of a personal God, of an aspect of God (Peace, Power, Silence), of identity with Brahman (I am He), or of utter dissolution in nirvana. The Scripture says: "Know ye not that ye are a temple of God, and that the Spirit of God dwelleth in you?" [93] God is within:

> The heavens are still—no sound.
> Where then shall God be found?
> Seek not in the distant skies:
> In man's own heart He lies. [94]

It is always a question of exceeding the limited human nature and growing into the Truth, the Right, the Vast. Man is at the meeting point of the physical and the metaphysical, and sums up in himself all physical nature and all the possibilities of angelic or divine nature.

The spiritual problem is to realise these possibilities. The mystic Jan Van Ruysbroeck says:

> He who seeks that gift to light him
> Must rise beyond his nature,
> To the highest height of being...
> Through his soul will flow
> The light of heavenly truth
> And he in it shall vanish... [95]

Another mystic, Plotinus, describes as follows his own experience:

> Often I have woken up out of the body to myself and I have entered into myself, going out from all other things. I have seen a beauty wonderfully great...I have lived to the full the best life and come to identity with the Divine. Set firm in It I have come to That Supreme Actuality, setting myself above all else in the realm of *Nous*... [96]

The battle is joined, and the aim is to transcend the tyranny of the material world, to go out "from all other things", to race beyond the bars of mere empirical knowledge. The *Rig Veda* declares: *Pādosya viśvā bhūtāni tripādasyāmṛtaṁ divi*; in other words, but a quarter of man the *Purusha* is in the apparent world, the remaining three quarters subsist above as Immortality. This assurance, like "the lark's morning thrill of humanity" (in Brunnhofer's words), has been at the root of man's strivings to invade the invisible, to defy his mortality, and to see in himself, "the conscious vice-gerent of God or responsible cooperator with a divine plan and purpose."[97] It is a trite saying that man partly is and wholly hopes to be; what he is, the appearance, is the one-quarter referred to by the *Rig Veda*. In so far as "we are at all", writes C.S. Lewis, "we have, so to speak, a root in the Absolute, which is the utter reality...we yearn, rightly, for that unity which we can never reach except by ceasing to be the separate phenomenal being called 'we.'"[98] These random witnessings and asseverations show clearly enough how, through all the ages of human history, there has manifested in man the desire for transcendence, the thirst for God, Light, Freedom and Immortality.

Sri Aurobindo's own yogic experiences and realisations may, for the sake of convenience, be said to have occurred roughly at four points in his life. No doubt what he experienced suffused his whole life, the Becoming flowed from the Being and returned to It; but these four shining land-marks in his spiritual life have also their particular significances. First came the experience of utter silence and calm and void when, under Yogi Lele's guidance, Sri Aurobindo, early in January 1908, learned in a room on the top floor of Sardar Mazumdar's house in Baroda to fling his thoughts back and create the desert of silence in his mind.[99] Writing about this, Sri Aurobindo says: "In three days—really in one—my mind became full of an eternal silence—it is still there."[100] The experiences of this point of time enabled Sri Aurobindo to, "see with a stupendous intensity the world as a cinematographic play of vacant forms in the impersonal universality of the Absolute Brahman."[101] This basic condition of silence seems to have continued for the rest of his life; that is to say, his subsequent activities—politics, journalism, authorship, etc.—proceeded as it were from the surface, without in any way affecting the deeper inward peace.[102]

Second came, not many months afterwards in his solitary cell in the Alipore Jail, his experience of the omnipresent Deity in the form of Narayana, Vasudeva. As he described his experience later in the course of the celebrated Uttarpara Speech delivered on 30 May 1909:

> I looked at the jail that secluded me from men and it was no longer by its high walls that I was imprisoned; no, it was Vasudeva who surrounded me...I looked at the bars of my cell, the very grating that did duty for a door, and again I saw Vasudeva. It was Narayana who was guarding and standing sentry over me. Or I lay on the coarse blankets that were given to me for a couch and felt the arm of Sri Krishna around me, the arms of my Friend and Lover. This was the first use of the deeper vision He gave me. I looked at the prisoners in the jail, the thieves, the murderers, the

> swindlers, and as I looked at them I saw Vasudeva, it was Narayana whom I found in these darkened souls and misused bodies.[103]

Although the ground is the absolute silence, there is structured above the many-chambered mansion of the divine manifestation *Sarvam khalvidam Brahma*: all is Brahman.

Third came, during the first four or five years of 'silent yoga' in Pondicherry, the experience of the glimpse of the possibility of the descent of Supermind into the earth-consciousness to create the conditions for the manifestation of the Life Divine here on the terrestrial base:

> I know that the Supermind is a truth…I believe the descent of this Truth opening the way to a development of divine consciousness here to be the final sense of the earth evolution.[104]

> No, the Supramental has not descended into the body or into Matter—it is only at the point where such a descent has become not only possible but inevitable; I am speaking, of course, of my experience.[105]

During the seven years (1914-21) when he edited *Arya*, Sri Aurobindo tried to project his vision of the supramental transformation in terms of philosophy, psychology, Vedic exegesis, etc. Presently he glimpsed the Overmind as a great intermediate power between Mind and Supermind and on 24 November 1926, known as the 'Day of *siddhi*' (Realisation), Sri Aurobindo had the experience of the descent of the Overmind, "in the physical, rendering possible the descent of the Supermind in Matter."[106]

As we have seen earlier, Overmind is a global consciousness and power, permitting variety and multiplicity but without denying the underlying unity; overmental activity can have multiple directions, but there will be no wasteful diffusion of effort, for the essential purpose, which is the divinisation of man and earth-nature, will not be ignored. Such was the power that Sri Aurobindo 'realised' through his yoga on 24 November 1926.

IX

PLANES OF CONSCIOUSNESS: STAIR OF WORLDS

The experience of, or should we rather say, disappearance in the unmanifest utter calm of the Spirit thus preceded the experience of the manifest God. Then came the vision of the possibility of man becoming God, of Nature becoming supernature. Last came the realisation of the Overmind, the important first step to the supramentalisation of man and Nature. These experiences, although apparently unconnected, were actually interlinked. The 'earthly paradise' was no mere dream now, but a sure, even if a distant, possibility. The world was to be accepted and transformed, that is, supramentalised, by stages:

> I am seeking to bring some principle of inner Truth, Light, Harmony, Peace into the earth-consciousness. [107]

> My Yoga can include indeed a full experience of the other worlds, the plane of the Supreme Spirit and the other planes in between and their possible effects upon our life and the material world... It is this view and experience of things and of the truth of existence that enabled me to write *The Life Divine*, and *Savitri*.[108]

Since the realisation, transformation or supramentalisation is to take place in stages, the ascending (and descending) planes, the world-stair, the receding inner countries, acquire a necessary importance in the yoga. Ever since his arrival in India from England in 1893, Sri Aurobindo had experiences of a sort—he had become vaguely conscious of "supraphysical worlds and planes with influences and an effect from them upon the material plane",[109] and later he made the "interpenetration of the planes...a capital and fundamental part of spiritual experience."[110] Now this was by no means peculiar to Sri Aurobindo. Planes, ascents, descents, explorations, although they evoke physical realities, have also corresponding nonphysical parallels.[111] It is thus not at all surprising that the imagery of ascent-descent and planes is employed purposively with regard to the mystic experiences as well. As Rufus M. Jones writes,

> The 'mystic way', 'this flight of the alone to the Alone', is described as steep and hard, lonely and arduous, a way of 'ladders' and 'steps' and 'ascents'. The historic 'grades' which divide the 'way' into well-marked levels, or heights of ascents, are the 'purgative', the 'illuminative' and the 'unitive' stages…the carefully labelled stages of the 'mystic way' only loosely sum up and recapitulate the unfolding processes of the soul on its way to God. [112]

In visualising Aswapati as the traveller of the worlds, Sri Aurobindo had not only such mystic or occult stairs or ladders or slopes in view, but he had also examples such as Dante's progress through Hell, Purgatory and Paradise in his *Divina Commedia*, Hanuman's passage through *Brahmaloka*, *Rajatalaya*, *Shakralaya*, *Brahmashiras*, *Vahnyalaya*, *Vaishravanalaya*, *Suryaprabha-Suryanibhandana*, *Brahmalaya* and *Vrisha* in the *Ramayana*,[113] and Gilgamesh's voyage through darkness in quest of immortality.[114] More recently, the Greek poet, Nikos Kazantzakis, in his colossal epic, *The Odyssey: A Modern Sequel*, has made his hero's travels symbolic of an upward movement spiralling towards increasing perfectibility. The Kingdoms and Godheads of the Little Life and of the Greater Life, the Paradise of the Life-Gods, the Kingdoms and Godheads of the Little Mind, of the Greater Mind and of the Greater Knowledge that cross Aswapati's path are no verbal abstractions but occult realities, and Sri Aurobindo has but tried to describe what he has himself seen or experienced. As Sir John Woodroffe writes,

> In the sensible world are a great variety of beings who form a number of orders and grades. These grades form a series, at one extremity of which lies that order of beings whose experiences are the most limited. From this grade upwards to man there is an ascending series, each successive order of which has experiences wider in range than those of the beings of the preceding order.

> Man stands at the head of this series. But there is no reason to suppose that he is the absolutely highest order. In fact he is limited and helped by Unseen Powers, Beings more powerful than he who exist in unseen forms. If what is supersensible in man can exist in an unseen form after death, why not other Beings who habitually exist in such forms? And if these Beings exist in unseen or super-sensible forms, then there are also states of existence or worlds which are also super-sensible and quite as real, if not in a sense more so than the gross world of ordinary experience. Experience reaches up to that of the Cosmic Mind which apprehends the world of universals as they exist in themselves.[115]

From 'inanimate' matter to the Overmind (and beyond): such is the cosmic range, and the human consciousness holds within itself the possibility of extension, above as well as below; there are verily more worlds above and below than are dreamt of in our normal consciousness! The idea of a journey, a climbing of planes, a quest after the Holy Grail of Truth or Love or Immortality, is really no more than a formalisation of an evolutionary process in which human beings are anyhow involved. For, as W. R. Inge says,

> Every one of us, in his short span of life, recapitulates and hurries through the whole gamut of creation. In the nine months before we see the light, we pass through the stages of evolution which in the race were spread over tens of millions of years. And in our upward progress may there not be some dim anticipations of another long period of growth, which the slow mills of God are grinding out without haste and without rest?...We can only know what is akin to ourselves, but there is that in us which is akin to God Himself.[116]

Out of this seeming mire must sprout forth the lotus plant of our evolving destiny, and the mystic bud of the lotus and its full blossoming in response to the sun's rays must be the destination of our journey. Alfred Noyes has sung:

Out of this earth, this dust,
Out of this flesh, this blood, this living tomb;
Out of these cosmic throes of wrath and lust,
Breaks the lost splendour from the world's blind womb. [117]

And A.E. asks wistfully:

Is there still in us
A heaven-descended ray
Of that which built the palaces
Of night and day?
Do our first works, sun, moon, and stars,
Shine on our clay? [118]

There *is* an evolving consciousness, we are acutely aware of it, we are ourselves participants in this drama of evolution; all this necessarily presupposes the involution of Consciousness—the highest imaginable—in mind, life, matter. Often the Truth is veiled. Consciousness is in a swoon; we see and do not see, or are afraid to recognise what we see; as R.W. Emerson once wrote, "Heaven walks among us ordinarily muffled in such triple or tenfold disguises that the wisest are deceived and no one suspects the days to be gods."[119] But the mystics are able to pierce the veil, terminate the swoon, tear away the disguises, and proclaim the truth:

I saw Eternity the other night,
Like a great Ring of pure and endless light. [120]

Eternity shut in a span!
Summer in winter! Day in night!
Heaven on earth! and God in man ![121]

Pico Della Mirandola tells an interesting fable: God took man as a creature indeterminate though of infinite possibility and, locating him in the middle of the world, told him that he had his future largely in his own hands; he could survey from earth to heaven, from heaven to earth; he would have the freedom alike to degenerate into the brutish lower forms of life and to ascend, out of his soul's judgement, to the higher forms which are divine.[122]

There is the natural order which we perceive through the senses and deduce through reason, and there is also the eternal order of the Spirit which we infer in the secrecies of our heart and soul. Worldly-wise people keep these 'orders' apart, but the mystic increasingly runs them together, and by jumbling the categories holds like Blake infinity in the palm of his hand and eternity in a second. To leap over the barriers of the material order, to storm the gates of eternity, to bring God to our midst: these are the mystic's, the *yogin*'s, preoccupations. Some mystics are content with losing themselves in God; others, like Sri Aurobindo, go further—they would bring the heavens down, realise the "Kingdom of Heaven *on earth*—'On Earth as it is in Heaven.'"[123]

It is implied, of course, that always there is a meeting of God's response and man's striving, for without this double movement no creative advance is possible. As Jacob Boehme has declared,

> I did not climb up into the Godhead, neither can so mean a man as I am do it; but the Godhead climbed up in me, and revealed such to me out of his Love, which otherwise I would have had to leave it quite alone in my half-dead fleshly birth.[124]

Sri Aurobindo clinches the point in a sentence: "He who chooses the Infinite has been chosen by the Infinite."[125] It is the Hound of Heaven, and Love is another name of this celestial Hound, that runs the quarry to its ultimate cave of awakening and acceptance. It was this Hound that drove Dante on and on till he came to the immediate presence of God. Such spiritual yearning, such Love, says C. G. Osgood, "is a reciprocal attraction, mutual between Infinite and Finite…As a sense of that love dawns in us by grace, and by the light of our best love for each other, so it increases in us, drawing us upward into a clearer vision of God."[126] Grace is the name of God's love, and a readiness to sacrifice is the proof of man's love, and when the two meet, there is an integration, a spiritual transformation.

In *Savitri* we have a double demonstration of the dynamics of spiritual awakening: Aswapati's odyssey of the occult worlds and Savitri's exploration of the countries of the soul, and the latter is as important as the former. Aswapati's occult and spiritual itinerary is at least remotely paralleled by Dante's, but Savitri's voyage of self discovery is almost unique. Of course, 'upward' and inward' are but physical terms to convey experiences that are supra-physical; 'The Kingdom of Heaven is within you', says the Scripture; and Browning says in *Paracelsus*:

> There is an inmost centre in us all,
> Where truth abides in fullness;

and F.W.H. Myers says in *A Cosmic Outlook*:

> Inward! aye deeper far than love or scorn,
> Deeper than bloom of virtue, stain of sin,
> Rend thou the veil and pass alone within
> Stand naked there and feel thyself forlorn!

Not forlorn, really, but accepting and being accepted in a transfiguring moment by Reality, *becoming* that Reality. "The first part of our journey towards reality," says J.J. Van Der Leeuw, "is the surrendering of our world-image and the turning inwards until we reach the centre of consciousness the second is to pierce through that centre and find the reality which, acting on that centre, produces the world-image in the cave of our consciousness."[127] In essence, this is what happens to Savitri when she journeys into the "inner countries". She discovers her secret soul, and she shares "the Superconscient's high retreat".[128]

Aswapati's *tapasya* and Savitri's *vrata* have undergone a tremendous extension in scope and significance at Sri Aurobindo's hands and become respectively an epic climb comprising divers occult worlds and a dramatic dive or entry into the inner countries of the spirit. While writing the relevant Books in *Savitri*, Sri Aurobindo must have (as already pointed out earlier) drawn largely from his own yoga and also from the spiritual experiences and realisations of his great collaborator, the Mother of the Sri Aurobindo Ashram at Pondicherry.

X

BATTLES OF THE SOUL

The third major ingredient of the epic, *Savitri*, is the prolonged trial of strength between Savitri and Death. In the original legend, Death (Yama) is no villain, no principle of primordial Evil, but a bright God, Dharma himself. In Sri Aurobindo's poem, he is referred to neither as Yama nor as Dharma, but only as Death. Savitri and Death meet by the side of prone Satyavan as antagonistic powers and personalities, and once the issue is joined, they struggle to the bitter end. A battle, whether symbolic or real, whether fought with material or other weapons, between the forces of Good and Evil can be as exciting as, perhaps even more exciting than, a voyage, a quest, a climb, in search of the lost Grail or the veiled God. The traditional stories of Siddharta the Buddha mention a prolonged battle that the Enlightened One gave to the forces of Evil (Mara) under the Bodhi Tree. Mara tempts Gautama Siddharta in various ways, including the offer of a world-wide Kingdom; failing in these attempts, Mara tries force, and fails again and flees with his hosts in disorder. There is a vivid description in Sir Edwin Arnold's *The Light of Asia*, culminating in a nobly articulate passage:

> Stars shot from heaven,
> The solid earth shuddered as if one laid
> Flame to her gaping wounds; the torn black air
> Was full of whistling wings, of screams and yells,
> Of evil faces peering, of vast fronts
> Terrible and majestic, Lords of Hell
> Who from a thousand Limbos led their troops
> To tempt the Master.
> But Buddha heeded not,
> Sitting serene, with perfect virtue walled
> As is a stronghold by its gates and ramps… [129]

Jesus too is likewise tempted in the wilderness after his forty days of fasting; the story of the temptation is detailed both by Matthew and Luke,[130] and elaborated into epic proportions by Milton in *Paradise Regained.* Following in the main Luke's version, Milton gives each temptation its particular stress, and it is not surprising that the second and main temptation—in which Satan offers Jesus all the kingdoms of the world—sprawls across more than one half of the whole poem. Frustrated and exasperated, Satan asks:

> Since neither wealth nor honour, arms nor arts,
> Kingdom nor empire, please thee, nor aught
> By me proposed in life contemplative
> Or active, tended on by glory or fame,
> What dost thou in this world? [131]

Back to the wilderness Jesus is therefore brought, though presently Satan begins "another method", bears Jesus through the air to Jerusalem and sets him on the "highest pinnacle" and challenges him either to stand or cast himself down. Jesus resists even this subtle temptation, and,

> So, strook with dread and anguish, fell the Fiend.[132]

Gautama Siddharta's and Jesus Christ's successful resistance of Mara's and Satan's offensives is rather prototypical of similar struggles presented in ancient and modern literature. For example, there is the description in the *Ramayana* of *Rishi* Vasishta and King Vishvamitra struggling for the possession of the divine cow, *Kamadhenu.* An early Latin poem, *Psycho-machia* by the Christian poet, Prudentius Clemens, describes a battle of Virtues and Vices for the soul, and this would appear to have proved somewhat of an archetype for many a later poem or 'morality', including John Bunyan's *The Holy War*, which is of course in prose. The situation is best described in Brutus' words:

> The Genius and the mortal instruments
> Are then in council; and the state of man,
> Like to a little kingdom, suffers then
> The nature of an insurrection. [133]

Christopher Marlowe introduces in *Dr. Faustus* the good and the bad angel, who strive for Faustus' soul. This theme is capable of endless variation and extension. But C.S. Lewis thinks that, "Seneca, with his imagery of life as a journey, was nearer to the mark than Prudentius... The journey has its ups and downs, its pleasant resting-places enjoyed for a night and abandoned, its unexpected meetings...and, above all, the sense of its goal...this represents more truly than any combat in a *champclos* the perennial strangeness, the adventurousness, and the sinuous forward movement of the inner life."[134]

It is not true in all cases that an *Odyssey* is better than an *Iliad*, a *Pilgrim's Progress* better than a *Holy War*. Besides, as Dr E.M.W. Tillyard points out, by way of retort, "the pilgrimage subject encourages diffuseness and endless episodes, whereas the martial subject encourages concentration."[135] In Sri Aurobindo's *Savitri*, the whole of Part III (omitting only the 'Epilogue'), comprising the Book of Eternal Night, the Book of the Double Twilight and the Book of Everlasting Day, is devoted to the 'struggle' between Savitri and Death. It is a symbolic struggle, but there is implied both a movement in space and a movement in time; and it is the struggle between Light and Darkness for "the soul of the world called Satyavan".

In the Buddha story and the Jesus story, there is a struggle, but the Buddha and Jesus are alike *passive*, and aim only at preserving the purity and calm of their inner paradise against the onslaughts of Mara and Satan respectively. In *Savitri*, the inner paradise, the realisation of her true Self, is the necessary preliminary to her *active* pursuit and worsting of Death; and this she does to rescue Satyavan "the soul of the world". In the Aurobindonian version though not in the original legend, Death plays a role not very different from that of Mara or Satan, and tries to act the sophist, beguiler, briber and perverter of truth, to make Savitri trip once, but all in vain.

Aswapati's Yoga (described in Part I of *Savitri*) prepares the way for Savitri's advent; Savitri's Yoga (described in Part II), which helps her to rear the impregnable fortress of the inner paradise of her true

Self, becomes the essential preliminary for the 'struggle' with Death and her ultimate victory (described in Part III); and the 'Epilogue' describes the return of Savitri and Satyavan to the earth, where they are now to build a new world, and live the Life Divine. Aswapati, on behalf of mankind and the earth, yearns for Light, Truth, Freedom, Immortality; Savitri first prepares and arms herself for the coming struggle with Darkness, Falsehood, Bondage, Death, and, when the struggle is actually joined, stands her ground resolutely and presses advantage upon advantage till complete victory is hers and the battle for mankind and the earth is finally won. Such is the rounded scheme of aspiration, preparation, struggle and fulfilment that is unfolded on the epic canvas of *Savitri*.

XI

'UPANISHADIC AND KALIDASIAN'

"The record of a seeing, of an experience..."; such is Sri Aurobindo's description of *Savitri*. He writes elsewhere: "When you see Light, that is vision; when you feel Light entering into you, that is experience; when Light settles in you and brings illumination and knowledge, that is a realisation."[136] Vision, experience, realisation; Aswapati, Savitri-Satyavan, the Earthly Paradise (the Life Divine): this is the ascending scale. And to Sri Aurobindo, "the path of Yoga has always been a battle as well as a journey, a thing of ups and downs, of light followed by darkness, followed by greater light."[137] It may therefore be assumed that much of what is poetically rendered in *Savitri* is based on Sri Aurobindo's own visions, experiences and realisations. Nor did he (and his spiritual collaborator, the Mother) rely on Faith alone, although it meant a good deal to them, but also, "on a great ground of knowledge which we have been developing and testing all our lives. I think I can say that I have been testing day and night for years upon years more scrupulously than any scientist his theory or his method on the physical plane."[138] *Savitri*, then, is a whole universe of knowledge and experience—physical and spiritual—presented in the dramatic form of a journey and a battle and a victory. It is, in the words of Krishnaprem (Ronald Nixon), "neither subjective fancy nor yet mere philosophical thought, but vision and revelation of the actual inner structure of the Cosmos and of the pilgrim of life within its sphere." [139]

So much for the 'thematic content' of *Savitri*. But the 'mystic' vision, experience, realisation is one thing, its expression in terms of poetry is a somewhat different thing. "The poetry of mysticism", says Evelyn Underhill, "may de defined on the one hand as a temperamental reaction to the vision of Reality: on the other, as a form of prophecy."[140] Of mystic poetry, with particular reference to *Savitri*, Sri Aurobindo writes:

> The mystic Muse is more of an inspired Bacchante of the Dionysian wine than an orderly housewife.[141]
>
> The mystic feels real and present, even ever present to his experience, intimate to his being, truths which to the ordinary reader are intellectual abstractions or metaphysical speculations. He is writing of experiences that are foreign to the ordinary mentality.[142]
>
> The attempt at mystical spiritual poetry of the kind I am at demands above all a spiritual objectivity, an intense psycho-physical concreteness. [143]

Mystic poetry like Sri Aurobindo's *Savitri* demands concentrated attention from the reader. Where it is most articulate it is charged with the overhead afflatus, and the apparent unconventionality may itself be the gateway to the new audience-chambers of revelation. Imagery is frequently resorted to and the idea is often presented in symbolic terms. Fire, lights, sun, moon, sky, stars, colours, sounds of bells, sea, dawn, gold, tree, snakes, diamonds, bird, flowers, fruits, cow, ass, horse, milk, mountain, elephant, lion the *aśwattha*, goat, bull, frog, fish, lotus, swan, peacock, flute, conch, pearl, the cross, the *cakra*, bow, etc., all have symbolic meanings. [144] And it is also the nature of mystic poetry to resort to multiple symbols, linked imagery and mixed metaphors. Above all, as in the opening canto, "...rapid transitions from one image to another are a constant feature in *Savitri* as in most mystic poetry."[145]

Besides the 'thematic content' and the symbolic language, there is the third element in overhead (indeed, all) poetry, namely the rhythm. The poetic line is really the miraculous fusion of idea, language and rhythm, and while we may no doubt desperately try to dissociate and study them separately, they are really the one-in-three, like *Sat-Chit-Ananda*! Of the metre and rhythm of *Savitri*, Sri Aurobindo wrote as follows:

> The structure of the pentameter blank verse in *Savitri* is of its own kind and different in plan from the blank verse that has come to be ordinarily used in English poetry. It dispenses with enjambement or uses it very sparingly and only when a special effect is intended; each line must be strong enough to stand by itself, while at the same time it fits harmoniously into the sentence or paragraph like stone added to stone; the sentence consists usually of one, two, three or four lines, more rarely five or six or seven: a strong close for the line and a strong close for the sentence are almost indispensable except when some kind of inconclusive cadence is desirable; there must be no laxity or diffusiveness in the rhythm or in the metrical flow anywhere, there must be a flow but not a loose flux.[146]

Sri Aurobindo had tried blank verse of the ordinary kind in his early poems, *Urvasie* and *Love and Death* and *Baji Prabhou*, as also the plays (including his translation of Kalidasa's *Vikramorvasie* as *The Hero and the Nymph*), but now his aim in *Savitri* was, "to catch something of the Upanishadic and Kalidasian movement, so far as that is a possibility in English."[147]

The Sanskrit *śloka*, or the popular verse in the *anuṣṭup* metre, has a clarity and edge of its own, a packed neatness and a crystalline power of suggestion; and a succession of great poets—Valmiki, Vyasa,

Kalidasa—have found in it almost an ideal, at least a wonderfully elastic, medium for poetic expression, inexhaustible in its potentialities, rather comparable to blank verse in the Age of Shakespeare or heroic verse (or the couplet) in the Age of Dryden and Pope. It is said that the *Adi-Kavi* (the 'first' poet), Valmiki, was walking on the shores of the Yamuna one morning when he perceived a pair of *krauñca* birds in sportive play on the branch of a tree. Even as he was feeling engrossed in the spectacle of the birds at play, an arrow as from nowhere struck the male bird and killed it, leaving the female disconsolate. Valmiki's humanity felt a deep wound, his anger flashed up for an instant, and he broke out into a curse—but the curse took a rhythmic form. The shock of tragedy and the welling up of pity had produced a sudden tension in Valmiki's mind which sought natural release in the form of the verse which was presently to provide the metrical norm—the *śloka* or the *anuṣṭup*—for his great epic, the *Ramayana.* [148]

The *śloka* is made up of four parts, each of eight syllables, and has proved a fit enough instrument for description and dialogue, for narration and discussion, for the highest poetry as well as the loftiest philosophy. A union of simplicity and strength, of grace and suppleness, is perhaps the chief claim of the *śloka* to unique distinction as a metrical form. The passion of the heroic figures, the agony of a Kausalya or of a Kunti, the clash of battle, the tasks of peace, the climb of philosophy, the revelation of Upanishadic wisdom, the lure of beauty, the enchantment of love, all have flowed into the handy and shining mould of the *śloka.* A passage made up of a series of *ślokas* is no massed Miltonic blank verse paragraph, but a clear-cut bricked-up wall where the unity of the whole doesn't quite obliterate the lines of the brick-laying. Here is a sample of dramatic blank verse from Sri Aurobindo's early (though only posthumously published) play, *Rodogune*:

Was Fate not satisfied
With my captivity? Waits worse behind?
It was a grey and clouded sky before
And bleak enough but quiet. Now I see

Fresh clouds come stored with thunder toiling up
From a black-piled horizon.[149]

Here is another passage, from the narrative poem, *Baji Prabhou*:

Clamorous, exultant blared
The Southron trumpets, but with stricken hearts
The swords of Agra back recoiled; fatal
Upon their serried unprotected mass
In hundreds from the verge the bullets rained,
And in a quick disordered stream, appalled,
The Mogul rout began.[150]

Sri Aurobindo's early blank verse achieved such effects of easy naturalness and nervous sinuosity with little apparent effort. *Savitri* must originally have been conceived as a companion piece to *Urvasie* and *Love and Death*, and written in blank verse of the same kind, with enjambement and shifting caesura and a tendency to form verse paragraphs in the Miltonic manner. Writing in 1934, Sri Aurobindo remarked: "*Savitri* is a work by itself unlike all the others. I made some eight or ten recasts of it originally under the old insufficient inspiration. Afterwards I am altogether rewriting it, concentrating on the first Book and working on it over and over again."[151] The "insufficient inspiration" doubtless covers both the absence of the overhead aesthesis and the currency of the old or "ordinary" blank verse. Here and there, especially in those later parts of the poem to which Sri Aurobindo could not perhaps give the final revision, the verse has still the traditional cast:

The wish to lessen
His suffering, the impulse that opposes pain
Were the one mortal feeling left.[152]

Savitri
Drew back her heart's force that clasped his body still
Where from her lap renounced on the smooth grass
Softly it lay, as often before in sleep
When from their couch she rose in the white dawn
Called by her daily tasks…[153]

On the other hand, there is no mistaking the sound of the new rhythm. In the projection of this blank verse which is Kalidasian not Miltonic-the syllabic energy is discharged, not continuously as in the above passages, but in linear quanta, in discrete bundles of about ten syllables as in

> Thus trapped in the gin of earthly destinies,
> Awaiting her ordeal's hour abode,
> Outcast from her inborn felicity,
> Accepting life's obscure terrestrial robe,
> Hiding herself even from those she loved,
> The godhead greater by a human fate. [154]

Each line stands almost by itself, and the series of six lines making a complete grammatical sentence moves with a graceful and dignified gait that is characteristic of poise and maturity and strength. In the following passage, however, we have a succession of 1, 1, 1, 1, 2, 1, 2, 4 line quanta respectively, the result being that there is a gradual heightening of expectancy and a mounting up of the rhythmic tension:

> A combatant in silent dreadful lists,
> The world unknowing, for the world she stood:
> No helper had she save the Strength within;
> There was no witness of terrestrial eyes;
> The Gods above and Nature sole below
> Were the spectators of that mighty strife.
> Around her were the austere sky-pointing hills,
> And the green murmurous broad deep-thoughted woods
> Muttered incessantly their muffled spell.
> A dense magnificent coloured self-wrapped life
> Draped in the leaves' vivid emerald monotone
> And set with chequered sunbeams and blithe flowers
> Immured her destiny's secluded scene. [155]

The first line states with utter succinctness that Savitri is a 'combatant'; the next line has a caesura which cuts the line into two, signifying thereby the 'dreadful lists'; then follow two more single lines of neat self-sufficiency and pointed brevity; the next two lines go together, and already the 'Gods above' and 'Nature' below are implicated in the drama; a single line, and two more lines, follow and these colourfully draw out the meaning of the word 'Nature'; now comes like a flood a four-line unit of verse which brilliantly fuses the imagery of Nature with Savitri's own purposive solitariness and strength. That such blank verse is Sanskritic and Kalidasian rather than Shakespearian or Miltonic does not make it a less elastic or less powerful instrument of poetic expression.

Professor Vivian de Sola Pinto has drawn my attention to the marked resemblance between Tennyson's blank verse at its best and the verse of *Savitri*. Writing of Tennyson in *The Future Poetry*, Sri Aurobindo remarked:

> There has been no more consummate master of the language, and this mastery is used with a careful, sure and unfailing hand. Whatever has to be expressed, whether it be of considerable, mediocre or no worth, is yet given a greater than its intrinsic value by a power of speech which without any such remarkable or astonishing energy as would excite or exalt the mind or disturb it from a safe acquiescence and a luxurious ease of reception, has always a sufficient felicity, curiously worked even when it affects simplicity, but with a chastened if not quite chaste curiosity... This art is that of a master craftsman, a goldsmith, silversmith, jeweller of speech and substance with much of the decorative painter in his turn...The spirit is not filled, but the outer aesthetic mind is caught and for a time held captive...His art suffers from the excess of value of form over value of content...He has left his stamp on the language and has given starting-points and forms for poets of a rarer force to turn to greater uses and pass beyond them to a new construction. [156]

A strictly judicial appraisement which notes the merits as well as the defects of Tennyson's verse, and notes too its limitations and possibilities. There is a sufficiency and beauty in the opening lines of *Tithonus*:

> The woods decay, the woods decay and fall,
> The vapours weep their burthen to the ground,
> Man comes and tills the field and lies beneath,
> And after many a summer dies the swan.

In *Oenone*, again, the verse moves smoothly in easy regular steps suggesting a superficial adequacy and fullness of articulation:

> O mother Ida, many-fountain'd Ida,
> Dear mother Ida, hearken ere I die.
> I waited underneath the dawning hills,
> Aloft the mountain lawn was dewy dark,
> And dewy dark aloft the mountain pine:
> Beautiful Paris, evil-hearted Paris,
> Leading a jet-black goat white-horn'd, white-hooved,
> Came up from ready Simosis all alone.

Morte d'Arthur has "some natural magic and vision", and the verse often has a taut quality, a noble clarity of utterance:

> And if indeed I cast the brand away,
> Surely a precious thing, one worthy note,
> Should thus be lost forever from the earth,
> Which might have pleased the eyes of many men.
> What good should follow this, if this were done?
> What harm undone? deep harm to disobey,
> Seeing obedience is the bond of rule...

But even at its best, the spirit is not quite filled, the content is not quite adequate, to the mould, and there is therefore—especially when Tennyson's verse is taken in long stretches—an impression of thinness, artificiality and mere prettiness. But Sri Aurobindo evidently found the Tennysonian mould itself useful, and his "starting-points and forms" helpful, and has turned them to greater uses and achieved a wholly "new construction" in *Savitri*.

The danger to all verse—and not least to blank verse of this kind—is monotony, which can be death. But Pope's verse, for all its 'correctness' and symmetry and geometrical patterning, seldom fails to tingle with life, even life with a touch of fiendishness or ferocity. To dismiss any verse as monotonous merely on *a priori* grounds can therefore be utterly wrong. By its effects alone we should judge verse like that of *Savitri*. There are lines that neatly divide, like a typical line of Pope's, into balanced halves:

> Near to earth's wideness, intimate with heaven… [157]
>
> Pain with its lash, joy with its silver bribe… [158]
>
> But wisdom comes, and vision grows within… [159]
>
> A deep of compassion, a hushed sanctuary… [160]
>
> A dense veil was rent, a mighty whisper heard… [161]
>
> The immobile lips, the great surreal wings… [162]
>
> Sunbelts of knowledge, moonbelts of delight… [163]
>
> Fair on its peaks, it has dangerous nether planes… [164]
>
> It plans without thinking, acts without a will… [165]
>
> Voices of prophets, scripts of vanishing creeds… [166]
>
> All Time is one body, Space a single book… [167]
>
> Objects are his letters, forces are his words… [168]
>
> Near, it retreated; far, it called him still… [169]

The appreciative comment that Lytton Strachey made in his Leslie Stephen lecture at Cambridge on Pope's neatly balanced single lines with their contrasted pairs of nearly antithetical words also fits lines like the above. 'Earth' and 'heaven', 'Pain…lash' and 'joy…bribe', and similar contrasted or balanced words and epithets give to the lines an epigrammatic edge and finish that bespeak a careful and consummate craftsman in verse. On the other hand, whereas such lines occur in Pope's verse with a frightening frequency, they appear but rarely in *Savitri*, and when they come, the effect is refreshing and most satisfying. Sri Aurobindo realised that what he was trying to do in *Savitri* was new as well as difficult; "You can't take that as a model," he wrote to a correspondent in 1932, "it is too difficult a rhythm-structure to be a model. I shall myself know whether it is a success or not, only when I have finished two or three Books."[170] Since he persevered with the experiment till almost the entire epic was recast or rewritten—and this must have occupied much of his spare time during the last twenty years of his life—it may be assumed that Sri Aurobindo himself was reasonably satisfied with the results of his labours.

A modern blank verse epic in about 24,000 lines, an epic that is a 'legend' and a 'symbol'; in blank verse, not of the ordinary, but of a special kind; and intended to be the living image of a vision, an experience, a realisation: such is *Savitri*. The old bardic story, as we have seen in the previous chapter, has also been conceived by Sri Aurobindo as a profound symbol, perhaps "a symbol of what can never be symbolised",[171] yet as a hint, a promise, of humanity drawing near to the Divine, and bringing the Divine to our midst. What is presented as a logical or dialectical possibility in *The Life Divine* and as being realisable in practice in *The Synthesis of Yoga* is now projected in *Savitri* as an experienced actuality, vivid and inspiring and alive.

It is said that *Rishi* Visvamitra, created by the power of his *tapasya* a new heaven, the *Triśaṅku Swarga*; and the wizard that the poet is creates likewise whole new worlds with the power of his aesthesis. In his own way a supreme lord of language, Sri Aurobindo summons the rhythmic word to his aid, charges it with semantic 'electricity', and out of it builds the Reality he has seen, experienced and realised. The great poet is thus not only the lord of language but also the lord of rhythm and the lord of architecture. The rhythmic unit in *Savitri* is the blank verse line, the iambic pentameter, and this has been likened by Lytton Strachey to,

> ...the Djinn in the Arabian Nights; it is either the most terrible of masters, or the most powerful of slaves. If you have not the magic secret, it will take your best thoughts, your bravest imaginations,

> and change them into toads and fishes; but, if the spell be yours, it will turn into a magic carpet and lift your simplest utterance into the highest heaven.[172]

Added to the inherent difficulty of the blank verse medium is Sri Aurobindo's decision to avoid enjambement as far as possible and to make walls of clearly discernible bricks rather than massed forms of reinforced concrete. The 'subject' or 'thematic content', being removed from everyday experience since it largely concerns the worlds of the occult and the Spirit, raises difficulties in comprehension rather out of the ordinary; and this was at least part of the reason why Sri Aurobindo decided upon this edged crystalline, in preference to the old overflowing, blank verse. The subject being apparently nebulous (nebulous, that is, to the large mass of readers), the verse should be as neatly pointed as possible, making it easier for the interested reader to concentrate, to follow the unfolding meaning with growing comprehension, to persevere hopefully towards a total apprehension of the revealed universe of Reality.

Densely packed yet illimitably suggestive, diamond-edged but also hard as diamond and often as richly brilliant: such is the model of this 'Kalidasian' blank verse which could be both studied in miniature and in the mass. Thus blank verse in *Savitri*, while it may strike the reader at first sight as rather mechanical and monotonous, will be seen on closer acquaintance to have its own characteristic beauty and rhythm. Within the limits of the generally end-stopped iambic pentameter, purposive variation and modulation, assonance and internal rhyme (though this is rare), bring out subtle effects of rhythm that cannot fail to appeal to the inward ear.[173] In *Savitri*, Sri Aurobindo frequently races beyond what is perceivable through the senses, what is organisable by the merely poetic intelligence, and hence he is often obliged, in his attempts to express the inexpressible, to resort to the potent—if also sometimes confusing—language of symbols and images. Evelyn Underhill rightly observes,

> The mystic, as a rule, cannot wholly do without symbol and

> image, inadequate to his vision though they must always be: for his experience must be expressed if it is to be communicated, and its actuality is inexpressible except in some side-long way, some hint or parallel which will stimulate the dormant intuition of the reader, and convey, as all poetic language does, something beyond its surface sense. Hence the large part which is played in all mystical writings by symbolism and imagery; and also by that rhythmic and exalted language which induces in sensitive persons something of the languid ecstasy of dream.[174]

The meaningful core of *Savitri* is the dynamics of the passage from Darkness to Light, Ignorance to Knowledge, Death to Immortality, from dark ignorant mortal humanity to the golden truth-conscious eternal Divine. This 'idea'—which is really idea, movement, action and realisation in one—fills the whole poem, as the ether fills all space and time. Even the epic similes come from this creative forge and reinforce the central meaning with astonishing force.

XII

SIMILES IN *SAVITRI*

The simile, already quoted on an earlier page, that describes the effect on the *yogin* of the mantra, in the context of Savitri's response to the word from Aswapati, is a remarkable example of the 'overhead' poetry; the Word is the Spirit, it is Power, it is creative joy, it is the aftermath of calm as well. The following simile compares Aswapati the pioneer and leader of the human race to a solitary star:

> As shines a solitary witness star
> That burns apart, Light's lonely sentinel,
> In the drift and teeming of a mindless Night,
> A single thinker in an aimless world
> Awaiting some tremendous dawn of God,
> He saw the purpose in the works of Time.[175]

Aswapati is the 'witness star', the solitary spark of Light, in the 'mindless Night' of Nescience. Here the symbol (a solitary star) and the thing symbolised (a single thinker, a solitary pioneer of the race) are explicitly related; likewise, in another simile, the effect of a search-light is compared to the burst of revelation when Aswapati gazes into the misty continent of the 'Little Life':

> As when a search-light stabs the Night's blind breast
> And dwellings and trees and figures of men appear
> As if revealed to an eye in Nothingness,
> All lurking things were torn out of their veils
> And held up in his vision's sun-white blaze. [176]

Not only do the consonants 's' 'st' 'b' and 'l' play at assonance in the first line to rich effect, the imagery itself is most striking; a sudden streak of light pierces the dark, the soul's penetrating gaze disperses the 'siege of mist'.

Again, in yet another simile, the dark-light antinomy is presented by invoking the suggestive symbol of the tunnel:

> As one who between dim receding walls
> Towards the far gleam of a tunnel's mouth,
> Hoping for light, walks now with freer pace
> And feels approach a breath of wider air,
> So he escaped from that grey anarchy. [177]

The tunnel-image is strikingly apt and memorably pictures Aswapati slowly groping his way from the Little Life to the Greater Life. Elsewhere, however, the Aurobindonian simile (or, rather metaphor) luxuriates with many a familiar detail drawn from our 'civilised' life; the veiled *Purusha* is the purblind man, he is the hesitant voyager, timid explorer:

> An expert captain of a fragile craft,
> A trafficker in small impermanent wares,
> At first he hugs the shore and shuns the breadths,
> Dares not to affront the far-off perilous main.
> He in a petty coastal traffic plies,

His pay doled out from port to neighbour port,
Content with his safe round's unchanging course,
He hazards not the new and the unseen.
But now he hears the sound of larger seas...
On a commissioned keel his merchant hull
Serves the world's commerce in the riches of Time
Severing the foam of a great land-locked sea
To reach unknown harbour lights in distant climes...
Or passing though a gate of pillar-rocks...
Steering on the trade-routes of Ignorance.
His prow pushes towards undiscovered shores,
He chances on unimagined continents...
He turns to eternal things his symbol quest...[178]

It is a sustained feat of elaboration starting from the description of the veiled *Purusha* as "the sailor on the flow of Time"; the sailor image suggests the rest, and the whole passage—extending to over a page—becomes a cunningly wrought piece of metaphorical ingenuity in which the experiencing *Purusha* and the voyaging mariner keep throughout abreast of each other.

The effect is hardly different in the following shorter but no less brilliantly executed expanded metaphor:

In the dim gleam of habit's passages,
In the subconscient's darkling corridors
All things are carried by the porter nerves
And nothing checked by subterranean mind,
Unstudied by the guardians of the doors
And passed by a blind instinctive memory,
The old gang dismissed, old cancelled passports serve,
Nothing is wholly dead that once had lived.
In dim tunnels of the world's being and in ours
The old rejected nature still survives...[179]

This is the picture of the hazy clashing confusion of our subconscious mind, and images like 'dim gleam' 'darkling corridors' 'sub-terranean mind' and 'dim tunnels' project this picture before us. Metaphorical language sometimes waxes into sheer violence as in:

> Agents, not masters, they serve Life's desires
> Toiling forever in the snare of Time.
> Their bodies born out of some Nihil's womb
> Ensnare the spirit in the moment's dreams,
> Then perish vomiting the immortal soul
> Out of Matter's belly into the sink of Nought. [180]

A few lines later, describing Savitri's safe passage through the 'valley of the wandering Gleam', Sri Aurobindo resorts to figurative language again:

> All this streamed past her and seemed to
> her vision's sight
> As if around a high and voiceless isle
> A clamour of waters from far unknown hills
> Swallowed its narrow banks in crowding waves
> And made a hungry world of white wild foam:
> Hastening, a dragon with a million feet,
> Its foam and cry a drunken giant's din
> Tossing a mane of Darkness into God's sky,
> It ebbed receding into a distant roar... [181]

In the first line 'streamed' and 'seemed' form a pair of internal rhymes; the current of life is the reality, the clamour of waters is its image, the simile; and presently the rush of waters becomes a dragon, all sound and fury, but signifying nothing in the end.

Imagery drawn from the sea is again effectively used while describing Death's arrogant confrontation of Savitri:

> As when the storm-haired Titan-striding sea
> Throws on a swimmer its tremendous laugh
> Remembering all the joy its waves had drowned,
> So from the darkness of the sovereign night
> Against the Woman's boundless heart arose
> The almighty cry of universal Death... [182]

A magnificent simile that almost sums up Death's speech and its wave upon wave of hysterical megalomaniac affirmation. Death has drowned with a laugh millions of life-enamoured mariners: as the waves strike down the swimmer, Death abridges human life; as the sea roars its defiance, so does universal Death. Sri Aurobindo returns to the imagery of the sea voyage in the passage where he describes how stray thoughts from a cosmic source come tranquilly to Savitri, only to be thrown back at once:

> As smoothly glides a ship nearing its port,
> Ignorant of embargo and blockade,
> Confident of entrance and the visa's seal,
> It came to the silent city of the brain
> Towards its accustomed and expectant quay,
> But met a barring will, a blow of Force
> And sank vanishing in the immensity. [183]

This is a typical simile, the comparison is properly proclaimed, and in true Homeric fashion it is worked out at some length and even with some extravagance ('embargo', 'blockade', 'visa', 'quay'). But, perhaps, the following passage with its triple simile insinuates its meaning with more subtlety and certainty:

> *As if* an old remembered dream come true
> She recognised...
> The mystic cavern in the sacred hill
> And knew the dwelling of her secret soul.
> *As if* in some Elysian occult depth,
> Truth's last retreat from thought's profaning touch,
> *As if* in a rock-temple's solitude hid,
> God's refuge from an ignorant worshipping world,
> It lay withdrawn... [184]

The triple simile is a means of reinforcing the holy hush and secrecy and inviolable loneliness of the ultimate home of Savitri's secret soul, and only such imagery can communicate so ineffable a spiritual experience. 'Mystic cavern', 'occult depth', 'God's refuge': either they are wholly opaque, or they are 'open sesames', 'charmed magic casements' opening on the threshold of Eternity. Three more similes may also be cited in illustration of Sri Aurobindo's mastery of imagery and metaphorical language:

As might a soul fly like a hunted bird,
Escaping with tired wings from a world of storms,
And a quiet reach like a remembered breast,
In a haven of safety and splendid soft repose
One could drink life back in streams of honey-fire,
Recover the lost habit of happiness,
Feel her bright nature's glorious ambiance,
And preen joy in her warmth and colour's rule... [185]

As one who spells illumined characters,
The key-book of a crabbed magician text,
He scanned her subtle tangled weird designs
And the screened difficult theorem of her clues,
Traced in the monstrous sands of desert Time
The thread beginnings of her titan works,
Watched her charade of action for some hint,
Read the NO-gestures of her silhouettes...
As if sitting near an open window's gap,
He read by lightning-flash on crowding flash
Chapters of her metaphysical romance
Of the soul's search for lost Reality... [186]

Then in Illusion's occult factory
And in the Inconscient's magic printing house
Torn were the formats of the primal Night
And shattered the stereotypes of Ignorance...
The skilful Penman's unseen finger wrote
His swift intuitive calligraphy... [187]

Everyday phenomena, mundane occurrences, facts and features in our mental, vital and physical life are thus touched up again, and again, and yet again, to yield meanings relevant to the vast spiritual drama unfolded in *Savitri*. The 'four basic elements' of metaphor have been named as *analogy*, *double vision*, *sensuous image* and *animistic projection*, although now one, now another element, is prominent in the conception of particular metaphors.[188] In Sri Aurobindo's similes and metaphors, however, the double vision is the base, and the rest are ancillary; one sees the two meanings at once, or almost at once: star and thinker, search-light and penetrating gaze, *Purusha* and voyager, and so on; first the double vision, then the corollaries, the ancillary analogies and sensuous images and vivid projections; and the whole complex of ideas and impressions and images builds a picture that delights and informs and carries many layers of meaning.

Middleton Murry says that, "metaphor appears as the instinctive and necessary act of the mind exploring reality and ordering experience. It is the means by which the less familiar is assimilated to the more familiar, the unknown to the known: it 'gives to airy nothing a local habitation and a name', so that it ceases to be airy nothing."[189] A poet like Sri Aurobindo who is engaged in communicating spiritual experiences and truths has a special need for metaphorical and symbolic language, for it is through such language alone that he can sting us into excitement and expectancy, and induce a condition that may prove responsive to the impact of 'news' from God, messages from the Infinite. *Savitri* verily speaks this language, it is heard almost everywhere, and while sometimes one is taken aback, or left rather bewildered, constant re-reading and listening with imaginative attention more often than not clear up ambiguities and reveal the intended vistas of meaning.

XIII

'TECHNIQUE' AND 'INSPIRATION' IN *SAVITRI*

If the neatly and meaningfully balanced single lines in *Savitri* recall Pope, the richly elaborated similies must be conceded to be in the true epic manner, almost Miltonic in their impact though not in their technical organisation. Milton himself thought that the virtue of blank verse lay in "apt numbers, fit quantity of syllables, and the sense variously drawn out from one verse into another." Can it be said that in *Savitri* the 'sense' is "variously drawn out from one verse into another?" Certainly, to judge from the passages quoted above, variety is not lacking, there is free modulation, and even an extra syllable at the end is not very uncommon. Of multiplication of vowel or consonant assonance and alliteration there are numerous examples:

> A hor*d*e of soun*d*s *d*efie*d* significance,
> A *d*issonant *c*lash of *c*ries and *c*ontrary *c*alls;
> A mob of vision*s* broke acro*ss* the *s*ight,
> A jostled *s*equence lacking *s*ense and *s*uite,
> Feelings *p*ushed through a *p*acked and burdened heart…[190]

A series of 'd's, followed by 'c's, then by 's's, and finally by two 'p's, give this passage an unusual opulence of sound. Scarcely less striking are the following:

> A *l*onely sp*l*endour from the invisib*l*e goa*l*
> A*l*most was flung on the opaque Inane…[191]
>
> A *v*anishing *v*estige like a *v*iolet trace…[192]
> Or whirle*d* in a *d*umb e*dd*y of meeting winds…[193]
>
> A beast of *p*rey that *p*auses in its *p*rowl…[194]
> And the fire and mystery of forbi*dd*en *d*elight
> *D*runk from the wor*ld*-*l*ibi*do*'s bottom*l*ess we*ll*,
> And the honey-sweet poison-wine of *l*ust and *d*eath,
> But *d*reamed a vintage of *gl*ory of *l*ife's *god*s,
> And fe*lt* as ce*l*estia*l* rapture's go*l*den sting.[195]

The last extract is, perhaps, the most interesting: here the 'd's, 'g's and 'l's play a prolonged game of hide and seek, and largely account for the cunning texture of the passage.

Admittedly difficult though this blank verse is—a difficulty only rendered still more difficult because of the nature of the subject—and although there are passages, whole pages perhaps, even whole cantos, that in the first instance prove unpromising and intractable, there can none the less be no question what-soever about the overwhelming effect of the verse as a whole or of the beauty and power of numerous passages and individual lines. Contemporary poetry, and more especially poetry like *Savitri* that is largely and professedly a creation of the overhead aesthesis, is only too apt to provoke detraction and it cannot be said that *Savitri* has quite escaped such attention. While K.D. Sethna, an ardent admirer, finds the canto in *Savitri* entitled 'The World-Soul' "a thrilled cry of mystical insight bringing up image on strange yet apt image of some hidden Heart of Hearts which in its many-toned unity carries all experience transfigured into bliss",[196] another critic, P. Lal, has singled out this very canto for particular denigration. After giving two extracts which describe the region of the World-Soul, the critic loftily comments as follows:

> Reading this passage has the effect of a gushy comical experience...The entire game is reminiscent of Roget's *Thesaurus*, where redundant familiars like 'soul', 'spiritual', 'subtle', 'deeps' and 'deathless' enjoy a private tea-party. I see nothing: there is nothing to hang on to...this kind of slushy verse is the most dangerous thing that infects our poetry today...a flutter of pretty epithets is to poetry what corrosive acid is to mosaic... [197]

And so on, as if flogged by a fanatic frenzy. The passage and the canto which provoke this wild onslaught occur almost at the end of the long Book, 'The Traveller of the Worlds', and since the subject is 'The World-Soul', earth's perfect antidote, there the "intimacy of God" is everywhere, one treads on soul-ground, one rises in soul-space, and one experiences soul-joy. But Lal, our critic, is allergic to the soul; he sees nothing, there is nothing for him to hang on to! This is but the expression of the Lilliputian point of view, and leaves the white radiance of *Savitri* wholly unaffected. Commenting on the great Russian novelists, Virginia Woolf says:

> In reading Tchekov we find ourselves repeating the word

> 'soul' again and again. It sprinkles his pages…Indeed, it is the soul that is the chief character in Russian fiction…The novels of Dostoevsky are seething whirlpools, gyrating sandstorms, waterspouts which hiss and boil and suck us in. They are composed purely and wholly of the stuff of the soul. Against our wills we are drawn in, whirled round, blinded, suffocated, and at the same time filled with a giddy rapture…It is the soul that matters, its passion, its tumult, its astonishing medley of beauty and vileness….[198]

Like many others, Virginia Woolf too is not quite at ease in this world of the soul, but she can see that it has its own tremendous reality; she doesn't close her eyes resolutely and proclaim: "I see nothing: there is nothing to hang on to." Answering a similar essay in detraction, Sri Aurobindo wrote: "I was not seeking for originality but for truth and the effective poetical expression of my vision. He (the critic) finds no vision there, and that may be because I could not express myself with any power; but it may also be because of his temperamental failure to feel and see what I felt and saw."[199] A poem that is the result of some decades of creative effort cannot be expected to yield all its meanings at once. Ordinarily we see only a small patch of the earth, only the present moment engages our attention; but a more comprehensive consciousness is possible. A global consciousness, even a cosmic consciousness, is not impossible; our own consciousness is by no means a static affair, for it evolves continually from lower limited forms into higher and more comprehensive forms.

"I used *Savitri*", Sri Aurobindo once wrote to Nirodbaran, "as a means of ascension. I began with it on a certain mental level, each time I could reach a higher level I rewrote from that level…In fact *Savitri* has not been regarded by me as a poem to be written and finished, but as a field of experimentation to see how far poetry could be written from one's own Yogic consciousness and how that could be made creative."[200] There can be hardly any doubt regarding the success of the experiment, and although there is much in *Savitri* that seems 'alien' to the average mentality, approached in the right spirit the poem sheds its strangeness and invites rewarding intimacy. It is truly and triumphantly "a new poetry with a new law of expression and technique."

When, after the first four or five years of 'silent Yoga', Sri Aurobindo decided to launch from Pondicherry the monthly philosophical journal, *Arya*, devoted to "a systematic study of the highest problems of existence", the burden of editorial labours fell mainly on him. The 'systematic' study had to be pushed in several directions at once, and much of the thinking and the writing had to be done by him. As he explained once,

> The spiritual experience and the general truths on which such an attempt should be based were already present to us... but the complete intellectual statement of them and their results and issues had to be found. This meant *a continuous thinking, a high and subtle and difficult thinking on several lines*, and this strain, which we had to impose on ourselves, we are obliged to impose also on our readers. [201] (italics mine)

The Life Divine, The Synthesis of Yoga, Essays on the Gita, The Secret of the Veda, The Ideal of Human Unity, The Psychology of Social Development (now known as *The Human Cycle*) and *The Future Poetry* were the major products of such "continuous...high and subtle and difficult thinking on several lines", and they demand from the reader both intellectual alertness and unflagging concentration.

While writing *Savitri*—or rather while making the final draft of the poem—Sri Aurobindo was really trying to translate all this thought, the essence of it at any rate, into poetry. The spiritual experience and the intellectual organisation of that experience were now to be taken to a further stage; idea was to become image, argument was to become prophecy. "Thinking is no longer in my line", he wrote in 1936, and added: "I don't bother about details while writing, because that would only hamper the inspiration...If the inspiration is the right one, then I have not to bother about the technique then or afterwards...If there is a defect I appeal to headquarters, till a proper version comes along...These things are not done by thinking or seeking for the right thing—the two agents are sight and call. Also feeling—the solar plexus has to be satisfied and, until it is, revision after revision has to continue...the object is not perfect technical elegance according to precept but sound-significance filling out the word-significance. If that can be done by breaking rules, well, so much the worse for the rule."[202]

Having done already all the thinking—continuous, high, subtle and difficult thinking on several lines—that was called for and imposed on his readers too such thinking, Sri Aurobindo was now drawing upon the powers—inspiration, sight, call and feeling —that were more appropriate to poetic expression. Besides he had to wait for the self-opening and proper functioning of the 'overhead' powers, for not otherwise could the spiritual experience that was now the subject suffer translation as poetry. "One has to wait", said Sri Aurobindo, "till the absolutely right thing comes in a sort of receptive self-opening and calling-down condition."[203] He claimed further that he had shown "an infinite capacity" for "waiting and listening for the true inspiration". It therefore follows that similar qualities are needed also in the *sahṛdaya* or the dedicated reader of *Savitri*. The strain of "waiting and listening" involving the sharpening of the 'sight', the response to the 'call' and the subtilising of the 'feeling', which the poet had imposed on himself, has to be accepted also by the reader.

In other words, *Savitri* cannot be read in a hurry; it is a sort of poetic source-book of the origins of the cosmos, a dramatisation of the present predicament, and a Book of Prophecy about the future; and so momentous and comprehensive a poetic relation of events and projection of future possibility demands austere attention from the reader and the strain of "waiting and listening", so that things may be seen with the inward eye and heard by the inward ear. The revelation cannot be total at once, for it is at first like straining one's eyes in darkness; many readings may be necessary; then there is the hint of a clue, the rays of light penetrate the darkness and the dusk, and one gradually feels the enveloping light. Parts of the poem are easier than other parts; the human story, the record of human history, the tale of striving and failure and partial victory, all these raise no serious problems of comprehension; it is the geography of the occult worlds and the drama enacted in the world of the Spirit that call for the special strain of "waiting and listening"; and the whole problem —which is at once a personal and a cosmic problem—is in a way summed up in the wonderfully sustained two opening cantos.

XIV

'DAWN' IN *SAVITRI*

There is no mistaking the vision that inspired, nor the voice that articulated, the magnificent 'Exordium', 'The Symbol Dawn':

> It was the hour before the Gods awake.
> Across the path of the divine Event
> The huge foreboding mind of Night, alone
> In her unlit temple of eternity,
> Lay stretched immobile upon Silence' marge.
> Almost one felt, opaque, impenetrable,
> In the sombre symbol of her eyeless muse
> The abysm of the unbodied Infinite;
> A fathomless zero occupied the world. [204]

The knot of opposing tenses ('was' and 'awake') in the first line must tease our thought for a while till thought itself is transcended. The night is darkest before dawn. The soul wallows in its dark night before it reaches the shore that is Aurora, the Sunrise to Eternity, Jacob Boehme's ultimate heaven. St John of the Cross saw as *night* the journey of the soul to God, for the pilgrim has but the razor's edge of Faith for his road, his starting-point is divorce from the world's claims, and the goal is as yet incomprehensible. Although we have now come to look upon the dispersal of night and the coming of day as a matter of course, to our Vedic ancestors the Dawn was "the first miracle and the greatest revelation the world has ever seen".[205] Usha in the Veda is also Ahana; Usha had her affiliations with the Greek Eos, and Ahana with Athene and Daphne; and these bright goddesses were the harbingers of light, life, beauty, joy.[206]

Throughout the Veda, according to Sri Aurobindo, Dawn as the daughter of Heaven, "...has always the same function. She is the medium of the awakening, the activity and the growth of the other gods; she is the first condition of the Vedic realisation."[207] Usha is thus at once the physical dawn, mental awakening, and divine illumination. On the other hand, Darkness could mean both inconscience and ignorance; and even when the darkness seems most oppressive, "even in the night of earth-consciousness, the force of Agni blazes again and again and with the glow of Usha radiates the light."[208] Night has her temple of eternity, but it is unlit, whence all the inertness, confusion or perversion; so impenetrable is night that it is like a thing opaque; nothing can be seen, nothing can be done; it is like the reign of everlasting Zero. The 'divine Event', which is the manifestation of the Divine Consciousness on the earth, is retarded by the reign of zero-night, but this reign will see the beginning of its end when Usha arrives and awakens "the activity and growth of the other gods". Again and again the issue is joined between Night and Day, and the most oppressive hour is also that which precedes the coming of Dawn and the awakening of the gods of the Day. As A.E. asks:

> From what dark martyrdoms, there spring
> The resurrection and the life,
> The glow within the psyche's wing?[209]

It is clear that the opening canto, even the opening line, is meant to convey in a succinct or quintessential form the meaning and message of the whole poem. Milton's "Of man's first disobedience", the marvellous opening phrase of his epic, at once projects the theme of *Paradise Lost*; so does the reference to the "wrath of Achilles" at the very beginning of *Iliad*. In *Savitri*, too, the opening line carries in itself, as a seed does the tree, the whole universe of this epic that is both a legend and a symbol. 'The hour' in the first line, and 'the path' and the 'Event' in the second line, have many layers of meaning, physical, mental, and spiritual. The temporary darkness that envelops man and Nature is to precede a new dawn and a new day. The bleak hour of Satyavan's death is to precede a renewal of life for him, and the flow of new happiness to him and to Savitri and to their parents. The dark hour of the body's inconscience and the soul's ignorance is to precede a new inrush of Light and the divinisation of man and Nature. The "divine Event" is decreed; the darkness is temporary; the Gods will now awake; Eternity will now meet Time.

That these wonderful opening lines of *Savitri* are surely from the 'overhead' planes will become clearer if we compare with them other earlier descriptions of Dawn in Sri Aurobindo. The fragment, *Chitrangada*, begins thus:

> In Manipur upon her orient hills
> Chitrangada beheld intending dawn
> Gaze coldly in. She understood the call.
> The silence and imperfect pallor passed
> Into her heart and in herself she grew
> Prescient of grey realities. [210]

In *Urvasie*, Pururavas is described as gazing,

> ...into the quiet maiden East,
> Watching that birth of day, as if a line
> Of some great poem out of dimness grew,
> Slowly unfolding into perfect speech.
> The grey lucidity and pearliness
> Bloomed more and more, and over earth chaste again
> The freshness of the primal dawn returned,
> Life coming with a virginal sharp strength,
> Renewed as from the streams of Paradise. [211]

In silence she comes, virgin Usha who is yet 'mother of life', and behind her come the youthful immortal nymphs, decked in morning's gold. There is the touch of the unearthly in both passages, and more is read into the physical phenomenon of day-break than actually meets the prosaic eye; in short, actuality is wedded to romance.

In the more mature *Ilion*, the description of Dawn with which the epic opens is charged with a new energy and force of utterance uniting the Homeric with the Aurobindonian:

> Dawn in her journey eternal compelling the labour of mortals,
> Dawn the beginner of things with the night for their rest or their ending,
> Pallid and bright-lipped arrived from the mists and the chill of the Euxine.
> Earth in the dawn-fire delivered from starry and shadowy vastness
> Woke to the wonder of life and its passion and sorrow and beauty,
> All on her bosom sustaining, the patient compassionate Mother… [212]

Ilion was to describe the course of the last day of the Trojan War, culminating perhaps in the death of Penthesilea at the hands of Achilles, Achilles at the hands of Paris, and the destruction of Troy at night, all to be presented with an Aurobindonian spiritual awareness matching the Homeric sense of imminent doom. *Ilion*, in short, was to be a tragedy, whereas *Savitri* is a paean of triumph celebrating Savitri's victory over Death. This vital difference is brought out also in the opening lines of the two epics. The 'dawn' over Ilion starts an action that is to end at night, but the 'symbol dawn' in *Savitri* leads to a night of struggle and victory, thus nursing in her bosom "a greater dawn". The Dawn in *Savitri* has thus a spiritual dimension in addition to the lower dimensions, and it is the sense of what may be called spiritual space and time, and above all spiritual light, that imparts to the opening lines of the poem an overhead movement and significance. The earth in *Ilion* is a "patient compassionate Mother"; in

Savitri, prone earth awaits "the divine Event", the imminent spiritual transformation.

The 'overhead' level at which the poem opens is sustained over almost the whole of the first and second cantos. The description is neither scientific nor fanciful but poetical and mystical. For example,

> Earth wheeled abandoned in the hollow gulfs
> Forgetful of her spirit and her fate.
> The impassive skies were neutral, empty, still. [213]

This is no scientific account of the earth going round the sun, but an "impressionistic symbol...of a partial and temporary darkness of the soul and nature". [214] Likewise, when Sri Aurobindo writes that "an unthought Idea.../Teased the Inconscient to wake Ignorance", he is not making play with mere abstractions, any more than Keats did with words like Beauty and Truth. "Men have not yet learned to recognise the Inconscient on which the whole material world they see is built", wrote Sri Aurobindo, "or the Ignorance of which their whole nature including their knowledge is built. But it is not so with me and I take my stand on my own feeling and experience."[215] Keats writes in his *Ode on a Grecian Urn* that it "dost tease us out of thought/As doth eternity". Sri Aurobindo writes that a still unthought Idea "teased the Inconscient..." What is dead—or to all appearance dead—has to be tickled and energised back to life. Obscure but potent forces start working:

> Into a far-off nook of heaven there came
> A slow miraculous gesture's dim appeal.
> The persistent thrill of a transfiguring touch
> Persuaded the inert black quietude
> And beauty and wonder disturbed the fields of God.
> A wandering hand of pale enchanted light
> That glowed along a fading moment's brink,
> Fixed with gold panel and opalescent hinge
> A gate of dreams ajar on mystery's verge.
> One lucent corner windowing hidden things

Forced the world's blind immensity to sight.
The darkness failed and slipped like a falling cloak
From the reclining body of a god. [216]

While making an attempt to elucidate his own 'Ode to the Confederate Dead', Allen Tate wisely says that a poem, if it is a real creation, is "a kind of knowledge that we did not possess before. It is not knowledge 'about' something else; the poem is the fullness of that knowledge." [217] An explanation or a paraphrase is no substitute for the poem itself, but it may stimulate appreciation, and help the reader to avoid false trails. Like Tate, Sri Aurobindo too has offered his own explanations of some of the passages in *Savitri*, especially in the earlier Books, and these are invaluable because they show us, just when we are extremely puzzled, the way to the "fullness of that knowledge". In defence of the double adjective 'slow miraculous' in the second line above, Sri Aurobindo cited Shakespeare's:

Wilt thou upon the *high and giddy* mast
Seal up the shipboy's eyes and rock his brains
In cradle of the *rude imperious surge*;

and as regards the line itself, with its obvious overhead charge of meaning and flow of rhythm, he wrote: "The 'gesture' must be 'slow miraculous'…it is the combination that renders the exact nature of the mystic movement, with the 'dimly came' supporting it, so that 'gesture' is not here a metaphor, but a thing actually done." [218] In the lines that follow, we start with the 'darkness' which, to give it a kind of symbolic solidity, is called "inert black quietude"; then a series of quick images follow, their cumulative effect being to suggest the falling back of darkness and the splendour of the new dawn:

> There is first a black quietude, then the persistent touch, then the first 'beauty and wonder' leading to the magical gate and the 'lucent corner'. Then comes the failing of the darkness, the simile used ['a falling cloak'] suggesting the rapidity of the change. Then as a result the change of what was once a rift into a wide

> luminous gap...Then all changes into 'a brief perpetual sign', the iridiscence, then the blaze and the magnificent aura. [219]

The whole passage is hard, but it is the hardness of a diamond, for the lights flash almost to blinding effect; from night we have made the passage to day, and it is a thrilling and glorious experience. Even the falling of the cloak was, for Sri Aurobindo, "not an image but an experience"; and unless we can feel it too as an experience rather than as an interesting figure of speech, we shall be missing the force and nuance of the passage.

The burst of sunrise fills the earth with beauty; and all earth responds in joyous adoration:

> A Form from far beatitudes seemed to near...
> Earth felt the Imperishable's passage close:
> The waking ear of Nature heard her steps
> And wideness turned to her its limitless eye,
> And, scattered on sealed depths, her luminous smile
> Kindled to fire the silence of the worlds.
> All grew a consecration and a rite.
> Air was a vibrant link between earth and heaven;
> The wide-winged hymn of a great priestly wind
> Arose and failed upon the altar hills;
> The high boughs prayed in a revealing sky.
> Here where our half-lit ignorance skirts the gulfs
> On the dumb bosom of the ambiguous earth...
> Our prostrate soil bore the awakening ray. [220]

The general sense is clear enough, as in Ralph Hodgson's *Song of Honour* [221]; but being emanations as it were of an overhead aesthesis, some of the lines raise difficulties to the ordinary mentality. What is meant by "the wide-winged hymn of a great priestly wind"? To an objection that Sri Aurobindo had transferred the 'wings' from the 'wind' to the 'hymn', he answered that he had done no such thing; the Vedic tradition gave no wings to the gods of the air. 'Wide-winged', on the other hand, was "proper to the voice of the wind which takes the form of a conscious hymn of aspiration and rises ascending from the bosom of the great priest."[222] The whole picture, Sri Aurobindo assures us, far from being artificial or cunningly made-up, was but a complete rendering of the experience that had actually come to him:

> The picture is that of a conscious adoration offered by Nature... The wind is the great priest of this sacrifice of worship, his voice rises in a conscious hymn of aspiration, the hills offer themselves with the feeling of being an altar of the worship, the trees lift their high boughs towards heaven as the worshippers, silent figures of prayer, and the light of the sky into which their boughs rise reveals the Beyond towards which all aspires. [223]

But the hard earth-crust is still an "anguished and precarious field of toil", which now receives the awakening ray that is both of the Sun and of the new Truth-Consciousness. Even the earth—frail and foul clay, as Hopkins calls it—agreeably responds to the revealing light; and this too is but a faithful transcription of Sri Aurobindo's own experiences at various times. [224]

XV

SAVITRI: HER POWER AND PERSONALITY

Gods and men and all Nature awake with the Dawn, and Savitri awakes too on this day of all days "when Satyavan must die". She is burdened by the foreknowledge about her Satyavan's fate, but she would share the burden with none; she cannot cry, she will not woo despair:

> Amid the trivial sounds, the unchanging scene
> Her soul arose confronting Time and Fate. [225]

The issue will soon be joined, and she must gather force and be ready. And she *is* ready. "All in her pointed to a nobler kind", for she might very well be "the forerunner or first creator of a new race."[226] Then follows a fifty-one line description of Savitri, as uniformly sustained a passage of overhead (even clearly overmind) poetry, unmistakably recognisable in rhythm and language, as anywhere else in the poem. The main effect is to project a divine-human power who symbolises a union of beauty and grace, strength and silence:

> Near to earth's wideness, intimate with heaven,
> Exalted and swift her young large-visioned spirit
> Voyaging through worlds of splendour and of calm
> Overflew the ways of Thought to unborn things.
> Ardent was her self-poised unstumbling will;
> Her mind, a sea of white sincerity,
> Passionate in flow, had not one turbid wave.
> As in a mystic and dynamic dance
> A priestess of immaculate ecstasies
> Inspired and ruled from Truth's revealing vault
> Moves in some prophet cavern of the gods,
> A heart of silence in the hands of joy
> Inhabited with rich creative beats
> A body like a parable of dawn
> That seemed a niche for veiled divinity
> Or golden temple door to things beyond.
> Immortal rhythms swayed in her time-born steps;
> Her look, her smile awoke celestial sense
> Even in earth-stuff, and their intense delight
> Poured a supernal beauty on men's lives.
> A wide self-giving was her native act…
> A deep of compassion, a hushed sanctuary,
> Her inward help unbarred a gate in heaven;
> Love in her was wider than the universe,
> The whole world could take refuge in her single heart...
> At once she was the stillness and the word,
> A continent of self-diffusing peace,
> An ocean of untrembling virgin fire:
> The strength, the silence of the gods were hers. [227]

There are other descriptions of Savitri, in other contexts, and

A. B. Purani has brought them all together in his valuable study.[228] There is, in the first place, the promise of a daughter to Aswapati:

> A music of griefless things shall weave her charm;
> The harps of the Perfect shall attune her voice,
> The streams of Heaven shall murmur in her laugh,
> Her lips shall be the honeycombs of God,
> Her limbs his golden jars of ecstasy,
> Her breasts the rapture-flowers of Paradise... [229]

There is, then, Aswapati's vision of full-grown virgin Savitri, who suddenly appears to him a goddess rather than a human being, an unearthly splendour of beauty rather than the daughter he had known and loved:

> There came the gift of a revealing hour...
> Annulled were the transient values of the mind,
> The body's sense renounced its earthly look,
> Immortal met immortal in their gaze...
> He saw through the familiar cherished limbs
> The great and unknown spirit born his child. [230]

The most impassioned description, however, is that by *Rishi* Narad when he sees Savitri returning after her meeting with Satyavan. Her eyes glow with the enchantment of love, she is the bride, the flame-born. Homer's Helen enslaves with her beauty Priam himself and all the Trojan elders; here, in Sri Aurobindo's poem, Savitri casts a spell on Narad the immaculate *Rishi* and celestial Bard! He flings on her "his vast immortal look", yet reins back knowledge and yields to the wonder of the moment:

> What feet of gods, what ravishing flutes of heaven
> Have thrilled high melodies round, from near and far
> Approaching through the soft and revelling air,
> Which still surprised thou hearest? They have fed
> Thy silence on some red strange-ecstasied fruit
> And thou hast trod the dim moon-peaks of bliss...[231]

There is also the great scene in the last canto of 'The Book of the Double Twilight' where Savitri assumes her *viśvarūpa* "in a flaming moment of apocalypse":

> Her forehead's span vaulted the Omniscient's gaze,
> Her eyes were two stars that watched the universe...
> Eternity looked into the eyes of Death.
> And Darkness saw God's living Reality. [232]

Savitri the redeemer, as the Supreme promised to fashion her; Savitri the flame-virgin, as her father glimpsed her; Savitri transfigured by Love, as *Rishi* Narad saw her; and Savitri, the body of the living Truth, showing Death his place at last: these are magnificent evocations, each striking and memorable in its own way. But the description of Savitri as she awakes on the fateful morning, self-poised with self-gathered force ready for the mortal challenge that is to turn into "the divine Event", is the apex, the Mount Kailas of the poem. It is when we read passages of sustained spiritual glow like the description of the 'Symbol Dawn' or of Savitri when as the World-Mother she, the young Bride awakes on the appointed day to meet and master Fate, that we come near to realising the truth of A. B. Purani's words:

> Sri Aurobindo does not get, as do some other great creators of beauty, intermittent glimpses of the supreme beauty; he seems to have his permanent station on those heights.[233]

If Milton in his 'mighty-mouthed' moments is inspired by the Higher Mind, if Shakespeare in his great dazzling moments of supreme utterance is the poet with the Illumined Mind, if Dànte's poetry is charged again and again with the marvellous revelatory power of the Intuitive Mind, then Sri Aurobindo's *Savitri* embodies the sovereignty of the Overmind and comes to us with the direct, potent and radiant force of the Upanishadic mantra, a sustained feat of poetic recordation never before attempted or achieved. [234]

SAVITRI: A COSMIC EPIC

The distinction of a poet—the dignity and humanity
of his thought—can be measured by nothing, perhaps,
so well as by the diameter of the world in which he lives;
if he is supreme his vision, like Dante's,
always stretches to the stars.

George Santayana

I

THE PROBLEM

An American Professor of Philosophy, Raymond Frank Piper, has referred to *Savitri* as "probably the greatest epic in the English language" and has also ventured the judgment that, "...it is the most comprehensive, integrated, beautiful, and perfect cosmic poem ever composed. It ranges symbolically from a primordial cosmic void, through earth's darkness and struggles, to the highest realms of supramental spiritual existence, and illumines every important concern of man, through verse of unparalleled massiveness, magnificence, and metaphorical brilliance...*Savitri* is perhaps the most powerful artistic work in the world for expanding man's mind towards the Absolute."[1] *Savitri* is a great epic, probably the greatest in the English language; it has a cosmic range and comprehension, and a beautiful and perfect articulation; and its effect on the reader is to expand his mind "towards the Absolute".

These are large claims which deserve to be carefully weighed and considered. Are epics possible at all in the modern world? Can we really describe *Savitri* as an epic? How does it compare with some of the great epics or epic compositions of the ancient and the modern worlds? What exactly is meant by a 'cosmic poem' or 'cosmic epic'? Is *Savitri* the last word yet in presenting in poetical terms the cosmic drama of the struggle between darkness and light, falsehood and truth, death and immortality, the drama of change and chance and defeat and victory? Does *Savitri* hew with the inevitability of art pathways to the Absolute, projecting before us the 'Divine Comedy' of the "yearnings and battles of mankind for eternal life", culminating in the victory, the certainty of "a greater dawn"?

II

EPICS, ANCIENT AND MODERN

"The epic in general, ancient and modern", writes C. M. Gayley, "may be described as a dispassionate recital in dignified rhythmic narrative of a momentous theme or action fulfilled by heroic characters and supernatural agencies under the control of a sovereign destiny. The theme involves the political or religious interests of a people or of mankind; it commands the respect due to popular tradition or to traditional ideals. The poem awakens the sense of the mysterious, the awful, and the sublime; through perilous crises it uplifts and calms the strife of frail humanity." [2] This is the greatest common measure of the epics, for whatever its origin, it is nothing if not a narrative poem involving heroic, even supernatural, actions and characters, sustained by tradition, implicated in the life-ways of the people, and enveloped in the aura of the unusual, the awful, and the sublime.

But there *is* a difference between the 'authentic' epics, the so-called communal or folk epics, the epics of tradition, on the one hand, and the more deliberate compositions, on the other, of a later day. Among the former are the *Iliad* and the *Odyssey*, *the Song of Roland*, *Beowulf*, and the Asiatic *Gilgamesh*; and among the latter, the *Aeneid*, the *Divina Commedia* (if it could be called an epic), Camoens' *Os Lusiadas*, *Paradise Lost*, and *Mahākāvya*s in Sanskrit like the *Raghuvamsa* of Kalidasa. Something is lost, and something is gained. The change is significant, but no more significant than the change from the Heroic Age to the more recent period of sophistication and organised civilisation. The old epics were evidently recited before groups of appreciative listeners, but the 'literary' epics are read more often than listened to, treasured in books rather than in men's memories. Striking a sort of balance-sheet between the old epics and the new, C. M. Bowra writes: "If the oral epic triumphs through its simplicity and strength and straightforwardness, through the unhesitating sweep of its narrative and a brilliant clarity in its main effects, the written epic appeals by its poetical texture, by its exquisite or apt or impressive choice of words, by the rich significance of phrases and lines and paragraphs."[3] We have as it were passed from the Gir forest in Kathiawar to the 'Hanging Gardens' on Malabar Hill. There is a diminution but also a refinement, there is less vitality, but more complexity.

The two great Indian epics, the *Mahabharata* and the *Ramayana*, however, defy easy description. They are more than epics, they are really called *itihasas*, reservoirs of traditional knowledge from which people can drink deep, and significantly form their minds and shape their lives. Their massiveness itself gives them a place apart: the *Ramayana* with its 44,000 lines and the *Mahabharata* with its 2,20,000 lines, by their very size, admit of an encyclopaedic range. Of course, mere length is no proof of vastness of conception or richness of content. As Lascelles Abercrombie perceptively puts it, "length in itself is nothing, but the plain fact is that a long poem, if it really is a poem,...enables a remarkable range, not merely of experience, but of kinds of experience, to be collected into the single finality of a harmonious impression: a vast plenty of things has been accepted as a single version of the ideal world, as a unity of significance."[4]

In both, but much more so in the *Mahabharata* than in the *Ramayana*, the personal, national and racial perspectives and the human, social and religious slants mingle and fuse to achieve a unity and universality of varied significance. Bowra is vaguely conscious of the difference between the Homeric and the ancient Indian epics, for he says that in these latter "a truly heroic foundation is overlaid with much literary and theological matter";[5] the essential contrast between the Western classical epics and the great Indian epics, however, goes rather deeper, though on the surface there is considerable similarity as well:

> These epics are...a highly artistic representation of intimate significances of life, the living presentment of a strong and noble thinking, a developed ethical and aesthetic mind and a high social and political ideal, *the ensouled image of a great culture*. As rich in freshness of life but immeasurably more profound and evolved in thought and substance than the Greek, as advanced in maturity of culture but more vigorous and vital and young in strength than the Latin epic poetry, the Indian epic poems were fashioned to serve a greater and completer national and cultural function...[6]

Devout Hindus to this day look upon these poems as scriptures, as *dharmaśāstra*s (Codes of Righteous Action); and the *Mahabharata* is often referred to as the fifth Veda. Together these two epics form a Book of Origins for much of the later literature in India, and classical dramatists like Bhasa, Kalidasa and Bhavabhuti as also poets of our own time like Subramania Bharati, Tagore and Sri Aurobindo have freely taken deep draughts from this veritable Ganga-Yamuna confluence of the great Indian epic tradition.

The literary epics from the days of Virgil in Europe and since the days of Kalidasa in India have carved no mean territory for themselves in the 'realms of gold'. Not all hill-ranges can be of equal immensity, nor can all rivers match the Mississippi or the Godavari in full and awesome flood. The latter-day epics have many things to recommend them, and they are cherished for one or another reason. Even so the doubt is often expressed that the world has now gone past the age of providing the right stimulus to the epic poet. Lyrics and satires and elegies, perhaps; perhaps, even, tragedies, though only occasionally; but epics—No! Yet, as J. K. Stephen jocularly remarked, genius finds out what it cannot do and then it goes and does it.

The great Polish poet, Adam Mickiewicz, turned history into epic poetry in his *Pan Tadeusz* (1834), in which, "the act of looking back is really a glimpsing beyond the semi-darkness to see the approaching new dawn of equality, justice and freedom."[7] There is Victor Hugo's *La légende des siècles*, which is said to have the true epic movement and quality. There have been other, though less successful, attempts too during the last one hundred and fifty years; and, besides, long poems like *The Prelude*, *Don Juan*, *The Ring and the Book*, Walt Whitman's *Song of Myself* and Bridges's *The Testament of Beauty* have also been sometimes loosely called 'epics', though epics with a substantial difference. And works of fiction like *War and Peace*, *A la Recherche du Temps Perdu*, *Ulysses* and perhaps even *Doctor Zhivago*, though written in prose, make a total impact that is not unlike the impact of epics on us. And what is one to say about a phenomenon like Goethe's *Faust* or Hardy's *The Dynasts*? The *Cantos* of Ezra Pound sets a similar problem: is it an epic, too, an epic still in progress? And we have, above all, Nikos Kazantzakis' colossal epic *The Odyssey: A Modern Sequel* [8] and Sri Aurobindo's *Savitri*. It cannot be the truth that the days of the epic are over.

An epic of our time cannot be exactly modelled on an *Iliad* or a *Mahabharata*; a modern epic must not be a mimicry of a great ancient epic. The 'race' may be essentially the same, but the 'milieu'—especially the climate of thought—must have changed a good deal in the course of the last two thousand years. The present moment in human history is truly pregnant with possibilities, and the poet must be acutely conscious of it all and desire to project his misgivings, his hopes, his nightmares, and his Pisgah visions in the form of poetry.

There are dramas like Maurice Maeterlinck's which shift the focus of the action from the outer world to the inner theatre of the soul, recalling the silent suffering of Job, Harischandra, or the great Prahlad who have defied evil with the calm strength of their souls. Cannot epics, too, be fashioned in the same way? After all, what *is* the 'action' in an epic, or an epyllion, like Milton's *Paradise Regained*? Satan tries to tempt Jesus, tries again and again, and fails. It is what Sir Arthur Quiller-Couch would have called the perfect 'static drama'.

The modern consciousness is obviously different from the 'heroic' consciousness of an Achilles or a Hector, of a Roland or a Karna; they were powers piled up in sheer strength, rather like masses of granite.

The modern consciousness partakes of the complexity of a Hamlet and the goodness of a Myishkin. Especially after the release of atomic power, man holds in his grip the means of complete self-annihilation and also the means of forging a new order of peace and plenty. Humanity now seems to be at the cross-roads of its destiny, damnation and salvation being both within the realm of immediate probability. The great epic poet of today cannot therefore content himself with jousts, dynastic rivalries, campaigns of conquest or wars on land, air and sea. His consciousness must penetrate further, it must boldly and justifiably pursue, in Milton's words, "things unattempted yet in prose or rhyme".

Discussing these possibilities, Sri Aurobindo wrote forty years ago:

> The epic is only the narrative presentation on its largest canvas and, at its highest elevation, greatness and amplitude of spirit and speech and movement. It is sometimes asserted that the epic is solely proper to primitive ages...This is to mistake form and circumstance for the central reality. The epic, a great poetic story of man or world or the gods, need not necessarily be a vigorous presentation of external action: the divinely appointed creation of Rome, the struggle of the principles of good and evil as presented in the great Indian poems, the pageant of the centuries or the journey of the seer through the three worlds beyond us are as fit themes as primitive war and adventure for the imagination of the epic creator. The epics of the soul most inwardly seen as they will be by an intuitive poetry, are his greatest possible subject, and it is this supreme kind that we shall expect from some profound and mighty voice of the future. His indeed may be the song of greatest flight that will reveal from the highest pinnacle and with the largest field of vision the destiny of the human spirit and the

> presence and ways and purpose of the Divinity in man and the universe.[9]

Even as man is purposefully participating in earth's evolutionary endeavour, cherishing ideals and dreams and visions, making experiments, pushing slowly ahead albeit along a difficult zig-zag course, man's creations too—his crafts, his arts, his political and social institutions—move towards these larger horizons of the future. The epics of today need not be patterned exactly on the epics of the past. New moulds, new motivations, a new organisation, a new colouring are possible. What is indispensable, however, is the largeness of the canvas, the height of elevation, the "greatness and amplitude of spirit and speech and movement".

In the course of his illuminating discussion on the 'Epic Spirit', Tillyard mentions the following requirements: high quality and high seriousness; "amplitude, breadth, inclusiveness, and so on"; "a control commensurate with the amount included", in other words "the structural ideal"; and the 'choric' quality, which means that, "the epic writer must express the feelings of a large group of people living in or near his own time."[10] Sri Aurobindo and Tillyard have both, the former succinctly and the latter with expansive elaboration, laid stress on the same qualities; whatever else is or is not there, these are quintessential to a true epic creation.

An epic cannot be a frivolous exercise, only a mock-epic (like *The Rape of the Lock*) can be that, and even a mock-epic generally aims at purging folly through laughter, which is a serious enough purpose. An epic cannot be close and constricted—wideness and largeness are its natural habitat. An epic speaks with a recognisable voice; it may tell us a hundred things but without confusing the main issue, it should be able at once to provoke the play of multiplicity and effectively to control it. Above all, there should be room in the epic for the slow significant rumbling of undertones, for what the Sanskrit rhetoricians call *dhwani*, so that always more is meant than meets the ear. As the centre of the action shifts from the visible outer arena of the battlefield to the mind and soul of man—the invisible promontories, the slippery ascents, the dark abysses—there is increasing need to imply more than to state, to send out waves of suggestion than raise walls of brick.

Even with regard to an early epic like the *Aeneid*, Bowra says that because Virgil, "wished to write a poem about something much larger than the destinies of individual heroes, he created a type of epic in which the characters represent something outside themselves, and the events displayed have other interests than their immediate excitement in the context."[11] Dante himself has explained that he wrote the *Commedia* in four senses: the literal, the allegorical, the analogical and the ethical. When viewed from the outside, it is the description of a journey; it is, in a deeper sense, a survey of states of mind, and, in a further sense, "a symbol of mankind's struggle upward out of ignorance into the clear light of philosophy…In a fourth sense, the *Commedia* is an expression of the laws of eternal justice; 'il contrapasso', the counterpass, as Bertran calls it or the law of Karma, if we are to use an Oriental term."[12] The transvaluation is from the visible to the invisible, from the material to the spiritual. As Stambler says, "Just as God uses the physical, temporal universe to convey to man, by analogy, the existence and the meaning of His universe, so does Dante the poet use narrative-in-time and detailed sense-experience to communicate to the reader *his* universe, a universe which the poet alone could comprehend simultaneously (in all its purposes) as well as sequentially."[13]

From our everyday experience of the space-time continuum we are subtly and surely transported by the power of Dante's poetic art into an imaginative participation in Dante's triple world which is really, in Scott Buchanan's words, "a rather complete integration of several great cultures with all their disparate and conflicting possibilities."[14] A point is reached when poetry must race beyond reason, as it does when Dante the mystic pilgrim feels as if he has "entered a still uncleft pearl", thereby as it were impearling himself. On this

Williams comments as follows: " How body enters body, dimension supports dimension (he says), we cannot tell; therefore we should more expressly long to understand the union of our nature with God's, that is, the Incarnation."[15] The *Commedia*, superficially, is as unlike the *Iliad* as cheese is unlike chalk; but what it loses in one way it gains in another; there is less of the blaze of action and assertion and more of the twilight revelation of inner striving and struggle and achievement.

Of the European epic poets between Dante and Milton, two Italians, Ariosto and Tasso, and the Portuguese, Camoens, stand rather in the forefront. Camoens's *Os Lusiadas* preceded by a few years Tasso's *Gerusalemme Liberata*, and was itself preceded by about sixty years by Ariosto's *Orlando Furioso*. There is more of the *Aeneid* than of the *Commedia* in these epics of the Renaissance. They are serious, they are expansive, and they are indelibly touched by the hues of romance and chivalry; above all, they are Christian in their main inspiration. In some respects, Camoens's epic is the most rewarding of the three. Like Dante, Camoens too—though with different results —acknowledges Virgil as his master. If Virgil sang of arms and the man, Aeneas, Camoens sang too of arms and the men—the men who carved out the Portuguese Empire and won the gorgeous East for Christ:

> The deeds I tell of are real, and far outstrip the fabled adventures of any Rodamonte, Ruggiero or Orlando, even granting that Orlando did exist. In place of these you will meet a valiant Nono Alvares, who did such notable service to his king and country, an Egas Moniz, a Fuas Roupinho, for whom alone I wish I had the lyre of Homer. The twelve knights Magrico led to England are more than a match for the paladins of France, the illustrious Vasco da Gama for Aeneas himself.[16]

It is clear Camoens is anxious to make out a case for his heroes as against the heroes celebrated by Ariosto and Virgil. But what is of particular significance in *Os Lusiadas* is that the scene of action has now overflowed Europe and the Mediterranean, and it is not merely a secular Empire that Camoens's heroes strive to establish, but also a spiritual Empire. "The Portuguese achievement, as Camoens saw it", writes William C. Atkinson, "was part of a great providential design to win the world for the true faith, the ulterior purpose of which clearly merged into God's purpose for the universe as a whole."[17] "They alone shall be my theme", declares Camoens towards the close of the seventh canto, "who for God and king adventured life itself and, losing it, won a larger life in the fame their works have so richly merited."[18] It is already a far cry from the world of the *Iliad*, it is some distance even from the world of the *Aeneid*. Camoens is ready to judge by other than pure terrestrial standards; he can already look a little beyond the unweeded garden that is the earth and see the Kingdom of God that is to be.

III

PARADISE LOST AND *SAVITRI*

When Milton, "long choosing and beginning late", decided at last to make the 'Fall of Man' the subject of his epic, he felt the need for an aggressive defence of his choice and so devoted the Exordium of Book IX to this purpose:

> Sad task! yet argument
> Not less but more heroic than the wrath
> Of stern Achilles on his foe pursued
> Thrice fugitive about Troy wall; or rage
> Of Turnus for Lavinia disespoused;
> Or Neptune's ire, or Juno's, that so long
> Perplexed the Greek, and Cytherea's son:...
> Not sedulous by nature to indite
> Wars, hitherto the only argument
> Heroic deemed....
> ...or to describe races and games,

> Or tilting furniture, emblazoned shields,
> Impresses quaint, caparisons and steeds,
> Bases and tinsel trappings, gorgeous knights
> At joust and tournament...
> ...Me, of these
> Not skilled nor studious, higher argument
> Remains...

He has a theme better in its own way and for his particular purpose than the themes of Homer and Virgil, of Ariosto and Tasso. Milton's ostensible aim is to "assert Eternal Providence,/And justify the ways of God to men." It is almost a theological aim; and he would therefore try to effect a marriage of theology and epic poetry.

"The Story of the Fall", writes Herbert Read, "is merely the kernel, or theme, round which he elaborates, firstly, a dramatic myth, and secondly, a philosophic thesis. Here the epic, we might say, is dominated by an idea."[19] It is not that the familiar paraphernalia of the old-time epics—elements like war councils, battles, single combats, domestic debates, scenes of temptation—are absent in *Paradise Lost*. They are memorably there, yet all these "are so transformed", says Bowra, "that their significance and even their aesthetic appeal are new...Before him the best literary epic had been predominantly secular; he made it theological, and the change of approach meant a great change of temper and of atmosphere."[20]

It would, perhaps, be truer to say that Milton tried to fuse Virgil and Dante, the epic manner of the former and the theological insights of the latter. This meant creating a new style, which is best summed up by the word 'sublime'. Analysing it, Gilbert Highet writes: "It was intended to be grand; to be evocative; and to be sonorous—three different aspects of sublimity, differing only in the means by which sublimity is achieved."[21] The epic casts a spell on the reader with the opening lines, and although one might now and then venture to murmur, the spell continues till the end. Hell, all Hell, the whole of Heaven and entire Earth are comprehended in the scheme of the poem; Milton makes good the promise:

> ...what surmounts the reach
> Of human sense I shall delineate so,
> By likening spiritual to corporal forms,
> As may express them best;[22]

and if, besides, we find in the end that the 'structural ideal' is not seriously impaired, the credit goes, partly at least, to the poetic style, to the power of its unifying harmony.

Highet's pointed emphasis on Milton's style in *Paradise Lost* is by no means misplaced. The hexameter of Homer and Virgil, the *anuṣṭup* of Vyasa and Valmiki, the terza rima of Dante, the symphonic blank verse of Milton, the crystalline iambic pentameter of *Savitri*, all play no mean part in charging these great epics with life and movement and a rounded significance. Ezra Pound makes an important point when he writes:

> When we know more of overtones we shall see that the tempo of every masterpiece is absolute, and is exactly set by some further law of rhythmic accord. Whence it should be possible to show that any given rhythm implies about it a complete musical form, fugue, sonata, I cannot say what form, but a form, perfect, complete. *Ergo*, the rhythm set in a line of poetry connotes its symphony, which, had we a little more skill, we could score for orchestra.[23]

Once the perfect metrical medium has been hit upon or shaped anew on the poet's creative forge, his inspiration can flow with comparative ease, and the disparate epic material can be held together as if by magic. The detractors of Milton's verse notwithstanding, this verse by its blending of beauty and power to the point of sublimity has given us what is to be found nowhere else in English poetry. Hell yawns before us, and chaos presently envelops us; and Satan and Beelzebub and Mammon and Moloch and Belial are vivid, almost apocalyptic, projections.

But there is a debit side as well, for as Sri Aurobindo points out, "Milton has seen Satan and Death and Sin and Hell and Chaos; there is a Scriptural greatness in his account of these things: he has not so seen God and heaven and man or the soul of humanity at once divine and fallen, subject to evil and striving for redemption; here there is no inner greatness in the poetic interpretation of his materials." Even so, it is a failure of vision not a failure of speech or rhythm, for Sri Aurobindo readily concedes that, "rhythm and speech have never attained to a mightier amplitude of epic expression and movement, seldom to an equal sublimity."[24]

Dante's poem 'covered' the triple worlds of Hell, Purgatory and Paradise; Milton's, likewise, sweeps across Hell, Chaos, Earth and Heaven. In these two epics, the scene of action is wider than the environs of Troy, and vaster than the Mediterranean or the great globe itself. We have to reckon with new dimensions and unknown modes of being. While there is thus an immense, an incalculable, extension in space and time, there is also—paradoxically enough—an amazing constriction, even an annihilation of space and time. There is a hint of it at least, though not the permanent, ineffable realisation of it. In the ultimate analysis, the stage—be it Hell, Earth, Chaos, Purgatory, or Paradise—is the human heart; the microcosm *is* the macrocosm.

Savitri may be said to be the third and final term in the series, of which the earlier terms are the *Commedia* and *Paradise Lost*. It is an attempt to, "reveal from the highest pinnacle and with the largest field of vision the destiny of the human spirit and the presence and ways and purposes of the Divinity in man and the universe." In 1920, such had seemed to him the worthy aim of "some profound and mighty voice of the future", a theme worthy of the future song of "greatest flight". It is difficult to say when exactly the idea of making this attempt himself came to Sri Aurobindo. At any rate we find him writing in 1931 with reference to *Savitri*: "There is a previous draft, the result of the many retouchings…"; in 1934 he wrote: "I made some eight or ten recasts of it originally under the old insufficient inspiration ."[25]

It is almost certain it was begun, along with or not long after *Urvasie* and *Love and Death*, in the Baroda period; he might have returned to it from time to time, retouching it here and there; but the decision to transform it altogether—"recasting the whole thing"—must have been taken sometime after 24 November 1926, the 'Day of Siddhi'. The 'recasting' was indeed very thorough. Although his handwriting was characteristic of him (being rather artistic) and he wrote clearly and apparently effortlessly, in his last years Sri Aurobindo too, like Milton, often dictated the additions to his epic to an amanuensis, but would on no account hurry through the job of revision. "What a revision!" reminisces Nirodbaran the amanuensis; "Every word must be the *mot juste*, every line perfect, even every sign of punctuation flawless. One preposition was changed five times; to change a punctuation-sign one had sometimes to read a whole section."[26] *Savitri* as we have it now is the fruit of almost twenty-five years' such intermittent labours, while the earliest draft might take us to a period twenty-five years earlier still.

IV

SONG OF MYSELF AND *SAVITRI*

While it is natural to see *Savitri* as a sort of continuation and fulfilment of the two earlier 'cosmic' epic narratives—*the Divina Commedia* and *Paradise Lost*—there were other formative influences as well, and some of these too deserve mention and even some scrutiny. The primary inspiration flowed no doubt from the fount of his own Yogic experiences and realisations; the 'overhead aesthesis' canalised this rush of afflatus into a blank verse that was Upanishadic in its packed clarity and Kalidasian in its light-glancing unhurried movement; and his sense of structure or power of architectural construction 'contained' the cosmic drama in the old legend of Savitri and Satyavan. But the Yogi and the metaphysician was also a student and critic of poetry, he was responsive to new movements in the world of poetry, and he was not unwilling to exercise, to experiment, in divers poetic moulds and modes.

We have seen in the previous chapter how Sri Aurobindo tried, with not a little success, to transplant some of the classical metres, and notably the hexameter, in the soil of English verse. If the profound Greek and Latin scholar in Sri Aurobindo felt attracted to these tried old classical metres, another part of him felt attracted, with a no less enthusiastic readiness, to a comparatively modern poet like Walt Whitman. Unlike his predecessors in America, Whitman had a giant individuality of his own and when he turned to the profession of poetry, he strove to find his bearings in the cosmos and to express himself and his new-found sense of freedom and power in a verse partaking of this freedom and this power.

Sir Aurobindo refers to Whitman as, "this giant of poetic thought with his energy of diction, this spiritual crowned athlete and vital prophet of democracy, liberty and the soul of man and Nature and all humanity."[27] In an audacious phrase, Sri Aurobindo calls Whitman "the most Homeric voice since Homer", because "he has the nearness to something elemental" and he has, "the elemental Homeric power of sufficient straight-forward speech, the rush too of oceanic sound though it is here the surging of the Atlantic between continents, not the magic roll and wash of the Aegean around the isles of Greece."[28] The magic, the disciplined grace, the unfailing beauty of Homer are absent, but there is energy, there is mass and amplitude. Whitman's *Song of Myself* is an attempt to "embody a universe in the rough";[29] in it the zero-self successfully grapples with and comprehends the infinite universe. Whitman is himself "a kosmos, of Manhattan the son", and at the height of his self-identification with his milieu and his ambience, he declares:

> I see something of God each hour of the twenty-four, and
> each moment then,
> In the faces of men and women I see God, and in my own
> face in the glass,

> I find letters from God dropt in the street, and every one is sign'd by God's name,
> And I leave them where they are, for I know that wheresoe'er I go,
> Others will punctually come forever and ever. [30]

Song of Myself is written in a new kind of verse and it is a new kind of epic; unabashed he announces that *he* is its central figure; but he derives his meaning and his power from the fact of his location in the universe, in the cosmos. "The end of *Song of Myself*", writes Roy Harvey Pearce, "the moral object which synchronises with its poetic object, is to know that the world is there, and in the knowing, to know itself as there; in effect, through such a transaction to create itself and the possibility for readers to create themselves."[31] The chronic malady that man suffers from is the malady of isolation, of feeling completely estranged from his environment, from the universe. To be in the universe yet feel no sense of belonging to it is a misery, or at least the boredom of a living death. D.H. Lawrence was thus right when he said that, "whoever can establish or initiate a new connection between mankind and the circumambient universe is, in his own degree, a saviour." [32]

Wordsworth in his best poetry (notably, *The Prelude*) and Whitman in his *Song of Myself*, in their different unique ways, have thus proved to be mankind's saviours. *Savitri* carries the process a stage further, and the sense of belonging is here included and exceeded by the sense of becoming. Heaven, not Hell, is our rightful habitat; we are required to be in this pestilential congregation of vapours no longer than our decision and determination to change it nearer our heart's desire. We can not only rise to any heaven that we ourselves choose but we can also change this Hell-infected earth itself into any heaven we choose. And when we take such a decision, when we will such a change, we shall receive adequate response from the higher powers of the Universe, and out of this meeting of the heart's desire and the Spirit's response a new heaven and a new earth can be brought here into being. Such, indeed, is the message of hope that *Savitri* embodies in the vast spaces of its symbolic action culminating in the decisive victory of Light over Darkness.

V

THE *CANTOS*

Apart from Whitman, whom Sri Aurobindo obviously admired, though with the necessary qualifications, he was doubtless also influenced as a practitioner of verse by the work of contemporaries like Yeats, Eliot and Ezra Pound. While the extent of the influence might not have been very appreciable, there can be no question about the reality of Sri Aurobindo's intelligent interest in contemporary English poetry. Passages from *The Hollow Men* are scanned in Sri Aurobindo's essay on quantitative metre as examples of the new 'ametric poetry', and once, in 1946, in defence of his use of the French word 'flasque' in *Savitri*, he said that he had done it "somewhat after the manner of Eliot and Ezra Pound".[33] Whether Sri Aurobindo had any close acquaintance with the *Cantos* it is difficult to say; but he certainly knew about this unique 'work in progress' in a general way, and any major poetic intelligence and endeavour is bound to exert some kind of pull on other contemporary poetic powers and intelligences.

A Draft of XXX Cantos appeared as early as 1933, though individual Cantos might have achieved magazine publication earlier still; in the course of the next twenty years came out in succession *Eleven New Cantos*, *The Fifth Decade of Cantos*, *Cantos LII-LXXI* and *The Pisan Cantos*, all preceding Sri Aurobindo's passing away in 1950; since then, two more instalments—*Section: Rock-Drill (LXXXV-XCV)* and *Thrones: XVI-CIX*—have come out. The piecemeal appearance of the *Cantos* and the piecemeal appearance of *Savitri* seemed to run parallel to each other, and even their 'obscurity' seemed to put them—widely different though they were from each other—in a class rather apart. The *Cantos* are evidently still in progress, and perhaps they are not meant ever to be concluded in a conclusive manner. What are the

Cantos about? Can they be viewed as a unity, as an epic, even as *the* American epic?

Two other American poets of our time—Hart Crane and Archibald MacLeish—have also tried their hands at epic poetry. Crane's ambitious poem *The Bridge* (1930) was an attempt to write something at once less personal and less universal than *Song of Myself*—something that was positively, almost objectively, American. The 'bridge' is the single spanning symbolic image that tries, though not altogether successfully, to hold together national myths like Pocahontas and Rip Van Winkle and the visible material realities of American civilisation. Structurally weak though often brilliantly evocative, *The Bridge* is said to approximate to a "highly sophisticated, highly syncopated local epic."[34]

MacLeish's *Conquistador* (1932) is a short epic written in the terza rima, a difficult measure which he handles with consummate mastery. The theme is the conquest of Mexico, but through resolved limitation MacLeish achieves both intensity and concentration; and all is presented from one angle: the emotion and memory of Bernal, the whilom hero (though only one of the minor ones) and the present aged narrator. The centre of interest has been adroitly shifted from the action to the memory of the action, from the tumult of the battle to the awakened private sensibility long after the event. It is said that MacLeish was himself influenced by the *Cantos*, at any rate the first Canto, when he wrote his *Conquistador*.[35] MacLeish would appear to have transferred to the war of conquest in Mexico the modern sensibility—the sensibility that we associate with the work of war poets like Wilfred Owen and Siegfried Sassoon—towards all war and the stupidity and the pity and the futility of war.

To return to the *Cantos*—for it is here if anywhere that the American epic is to be hailed—there can be no doubt regarding its polyphonic richness and its exasperating improvisations. What is the epic about? (And is it an epic, after all?) "The *Cantos* are talk, talk, talk", says Allen Tate, but he also adds: "The *Cantos* are a book of marvels—marvels that he has read about, or heard of, or seen... The *Cantos* are a sort of Golden Ass."[36] Writing again eighteen years later, Tate declared that his views had not changed; the *Cantos* remained "formless, eccentric, and personal".[37] But others, notably Hugh Kenner, have tried to infer the form underlying the apparent formlessness and incoherence. An epic certainly, though a "plotless" one. Waves start and swell and recede and subside and start again; there is a fusion of "logical independence and aesthetic interdependence of successive images", resulting in a new kind of unity. [38] It cannot be that all this poetic chatter and the many sudden bursts of imagery are about "nothing". The truth, perhaps, is that there is not one rigid form but the possibilities of many forms; as Kenner puts it, "a slight change in the angle of cut will reveal a wholly new surface". [39] Kenner's own analyses are very rewarding, especially the 'volitional' cut that reveals a *Divina Commedia* in the *Cantos*—with its own Inferno, Purgatorio and Paradiso.[40]

Nevertheless, the *Cantos* remain, on a first or second or even third reading, a maddening work. It is an important and immense poetic creation, a nodal point in contemporary English poetry. Crane and MacLeish, Eliot and Yeats, themselves considerable poets, have been influenced by the *Cantos* and the Poundian poetics and aesthetics. But there *must* be a clue to this labyrinth, however tenuous, however almost invisible; else the *Cantos* cannot have held the field so long. The opening of the first Canto is masterly:

> And then went down to the ship,
> Set keel to breakers, forth on the godly seas, and
> We set up mast and sail on that swart ship,
> Boresheep aboard her, and our bodies also
> Heavy with weeping, and winds from sternward
> Bore us out onward with bellying canvas,
> Circe's this craft, the trim-coifed goddess.

A voyage, then; Odysseus, obviously; and there is Circe, too. Is it the *Odyssey* again in a Poundian version, perhaps in all the four Dantean senses, the literal, the allegorical, the analogical, the ethical? We return to Odysseus from time to time:

> What have you done, Odysseus,
> We know what you have done... [41]
>
> 'What gain with Odysseus,
> 'They that died in the whirlpool
> 'And after many vain labours,
> 'Living by stolen meat, chained to the rowingbench,
> 'And lie by night with the goddess?' [42]
>
> Knowledge the shade of a shade,
> Yet must thou sail after knowledge
> Knowing less than drugged beasts...
> To the cave art thou called, Odysseus,... [43]

Allen Tate guardedly writes: "Mr. Pound's world is the scene of a great Odyssey, and everywhere he lands it is the shore of Circe, where men 'lose all companions' and are turned into swine. It would not do to push this hint too far, but I will risk one further point: Mr. Pound is a typically modern, rootless, and internationalised intelligence."[44] This is all journey and no destination, this world is all circumference and no centre. But the Odysseus-clue is valuable, although it will not do, as Tate warns us, to pull it too hard, lest it snap altogether. Kenner makes the further point that, even as Tiresias is central to the scheme of *The Waste Land*, Odysseus is to that of the *Cantos*:

> In one sense, the substance of the *Cantos* is what Odysseus sees, as that of *The Waste Land* is what Tiresias sees. The distinction between these two personae gives us one measure of Pound's poem. Tiresias the shade, foresuffering all, is capable only of psychic action...Odysseus, *polumetis*, many-minded, fertile in strategems, is engaged in active amelioration of conditions for himself and his men, involved in factive protagonist in what he sees.[45]

In the first Canto, when Odysseus sets out on his voyage, Tiresias tells him:

'A second time? why? man of ill star,
'Facing the sunless dead and this joyless region?
'Stand from the fosse, leave me my bloody bever
'For soothsay'.
And I stepped back,
And he strong with the blood, said then: 'Odysseus
'Shalt return through spiteful Neptune, over dark seas,
'Lose all companions'.

Is this really a parable of Pound's own adventure with the *Cantos*? Is it Tiresias warning Odysseus, or the Muse warning Pound? It may be both; and it is spoken with the accents of prophecy.

To Pound himself the *Cantos* are no more than "the tale of the tribe", the tale of the American people, the tale of the human race. Antiquity, the mediaeval world, the modern world: the West, the East: fact and fable: history and anecdotage: persons, ideas—all are thrown into these kaleidoscopic patterns of the tale of the tribe. Allusions and echoes both baffle and enrich the understanding, and the jostling together of poetry and banality, esoteric Chinese ideographs and dry notebook jottings, teases us to the point of exasperation. But Pound evidently feels that only through the cultivation of what Kenner has called "multiple foci of interest" the tale of so amazing a species as homo sapiens could be truthfully and adequately told.

Sri Aurobindo's preoccupation with Yoga led to his retirement from politics, and he spent the last forty years of his life in Pondicherry, in a sort of self-forged prison. Ezra Pound's open identification with politics during the Second World War led first to his isolation at Pisa and later to his relegation to St. Elizabeth's Hospital in Washington, D.C., on the recommendation of a commission of psychiatrists (he was ultimately released in 1958). Starting from opposite directions, as it were, these two great poets wrote some of their best work in isolation and seclusion.

Ezra Pound the pro-fascist and the anti-Semitist belongs to contemporary political history, but the creator of the *Cantos* can be considered as a figure apart. The *Cantos* continue their steady march, and continue to delight and intrigue by turns. *The Pisan Cantos*, which won for him the Bollingen Award, include passages like that on Vanity in the magnificent Canto LXXXI, which is even more articulate, being more direct, than the famous passage on Usury in Canto XLV.[46] Then came, from the asylum, *Section: Rock-Drill*, eleven more Cantos, which drew from Dudley Fitts the remark that the whole stupendous undertaking was but "a willed and perverse failure". More Cantos continued to appear (some in the *Hudson Review*), and the very latest bunch is *Thrones: XCVI-CIX*,

> In short, the cosmos continues
> and there is an observation somewhere in Morrison.
> leading to Remy?
> Bombs fell, but not quite on Sant Ambrogio.[47]

"The cosmos continues", that's the main thing. In Canto LXXXII, Pound openly merges with Whitman, feeling, "that he too is making the sort of cosmically penetrating poem towards which Whitman aspired."[48] *The Pisan Cantos*, in fact, more than the *Cantos* that preceded (except perhaps the first seven) or have so far succeeded them, seem to contain the essence of Pound's effort, "to make the past and present, memory, experience and learning, into a living whole which will sum up the whole work."[49] Its ambiguities admitted, this tremendous poetic adventure deserves to be hailed as "a Human Comedy in several dimensions and many voices",[50] an evolving epic of a cosmos still in a process of becoming. "It is as though", writes Roy Harvey Pearce, "Odysseus, or Aeneas, or Beowulf, or Mio Cid, or even Dante, under the *persona* of Adam (in whose fall/we sinned all) had been compelled, out of some dark necessity, to write his own history, and in writing it, to make it."[51] The *Cantos* may thus be almost called a sort of universal congress of epic heroes, or a junction where many epic highways meet, or even a Babel where many epic languages strive towards a basic unity of understanding and harmony.

VI

THE ODYSSEUS THEME

In a perceptive essay on 'The Odyssey and the Western World', George de F. Lord has tried to delineate Odysseus as a middle term between the Achilles of the *Iliad* and the Aeneas of Virgil's poem. Between Hamlet, father, the old-world heroic hero who smote the sledded Polacks on the ice, and Horatio the self-poised humanist who is not passion's slave, Shakespeare places Hamlet, the Prince, who is both his father's son and the scholar from Wittenberg.[52] At the risk of oversimplification, it may be said that heroes like Achilles (and Turnus in the *Aeneid*) fight for personal glory, while Aeneas is able to look beyond himself, and the present, and fight for a cause, and for a future. For a heroic poem, the *Aeneid* astonishes us by its sudden spiritual insights as, for example, in:

> First you must know that the heavens, the earth, the watery plains
> Of the sea, the moon's bright globe, the sun and the stars are all
> Sustained by a spirit within; for immanent Mind, flowing
> Through all its parts and leaving its mass, makes the universe work.[53]

God's ways so obviously mingle with man's that, as one reads the poem carefully, one feels in Tillyard's words that, "the multiplicity of the different manifestations of the numinous in the *Aeneid* works powerfully in securing for the poem the variety necessary for the true epic effect."[54] It is George de F. Lord's thesis that, although Odysseus begins as a heroic hero not unlike Achilles or Turnus, his wanderings school him in adversity, give a new dimension to his understanding, and gradually change him into a humane hero not unlike Aeneas. In a way, the turning point in his life is his being cast on the shore of peaceful Phaeacia and meeting the naive and chaste Nausicaa. When he narrates his adventures, and more particularly when he hears Demodocus tell the story of the wooden horse and the sack of Troy, he feels almost as Bernal feels in *Conquistador* when he recapitulates the conquest of Mexico. What price glory! Isn't the mere warrior a destroyer more than a creator? George de F. Lord concludes thus:

> This shift from power, which is accidental, to the principle of justice, which is in the reach of every man, marks the extraordinary moral revolution which occurs in the *Odyssey* and in the character of its hero... The power and excitement I find in the *Odyssey* stem in large measure from its testimony to the birth of civilisation in the emergence of charity and law and order out of the flux of passion and aimless brutality...The historical circumstan -ces of Odysseus' situation are so like ours that his restoration of the waste land within and outside him has the deepest relevance for ourselves."[55]

The whole point of the argument is that Odysseus is an evolving, not a static, character; he is ready and eager to experiment, to explore, to suffer, to change; it is only men like him that have the daring and the resilience necessary to carry forward the evolutionary destiny of man. Such are men of action doubled with thinkers, and they can even, if the occasion demands it, transcend both action and thought. It is not therefore surprising that Odysseus (or Ulysses) has become almost the archetype of the modern man. Tennyson's *Ulysses* first widely popularised the figure of the restless adventurer to whom ease is but sloth and who is determined "to strive, to seek, to find, and not to yield". The Poundian Odysseus of the *Cantos* voyages forth on the seas of the past, the present and the future, but the "swart ship" is seldom actually seen, it moves most of the time submarine-like under the water, but we are not long left in doubt regarding its reality. In his fine poem, *The Sail of Ulysses*, Wallace Stevens projects a "Symbol of the seeker, crossing by night/The giant sea", prospecting seas of thought, alone and unafraid:

> There is a human loneliness,
> A part of space and solitude,
> In which knowledge cannot be denied,
> In which nothing of knowledge fails…
> The right within us and about us,
> Joined, the triumphant vigour, felt,
> The inner direction on which we depend,
> That which keeps us the little that we are,
> The aid of greatness to be and the force.[56]

It is the first step in wisdom to race beyond the blaze of action and debate and seek out the sanctuary of silent thought where knowledge reigns undefiled and proves the ready helper. *What does* is exceeded by *what knows*, and action on a sure and sound basis of knowledge will be true creation, and this is how man the thinker becomes "the waver/Waving purpling wands", the magician who creates out of chaos a dancing star. But *what knows* has in its turn to be surpassed by *what is*;[57] the light of knowledge has to give place to the overhead illuminations, the utter Truth of Being:

> Yet always there is another life,
> A life beyond this present knowing…
> Not to be reached but to be known,
> Not an attainment of the will
> But something illogically received,
> A divination, a letting down
> From loftiness, misgivings dazzlingly
> Resolved in dazzling discovery.
> There is no map of Paradise.
> The great Omnium descends on us
> As a free race…

Always the cry is, in Eliot's words, not Farewell, but Fare forward! Leave the broken images behind; leave the symbols behind; leave "the rumours or speech-full domes" behind. In the realm of untainted sovereign Truth at last,

How then shall the mind be less than free
Since only to know is to be free?[58]

Such is Wallace Stevens' parable of the modern Ulysses' quest for freedom and felicity. The Ulysses myth has always proved a fecund source of inspiration to novelist and poet, and it seems to have (as George de F. Lord has affirmed) a peculiar relevance to the contemporary human situation. One of the latest variations of this tried old theme is Louis O. Coxe's sequence of six lyrics entitled 'The Last Hero', a series of backward glances at the life-career of Ulysses. When the hour of death approaches, Ulysses has no regrets;

Ready? aye, always. Always at my side
At kill or council, single eye that gathered
The heat of heaven to fire what I said
And did. Now let me die to what I fathered.[59]

He has been ruling "this island sea-surrounded, free,/Building, unbuilding", and now he is ready to go; he will become a ghost himself and haunt the places he has held dear. The prototypical picture of the heroic hero dying in ripe old age full of honour and years! But this is not how Nikos Kazantzakis, the great poet of modern Greece (and Crete), conceived the last years of Odysseus in *The Odyssey*: *A Modern Sequel*, the immense epic which has lately appeared, twenty-one years after its first publication in Greek, in an English translation by Kimon Friar. It is a natural, even a logical, transition from the *Cantos* of Ezra Pound to the modern *Odyssey* of Nikos Kazantzakis.

VII

KAZANTZAKIS' 'MODERN SEQUEL'

Sri Aurobindo was an Indian who mastered classical Greek and so completely entered into the spirit of Homer's poetry that he attempted, as we saw in the previous chapter, a 'sequel' to the *Iliad* in English hexameters. Nikos Kazantzakis was a Cretan Greek who became a European and a man of the world and tried to cram into his life and work divers realms and modes of experience. He knew (like Sri Aurobindo) many languages, he wrote fiction and poetry, he translated the epics of Homer, the *Commedia* and *Faust* into modern Greek, and (in 1945) he was for a time Minister of Education. Having come under Bergson's influence as a pupil, Kazantzakis was intrigued by the problem of evolution, and his life veered between action and introspection, and he tried mask after mask, pursued shadow after shadow. After following in vain various roads to happiness—love, scientific inquiry, philosophy, social action and literary creation—he resolutely turned back at last and sought asylum in Athos, a region untrodden by women and dedicated to the contemplative life. Here he had what must be called a mystical experience which may be given in his own words:

> I began a new Struggle. First of all I exercised my body in obedience to the spirit…Then I turned to the spirit; sunk in painful concentration, I sought to conquer within me the minor passions, the easy virtues, the cheap spiritual joys, the convenient hopes. Finally one night I started up in great joy, for I had seen the red ribbon left behind him in his ascent—within us and in all the universe—by a certain Combatant; I clearly saw his bloody footprints ascending from inorganic matter into life and from life into spirit.
>
> Then suddenly a great light was born within me: the transmutation of matter into spirit. Here was the great secret, the red ribbon followed by the Combatant…I now clearly saw the progress of the Invisible, and suddenly I knew what my duty was to be: to work in harmony together with that Combatant; to transmute, even I, in my own small capacity, matter into spirit, for only then might I try to reach the highest endeavour of man—a harmony with the universe.[60]

Kazantzakis was now an emancipated man, and he was free to collaborate with the 'Combatant'; being redeemed himself, he was free to participate in the movement for the redemption of the race. The Combatant is also God, he is the Life Force of Bernard Shaw, he is Bergson's *élan vital*, "the onrushing force through all of creation which strives for purer and more rarefied freedom."[61] God is a perpetual Becoming. One after another, the peaks have to be reached and passed, the veils of illusion torn and cast aside. Mind and heart are milestones on the path. The ego, the race, mankind itself, the circumambient universe, these too are but advancing exercises in identification, no sooner successfully accomplished than left behind and forgotten. Onward, forever onward,

> To follow knowledge, like a sinking star,
> Beyond the utmost bound of human thought.[62]

These and other ideas, mainly derived from his mystic experience on the Holy Mountain of Athos, were woven by Kazantzakis—no doubt with an admixture of strands of thought from Bergson and Nietzsche, and perhaps also Oswald Spengler—into a philosophical memoir in a poetical style entitled *Spiritual Exercises*: *Salvatores Dei*, which in the Kazantzakis canon perhaps corresponds to *The Synthesis of Yoga* and *The Life Divine* in the Sri Aurobindo canon. The tradition of retirement from the world for peace and meditation was already a long established one in India at the time of the Buddha, and it is an unbroken tradition to this day.[63] The surprising thing is that such an idea should have occurred to a modern Greek writer, and that such a retreat should have filled him with creative purpose for the rest of his life. One result, and indeed for us the chief result, of Kazantzakis' mystic experience is this stupendous 'Modern Sequel' to the *Odyssey*.

Like its Homeric model, Kazantzakis' poem too is an epic narrative in XXIV Books, but being 33,333 lines long, thrice as voluminous as the original. The metrical pattern too is his own, not a mere mimicry of the Homeric hexameter, but a verse of seventeen syllables with eight stresses, while Kimon Friar's English rendering is in lines of six iambic feet with the usual permissible variations. Whichever way one looks at the poem, whether the original or the translation, the experience (mystical and otherwise) that went into its making or the energy of the art that has made it what it is, this modern *Odyssey* should be adjudged a remarkable performance; "for its size and splendour and ambition alone",[64] it should claim and secure a place among the indubitable poetic triumphs of our time, taking a seat near *Savitri* and the *Cantos*.

Odysseus—who is at once Homer's hero, Kazantzakis' alter-ego, and the human spearhead of the evolutionary adventure—is the hero; his wanderings, his visions, his musings and his ravings, his successes and his failures including the ultimate holocaust of his death, form the mountainous thematic heap of the poem; and its philosophic base is provided by a Dionysian-Nietzschean-Bergsonian worldview that at its clearest and most perceptive moments becomes the 'Cretan glance', which is really no more than a new name for the Sophoclean capacity to see life steadily and see it whole, or even the old Stoic capacity for patient determined sufferance. Perhaps the 'Cretan glance' includes more of the joy of life than the Stoic or the Sophoclean, though quite as much of its clarity and strength and integrality.

Kazantzakis imagines (like Tennyson) that Odysseus, on his homecoming to Ithaca, neither pleases nor is pleased himself, and so sets out again on his wanderings with a few picked rugged companions. His first hop is at Sparta, and there he finds Menelaus' smugness repulsive. He abducts a not unwilling Helen, who is as beautiful as ever, but not because he desires her carnally but rather because he thinks that she too deserves release from the barred cage of false domesticity. The party arrives in Crete, where fertility rites are in progress. Odysseus actively helps the conspiracy against the decadent king, Knossos is now destroyed, and leaving one of his companions, Hardihood, behind to rule over Crete, he leaves with the others for Egypt. It is a singular irony that Helen should find real happiness at last in the arms of a barbarian, and that Crete's new king should be a ruffian like Hardihood.

In the meantime, Odysseus finds that the depraved Egyptian Empire too is in the throes of a rebellion, and gets quickly involved in it. But he is presently reduced to discomfiture and travels through darkest Africa to track the sources of the Nile. He and his companions reach at last the lake that is really Nile's source, and leaving them to rest for a while, Odysseus makes an ascent to a mountain-cave where for seven days he communes with himself and his God and whatever gods may be. An irresistible creative urge wells up in Odysseus, and he and his companions put forth sustained labours to build an Ideal City which, however, is destroyed by a sudden earthquake. One more illusion shattered, Odysseus turns an ascetic ("a figure more like an Indian Yogi", says W.B. Stanford), goes into a trance, and after resisting the assault of fresh temptations, he surrenders to a Dionysian dance of acceptance of everything. He wanders on towards the Cape, life idly or agitatedly passes him by, he encounters Tempters and Messiahs (including Prince Motherth and the gentle Fisher-Lad, who typify the Buddha and the Christ respectively), sets out towards the South Pole, and with a final supreme gesture of acceptance and affirmation he soars high and achieves the ultimate release.

Readers of poetry who petulantly complain that the *Cantos* tell no consecutive story, that Pound's is an epic without a plot, or that *Savitri* is an unconscionable inflation of a simple legend into the vast proportions of an epic, that it is a mass of obscurity, would find Kazantzakis' poem full of 'matter', full of the rugged manifoldness of life, peopled with a Dostoevskian variety of characters, full of the excitement of revolution, full of moving incidents, sudden transitions, and even audacious canters of thought. But the differences notwithstanding, all three contemporary epic creations share—though each in its own unique way and to the extent of the particular inspiration sustaining it—a high seriousness of purpose, a more or less total vision of man and Nature and the cosmos, and a profound anxiety about the future destiny of man. There is a down-to-the-earth realism, an uninhibited violence and downrightness, in Kazantzakis' poem which are in marked contrast to the zig-zag vagaries, exotic patterns and general obscurity of the *Cantos* or the occult distance and dreamy otherworldliness of large tracts of *Savitri*. But of any one of these three great poems (great, undoubtedly, though not all equally great) it may be said what one critic has said of one of them that its real effect is, "to bring forward (and with what unbelievable fullness!) the incalculable value of a total response to experience."[65]

VIII

SRI AUROBINDO AND KAZANTZAKIS

We saw in the previous chapter how *Savitri* begins with the dawn and the Symbol Dawn—"It was the hour before the Gods awake" —and how, after compressing the history of the cosmos into the events of a single day (including a cosmic revolution in the course of which Death is worsted), concludes with the assurance that "Night, splendid with the moon…in her bosom nursed a greater dawn". In the Preface to one of his charming Oriental tales, the late F.W. Bain, who spent many fruitful years in India and entered into the spirit of Indian culture as few had done before, has introduced a rhapsody to the Indian Dawn:

> First comes Night, and Chaos: and then, out of the black there arises, silently, imperceptibly, irresistibly, the glorious, the blushing, the beautiful, amber-clouded, opal-shredded, amethyst-bedappled Dawn. O Dawn, how I do love thee! How, after a night of blackness and distress, has thy delicious fragrance raised me from the dead, with its colour and the camphor and the nectar touch of its rosy finger, softer than flowers, cooler than sandalwood. Yes, it is necessary to be a dweller in the East, to taste and understand the religion of the Dawn.[66]

It is a wonderfully apt phrase: 'the religion of the Dawn'. The Sun, Surya, Savitri—in his four differentiated forms, Varuna, Mitra, Aryaman and Bhaga—is no doubt central to the Vedic religion, but the human approach to them is through the gateway of the Dawn. Kazantzakis, on the other hand, begins with a Prologue to the Sun and concludes with a lament because the Sun has set. Thus the Prologue:

> O Sun, great Oriental, my proud mind's golden cap…
> O Sun, my quick coquetting eye, my red-haired hound,
> Sniff out all the quarries that I love, give them swift chase…[67]

When the wheel comes full circle, when the Sun sets, when Odysseus is 'dead' (that is, when the body becomes spirit and the spirit becomes air), there is heard only, "the ultimate and despairing cry of Earth/ the sun's lament, but with no throat or mouth or voice."[68] The 'hollow hush' of this close merely insinuates the essential tragedy of the human situation, whereas the 'holy hush' of *Savitri's* close is the true meaning of that Divine Comedy.

This is not merely because Kazantzakis was a Greek and therefore heir to the great tradition of Attic tragedy whereas Sri Aurobindo was an Indian and therefore heir to the Kalidasian tradition, but also because of the different foundations on which they reared their respective epic edifices. Both of them believed in Evolution, and both had had mystic experiences. Kazantzakis, like Bergson, thought in terms of 'emergent evolution'; the *élan vital*, in their view, struggled and surged to achieve new forms of life. During his vigil on Mount Athos, Kazantzakis saw the Combatant pushing his way upward, and so achieving self-expression in newer and newer forms.

The Aurobindonian dialectic of ascent being met by a descent from above and the two achieving an integration and a new creation, and so preparing the way for the next rung, and the next, was quite different from the normal Western view of an irresistible evolutionary urge that knows not exactly whither it is going. Kazantzakis, in so far as he was a seer, still saw only with the mind; a general overhead vision hadn't opened to him; he saw some steps ahead, but darkness enveloped the rest. There is courage and cunning and resourcefulness and intellectual keenness and even moral earnestness in the story; but it is not touched by the Light from above, because he had not seen it; he had glimpsed the meteor-like ascending Combatant and the red trail left by him, but not the total splendour of the Descent nor the glow of the transformation effected by it. This necessarily colours also the quality and value of the two revelations. Impressive though the roll of the verse, vigorously and vividly evocative though the images, being for the most part but the projection of a vital and mental aesthesis, Kazantzakis' poem seldom rises to the sheer sublime, though rhetorical effectiveness and sensuous extravagance are rarely missed. There is a commendable virtuosity in a picture like that of the Ivory God with seven heads that a pedlar sells to Odysseus:

> Below, the most coarse head, a brutal base of flesh…
> Above it, like a warrior's crest, the second head
> clenched its sharp teeth and frowned with hesitating brows…
> The third head gleamed like honey with voluptuous eyes,
> its pale cheeks hallowed by the flesh's candied kisses…
> The fourth head lightly rose, its mouth a wetted blade,
> its neck grew slender and its brow rose tall as though
> its roots had turned to flower, its meat to purest mind.
> The fifth head's towering brow was crushed with bitter grief…
> Above it shone serenely the last head but one,
> and steadfast weighed all things, beyond all joy or grief…
> The final head shone, crystal-clear, translucent, light,
> and had no ears or eyes, no nostrils, mouth, or brow,
> for all its flesh had turned to soul, and soul to air![69]

These are vivid evocations of the successive stages in the evolution of man, from the ape-man through man the hero-fighter, the sensuous hedonist, the mental man, the man of sorrows who has a bottomless pity for mankind, the saintly man who has surpassed the dualities, and so to the disembodied soul. Odysseus fondles the seven heads and he is seized by the desire to "mount/the seven stories step by step and fade in flame", but all are but mental constructions, there is no overhead aesthesis here, no new revelation. The number 'three' fascinates Kazantzakis even more than the number 'seven'. On his return to Ithaca and after the destruction of the suitors, the minstrel sings how at the birth of Odysseus he had been blessed (or cursed) by Tantalus with a ravenous heart, by Prometheus with "the seed of a great light", his razor-edged mind, and by Heracles with "the unsated blaze", his restless spirit.[70] Next night he tells his father, wife and son that, in the course of his wanderings, Death had tried to tempt him in three forms:

> In cool Calypso's cave he came with laughing wiles...
> Heaven and its foundations swerved to serve us both,
> Stars vanished in the sea but others blazed with smiles,
> and we, two glowworms merged as one, gleamed on
> the sands. [71]

The second form Death took was that of Circe who lusted with him and infected his mind,

> for just as insects slowly sink and drown in amber,
> so in my turbid mind beasts, trees, and mortals sank. [72]

Last came the third form, the most dangerous of all, for now

> Death masqueraded like the virgin of a noble tribe
> who on the beach smiled softly at a shipwrecked man. [73]

Calypso, Circe, Nausicaa, these would, each in her own way, keep Odysseus chained to her, but to him life meant moving on and exploring and experimenting, not subsisting in the somnolence of any steady condition. The Combatant lures him on, but he would not "squander my soul's strength on worthless works".[74]

Savitri, too, is confronted in the course of her entry into the 'inner countries' by the 'triple soul-forces', namely the Madonna of Suffering, the Mother of Might, and the Madonna of Light, but these are apocalyptic visions though they can no doubt be roughly equated with certain characters in history or legend. Savitri is presented as the Goddess herself come down to effect the evolutionary change from Man to Superman, from terrestrial to the divine life. Coercing her godhead she has become a woman, and she is willing that the Master of Evolution should deal with her as is fit.[75]

Although Sri Aurobindo's mystic muse in *Savitri* is sometimes more of an intoxicated Bacchante-like mistress than a quiet and steady housewife, his heroine herself is an Appollonian, rather than a Dionysian, character. Her prime mark is "a union of strength and silence"[76] and she is "the forerunner or first creator of a new race".[77] Her glance is more than Cretan in its strength and steadiness and more than Apollonian in its purity and power. Once again, in the two protagonists of the developing evolution, we see in striking contrast the overhead aesthesis fashioning the one and a vital and mental aesthesis fashioning the other. Between Savitri and Odysseus there is all the difference between the purposive beauty of the Dawn and the fierce energy of a storm. When Odysseus becomes an ascetic after the destruction of his Ideal City, he no doubt transcends the dualities but, after all, it is a bleak enlightenment that cries:

> There is no master now on earth, the heart is free!...
> By the three-hundred-and-sixty-five joints knit to flesh,
> by the three-hundred-and-sixty-five snakes round
> the soul,
> no master-god exists, no virtue, no just law,
> no punishment in Hades and no reward in Heaven![78]

His wild dance to the tune of these negations merely scares away the pilgrims who have gathered round him for solace. It is the measure of Odysseus' limitation—as it is that of his creator, Kazantzakis—that they have reached only the Sahara of Negation, the icy desolation of the Antarctic, but have been unable to take us to the Well of Living Waters. The Everlasting No is a necessary stage in the journey, but not the final one; one must pass that milestone too, and reach the beckoning goal of the Everlasting Yea. This neither Odysseus nor

Kazantzakis does, and so *The Odyssey: A Modern Sequel* can only be called an incomplete or arrested revelation of the total cosmic drama. Neither in its total sweep of Space and Time nor in its insight into the real nature of the evolutionary drama is the 'Modern Sequel' as truly a 'cosmic epic' as Sri Aurobindo's *Savitri*.

IX

'A TRIPLE CHALLENGE'

Three such poems as the *Cantos*, *The Odyssey: A Modern Sequel* and *Savitri* are certainly a triple challenge to those who hold the view that the days of the long poem are gone. The *Cantos*, now numbering 109, probably make a bulk of nearly 800 pages; in the standard edition, *Savitri* too takes up 814 pages; and *The Odyssey*, with its 33,333 lines, is surely the longest and the most formidable (in mass) of the three. About thirty-five years ago a writer remarked in the course of a review, "It is possible that a long poem cannot be achieved out of the modern consciousness...but the question will continue to be mooted while poetry is a living art."[79]

Louis O. Coxe, who thinks that Kazantzakis' poem is wholly misconceived, fears that its failure to present "any unifying worldview" and its general miscarriage "may well be taken as proof that a long poem is no longer possible", but he also adds: "I cannot share any such notion. It proves only that the romantic approach to a long poem is not workable."[80] And T.S. Eliot says, though in an entirely different connection: "I by no means believe that the 'long poem' is a thing of the past; but at least there must be more in it for the length than our grandparents seemed to demand; and for us, anything that can be said as well in prose can be said better in prose. And a great deal, in the way of meaning, belongs to prose rather than to poetry."[81] It is true many long poems have been failures; and ambitious poems like Alfred Noyes' *The Torchbearers*, a sort of verse history of science, and even such a new species of poem like Bridges'

The Testament of Beauty, although it is impressive in theme as well as technique, have not hit the bull's-eye like *The Waste Land*, a much smaller poem that may almost be described as a modern epic in miniature.

But all this doesn't prove that a long poem, a modern epic, is impossible. The modern consciousness and an epic creation need not be a contradiction in terms; the reign of prose need not invalidate the parallel, or more sovereign, reign of poetry. What shall we look for in a long poem, a long poem that is an epic creation, a long poem that deserves to be acclaimed also a great poem? It is pertinent to cite in this connection the views of Abercrombie:

> When poetry is called great, it is not only on account of the *range* of its matter, though that is important: for we could not call poetry great which did not face the whole fact of man's life in this world, its wickedness and misery as well as its nobility and joy. But its greatness also consists in the *organisation* of its matter—and that, remember, is the evil as well as the good of life—into some consistent shapeliness or coherent unity of final impression; so that, whatever means have been taken to effect it, we have at last the sense of belonging to a life in which everything is related to everything else, in which nothing can intrude by chance, but all is required, even the evil is required, in the interest of the whole: nothing can there occur which does not belong to, and assist into being, one inclusive, harmonious orderliness of existence.[82]

Qualitatively a drop of milk is the same thing as a cup of milk or even the *kṣīra sāgara*, the ocean of milk; yet quantity, when quality is not divorced from it, is not to be ignored or despised. While a lyric and an epic are equally poetry, the latter is characterised by greater extension in space and time, greater comprehension, and hence greater universality of appeal. When the house is small, there is little elbow room, and there is bound to be a feeling of confinement. Intensity alone is not enough. By making room for characters and actions on a national, global or cosmic scale, the epic opens to us vast horizons of meaning and significance.

On the other hand, the immense chambers of the epic, its corridors, its stairways, its august approaches, its impressive backgrounds, also need to be made the stage of a vitally important drama of permanent human significance. The epic's is an all inclusive world: men, gods, demons, dreams, nightmares, ideas, all is assimilable epic 'material', all could be transformed into poetry. Neither mysticism nor philosophy, neither prophecy nor debate, need be excluded; only, they have to be processed into poetry. The view that maintains that content is of no consequence and the opposite view that content is everything alike miss the true nature of poetry.

Basil Willey is right when he says that, "so many Ph.D. theses go wrong...by treating a poet's 'thought' as if it were something which could be detached from the poetry, and discussed as part of the history of philosophy or ethics...If this nut were the only thing that mattered, the poet would have saved endless trouble by handing it to us in plain prose, like a man and a philosopher, instead of padding it round with a lot of obscure rhetoric."[83] But G. Wilson Knight is no less right when, while assessing the poetry of Pope, he studies "the total contents, as opposed to the style in isolation".[84] Elsewhere Wilson Knight writes: "Poetic language is an incarnation, not a transcription of thought: it is a seizing on truth beyond the writer's personal thinking through submission to the object."[85] Poetry, to beg the question, charges rhythmic language with a certain power and glory that it thereby becomes, in I.A. Richards' words, "the completest mode of utterance".[86]

X

DANTE AND SRI AUROBINDO

In *Savitri* Sri Aurobindo has tried to make poetry, partly out of his mystic experiences and realisations, partly out of the philosophy that he elaborated (mainly on the basis of these realisations) in *The Life Divine*, both sources of inspiration—the mystic and the philosophic—flowing into and filling with rich significance the mould of the ancient legend of Savitri and Satyavan. The question now arises: to what extent is mystic experience or philosophical statement amenable to transformation as poetry? It may be readily conceded that the rendering of mystical experience in terms of poetry, while it is perpetually necessary (for such poetry is the true nectar of man's rebirth in the spirit), is also perpetually unrealisable. The mystic has to express in words experiences that are beyond verbal expression. As Gilbert Highet perceptively says (he is thinking of poets like St John of the Cross, Holderlin, Valery, Donne and T.S. Eliot):

> These people had a certain experience of life which they found so complex, so dangerous and alarming, so much profounder than normal thought and living, that they *could not* communicate it in the ordinary speech—not even in ordinary poetic speech...only in poetry which was deliberately fragmentary and inadequate and symbolic;

but he makes an exception about Dante:

> That is why Dante is such a superb writer. He was one of the very few men in the world's history who have had such a vision and have been able to communicate it as a coherent whole... Most others cannot even think of making a complete exposition of such experiences.[87]

It is difficult, almost impossible, but it has been done once; it follows it could be done again if the circumstances are unusually propitious; and such circumstances may be said to have prevailed if the vision could be realised as an utterly adequate symbol or a linked system of symbols. The 'mirror' symbol in the *Paradiso* and the 'Dawn' symbol in *Savitri* are indeed such symbols, and they function as the *śruti* and the *swaras* or the background vibrations and musical tones that sustain and charge with rich significance the wonderful symphony.[88]

If mystical experience is difficult to render in poetry, philosophy too—though for the opposite reason—is an intractable subject for poetry. If mystical experiences are ineffable by their very nature, philosophical systems or statements may prove too arid or too severely logical for poetical transplantation. Middleton Murry, for example, takes Sir Henry Newbolt to task for thinking that McTaggart's philosophy of Time and Eternity[89] could provide a future poet with an inspiring faith to enable him to give solace and encouragement to ailing humanity, and declares that philosophy can do no such thing. In so-called philosophical poetry, as Arnold might put it, the poetry is the reality, the philosophy is the illusion; "the philosophy merely serves the same office in philosophical poetry as the plot or myth in other kinds. We give to the one as to the other 'that willing suspension of disbelief which constitutes poetic faith'; if the poet is great enough to create by means of his philosophy or his story, a significant order in the chaos of human experience, we ask no more from philosophy."[90]

The point of view here urged is that there is—there can be—no such thing as philosophical poetry; the substative alone is the reality. Love, Nature, politics, war, history, myth, philosophy, all could inspire the poet, but he would be writing only poetry! But Middleton Murry himself makes an exception in the case of Dante (even as Highet did): "The essential condition of philosophical poetry is that the poet should believe that there is a faculty of mind superior to the poetic; that was possible for Dante; but since Shakespeare lived and wrote it is not possible."[91] What is Murry driving at? Does he not mean to say that real philosophical poetry is superior to philosophy alone or poetry alone because it is the creation of a mind superior even to the poetic mind? Dante is the great exception. He has successfully turned mystical experience into poetry; he has triumphantly turned philosophy into poetry. The ineffable has been made vivid beyond words, the impossible has become triumphantly possible. "We feel not so much," says G.G.Coulton, "that he is relating, nor that he is creating, as that he stands by, removes a veil, and shows us a truth preexistent from all eternity and living to all eternity; a picture that impresses itself as irresistibly upon the mind as (to use his own simile) the seal impresses itself upon the wax."[92]

It was Quiller-Couch who categorically affirmed that, "philosophy and poetry work on different planes, and their terms belong to different categories. The one seeks to comprehend, the other to apprehend; the one moving round, would embrace the circumference of God's purpose, the other is content to leap from a centre *within* us to a point of the circumference, and seize it by direct vision."[93] On the other hand, T.S. Eliot bluntly says that, "nothing in this world or the next is a substitute for anything else; and if you find that you must do without something, such as religious faith or philosophical belief, then you must just do without it." The point Eliot is trying to make is that, while it may be possible to appreciate the *Commedia* or the *Bhagavad Gita* (which is "the next greatest philosophical poem" within Eliot's experience) as poetry without sharing the beliefs of the poet, yet, "actually, one probably has more pleasure in the poetry when one shares the beliefs of the poet."[94]

But he also immediately adds that, "there is a distinct pleasure in enjoying poetry as poetry when one does *not* share the beliefs"; whether one shares the beliefs or no, their presence must act either as a stimulant or an irritant. Eliot therefore concludes, in his characteristically guarded manner, that, "both in creation and enjoyment much always enters which is, from the point of view of 'Art', irrelevant."[95] It is when vision, idea and word—a whole world of direct mystic experience, a whole self-poised though complex pattern of ideas, and a whole stream of words in perfect rhythmical accord—fuse absolutely like Browning's conception of "three souls, one man" or, better still, Dante's vision of "three circles, of three colours and one magnitude",[96] it is when this miracle happens that we have a poem like the *Commedia*, the *Bhagavad Gita*, or *Savitri*.

The memory of the vision of Beatrice filled Dante's spiritual life, while the philosophy of St Thomas Aquinas filled his mental horizon;

in the fullness of time there was a fusion of these with his poetic aesthesis, and the result was the *Divina Commedia*. Were there comparable circumstances in Sri Aurobindo's life so that we may legitimately look for a repetition of the great miracle? Highet and Murry, starting from different premises, come nevertheless to the conclusion that Dante is the unique exception; Allen Tate says that Dante's poem, "is a vast paradigm of the possibility of the Beatific Vison",[97] and Eliot says that one learns, "from the *Inferno* that the greatest poetry can be written with the greatest economy of words... From the *Purgatorio*... that a straightforward philosophical statement can be great poetry; from the *Paradiso*, that more and more rarefied and remote *states of beatitude* can be the material for great poetry."[98] To repeat our question more succinctly: Was Sri Aurobindo the kind of poet who could have "done a Dante" and made of his *Savitri* another *Commedia*?

Before attempting to answer this very, very difficult question, let me preface my remarks with the following obiter dicta by Ezra Pound:

> Any sincere criticism of the highest poetry must resolve itself into a sort of profession of faith. The critic must begin with a 'credo', and his opinion will be received in part for the intelligence he may seem to possess, and in part for his earnestness.[99]

Continuous absorption in *Savitri* has convinced me of its greatness as a poem, but rationalising my conviction is not easy. Since the *Commedia* is the acknowledged *exemplum*, it is interesting to note that certain circumstances in the lives of Dante and Sri Aurobindo seem to strike a somewhat similar note. Dante, like Sri Aurobindo, was involved in active politics for a time; Sri Aurobindo left Calcutta in 1910, first for Chandernagore, and finally for Pondicherry, where he remained for the rest of his life, even as Dante left Florence in 1302, to spend the remaining nineteen years of his life in exile; and they were both about the same age (36-37) when this transplantation occurred, and they both left their wives behind, and did not meet them again.

The nodal event in Dante's life was his meeting Beatrice Portinari at her father's house when she was eight, and he but a few months older; they met off and on, and spoke once; and she died some sixteen years after they had first met. Although they had not married, she had kindled in Dante's heart a flame that was never again to be extinguished, that still burns with undiminished intensity in his *Vita Nuova*; it was also the flame that lighted up his path in the *Commedia*. There is no exact parallel to this nodal event in Sri Aurobindo's life. It is certainly true that India appeared to him, not simply as a geographical area or subcontinent, but as the Mother, verily as the Mother. He wrote to his wife in 1905 that a demon was sucking his Mother's blood, that he must strive to redeem Her from the demon's grasp.[100] He had a vision of the Lord as Narayana, as Vasudeva, in the Alipore Jail.[101] But there is no hint of a 'Savitri' in these experiences. We have to wait till 1914 for the first definite clue. In that year Madame Mira Richard, who had been seeking the Divine for years, came to Pondicherry, and under date 30 March she recorded:

> It matters not if there are hundreds of beings plunged in the densest ignorance. He whom we saw yesterday is on earth: His presence is enough to prove that a day will come when darkness shall be transformed into light, when Thy reign shall be indeed established upon earth.
>
> O Lord, Divine Builder of this marvel, my heart overflows with joy and gratitude when I think of it, and my hope is boundless. My adoration surpasses all words and my reverence is silent.[102]

On this passage Iyengar comments as follows: "This 'marvel', 'he whom we saw yesterday', was Sri Aurobindo."[103] Madame Richard presently became Sri Aurobindo's spiritual collaborator, and for about thirty years they were jointly the spiritual directors of the thousands of disciples who gathered around them in the Sri Aurobindo Ashram. When Sri Aurobindo passed away on 5 December 1950, to many of their disciples it was as though Satyavan himself had died, and Savitri had been left behind to carry on the fight with the forces of darkness.[104] One of the disciples, Nirodbaran, has also posed the leading question: "What is, after all, *Savitri* if not the inner life-episodes of the Mother and the Master?"[105]

XI

SAVITRI AND THE *COMMEDIA*

Sri Aurobindo's *Savitri*, in its earliest version,[106] must have approximated much closer to the 'legend' in the *Mahabharata* than to the present epic. The power of Savitri's radiant purity of purpose and fiery chastity confronts Yama; and Yama who is both the Lord of Death and the upholder of Dharma, being irresistibly awakened by her mere presence and the flow of apt speech from her to a realisation of his latter role, consents at last to release the 'soul' of Satyavan, and so the lovers return to their hermitage. It was during his early years at Pondicherry that Sri Aurobindo glimpsed clearly the possibility of the supramentalisation of man and Nature and the earth. Then came the meeting with Madame Richard (the Mother of the Sri Aurobindo Ashram), and the launching of the monthly journal, *Arya*, in which, during the next six years and a half, appeared the monumental philosophical sequence, *The Life Divine*, wherein Sri Aurobindo argued out with overwhelming force the possibility of the supramentalisation—the divinisation—of man and Nature and the earth. In 1920 Madame Richard returned from a prolonged visit to Japan, and finally settling down in Pondicherry assumed the general control of the Sri Aurobindo Ashram.

It was perhaps during the later twenties that Sri Aurobindo decided to give his *Savitri*—taken up for revision so often before but not brought to the actual point of publication—a wholly new orientation, to turn the 'legend' also into a 'symbol', in the light of his Yogic experiences, his newly formulated philosophy of the Life

Divine, and also his newly evolved theory and practice of 'overhead' aesthesis. The role of Beatrice in the *Commedia* is played as purposefully and more dynamically by Savitri in Sri Aurobindo's poem; Virgil is distantly paralleled by Aswapati, and even as Virgil leads to Beatrice, Aswapati leads to Savitri. And Savitri herself is at once the heroine of the legend and the symbol-force of the Supreme Creatrix assuming or incarnating in a human form—like the avatars of old—to effect the supramentalisation of man and his habitat.

The role of the philosophy of St Thomas Aquinas in Dante's poem is as fully and as creatively discharged by *The Life Divine* in Sri Aurobindo's poem.[107] That Sri Aurobindo 'used' a philosophy which he had himself evolved, partly no doubt in consonance with India's *philosophia perennis* but partly also in the light of his own Yogic realisations, whereas Dante had been content to 'use' the Thomist philosophy that was ready to hand doesn't essentially affect the parallelism between *Savitri* and the *Commedia*, for in one as in the other the philosophy is entirely consumed in the poetry. It is also more than a mere verbal coincidence that the key word 'Divine' should figure in both the title of Dante's great epic (*The Divine Comedy*) and in Sri Aurobindo's philosophical treatise (*The Life Divine*), which is itself a work of art in the 'other harmony' of prose, besides also providing the philosophical sustenance to *Savitri*.

There is, of course, danger in making facile comparisons, for they may sometimes mislead more than instruct us. Dante's Florence was a very small world compared with the Indian political stage on which Sri Aurobindo played so notable a part during 1906-10. Besides, while Dante was a religious man, Sri Aurobindo was a Yogi, a 'pilgrim of Eternity', a vassal of the Spirit. As philosophers, again, there can be no effective comparison between the Florentine and the Indian poet, for whereas the former had merely assimilated the Thomist philosophy, Sri Aurobindo's *The Life Divine* is an independent philosophical work mounting an impressive dialectic and charged with a high creative purpose.

Further, Dante left a completed epic behind him while Sri Aurobindo left *Savitri* apparently incomplete. Two of the projected cantos in Book VIII (The Book of Death) are missing. He evidently knew he had not long to live, and he was therefore particularly anxious to finalise Book VI (The Book of Fate); there was something of a race with time, and it was only after completing the revision of the long (and, in some respects, seminal) second canto of The Book of Fate that the tension relaxed and he felt relieved that it was over. On being told that the Book of Death and the last Book, the Epilogue, still needed to be cast in their final form, Sri Aurobindo seems to have remarked, "We shall see about that later on."[108] He could have revised those sections of the poem too had he cared, but he didn't; it was as though, so far as he was concerned, *Savitri* was finished. And, indeed, when we read this immense poem at a stretch, we do not get the feeling that it is in any real sense incomplete. It is unconcluded only in the quintessential sense that the cosmic drama of which the poem is no more than a symbol remains yet unconcluded; but merely as a poem, *Savitri* is a rounded fullness and completeness, verily a total revelation.

Some differences can also be noted with regard to the content and form of the two poems. The *Commedia* has a scheme of descent into Hell and ascent of Paradisal peaks *via* the slopes of Purgatory, which is, "closely similar to similar supernatural peregrination stories in Arabic and in old Persian literature—to say nothing of the descents of Ulysses and Aeneas",[109] to say nothing again of the wanderings of Rama, Sita and Lakshmana in the *Ramayana* and of the Pandavas in the *Mahabharata*. Aswapati's spiritual peregrination, described at considerable length in Book II (The Book of the Traveller of the Worlds), has a similar scheme, and can almost be detached from the rest of *Savitri*, though of course it is also integral to the total scheme of the epic. The occult-spiritual odyssey of Aswapati ends in the fourth canto of Book III (The Book of the Divine Mother), where he has the 'beatific vision' of the Mother who gives her consenting voice to his prayer on behalf of humanity.

There is also, in Book VII (The Book of Yoga), Savitri's entry into the inner countries of the spirit culminating in the finding of the soul; like Dante, she too realises in the end that she is at infinity's centre, she is in That without quite becoming That. There are thus two spiritual peregrinations in *Savitri*, the father's and the daughter's, and they are also a unity in difference. Yet, although important, they are only the background, for in the foreground is played the drama of Savitri and Satyavan, which is profoundly moving in the original legend, but here acquires a further spiritual dimension. Savitri is really the incarnation in human form of the Supreme Mother; there is the first test of her faith in love when Narad tries to warn her against marrying Satyavan, but she stands the test and is firm in her resolve. There is the later impact of Fate, the death of Satyavan, the temptation in the forest, the struggle with Death, and the ultimate victory. Since Death is viewed here as Evil, Ignorance and Darkness and Savitri as Light, Love and Goodness, the struggle between them is more in the nature of the struggle between Ravana and Rama in the *Ramayana* for the rescue of Sita, or between the Kauravas and the Pandavas in the *Mahabharata* for the righting of a wrong.

In the 'legend' Savitri solves her own personal problem, and in the process of regaining her Satyavan she also brings an accession of happiness to her parents and parents-in-law; in the epic, on the other hand, Savitri fights all the time the battle of mankind for a new life—the Life Divine—on earth, for Satyavan is really the "soul of the world". This is the new dimension given to the old story by the seer-poet of *Savitri*. In the *Commedia*, Dante, long separated from Beatrice, meets her again, but only on the "other side", not upon "this bank and shoal of time". Nevertheless, in the *Commedia* and *Savitri* alike, it is the heroine (the 'hero' in these two epics is about as positive or effective as the heroes in some of Shakespeare's great comedies) who takes the lead, who acts the role of *śakti*, who makes the divine transformation possible. Allen Tate truly says that, "what Dante achieved is an *actual* insight into the great dilemma, eternal life or eternal death."[110] The point may likewise be made that what Sri Aurobindo achieved and sought to dramatise in *Savitri* is an actual insight into the great dilemma: divine life on earth or death in the ignorance.

XII

SAVITRI AND SRI AUROBINDO'S EARLY NARRATIVE POEMS

It must be clear from the above that *Savitri* is a *Commedia* doubled with a *Ramayana*. The general scheme of the epic may now be indicated. "*Savitri* was originally written many years before the Mother came", wrote Sri Aurobindo to a correspondent in 1936, "as a narrative poem in two parts, Part I Earth and Part II Beyond...each of four Books—or rather Part II consisted of three Books and an epilogue."[111] The scheme was probably as follows:

Part I: Earth

Book I:	The Book of Birth and Quest
Book II:	The Book of Love
Book III:	The Book of Fate
Book IV:	The Book of Death

Part II: Beyond

Book V:	The Book of Night
Book VI:	The Book of Twilight
Book VII:	The Book of Day

Epilogue

Book VIII:	The Return to Earth

There was nothing in the early version corresponding to the present Book of the Traveller of the Worlds or to the cantos describing Savitri's Yoga; "rather Savitri moved through the worlds of Night, of Twilight, of Day—all of course in a spiritual sense—and ended by calling down the power of the Highest Worlds of Sachchidananda"; and Sri Aurobindo has also admitted that *at that time* he had no idea of what the supramental World would be like.[112]

Quite obviously, this early version of *Savitri* was written not long after *Urvasie* (1896) and *Love and Death* (1899), the two early narrative poems ('epyllions', Iyengar calls them)[113] in which Sri Aurobindo had essayed a somewhat similar theme. In *Urvasie*, the human hero Pururavas and the celestial nymph Urvasie come together, they are separated, and they come together again—and finally—when Pururavas is raised to the semi-divine status of a Gandharva. Not the death of Urvasie, but her withdrawal to heaven, causes the complication which is happily resolved when Pururavas too qualifies for life in that 'dream kingdom' of Gandharvas and Apsaras. An early poem, it is steeped in romantic sentiment and imagery, there is a 'temptation' at its heart, and an implied lesson. What though Urvasie were lost? All was not lost, there were his people, his kingdom, his responsibilities; not for personal enjoyment,

> But to the voice of Vedic litanies,
> Sacredly placed are the dread crowns of Kings
> For bright felicities and cruel toils.[114]

But no: Pururavas is "driven by a termless wide desire"; he can have no life without Urvasie. He gains his private felicity at last but at a heavy cost to his people and his kingdom:

> Then Love in his sweet heavens was satisfied.
> But far below through silent mighty space
> The green and strenuous earth abandoned rolled.[115]

In the companion poem, *Love and Death*,[116] there is described an Indian Orpheus (Ruru) regaining his lost Eurydice (Priyumvada); the roles of the Savitri story are here reversed, for it is the husband who by the power of his love regains his partner. Ruru, Sage Brigu's grandson, and Priyumvada, the Apsara Menaca's daughter, fall in love and marry. They lead the life of love's fulfilment, but the joy is short-lived. Priyumvada is bitten by a snake and dies. When the first shock is over, Ruru realises his grave loss and resolves to get back the living bride from Death's grim claws. The God of Love, Kama, tells Ruru that it may be Death will relent, but he would also drive a heavy bargain:

> Alone of gods Death loves not gifts: he visits
> The pure heart as the stained…
> Life the pale ghost requires: with half thy life
> Thou mayest protract the thread too early cut
> Of that delightful spirit…[117]

Ruru readily consents to the sacrifice, and so Kama shows the distracted husband the passage to the nether world,

> …to the grey waste,
> Hopeless Patala, the immutable
> Country, where neither sun nor rain arrives,
> Nor happy labour of the human plough
> Fruitfully turns the soil, but in vague sands
> And indeterminable strange rocks and caverns
> That into silent blackness huge recede,
> Dwell the great serpent and his hosts, writhed forms,
> Sinuous, abhorred, through many horrible leagues
> Coiling in a half darkness…[118]

This is like the descent into Dante's Hell, and Ruru is aghast when he sees the shapes and hears the cries in Death's Kingdom. But Ruru's resolve is unshaken, and he makes the inexorable bargain with Death, and Ruru and Priyumvada are permitted to renew their interrupted life on earth.

In both *Urvasie* and *Love and Death*, the hero, faced between two alternatives, unhesitatingly chooses love. Pururavas would rather be united with Urvasie in heaven than remain on earth and discharge his high obligations as a leader of the human race. Ruru would rather get back his Priyumvada even at the cost of half his own life than follow the higher calling of a Brahmin, and pursue (in the Dantean phrase) virtue and knowledge. Their single-minded love is worthy of all praise, but something is lost all the same; only that love is truly blessed that brings through its fulfillment happiness to all. Savitri, even in the legend, not merely regains her Satyavan, but brings undreamt of happiness to her own and Satyavan's parents. Already Sri Aurobindo was obscurely approaching the Savitri ideal of world redemption through love, for nobler still than Pururavas and Ruru and their successful defiance of fate was the defiance of Death on Savitri's part and all that came afterwards. In the words of K.D.Sethna,

> In *Urvasie* as well as *Love and Death* there is that struggle against mortality and the fate which circumscribes mundane life. Pururavas scales an Overworld to clasp the vanished Urvasie; Ruru descends into an Underworld to bring back Priyumvada killed before she was ripe. Earth's heart storming beyond earth to gain fulfilment, either by attaining the supra-terrestrial and remaining in its light or by invading the infra-terrestrial and reclaiming from its darkness what it has snatched and submerged —this is the psychological motif behind Sri Aurobindo's two most striking masses of achievement in blank verse during early life, and it renders his many-sided poetic masteries in them a kind of foreshadowing of the blank verse of *Savitri* in which today he is embodying his Yogic explorations of the Unknown in a more luminously mystical legend and symbol of love. [119]

Although this was written when *Savitri* was still in the process of revision, it is by no means an incorrect anticipation of the manifoldness of significance in the completed Legend *and* Symbol.

The new element which Sri Aurobindo introduced into the revised *Savitri* was his vision of the worlds up to the supramental and his conviction regarding the possibility of realising the Life Divine on earth. Much more now went into the first Book than there originally was, and ultimately most of the present Part I came to be newly added, while the present Part II and Part III are really revised versions of the old Parts I and II respectively. The main additions, then, relate to Aswapati's Yoga in Part I (Books I-III) and Savitri's Yoga (Book VII). The piece d'resistance in the whole poem is Book II, with its fifteen cantos, in which Aswapati's 'odyssey' through the 'worlds' is described.

In 1938 Sri Aurobindo took up the 'Worlds' seriously, and by 1946 "the small passage about Aswapati and the other worlds" became an enormous Book, and besides the poem as a whole also was fast taking its final shape. Although in the meantime he had developed his theory of the overhead aesthesis and was in practice often writing in response to the movements in the higher planes of consciousness, he was nevertheless aware of inequalities of level in the still widening expanse of the poem. "In so large a plan", he wrote in 1946, "covering most subjects of philosophical thought and vision and many aspects of spiritual experience there is bound to be much variation of tone: but that is, I think, necessary for the richness and completeness of the treatment."[120] Anyhow, by October or November 1950, the poem in its present form was ready, and Sri Aurobindo was content to leave it there. He knew that a poem like *Savitri* could not hope to be understood at once. His best hope was expressed in these terms in a letter written in 1947: "It took the world something like a hundred years to discover Blake; it would not be improbable that there might be a greater time-lag here, though naturally we hope for better things. For in India at least some understanding or feeling and an audience few and fit may be possible. Perhaps by some miracle there may be before long a larger appreciative audience."[121]

XIII

SAVITRI AND *FAUST*

A poem like *Savitri* that was, as we have seen, some fifty years a-growing, a poem that attempts to present at one and the same time a human and a cosmic drama, a poem besides that reveals some of the features of a tantalising palimpsest, must needs, as Sri Aurobindo himself has admitted, show traces of variations in tone and changes in style. In this respect, as also in others, *Savitri* challenges comparison with another great poetic masterpiece, Goethe's *Faust*,[122] which was years a-growing. Sri Aurobindo greatly admired Goethe and once wrote to a disciple:

> Yes, Goethe goes much deeper than Shakespeare; he had an incomparably greater intellect than the English Poet and sounded problems of life and thought Shakespeare had no means of approaching even. But he was certainly not a greater poet; I do not find myself very ready to admit either that he was Shakespeare's equal. He wrote out of a high poetic intelligence but his style and movement nowhere came near the poetic power, the magic, the sovereign expression and profound or subtle rhythms of Shakespeare... There is too a touch mostly wanting—the touch of an absolute, an intensely inspired or revealing inevitability...[123]

Sri Aurobindo thus knew his *Faust* even as he knew the *Commedia* intimately, and he might even have seen—as Kuno Fischer and others have—resemblances between the two poems. In the earliest version dating from 1773, Goethe seems to have laid the stress on the heroine, Gretchen, while Faust was no more than the Faust of the old legend. It was almost twenty-five years later that—perhaps under the influence of Schiller—the characterisation of Faust acquired deeper symbolic hues and that he was raised to a higher philosophical plane. The Second Part, written during the last eight years of his life when he enjoyed the friendship of Eckermann, gave the play a further dimension and made the whole work a philosophical poem of imperishable value, though there will always be people who prefer the First to the Second Part. For example, A.C. Bradley says,

> Goethe himself could never have told the world what he was going to express in the First Part of *Faust*: the poem told *him*, and it is one of the world's greatest. He knew too well what he was

> going to express in the Second Part and with all its wisdom and beauty it is scarcely a great poem.[124]

As *Faust* added new dimensions in the Second Part, so did *Savitri* in its final revised form. These additions to *Savitri* and the new accent given to her character owe their origin, as already pointed out, partly to Sri Aurobindo's Yogic experiences and the philosophy that he outlined on their basis, and partly also to his association with the Mother during the last thirty years of his life. What Karl Breul says in his 'Introduction' to the Bohn's Series edition about Part II of *Faust* may also be said of Book II of *Savitri*: "...although sometimes difficult, yet by no means abstruse and incomprehensible, not a whit harder to understand in general motive and outline." The Aurobindonian view that when right aspiration wells up from man's troubled or unsatisfied heart it is met by an answering response from Above, is also found enunciated towards the close of Goethe's poem at the climactic point of Faust's redemption:

> Saved is this noble soul from ill,
> Our spirit-peer. Who ever
> Strives forward with unswerving will,—
> Him can we aye deliver;
> And if with him celestial love
> Hath taken part,—to meet him
> Come down the angels from above;
> With cordial hail they greet him.[125]

Besides, it is worth noting that, before his death, Faust realises that permanent happiness could come only if man works, not for himself, but for humanity. This is paralleled by the Aurobindonian view that one should work only for the Divine, the Divine, of course, including humanity also. Further, it is a striking parallelism between the *Commedia* and *Faust* that even as it is Beatrice who conducts Dante through Paradise, it is Gretchen who finally comes forward to guide Faust to the higher spheres:

To guide him, let it be given to me;
Still dazzles him, the new-born day.[126]

In Sri Aurobindo's epic, likewise, it is Savitri who saves Satyavan ('the Soul of the World') from the death-trap and guides him back to the world of man to greet another Dawn. Whether in the *Commedia*, *Faust* or *Savitri*, Woman—the blessed feminine—is the ultimate Redeemer; she is Love, she is Wisdom, and she is Strength.

It will be clear, then, that the Faustian consciousness as presented by Goethe is verily an expanding and an evolving consciousness that tries to comprehend all ranges and gradation of human life; and it even extends, says Ronald Peacock, "to human experience over many centuries, since Goethe includes later in his play a deep vista of ancient culture and a sense of historical evolution."[127] Just as Faust tries to go beyond books and magic to explore the deep perennial springs of human life, so also Savitri, by exploring the "inner countries of the mind and heart", covers the whole gamut of possible human experience and penetrates to the secret Self that includes all and transcends all.

XIV

SAVITRI: ITS ARCHITECTURAL DESIGN

On a first view it cannot be denied that the original scheme of *Savitri* in two parts had a neat simplicity, even as the scheme of the *Divina Commedia* (Hell: Purgatory: Paradise) has an obvious rounded completeness. However, a closer view will show that the revised *Savitri* too is not lacking in a firm architectural design. The poem begins, as Western epics often do, at a critical point; it plunges into the middle of things—*in medias res*. Retrospective narration follows (as in *Paradise Lost*); the thread of the story is taken up again, and now we follow it without any further interruption, till the unfolding of the triumphant conclusion. If we leave aside the period covered by the retrospective narration (a period of about forty years in actual time, which includes the eighteen years of Aswapati's Yoga, the years of Savitri's birth and childhood and girlhood and the 'Quest' which follow, as also the first year of her married life with Satyavan), the drama outlined in the poem extends over a single day (as, for example, in a modern 'prose epic' like James Joyce's *Ulysses*). The scheme of the poem may be indicated accordingly as follows:

DAWN

(The 'dawn' of the fateful day in Savitri's life, and in the life of evolving humanity: Book I, Cantos 1 and 2.)

Backgrounds and Antecedents:
(Retrospective Narration)

I. Aswapati's Yoga that led to Savitri's incarnation:

(i) Aswapati's spiritual fulfilment as an individual. (Book I, Cantos 3, 4 and 5).

(ii) Aswapati's ascent as a typical representative of the human race to win the possibility of discovery and possession of all the planes of consciousness. (Book II, Cantos 1-15).

(iii) Aswapati's voicing his (and humanity's) aspiration for a universal realisation and a new creation, and the promise of the Incarnation. (Book III, Cantos 1-4).

II. Savitri's earlier story (including her Yoga):

(i) Childhood and Girlhood. (Book IV, Cantos 1-2).

(ii) The seeking and the finding of Love (Satyavan) in the Forest. (Book IV, Cantos 3-4 and Book V, Cantos 1-3).

(iii) The warning of the challenge of Fate given by Narad, and Savitri's acceptance of the challenge. (Book VI, Cantos 1-2).

(iv) Marriage of Savitri and Satyavan; her bitter-sweet ordeal. (Book VII, Canto 1).

(v) Savitri's Yoga and preparation to meet the threatened challenge of Fate. (Book VII, Cantos 2-7).

DAY

(Savitri, with her knowledge of what is to happen on this fateful day, persuades her parents-in-law to allow her to accompany Satyavan on his usual fruit-and-fuel gathering mission to the forest. There, at the destined hour, Satyavan is racked by headache, lies on the ground with his head on Savitri's lap, and presently life is extinct in him: Book VIII, entitled 'The Book of Death'.)

The Struggle Between Savitri and Death

(The Divine Manifestation *vs.* the Old Dispensation; Supramental Light *vs.* the Night, the Falsehood and the Ignorance)

I. Eternal Night (Book IX)

II. The Double Twilight (Book X)

III. Everlasting Day (Book XI)

NIGHT

(Savitri and Satyavan start returning to the hermitage, and on the way are met by his father, who has recovered his eyesight and his kingdom. All is well now, and as they retire for the night's rest at long last, they know that a great new Dawn awaits them: Book XII, the Epilogue.)

Since the poem is both a Legend and a Symbol, the above simple scheme may now be presented in a somewhat different way also so as to bring out the dual aspects side by side:

	LEGEND **EARTH** (Action in Time)	**SYMBOL** **BEYOND** (Timeless Action)
DAWN	Dawn of the fateful day in the life of Savitri and Satyavan: the Day foretold by *Rishi* Narad— "Savitri too awoke" (p. 6).	Symbol Dawn of the day when the issue between Life and Death, Light and Darkness, is to be joined, and finally decided —"It was the hour before the Gods awake." (p.1).

ALL THE YESTERDAYS

The Yoga of Knowing

1. Aswapati's Yoga: as an individual, leading to self-knowledge; as the leader of the race, summing up its achievements, and embodying its hopes; voicing his and the race's aspiration and invoking a new Incarnation.

1. The exploration of the occult and symbol worlds: voyaging through the World-Stair—The Kingdom of Subtle Matter; The World of the Vital, the Glory and the Fall; The Kingdoms and Godheads of the Little Life—the Powers of the Ignorance; The Kingdoms and Godheads of the Greater Life—the Hero, the Artist, the Superman.

DESCENT

Into the Abyss of the Night; Reign of Falsehood, Evil and Darkness; Life's worst Perversions; Hell's deepest Hole.

ASCENT

The Paradise of the Life-Gods; The Kingdoms and Godheads of the Little Mind: Mind's Loyal Serfs—Thought, Intelligence, Reason; The Kingdoms and Godheads of the Greater Mind—the Overhead Powers with their increasing Truth-Consciousness; The Heavens of the Ideal; In the Self of Mind; The World-Soul; The Greater Knowledge, and the route to the Unknowable; The Beatific Vision and the nectarean Boon.

	2. Savitri's birth, and growth, and Quest, and marriage to Satyavan:	2. The journey into the "inner countries" of the mind and the heart in search of the true Soul and the Self:
	Savitri's Yoga of preparation for the threatened event.	The World of Appearance; Beyond Appearance; World within World; Behind the veil of Forms; The triple soul-forces: Sorrow, Might, and Light; The Soul's Mystic Cave; The Secret Soul.
The Yoga of Readiness		The invasion of Nihil; The Cipher of God; Beyond the Nihil; The Power and the Glory of Ananda.
DAY	Death of Satyavan in the Forest; Savitri and Death; the vigil and the victory.	'Darkness at Noon': the struggle between Light and Darkness, Love and Death, in the symbol realms of Eternal Night, the Double Twilight, and Everlasting Day.
NIGHT	The Night of Fulfilment, leading to a Greater Dawn; the Yoga of Knowing (Aswapati's) and the Yoga of Readiness and Striving (Savitri's) are now followed by the	

> Yoga of Becoming and Being, in which both Savitri and Satyavan participate and enact the Life Divine on Earth.

Any attempt to picture the cosmos should take note of its three inherent laws: the Law of Variety, the Law of Change, and the Law of Order and Purpose that gives meaning to the Variety and the Change. Dante's universe is carefully localised: Earth at the centre, and Hell, with its circles burrowing and penetrating, and Purgatory, with its rising slopes, on either side of the Earth; then the nine heavenly spheres, and, beyond them, the Empyrean, the Rose of the Blessed, the nine Angelic Circles, and so on to the Ultimate Vision. Order and hierarchy are purposively related, and from the Lowest to the Highest, from prime matter to pure intelligence, is a continuous chain, a logical sequence and pattern. Sri Aurobindo's Cosmos, on the other hand, takes a modern rather than a mediaeval view; the picture presented by science is not denied, and the insights of psychology are fully pressed into service. Dante himself is now seen to be more modern than he appeared to be during the last five or six centuries, but Sri Aurobindo *is* modern, and his picture of the cosmos has a poetical and philosophical as well as a scientific and psychological validity and sufficiency.

XV

SAVITRI: ITS SYMBOLIC ACTION IN A COSMIC BACKGROUND

A comparison of the extended scheme of *Savitri* with that of the earlier narrative poem will make clear that the major additions are Aswapati's Yoga, Savitri's Yoga and the new accent or dimension given to the struggle between Savitri and Death in Book IX, X and XI. The intention behind these additions and changes is to impose on the simple austere ambrosial human drama a vast symbolic dimension so that what happens in an apparently obscure place on earth may be made to carry implications on a truly cosmic scale. The opening line in canto three of Book I: "A world's desire compelled her mortal birth," succinctly prepares us for this shift from the individual to the general or universal context. Aswapati sought an heir to his kingdom through *tapasya*, which extended over a period of eighteen years: thus the old legend.

What does *tapasya* mean? Spiritual knowledge may be acquired from scriptures and from one's teachers; it comes also as the result of one's own turning inwards and seeking the light of the Infinite. Knowledge of the former kind can lead to the latter, and experienced knowledge can lead to the former. Aswapati turns from the first phase of his spiritual awakening to the Book of the Secret Knowledge; and this in turn equips him for a fresh spiritual quest. Aswapati's consciousness now ranges from heaven to earth, from earth to heaven, all planes of life are traversed, all possibilities are assessed. Of course, although Aswapati is the *tapasvin* of the story, what is recorded is really the vision of the poet which, like a searchlight, guides us through the World-Stair. Like a great Dragon stationed near the approaches to a beautiful house, this part of *Savitri* is apt to scare away the average reader. What is it all about, he may ask in exasperation, and turn away, without waiting for an answer which, in any case, can be neither easy nor short.

A thinker who tries to take stock of the human and cosmic situation may very well pose the fundamental questions: Where do I stand? What is my goal? How may I reach it? These roughly correspond to the traditional Hindu categories of *tattva*, *hita* and *puruṣārtha*, and, again, to Kant's celebrated questions: What can I know? What ought I to do? What may I hope for? These primary questions have thus occurred to thinkers of the East as well as the West, and since Sri Aurobindo was in some respects a unique synthesis of what was best in the culture of India and the culture of the West, he could not but view these questions with a new integralised vision and creative purpose.

"The tendency of Eastern thinkers", writes W.R. Inge, "is to try to gain a view of reality as a whole, complete and entire: the form under which it most readily pictures it is that of *space*. The West seeks rather to discover the universal laws... The form under which it most readily pictures reality is that of *time*."[128] It would, perhaps, be no over-simplification to say that Sri Aurobindo's philosophical thought was a fusion of the two approaches to Reality, for both *space* and *time* came into his calculations. He was less interested in losing himself in infinity than in realising, if possible *here* and *now*, an earthly paradise. He was no absolute monist enamoured of Nihil, but an evolutionist who thought that man could evolve into God. He sought in this pluralistic temporal world itself the inspiration to build the Life Divine. A poem entitled *The Human Power* by Elder Olson expresses this idea very well:

> Not in God's image was man
> First created, but in
> Likeness of a beast;
> Until that beast became man,
> All travailed in death and pain
> And shall travail still
> Till man be the image of God...
> And this I believe is God's will.[129]

Beast to man, man to God; or average ordinary man to the evolved spiritually awakened saint: how is this progression started, how achieved? "Spiritual evolution as distinct from revolution", says Hugh I' Anson Fausset, "consists of this gradual dying to the old life of the divided senses and gradual growing of the new life of wholeness within the decaying body of the old. It is a growth, often imperceptible, in the knowledge of spiritual reality, at each stage of which the material world loses something of its delusive appearance as the veils of partial sense are withdrawn until at last its true spiritual form is perceived."[130] Spiritual growth is also growth in freedom, and freedom is power; the lower life is the life of the slave, the highest life is the life of the saint, and just as all art is said to aspire to the condition of music, all humanity must aspire to the condition of utter freedom which is the saint's prerogative.[131] Since it is the privilege of civilised humanity to retain the memories of the race, it is often possible to achieve in a short time what took thousands of years for our ancestors to accomplish.

It is, of course, understood that, whatever the materialists may say, the advance of the race is brought about as much by man's aspiration as by the answering response of God. John Elof Boodin says that, "God must be conceived as an energising spirit in the universe who furnishes the inspiration for creating an ideal realm of values—a kingdom of heaven—in a distressed and struggling world"; on the other hand, the individual also, "has a say in the comedies and tragedies enacted in the cosmos, whether the individuals be electrons or human beings or stars."[132] Emergent evolution, in the sense that new things somehow come out of the old things, doesn't make sense; nothing can come out of anything unless it is there already, in however nascent a condition; it would thus be necessary to assume that all energy is, in the final analysis, "an expression of the universal mind...and it would then seem to be true that all development is of the nature of emergence. It contains from the first the 'promise and potency' of the higher forms of life."[133] Boodin also makes the same point, but even more emphatically, when he says that, "the higher level in the advance of life does not merely emerge from below, but implies a stimulus from beyond and the creative response of the finite to this stimulus... Best of all, the consciousness of the divine may come to us as a sense of communion with God and in rare moments as a beatific Vision..."[134]

From the above religious insights it is clear that man has a dynamic destiny, he is in a field of forces with a cosmic range, his destiny and the destiny of the cosmos are together involved in a "general plan" projected by the Universal Mind;[135] it is clear too that freedom and power in a spiritual sense really mean the capacity to participate in the Plan and further it, and this can best be done if man, a creature of the 'natural order', makes himself the instrument of God, who is the source of the 'divine order'.[136]

When Sri Aurobindo describes Aswapati as journeying through the several occult realms in the World-Stair, he is not luxuriating in pseudo-romantic escapism but merely recording, with painstaking accuracy, in the light of his own visions and experiences, the various levels and gradations of consciousness which comprise the cosmos. Samuel Alexander says that, "within the all-embracing stuff of Space-Time, the universe exhibits an emergence in Time of successive levels of finite existences, each with its characteristic empirical quality."[137] Man to Deity is, according to Alexander, the next spurt in evolution, but he too doesn't relate the idea of evolution with the idea of the Divine being already involved in the lower forms of existences; an endless epic of emergent evolution can be played by a Force more akin to Kazantzakis' Combatant and Shaw's Life Force than a power like Sachchidananda, from which all involution emanates and towards which all evolution strives. The views of two Western spiritualists too may be give here; thus F.W.H. Myers:

> I imagine that the continuity of the universe is complete; and that therefore the hierarchy of intelligences between our minds and the World-Soul is infinite, and that somewhere in that ascent a point is reached where our conception of time loses its accustomed meaning...[138]

and Sir Oliver Lodge also speaks to the same effect:

> ...there must be grades of existence higher as well as lower than man; and it is reasonable to suppose that such grades of existence extend upward at least as far as they extend downward; they can hardly have a limit short of infinity. The Infinite Being we call God, and we seek after him...[139]

The universe is, first of all, a cosmos; secondly, it is a living, not a dead, cosmos. From these premises may be drawn other conclusions. Not only of humanity can it be said that we are members of one another; of the cosmos, too, it should be said. A living cosmos means, besides, a cosmos capable of change and growth; growth carrying the seeds of decay, decay and 'death' carrying the seeds of new life. The one may unfold as the many, the many may enclose as the one. In trying to explain this mystery—or this mystic truth at the heart of the cosmos—writers are obliged to resort to symbolism, as for example in the Chinese Book of Life, which speaks of the unity of *hsing-ming* or 'essence' and 'life', "inseparably mixed like the seeds of fire in the refining furnace", on which C. G. Jung comments:

> This symbolism refers to a sort of alchemic process of refining and 'ennobling'; darkness gives birth to light; out of the 'lead' of the water-region, grows the 'noble' gold; the unconscious becomes conscious in the form of a process of life and growth. (Hindu *Kuṇḍalinī* Yoga affords a complete analogy.) In this way the union of consciousness and life takes place.[140]

With whatever variations in idea or symbol, seers both of the West and the East have thus seized the quintessential truth regarding the efflorescence of divinity out of the bud sprouting from the seeming ooze of the world. But the evolutionary advance asks for a sense of adventure, a readiness to dare all and lose all to be able to gain all. "The step to higher consciousness", says Jung again, "leads away from all shelter and safety. The person must give himself to the new way completely, for it is only by means of his integrity that he can go farther."[141] Death itself may have to be faced; if the supreme encounter is avoided, it may prove to be a compromise, a retreat, not a victory and an advance. Christ was victorious in one way, Savitri in another; neither was *afraid* of death, nor wished to bypass it.[142] If egoism denies more and more, retreats more and more into the stifling prison-house of the selfish life, love affirms more and more, advances further and further, embracing all the universe in its affectionate grasp.

Egoism is the real prelude to death while love is the way of freedom and immortality. In Edward Carpenter's words,

> Love indicates immortality. No sooner does the human being perceive this divine nucleus within himself than he knows his eternal destiny. Plunged in the matter and gross body he had learned the lesson of identity and separateness. All that the devil can teach him, he has faithfully absorbed. Now he has to expand that identity, forever unique into ever vaster spheres of activity—to become finally a complete and finished aspect of the One.[143]

The Mother has recorded how, as a child of thirteen, every night she used to undergo an extraordinary experience; she saw herself coming out of her body and rising up above the house and the town, with a magnificent robe covering the town like an immense roof:

> Then I would see coming out from all sides men, women, children, old men, sick men, unhappy men; they gathered under the outspread robe, imploring help, recounting their miseries, their sufferings, their pains. In reply, the robe, supple and living, stretched out to them individually, and as soon as they touched it, they were consoled or healed...Nothing appeared to me more beautiful, nothing made me more happy; and all the activities of the day seemed to me dull and colourless, without real life, in comparison with this activity of the night which was for me the true life...[144]

Her love had acquired vast dimensions, and this was one measure of the reality of her spiritual life. If love can thus extend from the narrow confines of a home and embrace a whole city, or all humanity, we need put no limits whatsoever to its full extension in space and time. Not the fact of such love alone, but the results of such love also, must beggar human calculation.

Consider a building: the physical frame (itself made up of steel, cement, brick, stone, timber, etc.), the electrical wiring, the pipes conveying water, photographs and pictures on the walls, flower-vases, furniture, utensils, people (themselves built of or run by chemical, electrical and psychic systems), all co-exist, and various currents—material, intellectual, emotional, psychic—set up by this conjunction of elements, all together, in their diversity and change and control and unity, make the house, which is the home of a family. Is it not so with the cosmos as well? "In the cosmos we must suppose", writes Boodin, "a far greater range of fields—electro-magnetic fields, gravitational field, chemical fields, organic fields, psychological fields, and, over and above them all, the supreme spiritual fields which prescribes the architecture of all the subordinate fields, which in turn make their variant individual adjustments according to their own relativity."[145]

The infinitely small and the infinitely vast, the infinitely near and the infinitely distant, are strangely enough related and poised in the cosmos. The fission of an atom releases energies sufficient to destroy a city. Why should not then the release of spiritual energy, which must be the ultimate source of *all* energy, be capable of effecting a revolution in our earth-nature and setting it in the direction of supernature? A house is sunk in darkness; a switch is put on, and the house is flooded with light. We know how it happens; there is the electrical system; and there is the power house from which energy flows to the house. Where are the power houses of the spirit? How is such power canalised? Are there worlds where spiritual energy is as freely current and for as manifold purposes as electrical energy is current in our modern cities? Further, as man is simultaneously a chemical, an electrical and a psychic system, and as the cosmos also is simultaneously several systems, cannot these be isolated for purposes of observation and study?

Can we have, in short, a cosmic view that takes note both of the infinitely small and the infinitely great, of all grades of existence, all possible levels of evolved or evolving life; that takes note also of all recent scientific discoveries and technological achievements, and even future possibilities; and, above all, posits the enveloping reality of the Spirit, the overall spiritual control of the universe?

Being a cosmos there is some order and harmony behind it all; but it is a still living and changing and evolving cosmos, and hence the order and the harmony do not preclude tensions and struggles, memories and regrets, dreams and hopes, aspirations and realisations. As Sri Aurobindo affirmed in one of his early poems:

> Time is a strong convention; future and present
> Were living in the past...
> And even from this veil of mind the spirit
> Looks out sometimes and sees
> The bygone aeons that our lives inherit,
> The unborn centuries...[146]

Such is the vision behind the symbolic action unfolded in *Savitri*. It is no poetic fiction, no projection of the probable impossible; on the contrary, what is here dramatised is an actually developing and fulfilling action with man as protagonist and the Divine as the goal.

XVI

SAVITRI AND THE 'SONNETS'

Some of the key-ideas projected vividly in *Savitri*, and especially in the Book of the Traveller of the Worlds, are not only elaborately expounded in *The Life Divine* but are also succinctly and poetically expressed in the series of sonnets that Sri Aurobindo wrote during the thirties and the forties, roughly contemporaneously with the composition of *Savitri* in its present form. Indeed, K.D. Sethna goes so far as to say that, "in many respects the Sonnets are the best brief approach for us to *Savitri*", and in many of these sonnets we have broad clues to the worldview inherent in the drama of *Savitri* as also, "the element of spiritual autobiography that is found worked in a non-personal narrative shape into that poem in detailed abundant vividness."[147] One of the last sonnets, *Evolution*, is an incandescent summing-up of the Aurobindonian worldview:

I passed into a lucent still abode
And saw as in a mirror crystalline
An ancient Force ascending...
Earth was a cradle for the arriving God
And man but a half-dark half-luminous sign
Of the transition of the veiled Divine
From Matter's sleep and the tormented load
Of ignorant life and death to the Spirit's light.[148]

The ascending Force is not unlike Kazantzakis Combatant, but it is also the veiled Divine, the beckoner of the arriving God. The entire Aurobindonian dialectic of the supramentalisation or divinisation of man and the earth is here presented in sharp miniature. In this drama of transformation, man plays a protagonist's role:

Yet his advance,
Attempt of a divinity within,
A consciousness in the inconscient Night,
To realise its own supernal Light
Confronts the ruthless forces of the Unseen.
Aspiring to godhead from insensible clay
He travels slow-footed towards the eternal day.[149]

But this insensible clay is yet the home of the veiled Spirit, and from where it is hid, it may emerge when the occasion is ripe. Even the electron is the Spirit's minute particle of movement and power:

The electron on which forms and worlds are built,
Leaped into being, a particle of God.
A spark from the eternal Energy split,
It is the Infinite's blind minute abode.
In that small flaming chariot Shiva rides.
The One devised innumerably to be;
His oneness in invisible forms he hides,
Time's tiny temples of eternity.[150]

'Dead' matter, they said once; we now know that matter, being made up of these flaming whirling electrons and other infinitesimal particles that are really minute bundles of energy, is not 'dead' but wonderfully 'alive' under the surface. It is clear, then, that darkness, death, inconscience cannot be real, cannot be final:

> What stark Necessity or ordered Chance
> Became alive to know the cosmic whole?
> What magic of numbers, what mechanic dance
> Developed consciousness, assumed a soul?
> The darkness was the Omnipotent's abode,
> Hood of omniscience, a blind mask of God...[151]
> As with the figures of a symbol dance
> The screened Omniscient plays at Ignorance.[152]

What's the point of it all, it may be asked. We have to fall back on the explanation that all is God's play, the *lila* of the Supreme:

> One who has made in sport the suns and seas
> Mirrors in our being his immense caprice.[153]

Call it *lila* or the 'infinite adventure' of Becoming: the seeming opposites clash, the contrasts meet and merge, and there is no end to the rapture of the play. When the "skiff is launched", it leaves its sheltered harbour-home, and must surrender to the Unknown completely, though there is an all-knowing Captain who will invisibly control the rudder and guide the bark through the threatening abysses to the safe thither shore.[154] When consciousness exceeds the cribbed average mentality and scours the oceans of the Unknown, when the mind breaks through its prison-house and engages in a cosmic task, when man's courageous soul makes "an assignation with the Night" and comes to woo "her dark and dangerous heart", man then achieves a vast extension in his being and his power:

> This mute stupendous Energy that whirls
> The stars and nebulae in its long train...
> It rises from the dim inconscient deep
> Upcoiling through the minds and hearts of men,

> Then touches on some height of luminous sleep
> The bliss and splendour of the eternal plane.[155]

It is a preparation for the possession of 'cosmic consciousness', a prelude to the exercise of such sovereignty; nothing is now hidden from view, neither the origins nor the course of events, neither the glory of Shiva in his "mystic loneliness of nude ecstasy" nor the passion of Krishna's flute and the beauty of his immortal eyes:

> I have wrapped the wide world in my wider self
> And Time and Space my spirit's seeing are.
> I am the god and demon, ghost and elf,
> I am the wind's speed and the blazing star.
> All Nature is the nursling of my care,
> I am its struggle and the eternal rest;
> The world's joy thrilling runs through me, I bear
> The sorrow of millions in my lonely breast.
> I have learned a close identity with all,
> Yet am by nothing bound that I become;
> Carrying in me the universe's call
> I mount to my imperishable home.
> I pass beyond Time and life on measureless wings,
> Yet still am one with born and unborn things. [156]

Such is 'Cosmic Consciousness'; there is an edged intellectual clarity, but it by no means destroys the nuances of powerful suggestion, the rumbling undertones of *dhvani*.

These sonnets are, of course, no more than stray 'sparks' from the fiery Aurobindonian forge that was mainly engaged in the creation of *Savitri*. The neat turns of phrase, the apt imagery, the striking symbolism in some of these sonnets are a tribute to Sri Aurobindo's poetic powers and artistic integrity. But as a sample and a foretaste of the characteristic philosophical poetry of *Savitri* and of its mystical muse, these sonnets are no less valuable.

XVII

ADVOCATUS DIABOLI AND ADVOCATUS DEI

Admittedly the experience that has gone into a poem of such magnitude may be both authentic and of profound significance. The philosophical worldview that serves as the frame-work of the poem may be both impressive and intellectually satisfying. The human drama played in the foreground may be capable of making an immediate appeal to our emotions; it may be sanctified by tradition, it may have a perennial human significance. The symbols employed in the poem may likewise hark back to the glorious childhood of the human race, the Age of the Veda, when the *rishi*s looked out upon Nature with wonder and wild surmise and created the great myths of the race.

The race, the milieu, the moment may all create a favourable context for the poet who would sing of man and his developing destiny in the cosmos. But in spite of all these propitious circumstances, a great epic may fail to arrive. Is *Savitri* the supreme achievement in the epic genre, or is it a noble effort gone awry? Is it the one great cosmic poem of our time and of all time, or is it no more than a tour-de-force, worthy to be praised because it was undertaken at all, and not because it has been successfully accomplished? Only posterity can give the final answer to these questions but we too cannot shirk our responsibility to face the questions boldly and formulate our answers. The traditional Hindu dialectic has been to state first the Purvapaksha and then only the Siddhanta; in other words, first to allow the Devil's Advocate to have his worst say, and then only to give a chance of reply to the God's Advocate. It would not be amiss if such a method were followed here as well. There is an incidental advantage too, for it is often possible to hear Sri Aurobindo himself in defence of his aims and methods.

The criticisms may be ranged, for the sake of convenience, under five heads. First, then, about the size and structure of the poem. *Savitri* is a poem running into 23,813 lines, longer even than Browning's *The Ring and the Book*, twice as long as *Paradise Lost*, and more than one-half the size of the *Ramayana*. Even so, Sri Aurobindo left it 'incomplete'. Not only is the poem unconscionably long, it has also a lop-sided structure. Retrospective narration takes up about three-fourths of the entire bulk of the poem; and even there, Aswapati's Yoga is given a disproportionate importance, and extends over nearly 400 (out of the total of 814) pages. For so voluminous an epic poem, there is insufficient matter, the fable is too thin, the characters are too few, the incidents too hazy.

So much for the Purvapakshin; and now for the Siddhantin. Appearances may be deceptive, as they *are* deceptive here. Length in a poem is by itself neither a virtue nor a blemish; the question to consider is how far length is related to amplitude. Objective measurements should thus be related to functions and not discussed in a kind of critical vacuum. Tillyard asks for "amplitude, breadth, inclusiveness, and so on", as also "a control commensurate with the amount included"; do we find these in *Savitri*? Likewise, Abercrombie asks for *range* as well as *organisation*; do we have these in *Savitri*? An affirmative answer is called for because *Savitri*, looked at from one angle, is a history of the cosmos itself, and the epic includes within its purview the past, the present and the future.

Man's life in the cosmos is the theme of the poem, and life, while it is forward-looking has to take frequent backward-glances as well. The past determines the present, and together they will determine the shape of things to come. Aswapati reviews the aeons of human endeavour in the past, the zig-zag course of human history, the many failures and the few significant advances; and he penetrates the mystery of the cosmos to seek the clue both to man's past failures and to the possibility of future victory. Yeats says that, "our little memories are but a part of some great memory that renews the world, and men's thoughts are not, as we suppose, the deep but a little foam upon the deep."[157] Aswapati, however, skims the foam and dives much deeper, touching the very bottom; and soars high above the clouds, reaching the highest heights. He is able therefore to see behind veil upon veil of appearance and reveal the stairway of the occult worlds.

Even as there is amplitude, breadth, inclusiveness (it is the cosmic play itself that is here recorded), there is also the necessary organisation, as already explained in the two complementary schema given earlier. As in the human body the mere size of the respective organs—hands, legs, eyes, brain, heart—bears little proportion to their intrinsic or functional importance, and living man is a whole, a power and a personality, so too in an epic like *Savitri* it is not altogether relevant to talk of the relative size of this or that section of the poem; the total contents and the total impression are what matter ultimately, and *Savitri*, judged by such criteria, would be found to fulfil the 'structure ideal' at least as much as other poems of similar size and scope.

The criticism of length—"unconscionable length"—has been made, not only against *Savitri*, but against Sri Aurobindo's major works generally. It was the reviewer in the *Times Literary Supplement* who in an otherwise eulogistic appreciation of *The Life Divine* found it also to be of "unconscionable length".[158] The reviewer of *Ilion* in the *Hindu* found in it "descriptions, embassies, debates of desolating length…typically Aurobindo-esque."[159] That Sri Aurobindo could be pointed, that he could give his statements a diamond-edge and brilliance, that his correspondence is full of the play of wit, humour, repartee and epigram, that he knew the virtue of brevity and succinctness in expression, must be clear to readers who are familiar with all parts of the Aurobindo canon. But there is no doubt that *Savitri* is a long poem, even as *The Life Divine* is a 'bulky' treatise. What is Sri Aurobindo's own defence? In the course of a long apologia written in 1947 he pleaded:

> Its length is an indispensable condition for carrying out its purpose and everywhere there is this length…in every part, in every passage, in almost every canto or section of a canto.

> It has been planned not on the scale of *Lycidas* or *Comus* or some brief narrative poem, but of the longer epical narrative, almost a minor, though a very minor *Ramayana*; it aims not at a minimum but at an exhaustive exposition of its world-vision or world-interpretation...omitting nothing that is necessary, fundamental to the completeness...It will of course seem much too long to a reader who does not understand what is written or, understanding, takes no interest in the subject; but that is unavoidable.[160]

Of any long poem whatsoever some people would say in exasperation: "None wished it longer than it is!" And even a comparatively short poem like *The Waste Land*, notwithstanding whole hillocks of exegesis, might still baffle us with regard to its 'meaning' and 'structure'. Not all the evidence is available at once, and one is often burdened by preconceived notions of what is proper. If when facing a swan we start looking for a duck we shall only pronounce it an ugly duckling! Poetic appreciation, as Ezra Pound has reminded us, is a sort of profession of faith; but, of course, the 'profession' itself is preceded by a genuine first response to the poem, and should be followed by a patient examination of the total contents. If impatience or intolerance dictates a hasty conclusion, it should not be taken very seriously.

Secondly, *Savitri* is assailed because it carries insufficient human interest. The human characters are few—Aswapati, Savitri, Satyavan, Dyumatsena; a few more perhaps, but they are of little consequence; and Narad is hardly of this earth, and certainly not earthy. What sort of epic can you make of these people? There is no 'physical' action either. There is the Yoga of the King, there is the Yoga of the Wife, and there is the Yoga of Struggle and Victory. We don't know whether we stand on our feet (the legendary story) or our heads (the symbol). We move from the 'symbol dawn' to the stairway of the occult worlds; the interior countries are symbolic; the Void is symbolic, the Double Twilight and the Everlasting Day are symbolic. What are we to make of such a poem? We have heard this sort of criticism before, about *Paradise Lost*, for example. Every time it is made, it sounds impressive, and must be answered. People say again: "I see nothing: there is nothing to hang on to. It is all too much in the air. The story has no contemporaneous relevance. It doesn't speak to *us*!"

Savitri is admittedly a legend *and* a symbol, answers the Siddhantin. But there is no jugglery about it: Savitri is the human character, and Savitri is the symbol; one goes back to the *Mahabharata*, the other goes back to the Veda, and both are as contemporaneous as the Sun that is shining today. The human and the cosmic action, too, centre in Savitri. "The great human appeal of idealism", writes Boodin, "has been a call to recreate the world into a better world, with the assurance that a power, greater than ourselves, is on the side of the creators. This call to creativeness involves the challenge that all is not well with the world—that the world needs to be made over."[161] Savitri is both a human power (which is the appearance) and the incarnation of a power greater than ourselves; she is one of the two protagonists in the struggle that she wages, both as a human and as a cosmic power, and the resulting victory too has consequences both on the individual and the cosmic planes.

Of Beatrice, who plays in the *Divina Commedia* a role not unlike Savitri's in the Indian epic, Charles Williams writes: "Let us say then that this was the effort—the union of virtue and beauty. It is, I think, true that virtue eventually runs away with the book... Philosophy—lady or no lady—is the vaster subject matter. But his (Dante's) descriptions and explanations of philosophy are often put in terms applicable to the woman, and sometimes astonishingly so."[162] Savitri is likewise the "union of strength and silence"; she is "an incarnation of the Divine Mother"; she is "the forerunner or first creator of a new race".[163] The dialectic of world transformation, the change of darkness into light, of death into immortality, is the vaster subject matter; but the human drama of the young wife ready to fight for and save her immaculate husband is no less significant. Savitri is human though out of the ordinary, her love for Satyavan is human though it acquires a new dimension of protective power, and her anxiety is human though her silent strength is verily superhuman. Savitri is both herself and a power beyond her apparently limited human self. She is at one and the same time conscious of her humanity and of her potential divinity:

> For I know now why my spirit came on earth
> And who I am and who he is I love.[164]

Finding that there is no other way, she is obliged to show Death her cosmic form:

> Her forehead's span vaulted the Omniscient's gaze,
> Her eyes were two stars that watched the universe.[165]

With a tone of unquestionable authority she now commands Death:

> Release the soul of the world called Satyavan...[166]

Savitri and Satyavan are Shakti and Shiva, they are Power and Truth; the victory certain, now they will realise its fruits on earth:

> I know that I can lift man's soul to God,
> I know that he can bring the Immortal down...
> To bring God down to the world on earth we came,
> To change the earthly life to life divine...
> I sacrifice not earth to happier worlds.[167]

Urban says truly that the religion of the mystics is, "that the love of man for God is also a love for all humanity...our human love, both for God and man, is also a witness of the love of God for us. In this love divine, all loves excelling, we know the oneness of the Good and of Being which our human reason, while it can demonstrate it as reasonable belief, can never completely prove. And in this knowledge all our other knowledge finds its fulfilment and its crown."[168] Savitri's love is of this kind: she loves God and therefore humanity, and she is the divine inhabiting a human tenement.

The criticism that *Savitri*, even if it should be conceded to have some kind of human interest (for, after all, the Savitri story *is* human), is nevertheless spoilt as a poem because of the intrusion of too much philosophy and mysticism, is as little justified as the criticism that it lacks human interest and contemporary urgency. We have seen earlier that although mysticism and philosophy seldom prove tractable to poetic treatment at some length, yet Dante has somehow performed the miracle; if Dante, why not Sri Aurobindo? Dante, with great power of flight, describes the journey of the "two high creatures" through the nine heavens to the Empyrean, and we see that they "move in space and time still, but also through increasing knowledge of heaven."[169] Though expressed with other figures, such too is the Aurobindonian dialectic of growth in spiritual knowledge, which is very different from the blind alleys of modern Existentialism. As Guido de Ruggiero brilliantly argues,

> Positing an activity at the source of becoming not only gives it a true protagonist, but explains also the levels which existence assumes through the various stages of the journey…The multiplication of planes and the activity of the protagonist, which is never satisfied with single stages that have been attained but continually surpasses them, creates in their intermingling dialectic the variety and richness of spiritual life. In Existentialism, on the contrary, all this relief vanishes and we get only a process deprived of significance and value…[170]

Savitri is presented in the poem as the central figure in the great drama of Becoming. Aswapati's effort, which is really the culmination of the effort of all of our yesterdays, the gathered energy of all the aeons of the past, is the necessary prelude to the Divine Mother agreeing to be a human incarnation as Savitri. From Savitri radiate the lines of mankind's and earth's future destiny. Past, present and future thus meet in Savitri, and it may be said of her and of the epic to which she gives her name:

> Time present and time past
> Are both perhaps present in time future,
> And time future contained in time past.[171]

Kindled and quenched and kindled again, the cosmic creative fires blaze and subside and blaze again, and Sri Aurobindo has *seen* this cosmic play and tries also to reason out the probable purposes behind it all and infer the probable directions of future advance. "The philosophy of *Savitri*", writes Sri Aurobindo, "expresses or tries to express a total and many-sided vision and experience of all the planes of being and their action upon each other. Whatever language, whatever terms are necessary to convey this truth of vision and experience it uses without scruple or admitting any mental rule of what is or is not poetic."[172] The mystic experience, the philosophy of transcendence (from the mental to the supramental), and the poetic recordation of the vision and the idea all fuse in the figure of Savitri, the chaste wife whose silent strength is the sole visible reality.

F.W. Bain tells an interesting story: A wife separated from her husband for some years lets a lighted lamp afloat on the waters of the Ganges. If the light burns, her husband is alive; if the light extinguishes, he is no more. A storm that is brewing subsides, and the waters are absolutely calm; the sky and the stars are reflected in the water. The sky thinks that the reflection is an illusion; the Lord therefore tells him: "Thou foolish sky, know that thou art thyself, with all thy stars, no less an illusion than is that other sky below. The sole reality of all is yonder little lamp, that floats midway, poised between the infinity above and that below. For it embodies the good quality of a faithful wife."[173] Savitri is the reality, and she makes real the mysticism and the philosophy that sustain, like the overhanging sky and the reflected sky, and give cover and rich significance to the little floating lamp on the still waters of the Ganges on a clear night.

The fourth group of critics assail *Savitri*, not on the score of its size or structure or matter or meaning, but on account of its imperfect articulation. The language is too dry and too abstract, or too sentimental and too rhetorical. There is too much repetition, and too much repetitive elaboration. The same features recur (journeys, expositions, forecasts), and certain words—tenebrous, golden, nude, plan, lone, bright, moon, sun, dark, soul, spirit, self, space, depth, etc. tend to occur again and again. The use of words is not imaginative enough, the rhythm chosen (namely the iambic pentameter) is used with insufficient elasticity, and there are individual word-combinations, especially line-endings, which are harsh and uncouth. "Self-space" occurs twice (123, 206); in the course of two consecutive pages (330-1) occur the combinations "spirit-depths", "soul-stuff", "soul-ground" and "soul-joy". Many of these line-endings—sun-march, soul-signs, spirit-sense, swim-range, heart-pulse, life-drift, world-scheme, life-plan, self-search, world-cloak, dream-brush, life-wants, soul-change, thought-hue and field-paths—make the rhythmic movement difficult, and have often to be read as spondees. There is, finally, a certain inequality in the style, sometimes descending to mere prose, though there are occasional elevations and crests as well. *Savitri* fails ultimately because its language fails and its rhythm fails to rise to the true pitch of epic utterance. One critic, himself a writer of magazine verse, has indeed gone to the extent of condemning the verse of *Savitri* as "slushy" and has roundly condemned "the temptation to slip into greasy, weak-spined and purple-adjectived 'spiritual' poetry".[174] And a Western journalist has called *Savitri* one of the "longest and worst epic poems of all time".[175]

What is distinctive and new, what is probably unique, in Sri Aurobindo's use of language and rhythm has been discussed towards the end of the previous chapter on 'Overhead' poetry and *Savitri*, and it is not therefore necessary to cover the entire ground once again. Here is a passage not untypical of *Savitri*:

> Distrust was thrown upon Mind's instruments;
> All that it takes for reality's shining coin,
> Proved fact, fixed inference, deduction clear,
> Firm theory, assured significance,
> Appeared as frauds upon Time's credit bank
> Or assets valueless in Truth's treasury.
> An Ignorance on an uneasy throne

Travestied with a fortuitous sovereignty
A figure of knowledge garbed in dubious words
And tinsel thought-forms brightly inadequate.[176]

Is it too dry and abstract, too inarticulate, or too ineffective? Is 'fortuitous sovereignty' too "pompous and bombastic"? Is the simile too obvious? Is the personification of Ignorance untenable? In itself and in its particular context, the passage seems to be edged and clear and evocative and effective. "The whole passage", explains Sri Aurobindo, "is of course about mental movements and mental powers, therefore about what the intellect sees as abstractions, but the inner vision does not feel them as that. To it mind has a substance and its energies and actions are very real and substantial things."[177] He always claimed the right to use words, not in terms of any notion of 'poetic diction' or any set so-called poetical rule, but by an intuitive feeling, leaving the final judgement to posterity. He has freely used scientific and technical words like plasm, wave particles, atom, proton, photon, robot, chemic, cells, stratosphere, morse, fractions, integers, decimals, camera, fifth-columnist, logarithmic-table, quantum, television, and various others drawn from the whole world of modern life and thought, but always with a clinching or suggestive appropriateness.

Repetition there no doubt is, plenty of it, but this, after all, is a characteristic feature of all epic poetry. Besides, Sri Aurobindo makes the legitimate claim that the repetitions of, "the same key ideas, key images and symbols, key words or phrases, key epithets, sometimes key lines or half-lines...give an atmosphere, a significant structure, a sort of psychological frame, an architecture"; the poet, especially the mystic poet, can thus resort to *āvṛtti*, repetition, "as one of the most powerful means of carrying home what has been thought or seen and fixing it in the mind in an atmosphere of light and beauty."[178] Eliot uses repetition to almost hypnotic effect in the *Choruses from the 'Rock'*, *Four Quartets*, and several other poems; in fact most poets of the first order are adepts at exploiting the 'uses' of repetition.

And often, in expert hands, repetitive elaboration casts a spell by purposefully running unity and variety together, as for example in *sangathi*s (improvisations) while rendering *kriti*s (songs) in classical South Indian music or in the repetition of motifs in Indian temple architecture or in the Ajanta paintings. Things are not to be judged on *apriori* grounds but only by their valid effects upon us.

'Rhetoric', of course, is another ready stick to brandish, but it is apt more often than not merely to claw the air. Speeches in epic poetry generally acquire a rhetorical cast (somewhat like speeches in Greek tragedy), though now and then they may be lifted up by a superlative emotional intensity or they may acquire a fluid charm or whispering cadence or dance of joy or haunting moan on account of the emotional nuances involved. When an Aswapati addresses the Divine Mother, how does he talk? How does the Divine Mother respond? Sri Aurobindo doesn't avoid the situation; he is willing to dare the impossible and find words to fit the situation. Thus Aswapati says:

> O radiant fountain of the world's delight…
> Let thy infinity in one body live,
> All-Knowledge wrap one mind in seas of light,
> All-Love throb single in one human heart…
> Pack with the eternal might one human hour
> And with one gesture change all future time.
> Let a great word be spoken from the heights
> And one great act unlock the doors of Fate.[179]

And the Divine Mother vouchsafes the answer:

> O strong forerunner, I have heard thy cry.
> One shall descend and break the iron Law,
> Change Nature's doom by the lone Spirit's power…
> A seed shall be sown in Death's tremendous hour,
> A branch of heaven transplant to human soil;
> Nature shall overleap her mortal step;
> Fate shall be changed by an unchanging will.[180]

Words have to be found to express the movements of aspiration and response, and since a total correspondence is neither here nor there, a lucid and luminous clarity is here successfully attempted. The rhythm is a gentle swaying one, Kalidasian in its lilt, regular but not lacking in variation within the line. Like words and phrases and images, situations too seem to repeat themselves, but it is repetition always with a difference. For example, there is Aswapati's Yoga and there is Savitri's; the difference is more important than the similarity. Seekers of God sometimes seek him without, sometimes within, and sometimes in his own abode or as the transcendent; the destination is the same though the path-ways may be different.[181] The situations, the imagery, the words thus seem to recur, but it is not due to a failure of the creative energy but for special purposes.

How about the uncouth word-combinations? The effects intended seem to be deliberate, for such expressions (recalling sometimes the practice of a poet like Hopkins) come so frequently that they cannot be explained away as chance occurrences. Might it be that Sri Aurobindo found the need to hammer out these word-combinations much as the old Anglo-Saxon poets felt the need to coin their 'kennings'? According to Douglas C. Collins, "In essence a kenning is a metaphorical expression: it is because the Anglo-Saxon mind did not make the comparison in the obvious way that there are few similes. The comparison is much closer: the Anglo-Saxon poet saw the comparison not as *like* something else but *as* something else—the idea was completely assimilated."[182] The poet thus aimed at a 'unity of meaning', as in *sund-hengestas* (ocean-steeds) and *ydhmearas* (stallions of the waves); sometimes with a hyphen, sometimes without, the unity was effected by telescoping two words to yield a new meaning. It is remarkable how often Sri Aurobindo produces like effects:

> The world's *thought-streams* traveled into his ken…[183]
> Climbing with *foam-maned* waves to the Supreme…[184]
> The brilliant *time-flakes* of eternity…[185]
> Its *gold-horned herds* trooped into earth's *cave-heart*…[186]

Numerous are such audacious hyphenated combinations: 'sun-herds and moon-flocks', 'thought-food', 'sleet-drift', 'world-kindergarten', 'sea-heart', 'sun-laugh', 'soul-nature and mind-sense', 'star-field space', 'dense-maned monsoon', 'flower-mouth', 'Sun-word', 'heaven-bliss', etc. Even as the Anglo-Saxon poet had somehow to convey in the most vivid or picturesque way possible his ideas and feelings about the sea and the heroic exploits of Beowulf, Sri Aurobindo too had somehow to get across his impressions of the cosmos, to snap the vicissitudes of the cosmic play, and to convey his unique spiritual insights. He would, in defiance of euphony and convention if need be, make his images concrete and living and apt. The epithets are meant to grip our understanding by main force, and an expression like 'soul-space' or 'self-space' occurs more than once. The promiscuous use of such expressions may hinder more than help the aims of the poet, but it cannot be said that Sri Aurobindo overdoes these 'kennings' or rather curtal metaphors.

The ultimate detraction is that *Savitri* is a tour-de-force, not a supreme poetic creation. "This sort of thing, well, impressive though it may be, once is enough!" At least, once is necessary! Of Tillyard's four criteria, two—'amplitude, breadth and inclusiveness' and 'the structural ideal'—are exemplified in *Savitri*. There are, then, the remaining criteria of 'high quality and high seriousness' and the 'choric' quality. High quality and high seriousness of purpose may also be allowed readily enough, but does *Savitri* speak with a 'choric' voice of general acceptance? Here, too, the answer must be 'yes'—at any rate in India, for Savitri speaks to the Hindu woman, and the quintessential Hindu woman speaks through Savitri. The philosophical ideas and the mystic experiences that help Savitri to speak with such amazing insight and such passionate intensity are, on a general view, by no means foreign to the Indian way of thinking and feeling about these profound problems of life and fate and death and immortality.

And even as regards the language and the versification, there is no need to be apologetic. "In total impact his (Sri

Aurobindo's) blank verse—thousands of lines...—is Miltonic", said the *Poetry Review* of London.[187] Not an altogether apt description, but at least it is meant to be complimentary. It would, however, be more accurate to describe *Savitri*, borrowing a phrase of Boodin's though in an entirely different context, as a "celestial chorus of ideals".[188]

XVIII

CONCLUSION: TOWARDS A GREATER DAWN

We have tried in the preceding pages to approach *Savitri* from various directions, to observe it from various stances, to make pointer readings from various positions of vantage. These pathways are seldom straight, and one has to zig-zag one's way through thickets and even jungles of controversy to the beckoning Holy Mount; and wherever we may take our stance, the view is obscured by sudden mists and passing clouds. There is no substitute for utter imaginative identification with the world of *Savitri* and with the power and personality of Savitri. Indeed, a total surrender to its ambrosial spiritual symbolism is called for, and a surrender also to the Creatrix in her marvellous human incarnation. But these are beyond the purview of literary criticism. Besides, intellectual approaches cannot be wholly avoided, and they may even prove useful within limits; analysis, comparison, contrast, aetiology, 'poetolatry'—inevitably these too invade our studies, and so long as they can be kept in their place, they may help to promote the final reality of poetic appreciation. Let me now make a final attempt to gather together some of the tentative conclusions of the preceding pages.

From one point of view, *Savitri* may be described as a significant knot, a converging point, of divers threads and movements in Sri Aurobindo's own life and thought. His spiritual and artistic life, his yoga and his philosophy, his politics and his aesthetics, all find in *Savitri* their splendorous fulfilment. In this respect, what Wilson

Knight says about Shakespeare and *The Tempest* is far more, and more truly, applicable to Sri Aurobindo and *Savitri*:

> ...But poetry works to render fully objective the deepest 'I'-intuition...whether in plot or person, imaginative description and atmosphere, or in the minutest details of imagistic impression; in words themselves handled as rounded and worthy things well-charged with meaning; in all this the literary artist, in either verse or prose, attains the highest realisation, something more real than either philosophy or science. This realisation is, moreover, superpersonal and therefore universal.[189]

We may start from Sri Aurobindo's first mystic experiences on his arrival in India, and trace the course of his spiritual life with the aid of such external sign-posts—his poems and his letters, for example—as are available: his experience of cosmic silence under Yogi Lele's guidance; his beatific vision of Narayana the Omnipresent God in the Alipore Jail; his experience of the besieging of his fields of trance by the cosmic ignorance; his spiritual association with Madame Richard, the Mother from 1914 onwards; his rendezvous with Night; his vision of the Paraclete, Thought, and of the ecstasy-laden *Rose of God*; and other experiences too, both before and after the climactic realisation of 1926, the *Siddhi*—and all achieve poetic recordation in *Savitri*.

We may start, again, from Sri Aurobindo's early experiments in lyric and narrative poetry—*Songs to Myrtilla*, *Urvasie*, *Love and Death* and follow his career as a poet; his renderings from the *Ramayana* and the *Mahabharata*—the fragments, *Nala* and *Chitrangada*, the 'heroic' *Vidula* and *Baji Prabhou*, the blank verse dramas, the many philosophical poems culminating in *Ahana*—the numerous 'mystical' pieces included in the 1941 volume and in *Last Poems*—the varied experiments in quantitative metre culminating in the tour-de-force, *Ilion*: again, all these channels of poetic activity, lyrical, heroic, dramatic, mystical, philosophical, experimental, all flow into and merge in the epic ocean of *Savitri*.

His Yoga of the Life Divine, the 'integral Yoga' that sought to fuse into a potent engine of transformation the old disciplines that were centred on will, works, knowledge, love, any one of them alone; his own and the Mother's travail of spiritual voyage and vigil and defeat and discovery and ultimate victory; his hopes and visions and forecasts of the future: these too achieve vivid poetic expression in *Savitri*.

So in due measure with Sri Aurobindo's philosophical worldview as well: the ground-plan in *The Life Divine*; the speculations about the future world polity, the future human society and the future poetry as elaborated in *The Ideal of Human Unity*, *The Human Cycle* and *The Future Poetry*: these also find their reflection or fulfilment or promise of ultimate realisation in the vast spaces of *Savitri*. Youth and age, wise passivity and creative dynamism, the bareness of the hermitage and the splendour of the court, love and fate and death and immortality, the real and the symbol worlds, visible and invisible powers: all are comprehended in *Savitri*, and earth meets heaven, and Time intersects Eternity, and for a blissful term there is the collapse of Time and the reign of Eternity.

Savitri's sum of excellences is thus no measurable quantity. One might say with ample justification that *Savitri* was Sri Aurobindo's *Faust*, his *Song of Myself* and his Song of the Mother rolled into one; his Testament of Beauty and Love and his testament of truth and power; his Odyssey of self-discovery and world-discovery; his lyric of the evolving soul of humanity and his epic of the cosmos. It is not therefore surprising that, when a few days before he passed away, he dictated the final additions to The Book of Fate, he felt relieved—as the Venerable Bede had felt when he concluded his *Ecclesiastical History of England*—and said to his scribe with a smile of sovereign contentment, "Ah, it is finished!"

It would, however, be no less fruitful to see *Savitri* in close relation to other epics and other philosophical poems than to see it in relation to Sri Aurobindo's own life and work. Albeit a new epic, the epic of the coming supramental age in human history, *Savitri* has its affiliations with the epics and epic narratives of other times and of our own time. Thus we may start with the Veda, follow the symbolism of Ahana, Usha, Savitri, Aswin, the lost herds and their ultimate recovery, linger on the *Mahabharata* story of Savitri and Satyavan, linger too near the field of battle where Krishna and Arjuna enact the dialectic of the *Bhagavad Gita*, and find ourselves at last in the world of *Savitri* wherein the old Vedic symbolism, the simple bardic story, and the dialectic of doubt and faith, inaction and right action, are brought together in terms of rich significance to *sahṛdayas* and spiritual seekers alike.

Other similar approaches to *Savitri*, too, are possible. We have viewed it, for example, alongside of *Faust*. We have, again, seen it as the third term of a series whose first two terms are *The Prelude* and *Song of Myself*. There is also Bridges's long poem, *The Testament of Beauty*. *The Prelude*, apart from its fine mystical insights, is really an account of the growth of a poet's mind from childhood to early manhood, while the *The Testament of Beauty* is the philosophical stock-taking of a poet past eighty; chronologically coming in between these two poems, *Song of Myself* is somewhat 'alien' in cast and almost explosive in utterance; its range, too, is wider, and its sweep approaching the cosmic. All three are 'autobiographical' poems, though each has its own distinctive quality. What these share with *Savitri*, however, is an earnestness and integrity in facing the problem of man set in a universe which he would fain understand and in which he would like to feel at home. On the other hand, *Savitri* is less consciously or deliberately subjective than the *Song of Myself* or *The Prelude*, and the equation that man and his cosmos are quintessentially one, forever changing and yet forever the same, is more central to the scheme of *Savitri* than that of the others.

Or we may approach *Savitri* by yet another road, passing on the way the two formidable milestones, the *Cantos* of Ezra Pound and Kazantzakis' 'modern sequel' to the *Odyssey*. The modern American-

European, the modern Cretan-Greek, the modern Hindu with an English education: all three poets—Pound, Kazantzakis and Sri Aurobindo—are masters of many languages and heirs to more than one cultural tradition, and each in his magnum opus has tried to explore human history, human experience or human consciousness to the utmost possible limits. But since Sri Aurobindo as man and as thinker experienced and comprehended more, since as yogi and as philosopher he outdistanced the other two in the range of his vision and the reach of his understanding, and since as poet he evolved an overhead aesthesis which was quite beyond the scope of their poetic utterance, *Savitri* has a new dimension of understanding and a piercing total power of revelation to which the other two poems cannot lay claim.

Or, finally, we may start again with stories of old like the wanderings of Odysseus, the mission of Hanuman to Lanka in the *Ramayana*, or Gilgamesh's voyage through Darkness, follow the peregrination motif as it found expression in the epics of later times, notably in the *Divina Commedia*, mark its variation in Satan's voyage across Chaos in *Paradise Lost*, and observe how the motif is treated in *Savitri*, first in the description of Aswapati's Yoga, apparently (though not really) an 'exteriorised' journey through the worlds, and secondly in Savitri's Yoga, an apparently (and also really) 'interiorised' exploration of the inner countries of the mind, heart and soul.

But here we must pause a little. Dante and Milton are great figures in poetry, and it would of course be wrong to include them as mere steps in an argument in any cavalier fashion. Both Dante and Milton had an exalted view of their poetic function and responsibilities. They tried, in fact, to "assert Eternal Providence, and justify the ways of God to men"; they wished, like the Seer-Poets of old, to *see* the inner structure of the Cosmos—the wires, the machinery, the currents, the processes, the powers—and to use the "magic of the divine Logos" to describe what they had seen. Did Dante succeed? Did Milton succeed? To quote Sri Krishnaprem,

> Perhaps the last great Western poet to have made any real attempt to grasp the inner unity was Dante, and even he made use of merely traditional myth—and somewhat degenerated myth at that—for most of his structure, while Milton who came later used even more degenerated myth for purposes which it is not unfair to describe as theological apologetics. Still later, Blake, a genuine but undisciplined seer, attempted to recover the lost unity but lost his way in uncharted private worlds.[190]

The *Commedia* and *Paradise Lost* are among the half a dozen great epics of the Western world; the criticism in the above passage is thus directed, not against the poems as poems, but against their insufficiency as *cosmic* poems. Ultimately the intellect rules both Dante and Milton, and the intellect alone is not enough. Neither can the modern man dispense with the intellect. It is because Sri Aurobindo has been able to reach and function from the overhead—the above-mind—planes and write in terms of an overhead aesthesis that what was not possible even for Dante and Milton has been largely possible for him. He has relied on the age-old myth of Savitri whose meaning is as fresh and invigorating today, and literally so, as the freshness and brightness of the morning Sun. For the rest, he has avoided heavy or cumbersome mythology. Death is referred to as Death throughout, not as Yama. The worlds, the powers, the symbol kingdoms—almost as in *The Pilgrim's Progress*—have tell-tale names: Subtle Matter, Little Life, Greater Life, Pigmy Thought, Night, Falsehood, Life-Gods, Little Mind, Greater Mind, Heavens of the Ideal, World-Soul, and so on. What is *seen* directly, with no haze or ambiguity, is presented as directly, the right words (even when they seem unpoetic to *us*) being chosen and arranged in the right rhythm. In short, the *poetic* is welded and fused with the *actual*, subjective truth with objective reality. The Irish poet, A.E., once wrote to Dilip Kumar Roy that the English language was pitifully ill-equipped to convey spiritual ideas; but Sri Aurobindo could not subscribe to this view:

> ...this seems to me a reasoning from the conventions of a past order which cannot apply to a new poetry dealing with spiritual things. A new art of words written from a new consciousness demands a new technique...Truth first—a technique expressive of the truth in the forms of beauty *has* to be found if it does not exist. It is no use arguing from the spiritual inadequacy of the English language. It has been plastic enough in the past to succeed in expressing all that it was asked to express, however new: it must now be urged to a farther new progress.[191]

It was a challenge which Sri Aurobindo felt bound to accept, and *Savitri* is the astonishing result.

The title itself, at any rate to Hindu ears, is charged with untold significance. A very gem of a title, *Savitri* has a self-sufficing beauty of its own; trisyllabic, trinitarian, a union of light, strength and silence, three circles radiating from one centre, love. Again, Savitri, being the other name of the holiest and hoariest of the Vedic mantras—the *Gāyatrī*—which for some thousands of years Hindus have chanted morning, noon and evening, at once starts psychic vibrations of incommensurable potency. There are endless overtones and undertones from the Vedic and Upanishadic structures of myth and symbolism and spiritual knowledge. Then the story itself; the tremendous issue and its vast implications; the human and the cosmic backgrounds; and the struggle and the victory. In all this *Savitri* does convincingly project before us a human and a cosmic drama, and we are able to respond at once to this impact of poetry and this invasion of cosmic actuality. To quote Sri Krishnaprem again,

> *Savitri*...is neither subjective fantasy nor yet mere philosophical thought, but vision and revelation of the actual inner structure of the Cosmos and of the pilgrim of life within its sphere—Bhu, Bhuvar, Swar: the Stairway of the Worlds reveals itself to our gaze—worlds of Light above, worlds of Darkness beneath—and we see also ever-circling life ('kindled in measure and quenched in measure') ascending and descending that Stair under the calm

> unwinking gaze of the Cosmic Gods who shine forth now as of old…Poetry is indeed the full manifestation of the Logos, and when, as here, it is no mere iridescence dependent on some special standpoint, but the wondrous structure of the mighty Cosmos, the 'Adorned One', that is revealed, then in truth does it manifest in its full, its highest grandeur.[192]

We have here gone beyond logic and metaphysics, ethics, politics and philosophy; beyond debate and argument, theorising and demonstration; the thing itself—the cosmos—is there before us, it awes and dominates us, it seizes and possesses us. And, wonder of wonders, the Infinity which Aswapati spans across as he races up and down the Stairway of the Worlds and the Zero that Savitri tracks down in its innermost cave of the inner countries—they are the same! How can the mere mind grasp these paradoxes of cosmic sovereignty?

In the childhood of the human race, before self-conscious mind—that "dwarf three-bodied trinity"—started governing the affairs of man, poets like the Vedic *rishi*s glimpsed the great truths relating to the matrix of universal life in sudden lightning flashes of illumination and expressed them through myth and symbol, in mantric incantation and song. If poetry is to be written again with such inner certainty and total cosmic vision, the new poet has both to return to those ancient wells of integral knowledge and to be a master of the mental knowledges of our age of advancing science and technology; he has to master the variety of all this specialised and compartmentalised knowledge, yet impose on it all the unity of the Spirit with the aid of a new faculty, the spiritual power of the supermind, or at least an overmental vision and power.

The claim has to be made on behalf of Sri Aurobindo and *Savitri* that this great task of the modern age has been at last boldly attempted and impressively accomplished. *Savitri* is more than a poem, more even than a cosmic poem, for it is not about the dawn, or about light, or about the Life Divine; *Savitri* is the Dawn itself, it is Light, it is Life. There is so much darkness and despair in the world today; the remedy can only be a new invasion of Light and Hope, a new incarnation of Love, and *Savitri* is such an invasion, it is nothing less than such a revelation of receding Night and the imminent arrival of a greater Dawn.

REFERENCES

Preface to the First Edition

1. *The Hudson Review*, Winter 1959-60, p.507.
2. *Dante the Philosopher*, tr. By David Moore, pp. ix-x
3. Quoted by J.B. Leishman in his Introduction to *Poems* 1906 to 1926.
4. *The Dawn Eternal*, pp.37-8
5. 18 April 1958
6. Quoted in Purani, '*Savitri*': *An Approach and a Study*, p. 1
7. *Rig Veda*, V 80, 1

Sri Aurobindo: His Life and Work

1. Translated from the original Bengali by Kshitish Chandra Sen (*Sri Aurobindo Mandir Annual*, 1944, p. 2).
2. Quoted in K.R. Srinivasa Iyengar, *Sri Aurobindo,* pp. 7-8.
3. *The Air-Conditioned Nightmare*, p. 18.
4. Quoted from *Prophets of the New India* in D.S. Sharma's *The Renaissance of Hinduism*, p. 305.
5. Quoted from *India on the March* in Iyengar's *Sri Aurobindo*, p. 8.
6. Quoted from *Dawn Over Asia* in Iyengar's *Sri Aurobindo*, p. 200.
7. See Iyengar, op. cit., p. 8.
8. Issue dated 8 July 1944.
9. I am mainly indebted, for this section, to the standard biographies by K.R. Srinivasa Iyengar and A.B. Purani. While Iyengar's *Sri Aurobindo* is a 'composite study', Purani's *Life of Sri Aurobindo* is an indispensable biographical source book.
10. See Purani, *Life*, p. 23.
11. *ibid.*, pp. 24-5.
12. *Sri Aurobindo on Himself and on the Mother*, p. 12.
13. *ibid.*, pp. 18-9.
14. Iyengar, *Sri Aurobindo*, p. 194.
15. *ibid.*, p. 194.
16. *ibid.*, pp. 396-7.
17. *ibid.*, pp. 113-4.
18. *Sri Aurobindo on Himself and on the Mother*, p. 127.
19. Letter to Joseph Baptista, quoted in Purani, *Life of Sri Aurobindo*, p. 162.
20. For example, the five-act blank verse play, *The Viziers of Bassora*, which was Exhibit 299/3 in the Alipur Case, was spotted just when the MS was about to be sold as waste paper to the Government Contractor.
21. Quoted in P.C. Ray, *Life and Times of C.R. Das*, pp. 63-4.
22. *The Religion of Man*, pp. 81-2.
23. *The Varieties of Religious Experience*, p. 349.
24. Quoted in F.O. Matthiessen's *American Renaissance*, p. 488.
25. Letter to Baptista, quoted in Purani, *Life of Sri Aurobindo*, p. 163.

26. Vide *Evening Talks with Sri Aurobindo*, First Series, Recorded by A.B. Purani.
27. *ibid.*, p. 15.
28. Iyengar, *Sri Aurobindo*, Appendix, pp. 395-7.
29. See Iyengar, *On the Mother*, p. 124.
30. *ibid.*, p. 125.
31. Italics mine. Vide *Sri Aurobindo on Himself and on the Mother*, p. 68.
32. J.H. Cousins and M.E. Cousins, *We Two Together* (1951)
33. *Mother India*, December 1953, p.121. This is a part of his long poem, *New Roads*, which begins with the following 'Dedication to Sri Aurobindo.'
The world knows not, nor yet could it conceive
The mighty holocaust Thy Light has flung
Upon the vast Asuric thoughts of Hell… (*ibid.*, p. 120).
34. *Aspects of Sri Aurobindo* (1953)
35. *The Synthesis of Yoga*, p. 4
36. *Sunrise to Eternity*, p. 65
37. *On Yoga II*, Tome One, p. 477
38. *Sri Aurobindo on Himself and on the Mother*, p. 221
39. Stace, *Time and Eternity*, p. 131
40. *On Yoga*, II, Tome One, pp. 107-8.
41. *Sri Aurobindo on Himself and on the Mother*, p. 408.
42. *ibid.*, p. 245.
43. *ibid.*, p. 248.
44. *On Yoga*, Tome One, p. 129.
45. *ibid.*, Tome Two, p. 717.
46. *ibid.*, p. 708.
47. *The Synthesis of Yoga*, pp. 699-700.
48. *The Mother*, pp. 11-13.
49. *Isha Upanishad*, pp. 150, 16.
50. *Sri Aurobindo on Himself and on the Mother*, p. 337.
51. *Essays on the Gita*, p. 482.
52. *ibid.*, p. 529.
53. Purani, *Life*, p. 86.
54. *The New Spirit in India* (1908), p. 226.
55. *Sri Aurobindo*, pp. 121-2.
56. *Sri Aurobindo on Himself and on the Mother*, p. 289.
57. *ibid.*, p. 349.
58. A.B. Purani, *Evening Talks*, First Series, p. 127.
59. *The Life Divine*, p. 947.
60. *Sri Aurobindo on Himself and on the Mother*, p. 333.
61. *Times Literary Supplement*, 8 July 1944.
62. *The Renaissance of Hinduism*, p. 305.
63. *Laureate of Peace*, p. 173.
64. This para is very largely derivative and mainly draws upon S.K. Maitra's *The Meeting of the East and the West in Sri Aurobindo's Philosophy* (1956).
65. See Kenneth Walker, *A Study of Gurdjieff's Teaching*, pp.131-2.
66. *The Spectator*, 28 April 1950, pp.586, 588.
67. From an unpublished letter to K.R. Srinivasa Iyengar dated 14 November 1950.
68. From a letter to K.R. Srinivasa Iyengar, dated 8 September 1952.
69. *The Phenomenon of Man* (translated from the original French by Bernard Wall), p. 300.
70. *ibid.*, p. 210.
71. See *The English Mystics*, pp. 220-2.
72. Quoted in Iyengar, *Sri Aurobindo*, p. 334.
73. *The Phenomenon of Man*, p. 72.
74. *ibid.*, p. 301.
75. *ibid.*, p. 258.
76. *ibid.*, Appendix.
77. *ibid.*, p. 28.
78. I wrote the above in April 1960, and I am glad to find corroboration in a recent study by Ninian Smart and also in a biography of Pierre Teilhard de Chardin. Writing about 'Sri Aurobindo and History' in the current (1961) number of *Arts and Letters* (issued by the Royal India, Pakistan and Ceylon Society), Ninian Smart finds like me "some striking likenesses to Sri Aurobindo's position" in Fr. de Chardin's book: "both see man as the crest of the on-sweeping wave of development; it is out of man's

potentialities that the luminous future will be fashioned." It is no less interesting to read in the recently published Nicolas Corte's *Pierre Teilhard de Chardin: His Life and Spirit*, translated by Martin Jarrett-Kerr, that during his years of theology at Hastings, in Sussex, de Chardin grew little by little, "more and more conscious, less as an abstract notion than as a *presence*, of a profound, ontological total drift of the Universe around me: so conscious of this that it filled my whole horizon." It was evidently this experience that Fr. de Chardin later translated into the affirmations of *The Phenomenon of Man*.

79. Letter to C.R. Das dated 18 November 1922.
80. Translated from the original German by Medhananda (*The Advent*, April 1958, pp. 68, 71).
81. See A.B. Purani, *Life of Sri Aurobindo*, p. 167.
82. *The Human Cycle*, p. 273.
83. *The Ideal of Human Unity*, p. 167.
84. *ibid.*, p. 323.
85. K.D. Sethna, *The Poetic Genius of Sri Aurobindo*, p. 1.
86. *Collected Poems and Plays*, Vol. I, p. 36.
87. *ibid.*, p. 122.
88. P.M. in *The Hindu*.
89. *Collected Poems and Plays*, Vol. II, p. 281.
90. *ibid.*, p. 287.
91. *ibid.*, p. 302.
92. *ibid.*, p. 363.
93. *ibid.*, p. 371.
94. *The Future Poetry*, p. 46.
95. *Evening Talks*, First Series, p. 292.
96. *ibid.*, p. 299.
97. *Last Poems*, p. 44.
98. *ibid.*, p. 27.
99. *Collected Poems and Plays*, Vol. II, p. 374.
100. *Last Poems*, p. 41.
101. *Collected Poems and Plays*, Vol. I, p.17.
102. *Sri Aurobindo*, p. 49.
103. *Collected Poems and Plays*, Vol. II, p. 273.
104. *ibid.*, p. 65.
105. *ibid.*, Vol. I, pp. 173-4.
106. *ibid.*, p. 306.
107. *Rodogune*, p. 105 *Cf.* Cleopatra in Shakespeare's play:
    Dost thou not see my baby at my breast
    That sucks the nurse asleep? (V, ii, 307-9)
108. *ibid.*, p. 116 *Cf.* Cleopatra again:
    Give me my robe, put on my crown; I have
    Immortal longings in me. (V, ii, 278-9).
109. *ibid.*, p. 105.
110. My account of the *Viziers* is mainly based on my own review of the play in the *Indian P.E.N.*, January 1960, pp. 27-8.
111. *Eric: A Dramatic Romance*, p. 67.
112. My account of *Eric* is largely based on my review of the play in *The Aryan Path*.
113. *Prince of Edur*, p. 91.
114. *ibid.*, p. 18.
115. *Collected Poems and Plays of Rabindranath Tagore*, pp. 409-10. See Iyengar, *Urvasi* (*Sri Aurobindo Mandir Annual*, 1949).
116. *Collected Poems and Plays*, Vol. I, p. 42.
117. *Sri Aurobindo Mandir Annual*, VIII, p. 123.
118. See A.B. Purani, *Evening Talks*, First Series p. 280; also Purani, *Life of Sri Aurobindo*, p. 26.
119. *Collected Poems and Plays*, Vol. II, p. 163.
120. *The Aeneid of Virgil*, translated by C. Day Lewis, p. 64.
121. *Ilion*, p. 125.
122. My account of *Ilion* above is largely based upon my own review-article in the *Indian P.E.N.*, December 1958, pp. 399-401.
123. 'The Interpretation of Ancient Greek Literature'.

124. *The Name and Nature of Poetry*, p. 12.
125. pp. 157-8.
126. *Savitri*, p. 910. (The page-references are throughout to the standard edition of *Savitri* in Sri Aurobindo International University Centre Collection published in 1954).

The Exordium

1. *Savitri*, p. 3.
2. *ibid.*, p. 3.
3. *ibid.*, p. 4.
4. *Cf.* Robert Bridges :
And since we observe in all existence four stages
Atomic, organic, sensuous, and self-conscient
and must conceive these in gradation, it was no flaw
in Leibnitz to endow his monad-atoms with Mind. (*The Testament of Beauty*, Bk. I, II. 427-30).
5. *Savitri*, p. 6.
6. *ibid.*, p. 11.
7. *ibid.*, p. 11.
8. *ibid.*, p. 4.
9. *ibid.*, p. 6.
10. *ibid.*, p. 729.
11. "*tishtanthi chaiva Sāvitri kāshtabhūteva lakshyate* : And Savitri, who was fasting, looked (unperturbed) like a block of wood." (From 'Savitri Upakhyana' in the *Vana Parva* of the *Mahabharata*).
12. *Savitri*, p. 14.
13. *ibid.*, p. 14.
14. *Cf.* Fr. D'Arcy : "Without struggle... the ascent of Man is almost impossible." (*The Pain of this World and the Providence of God*, 1935).
15. The Puranic story is that when the *devas* (Gods) and the *asuras* (Demons) churned the ocean of milk, poison came first and then came nectar.
16. *Savitri*, p. 15.
17. *ibid.*, p. 15.
18. *ibid.*, p. 16.
19. *ibid.*, p. 16.
20. *ibid.*, p. 16.
21. *ibid.*, p. 16.
22. *ibid.*, p. 18.
23. *ibid.*, p. 18.
24. *ibid.*, p. 18.
25. *ibid.*, p. 19. Sri Aurobindo comments on these lines as follows : "The line about the 'stillness' and the 'word' gives us the transcendental element in *Savitri*, for the Divine Savitri is the word that rises from the transcendental stillness; the next two lines render that element into the poise of the spiritual consciousness; this last line brings the same thing down to the outward character and temperament in life." (*ibid*, pp. 766-7).
26. *ibid.*, p. 21. *Cf.* Hamlet : To be, or not to be that is the question; Whether' its nobler in the mind to suffer The slings and arrows of outrageous fortune, Or to take arms against a sea of troubles And by opposing end them ?
27. *Savitri*, p. 21.
28. *ibid.*, p. 24.
29. *Cf. jwalati chalithendhanognirviprarutha-ha pannagaha phanām kurute : prāyaha-swammahimānamkshobātpratipadyate hi janah.* "The fire blazes when the fuel is stirred ; the serpent, when provoked, expands its hood ; for a man generally regains his proper greatness, under some provocation." (Matali in Kalidasa's *Sakuntalam*).
30. *Savitri*, p. 25.
31. *ibid.*, p. 21.

Backgrounds and Antecedents

1. *Savitri*, p. 30.
2. *ibid.*, p. 38. In the course of this long chapter (in two parts, seven sections, and almost forty sub-sections) as also in the next chapter, there are necessarily numerous references to the text of *Savitri*. As I do not wish to burden the pages with too many footnotes and page references, I have

given citations only to the longer extracts from the poem: where phrases or single lines alone are taken, I have used the double quotation marks, and from their situation it would not be difficult to locate them in the poem. As title-headings for the sections and sub-sections in this chapter and the next, I have given the titles of Books and cantos respectively in the poem itself: hence the single quotes.

3. *ibid.*, p. 44.
4. *ibid.*, p. 46.
5. *ibid.*, p. 48. *Cf.* Shakespeare:
   The expense of spirit in a waste of shame
   is lust in action. (Sonnet 129).
6. *ibid.*, p. 50.
7. *ibid.*, p. 51.
8. *The Aryan Path*, August 1959, pp. 338-9.
9. *Savitri*, p. 57.
10. *ibid.*, p. 62.
11. *An Essay on Man*, II.
12. *Savitri*, p. 65.
13. *Collected Poems and Plays*, Vol. II, p. 284.
14. *Savitri*, p.67.
15. *Cf.* W.B.Yeats:
    O body swayed to music, O brightening glance,
    How can we know the dancer from the dance? (*Among School Children*)
16. *Savitri.*, p. 72.
17. *ibid.*, p. 72.
18. *ibid.*, p. 74.
19. *ibid.*, p. 75.
20. *Cf.* Sri Aurobindo's *A God's Labour*:
    He who would bring the heavens here
    Must descend himself into clay
    And the burden of earthly nature bear
    And tread the dolorous way. (*Poems Past and Present*).
21. *Savitri*, p. 82.
22. *Cf.* Subramania Bharati's Tamil poem *Oozhi-k-koothu*, which he evidently wrote under the influence of Sri Aurobindo. The last stanza may be translated as follows:
    When Time and the three
    Worlds Have been cast in a ruinous heap,
    When the frenzy has ceased
    And a lone splendour has awakened,
    Then auspicious Shiva appears
    To quench your terrible thirst.
    Now thou smilest and treadst with him
    The blissful Dance of Life!
    Mother, Mother, You've drawn me
    To see thee dance !
23. *Savitri*, p. 83.
24. *ibid.*, p. 84.
25. *ibid.*,p.85.
26. *ibid.*, p. 88.
27. *ibid.*, p. 89.
28. I am giving to 'Catharsis' the meaning 'beyonding' suggested by Kenneth Burke. (*The Kenyon Review*, Summer 1959).
29. *Savitri*, p. 91.
30. *ibid.*,p. 92.
31. *ibid.*, p. 94.
32. *ibid.*, pp. 98-9.
33. *ibid.*,pp. 100-1.
34. *ibid.*, pp. 103-4.
35. *ibid.*, p. 882.
36. In an early poem, *The Rishi*, King Manu seeks Knowledge from the *Rishi* of the Pole, who exhorts the King finally:
    Perfect thy human might,
    Perfect the race. (*Collected Poems and Plays*, Vol. I, p. 162).
37. *Savitri*, p. 823.
38. *ibid.*, p. 826.
39. *ibid.*, p. 827.
40. *ibid.*, p. 110.
41. *ibid.*, p. 111.
42. *ibid.*, p. 113.
43. *ibid.* p. 115.
44. *ibid.*, p. 117.
45. *ibid.*, p. 120.
46. *ibid.*, p. 123.
47. *ibid.*, p. 127.
48. *ibid.*, p. 127.
49. *Cf.* Shelley: Thou lovest—but ne'er knew love's sad satiety. (*To a Skylark*).

50. *Savitri*, p. 128.
51. *ibid.*, p. 135.
52. *ibid.*, pp. 140-1.
53. *ibid.*, p. 145.
54. *ibid.*, p.150.
55. *ibid.*, p. 152.
56. *ibid.*, pp. 152-3.
57. *ibid.*, p. 157.
58. *Cf.* Coleridge:
    Beyond the shadow of the ship,
    I watched the water-snakes…
    O happy living things!
    no tongue Their beauty might declare:
    A spring of love gushed from my heart,
    And I blessed them unaware:
    Sure my kind saint took pity on me,
    And I blessed them unaware. (*The Rime of the Ancient Mariner*).
59. *Savitri*, p. 160.
60. *ibid.*, p.163.
61. *ibid.*, p. 167.
62. *ibid.*, p. 169.
63. *ibid.*, pp. 169-70.
64. *ibid.*, p. 171.
65. *ibid.*, p. 173.
66. *ibid.*, p. 176.
67. *ibid.*, p. 180.
68. *ibid.*, p. 181.
69. *ibid.*, p. 183.
70. *ibid.*, pp. 193-4.
71. *ibid.*, p. 194.
72. *ibid.*, p. 200.
73. *ibid.*, p. 203.
74. *ibid.*, p. 206.
75. '*God's Grandeur*'
76. *Savitri*, p. 213.
77. *ibid.*, p. 215.
78. *ibid.*, p. 219.
79. *ibid.*, pp. 224-5.
80. *ibid.*, p. 228.
81. *ibid.*, p. 230.
82. *ibid.*, p. 234.
83. *ibid.*, p. 239.
84. *ibid.*, p. 241.
85. *ibid.*, p. 243.
86. *ibid.*, p. 244.
87. *ibid.*, p. 245.
88. *ibid.*, p. 251.
89. G.M. Hopkins' Sonnet.
90. *Savitri*, p. 253.
91. *ibid.*, pp. 256-7.
92. *ibid.*, p. 262.
93. *ibid.*, p. 264.
94. *ibid.*, p. 271.
95. *ibid.*, p. 273.
96. *ibid.*, p. 274.
97. *ibid.*, p. 278.
98. *ibid.*, p. 281.
99. *ibid.*, p. 283.
100. *ibid.*, pp. 284-5.
101. *ibid.*, p. 286.
102. *ibid.*, p. 289.
103. *ibid.*, p. 290.
104. *ibid.*, p. 298.
105. *ibid.*, p. 300.
106. American Edition, p. 833.
107. *Savitri*, p. 304.
108. *ibid.*, pp. 304-5.
109. *ibid.*, p. 307.
110. *ibid.*, p. 309.
111. *ibid.*, p. 310.
112. *ibid.*, p. 312.
113. *ibid.*, p. 313.
114. *ibid.*, p. 313.
115. *ibid.*, p. 313.
116. *ibid.*, p. 314.
117. *ibid.*, pp. 314-5.
118. *Collected Poems and Plays*, II, p. 301.
119. *Savitri*, p. 317.
120. *ibid.*, pp. 317-8.
121. *ibid.*, p. 319.
122. *ibid.*, p. 319. *Cf.* T.S.Eliot:
     "When the tongues of flame are in-folded
     Into the crowned knot of fire
     And the fire and the rose are one."
     (*Little Gidding*).
123. *Savitri*, p. 321.
124. *ibid.*, p. 322.
125. *ibid.*, p. 324.
126. *ibid.*, p. 325.
127. *ibid.*, p. 326.
128. *ibid.*, p. 327.
129. *ibid.*, p. 328.
130. *ibid.*, p. 328.
131. *ibid.*, pp. 332-3.
132. *ibid.*, pp. 333-4.
133. *ibid.*, p. 334.

134. *ibid.*, p. 335.
135. *ibid.*, p. 339.
136. *ibid.*, pp. 341-2.
137. *ibid.*, p. 347.
138. *ibid.*, p. 348.
139. *ibid.*, pp. 349-50.
140. *ibid.*, p. 352.
141. *ibid.*, p. 356.
142. *ibid.*, p. 358.
143. *ibid.*, p. 359.
144. *ibid.*, p. 361.
145. *ibid.*, pp. 367-8.
146. *ibid.*, pp. 370-2.
147. *ibid.*, p. 374.
148. *ibid.*, p. 375.
149. *ibid.*, p. 377.
150. *ibid.*, p. 379.
151. *ibid.*, pp. 385-6.
152. *ibid.*, p. 386.
153. *ibid.*, p. 390.
154. *ibid.*, pp. 390-1.
155. *ibid.*, pp. 391-2.
156. *ibid.*, p. 394.
157. *ibid.*, p. 397.
158. *ibid.*, p. 399.
159. *ibid.*, p. 400.
160. *ibid.*, p. 404.
161. *ibid.*, p. 405.
162. *ibid.*, p. 406.
163. *ibid.*, p. 407.
164. *ibid.*, p. 405.
165. *ibid.*, p. 408.
166. *ibid.*, p. 411.
167. *ibid.*, p. 412.
168. *ibid.*, p. 415.
169. *ibid.*, p. 417.
170. *ibid.*, p. 416.
171. *ibid.*, p. 420.
172. *ibid.*, pp. 422-3.
173. *ibid.*, pp. 425-4
174. *ibid.*, p. 430.
175. *ibid.*, p. 432.
176. *ibid.*, p. 434.
177. *ibid.*, p. 435.
178. *ibid.*, p. 438.
179. *ibid.*, p. 441.
180. *ibid.*, p. 442.
181. *ibid.*, p. 443.
182. *ibid.*, p. 444.
183. *ibid.*, p. 445.
184. *ibid.*, p. 447.
185. *ibid.*, p. 448.
186. *ibid.*, p. 448.
187. *ibid.*, p. 449.
188. *ibid.*, p. 451.
189. *ibid.*, p. 452.
190. *ibid.*, p. 454.
191. *ibid.*, p. 455.
192. *ibid.*, p. 457.
193. *ibid.*, p. 459.
194. *ibid.*, pp. 462-3.
195. *ibid.*, pp. 463-4.
196. *ibid.*, p. 445.
197. *ibid.*, p. 445.
198. *On Yoga*, II, Tome Two pp. 840-1
199. *The Life Divine*, p. 721
200. *Essays on the Gita*, p. 202
201. *On Yoga*, II, Tome Two, p. 849
202. *ibid.*, Tome One, p. 420
203. *Savitri*, p. 471.
204. *ibid.*, p. 473.
205. *ibid.*, p. 474.
206. *ibid.*, pp. 475-6.
207. *ibid.*, p. 477.
208. *ibid.*, p. 479.
209. *ibid.*, p. 481.
210. *ibid.*, p. 482.
211. *ibid.*, p. 482.
212. *ibid.*, p. 484.
213. *ibid.*, p. 484.
214. *ibid.*, p. 485.
215. *ibid.*, p. 486.
216. *ibid.*, p. 486.
217. *ibid.*, p. 487.
218. *ibid.*, p. 488.
219. *ibid.*, p. 489.
220. *ibid.*, p. 490.
221. *ibid.*, p. 490.
222. *ibid.*, p. 491.
223. *ibid.*, p. 491.
224. *ibid.*, p. 493.
225. *ibid.*, p. 493.
226. *ibid.*, p. 494.
227. *ibid.*, p. 496.
228. *ibid.*, p. 496.
229. *ibid.*, p. 496.
230. *ibid.*, p. 497.
231. *ibid.*, p. 498.
232. *ibid.*, p. 498.
233. *ibid.*, p. 498.

234. *ibid.*, p. 499.
235. *ibid.*, p. 501.
236. *ibid.*, p. 501.
237. *ibid.*, p. 502.
238. *ibid.*, pp. 502-3.
239. *ibid.*, p. 503.
240. *ibid.*, p .503. *Cf.* Francis Thompson:
Ah ! must—
Designer infinite !—
Ah! must Thou char the wood ere Thou canst limn with it? (*The Hound of Heaven*).
241. *Savitri*, pp. 504-5.
242. *ibid.*, p. 505.
243. *ibid.*, p. 508.
244. *ibid.*, p. 509.
245. *ibid.*, p. 510.
246. *ibid.*, p. 511.
247. *ibid.*, p. 514.
248. *ibid.*, p. 516.
249. *ibid.*, p. 517.
250. *ibid.*, p. 518.
251. *ibid.*, p. 520.
252. *ibid.*, p. 521.
253. *ibid.*, p. 522.
254. *ibid.*, p. 522.
255. *ibid.*, p. 523.
256. *ibid.*, p. 523.
257. *ibid.*, p. 527.
258. *ibid.*, p. 527.
259. *ibid.*, p. 531.
260. *ibid.*, p. 531.
261. *ibid.*, p. 532.
262. *ibid.*, p. 533.
263. *ibid.*, p. 534.
264. *ibid.*, p. 535.
265. *ibid.*, p. 536.
266. *ibid.*, p. 539.
267. *ibid.*, p. 539.
268. *ibid.*, p. 540.
269. *ibid.*, p. 541.
270. *ibid.*, p. 542.
271. *ibid.*, p. 545.
272. *ibid.*, p. 547.
273. *ibid.*, p. 547.
274. *ibid.*, p. 549.
275. *ibid.*, pp. 551-2
276. *ibid.*, p. 552.
277. *ibid.*, p. 556.
278. *ibid.*, p. 559.
279. *ibid.*, p. 561.
280. *ibid.*, p. 563.
281. *ibid.*, p. 568.
282. *ibid.*, pp. 569-70. *Cf.* M.P. Pandit: "He (Brahman) is to be sought behind the veil of forms and the search must proceed and be pursued from the more dense to the less dense layers of existence…until one arrives at the sheer core of things where hidden in the secrecy of the supreme ether Brahman awaits to be cognized and realised". (*The Advent*, August 1956, pp. 18-9).
283. *Savitri*, p. 570.
284. *ibid.*, p. 571.
285. *ibid.*, p. 572.
286. *ibid.*, p. 574.
287. *ibid.*, pp. 578-9.
288. *ibid.*, p. 584.
289. *ibid.*, p. 586.
290. *ibid.*, p. 587.
291. *ibid.*, p. 588.
292. *ibid.*, p. 590.
293. *ibid.*, p. 591.
294. *ibid.*, p. 592.
295. *ibid.*, p. 593.
296. *ibid.*, p. 594.
297. *ibid.*, p. 595.
298. *ibid.*, p. 596.
299. *ibid.*, p. 598.
300. *ibid.*, p. 603.
301. *ibid.*, pp. 604-5.
302. *ibid.*, pp. 607-8.
303. *ibid.*, p. 610.
304. *ibid.*, p. 611.
305. *ibid.*, pp. 612-3.
306. *ibid.*, pp. 613-4.
307. *ibid.*, p. 614.
308. *ibid.*, p. 615.
309. *ibid.*, p. 619.
310. Sri Aurobindo gave no title to Book VII, canto 7: I have accordingly given 'Rose of God' (itself the title of one of his poems) as the heading of this sub-section.
311. *Savitri*, p. 628.
312. *ibid.*, pp. 628-9.
313. *ibid.*, p. 630.
314. *ibid.*, p. 631-2. *Cf.* Rose of God:

Leap up in our heart of humanhood,
O miracle, O flame,
Passion-flower of the
Nameless, bud of the mystical Name…
Transform the body of the mortal like a sweet and magical rhyme;
Bridge our earthhood and heavenhood,
make deathless the children of Time.
(*Collected Poems & Plays* Vol. 11, p. 302).

The Struggle and the Victory

1. This refers to the 1954 edition.
2. *Savitri*, p. 635 fn.
3. *ibid.*, p. 635.
4. *ibid.*, p. 637.
5. *ibid.*, p. 638.
6. *ibid.*, p. 639.
7. *ibid.*, p. 639.
8. *ibid.*, p. 640.
9. *ibid.*, p. 646.
10. *ibid.*, p. 647.
11. *ibid.*, pp. 648-9.
12. *ibid.*, p. 650.
13. *ibid.*, p. 651.
14. *ibid.*, p. 656.
15. *ibid.*, p. 657.
16. *ibid.*, p. 659.
17. *ibid.*, p. 665.
18. *ibid.*, p. 668.
19. *ibid.*, p. 669.
20. *ibid.*, p. 671.
21. *ibid.*, p. 671.
22. *ibid.*, p. 672.
23. *On the Veda*, pp. 277-8.
24. *ibid.*, p. 617.
25. *Savitri*, p. 675.
26. *ibid.*, p. 676.
27. *ibid.*, pp. 676-7.
28. *ibid.*, p. 680.
29. *ibid.*, p. 683.
30. *ibid.*, p. 683.
31. *ibid.*, p. 685.
32. *ibid.*, p. 687.
33. *ibid.*, p. 611.
34. *ibid.*, p. 689. *Cf.* Sri Aurobindo's *Ahana*:
   Brindavan arching o'er us where Shyama sports and rejoices.
   Inly the miracle trembles repeated; mistwalls are broken
   Hiding that country of God…
   (*Collected Poems & Plays* Vol. 11, p. 157).
35. *ibid.*, p. 694.
36. *ibid.*, p. 696.
37. *ibid.*, p. 698.
38. *ibid.*, p. 699.
39. *ibid.*, p. 700.
40. *ibid.*, p. 700. *Cf.* Subramania Bharati:
   Many a joy hast thou devised,
   O Lord !
   …Through the play of consciousness in matter
   You have designed this wonderful universe:
   These myriad multi-coloured worlds
   You have structured in terms of beauty. (*Bharati in English Verse*, p. 77).
41. *ibid.*, p. 701.
42. *ibid.*, p. 702.
43. *ibid.*, p. 706.
44. *ibid.*, p. 707.
45. *ibid.*, p. 710.
46. *ibid.*, p. 711.
47. *ibid.*, p. 712.
48. *ibid.*, p. 714.
49. *ibid.*, p. 717.
50. *ibid.*, p. 718.
51. *ibid.*, p. 719.
52. *ibid.*, p. 721.
53. *ibid.*, pp. 723-4.
54. *ibid.*, p. 727.
55. *ibid.*, pp. 727-8.
56. *ibid.*, p. 731.
57. *ibid.*, p. 731.
58. *ibid.*, p. 732.
59. *ibid.*, p. 735.
60. *ibid.*, pp. 737-8.
61. *ibid.*, p. 739.
62. *ibid.*, p. 741.
63. *ibid.*, p. 743.
64. *ibid.*, p. 744.
65. *ibid.*, p. 745.
66. *ibid.*, p. 748.
67. *ibid.*, p. 749.

68. *ibid.*, p. 754.
69. *ibid.*, p. 755.
70. *ibid.*, p. 757. *Cf.* Keats:
Charmed magic casements opening on the foam,
Of perilous seas in faery lands forlorn. (*Ode to a Nightingale*).
71. *ibid.*, p. 759.
72. *ibid.*, p. 760.
73. *ibid.*, p. 762.
74. *ibid.*, p. 765.
75. *ibid.*, p. 765.
76. *Cf.* A.B. Purani: "Death was transfigured into Love. Virat, Hiranyagarbha, Chaitanya, Ghana, Ananda — the four aspects of the Reality worked harmoniously in the everlasting Day." (*Savitri: An Approach and a Study*, p. 252).
77. *Savtitri*, p. 768.
78. *ibid.*, p. 770.
79. *ibid.*, p. 773.
80. *ibid.*, p. 775.
81. *ibid.*, p. 777.
82. *ibid.*, p. 779.
83. *ibid.*, pp. 780-1.
84. *ibid.*, p. 781.
85. *ibid.*, p. 783.
86. *ibid.*, p. 783.
87. *ibid.*, p. 784.
88. *ibid.*, p .788.
89. *ibid.*, p. 792.
90. *ibid.*, p. 793.
91. *ibid.*, p. 798.
92. *ibid.*, p. 799.
93. *ibid.*, p. 800.
94. *ibid.*, p. 804.
95. *ibid.*, p. 805.
96. *ibid.*, p. 806.
97. *ibid.*, p. 808.
98. *ibid.*, p. 809.
99. *ibid.*, pp. 810-1.
100. *ibid.*, p. 812.
101. *ibid.*, p. 813.
102. *ibid.*, p. 814.

The 'Legend' and the 'Symbol'

1. *Sri Aurobindo Mandir Annual*, No. 5. An off-print was also published as a Fascicule.
2. K.D. Sethna's article in *Sri Aurobindo Mandir Annual*, 1942.
3. This is the scene visualised by Sri Aurobindo in his *Savitri*, Book IV, canto 3.
4. See Pratap Chandra Roy [Tr.], *The Mahabharata* Vol II, p. 629 fn. Also John Brough *Selections From Classical Sanskrit Literature* p.148 (Notes to II. 301-8).
5. Letter dated 8 March 1899 Romesh Chunder Dutt (Quoted in J.N. Gupta's *Life and Work of Romesh Chunder Dutt, C.I.E.*,1911, p. 268), Romesh Chunder included *Savitri* in his verse rendering of the *Mahabharata* (1898) but portrayed her as weeping and so "took away the very strength of which Savitri is built" (*Evening Talks with Sri Aurobindo*, First Series p. 294).
6. *Disjecta Membra: Studies in Literature and Life*, p. 61.
7. *A History of Indian Literature*, Vol. I, (Tr. by Mrs. S. Ketkar), p. 397.
8. *ibid.*, p. 398.
9. *ibid.*, p. 398.
10. *Vyasa and Valmiki*, p. 22. Sri Aurobindo seems to have attempted a rendering of the Nala story too, but only an unrevised fragment remains, and it has been posthumously published in *Mother India*, December, 1953, pp. 96-9. It is interesting to note that this version also is in blank verse, though with enjambment as in *Urvaise* and *Love and Death*.
11. *Savitri* p. 827.
12. *ibid.*, pp. 818-820 (Note). See also Nirodbaran's article in *Mother India*, 19 May 1951.
13. Louis O. Coxe, in *Poetry* (December I959), p. 180.
14. *Savitri*, p. 907.
15. *ibid.*, p. 829.
16. *ibid.*, p. 823.
17. Max Muller writes: "Though Savitri is a name applied to the sun in general, it is most frequently used as the name of the rising and life-

and-light-giving sun. Nor must it be supposed that Savitri is simply an appellative of the solar globe. Savitri has become a divine name or a divine *numen* as full of life and personality as any other *Deva*." (*Auld Lang Syne*, p. 210).

18. *The House of the Titans*, pp. 1-2.
19. *Essays in Literary Criticism*, edited by Irving Singer, p. 403.
20. *ibid.*, p. 405.
21. See Wellek & Warren, *Theory of Literature*, p. 195.
22. Quoted in Cassirer, *Language and Myth*, p. 5.
23. *Collected Essays in Literary Criticism*, p. 101.
24. *Language and Myth*, p. 99. See also Berdyaev: "The human consciousness reflects and repeats the historical and cosmogonic processes of nature, which take the form of mythology in its primal stages. The mythological consciousness is thus full of cosmic myths in which man is revealed as a natural being related to the spirits of nature. These myths also disclose the ties uniting man with the primary process of world creation and formation, which go back much further than the consolidation of matter from which science, later, dates its study of world evolution... Mythology is the original source of human history." (*The Meaning of History*, pp. 80-1).
25. *Coleridge on Imagination*, pp. 171-2.
26. See Allen Tate, *The Man of Letters in the Modern World*, pp. 62-3.
27. Bernard Blackstone, *The Consecrated Urn*, p. 134; see also Charles Williams, *The Figure of Beatrice*, p. 56, Wellek & Warren, *Theory of Literature*, p.196, and Ezra Pound, *The Spirit of Romance*, p.127.
28. *On the Veda*, pp. 8-9.
29. *ibid.*, pp. 277-8
30. *ibid.*, p. 11
31. *Savitri* p. 275-6, See also A.B. Purani, *Savitri: An Approach and a Study*, p. 208.
32. *The Meaning of History*, pp. 52-3.
33. Sri Aurobindo, *On the Veda*, p. 254.
34. See Urban, *Humanity and Deity*, p. 81.
35. *Dante's Other World*, p. 75.
36. *Complex, Archetype, Symbol*, pp. 76-7.
37. *Time and Eternity*, p. 63.
38. Carlyle, quoted in Baker, *The Sacred River*, p. 208.
39. See Gai Eaton, *The Richest Vein*, pp. 186-7; also Cassirer, *Language and Myth*, p. 38.
40. *Complex, Archetype, Symbol*, pp. 77-8.
41. Baker, *The Sacred River*, p. 211.
42. *The Richest Vein*, p.45.
43. *Humanity and Deity*, p. 89.
44. Jacobi, *Complex, Archetype, Symbol*, p. 91.
45. See Abinas Chandra Das, *Rig-Vedic India* Vol. I, pp. 420-1.
46. *Rig Veda*, V, 81, 5 (Tr. by Sri Aurobindo).
47. *ibid.*, V, 82, 4 (Tr. by Sri Aurobindo).
48. Sri Aurobindo, *On the Veda*, p. 347.
49. *Rig Veda*, III, 62, 10.
50. Sri Aurobindo, *On the Veda*, pp. 575-7.
51. *ibid.*, p. 554.
52. *ibid.*, pp. 433-4. Cf. C. M. Bowra on the Greek gods and *their* relations with humanity: "The essence of Greek religion is its assumption that gods and men belong to a single world, that they resemble one another in many important respects, even if the gods live forever and enjoy eternal youth, that relations between them can be those of human friendship with its loyal ties and obligations, that the best things in life are those in which men come close, if only for a moment, to a felicity of the gods." (*The Sewanee Review*, Spring 1955, p. 340).
53. *ibid.*, p. 525.
54. *ibid.*, p. 526.
55. *Essays on Indo-Aryan Mythology*, pp. 90-1.
56. *ibid.*, p. 92.
57. *The Colossus of Maroussi.*

58. American Edition, p. 944.
59. *The Mother*, p. 84.
60. *ibid.*, pp. 789-90.
61. *The Sale of Saint Thomas* (1931), p.33.
62. K.D. Sethna, *The Poetic Genius of Sri Aurobindo*, p. 119.
63. *Savitri*, p. 797.
64. *The Mother*, pp. 84-5.
65. *On the Veda*, p. 427.
66. *ibid.*, p. 428
67. *ibid.*, p. 432
68. ibid., p. 441
69. Sri Aurobindo, *On the Veda*, pp. 462-3
70. ibid., P. 167. Cf. F.W. Bain. "What is the secret of the rooted affection of the Aryan and Iranian, the Veda and the Avesta, for the Cow? Partly, no doubt, its utilitarian value. But they are deceived, who think that this is all. There is religion in it, mysticism, aesthetic affection. The Cow is an Idea...." After describing a memorable experience of the sudden unexpected confrontation of a Cow in the Rajaputana desert, Bain continues: "Since then, every heifer, and for the sake of the heifer, even every ox, has possessed for the writer a touch of divinity". (A Heifer of the Dawn, pp. viii, x).
71. A.B. Purani, *Savitri: An Approach and a Study* p. 3. See *The Human Cycle*, pp. 297-9.
72. Tr. by Sri Aurobindo, *On the Veda*, pp. 371-72.
73. *ibid.*, pp. 373-77.
74. *ibid.*, p. 378.
75. *ibid.*, p. 378.
76. Kenneth Burke, *Counter-Statement* (1931).
77. *Savitri*, p. 20-1.
78. Collected Poems & Plays, Vol.11, p. 279-80.
79. *Savitri*, p. 873.

'Overhead' Poetry and *Savitri*

1. *Savitri*, p. 920.
2. *ibid.*, p. 831.
3. *Common Sense About Poetry*, pp. 10-1
4. *Cf.* Ezra Pound: "It doesn't, in our contemporary world, so much matter where you begin the examination of a subject, so long as you keep on until you get round again to your starting point. As it were, you start on a sphere, or a cube; you must keep on until you have seen it from all sides." (*ABC of Reading*, p. 29).
5. p. 1017.
6. *The Life Divine*, pp. 155-6.
7. *The Synthesis of Yoga*, p. 321.
8. *ibid.*, p. 584. Cf.: "To find highest beauty is to find God; to reveal, to embody, to create as we say, highest beauty is to bring out of our souls the living image and power of God (*The Human Cycle*, p.160). Also Robert Lynd: "It (poetry) enables him (man) to escape out of the make-believe existence of everyday in which perhaps an employer seems more huge and imminent than God, and to explore reality, where God and love and beauty and life and death are seen in truer proportions, and when the desire of the heart is at last brought within sight of a goal." (*On Poetry and the Modern Man*, 1921).
9. *The Life Divine*, p. 151
10. *The Mother*, p. 1.
11. *The Life Divine*, pp. 833-46.
12. *ibid.*, p. 840.
13. *ibid.*, p.842.
14. *ibid.*, p. 844.
15. *ibid.*, p. 846.
16. *Savitri*, p. 937.
17. *ibid.*, p. 937.
18. *ibid.*, p. 926.
19. *ibid.*, p. 930. *Cf.*:
A new aesthesis of Inferno's art
that trained the mind to love what the soul hates,
Imposed allegiance on the quivering nerves
And forced the unwilling body to vibrate. (*Savitri*, p.242). See also V.K. Gokak's 'Sri Aurobindo and Aesthetics', *Mother India*, (January, 1954), p. 22
20. *The Life Divine*, p. 74.

21. *ibid.*, p. 95.
22. *Savitri*, p. 931.
23. *The Life Divine*, p. 98.
24. *Savitri*, pp. 931-2.
25. *Twelfth Night*, II, iv, 22. 113-4.
26. *Savitri*, p. 934. See also *The Human Cycle*, pp.153-4.
27. *ibid.*, p. 935.
28. *ibid.*, p. 426.
29. *The Future Poetry*, p. 393.
30. H.L. Sharma in his article on 'Indian Aesthetics' (*The Journal of the Ganganath Jha Research Institute*, May-August I958, pp.196-9).
31. See K.D. Sethna, *The Poetic Genius of Sri Aurobindo*, p. 89.
32. *Encyclopaedia of Religion and Ethics*, Vol. IX.
33. Quoted in W.R. Inge, *Christian Mysticism*, p. 339.
34. *The Wisdom of India*, p. 17.
35. See McTaggart, *Philosophical Studies*, p. 47. *Cf.* Alfred Noyes:
    Man is himself the key to all he seeks.
    He is not exiled from this majesty,
    but is himself a part of it.
    To know himself, and read this Book of Earth aright,
    flooding it as his ancient poets, once,
    illumed old legends with their inborn fire,
    were to discover music that out-soars his plodding thought,
    and all his fables, too.
    A song of truth that deepens,
    not destroys the ethereal realm of wonder. (*The Book of Earth*, pp. 16-7).
36. Raynor C. Johnson, *The Imprisoned Splendour*, p. 401.
37. *The Pursuit of Death*, p. 264. See also Montague, *The Ways of Knowing*, p. 58: "If the cosmos...were possessed of a psychic concomitant or mind as much vaster than our minds, as the matter of which it is composed is vaster than the matter of our bodies, there would be the possibility of a rapport between the larger cosmic life and the lesser lives of the individuals contained within it. The intuitions and the revelations of the mystic would then be grounded not only upon subconscious memory and instinct, but also upon the influx of energy from a larger Self."
38. *Collected Essays in Literary Criticism*, p. 44.
39. Quoted in *The Imprisoned Splendour*, p. 81.
40. *The Destiny of the Mind*, p. 122. Also Robert Graves: "... it is not too much to say that all original discoveries and inventions and musical and poetical compositions are the result of proleptic thought—the anticipation, by means of a suspension of time, of a result that could not have been arrived at by inductive reasoning—and of what may be called analeptic thought, the recovery of lost events by the same suspension..." (*The White Goddess*, p. 280).
41. R.G. Collingwood, quoted in Wimsatt & Brooks, *Literary Criticism*, p. 603.
42. Erich Kahler, in *Problems in Aesthetics* (Ed. by Weitz), p. 171.
43. Brockington, *Mysticim and Poetry*, p. 124.
44. *Cf.* Sri Aurobindo: "The soul of beauty in us identifies itself with the soul of beauty in the thing created and feels in appreciation the same divine intoxication and uplifting which the artist felt in creation. Criticism reaches its highest point when it becomes the record, account, right description of this response; it must become itself inspired, intuitive, revealing." (*The Human Cycle*, p. 158). Also Boris Pasternak: "...although the artist is of course mortal like everyone else, the joy of living experienced by him is immortal and can be felt by others through his work, centuries after his death, in a form approximating to that of his original, intimately personal experience." (*An Essay in Autobiography*. Tr. by Manya Harari, p. 69).

45. *Savitri*, pp. 568-9.
46. *Countries of the Mind*, Second Series, p. 10.
47. Dr. Tillyard quotes a four-line passage in which this phrase occurs and comments thus: "The famous third line is popularly taken from its context and misunderstood in a general sense, which is that life is a melancholy affair for men. In the whole context *hic* is the important word. *Here*, in a work of art, in the different realm of the artist, merit, however unfortunate, is recognised; *ere* there is sympathy and pity for the affairs of men." (*The English Epic and Its Background*, p. 80).
A clear echo, "touch of tears in mortal things," occurs on p. 87 of *Savitri* and an echo of Wordsworth, "And great burning thoughts voyaged through the sky of mind", on p. 88.
48. *Savitri*, p. 924.
49. *ibid.*, p. 924.
50. *Selected Poems* (1939), p. 5.
51. *Sohrab and Rustum*, II. 322-4.
52. *Measure for Measure*, III, i, .II 119-33.
53. *Savitri*, p. 923.
54. 'Dedication' to *Selected Poems.*
55. 'Romance' (*Selected Poems*), pp. 3-4.
56. *Ode to a Nightingale.*
57. *Collected Poems*, pp. 97-8.
58. *That Nature is a Heraclitean Fire.*
59. *After a Great Pain a Formal Feeling Comes.*
60. *Ode to the Confederate Dead.*
61. *Luke Havergal.*
62. *East Coker.*
63. *Sunday Morning.*
64. Sri Aurobindo, *The Future Poetry*, pp. 7-8.
65. *Maud*, ii. 82-3.
66. Letter to Nirodbaran (*Mother India*, June 1957, p. 3).
67. *Cf.* Bhavabhuti's *Uttararāmacarita: Laukikānāṁ tu sādhūnām arthāṁ vāk anuvartate, ṛṣiṇaṁ punarādyanaṁ vācam arthonu dhāvati.*
68. *English Critical Essays*, XX Century, Second Series, p. 73.
69. Allen Tate, in his rewarding essay on *Longinus and the New Criticism*, ably argues that 'transport' does not mean 'romantic shudder'; Longinus' own words are (as quoted by Tate): "...If a work of literature fails to disclose to the reader's intelligence an outlook beyond the range of what is said, when it dwindles under a careful and continuous inspection, it cannot be truly sublime, for it has reached the ear alone...For that is truly grand of which the contemplation bears repeating."
"There must be, in short", Tate adds, "a total quality of the work which abides its first impact to that total quality he gives the name of composition....Longinus' location of rhythm in the total composition, as binding and bound up with it, is perhaps the best critical insight of its kind before Coleridge." (*The Man of Letters in the Modern World*, pp. 169-70).
70. See Lytton Strachey, *Literary Essays* 1948), p. 16.
71. Okakura Kakuzo, *The Book of Tea* (Charles E. Tuttle Company, Tokyo, 1957), p. 78.
72. Mr C.S. Lewis has recently made a strong plea in favour of the classical terminology: "... it is surely time to re-avail ourselves of the enormous advantages which the classical terms offer." (*A Review of English Literature*, January 1960, p. 49).
73. *Collected Poems and Plays*, Vol. II, pp. 303-4.
74. *ibid.*, p. 334.
75. *ibid.*, pp. 160-1.
76. *Ilion*, p. 6.
77. *The Poetic Genius of Sri Aurobindo*, p. 74.
78. *Ilion* (Appendices), p. 169.
79. K.D. Sethna, *The Poetic Genius of Sri Aurobindo*, p. III.
80. *Collected Poems and Plays*, Vol. II, p. 368.
81. *ibid.*, p. 373.

82. *ibid.*, p. 300.
83. *The Concise Oxford Dictionary.*
84. *Savitri*, p. 913.
85. *Cf.* Henry Adams:
"Life, Time, Space, Thought, the World, the Universe
End where they first begin, in one sole Thought
Of Purity in Silence."
86. *Savitri*, p. 827.
87. *ibid.*, p. 835.
88. *ibid.*, p. 852.
89. *ibid.*, pp. 901, 909.
90. *ibid.*, p. 910.
91. *ibid.*, p. 911.
92. *ibid.*, p. 917.
93. *ICor*, iii, 16.
94. Shao Yung (Tr. by H.A. Giles).
95. Tr. from the Flemish by Jane T. Stoddart.
96. A.H. Armstrong, *Plotinus* (I953), p. 131.
97. Charles Gore, *The Philosophy of the Good Life*, p. 215.
98. *Surprised by Joy*, pp. 221-2. Cf. Dadu the Indian mystic: "From separation I have come to Union. The bonds of self are loosened, all error has fled, and the light of the Brahman shines upon my soul." (Quoted in Sen, *Medieval Mysticism of India.*, p. 173).
99. See Purani, *Life*, p. 104; also Iyengar, *Sri Aurobindo*, p. 140.
100. *Sri Aurobindo on Himself and on the Mother*, p. 131.
101. *ibid.*, p. 127.
102. See Purani, *Life*, p. 106.
103. See Iyengar, *Sri Aurobindo*, pp. 159-60.
104. *Sri Aurobindo on Himself and on the Mother*, p. 214.
105. *ibid.*, p. 215.
106. See Purani, *Life*, p. 212.
107. *Sri Aurobindo on Himself and on the Mother*, p. 214.
108. *ibid.*, p. 149.
109. *ibid.*, p. 148.
110. *ibid.*, p. 180.
111. In her recent book Dr Payne has given a tone plotting scale for the evaluation of any type of man: the tone ranges from o.o, which signifies mere reflex activity or 'death', passes on through 0.5 (apathy), 1.0 (fear), 1.5 (anger), 1.8 (pain), 2.5 (boredom), 3.0 (conservation and respectability), 4.0 (enthusiasm), 8.0 (exhilaration), 22.0 (optimum activity, freedom from self-concern), 40.0 (serenity and self-awareness); the range 40-100 is left unexplored, and we may take it that above 40.0 are the 'overhead' planes of consciousness. (*Creative Education*, pp. 22-9). It may be added that the 'tone' plotting scale is the invention of Dr. L. Ron Hubbard, the noted psychiatrist, nuclear physicist and 'scientologist'.
112. *Encyclopaedia of Religion and Ethics*, Vol. IX.
113. See H.P. Sastri, *The Ramayana of Valmiki*, Vol. III, p. 218.
114. See G.R. Levy, *The Sword from the Rock*, pp. 134-40.
115. *The World as Power*, Section 'Reality', pp. 95-6.
116. *Personal Idealism and Mysticism*, pp. 2-3.
117. *The Book of Earth*, p. 68.
118. *The House of the Titans* (1934), p. 64.
119. Quoted in F.O. Matthiessen, *American Renaissance*, p. 55.
120. Henry Vaughan. Cf. Sri Aurobindo:
I saw the spirit of the cosmic Ignorance;
I felt its power besiege my gloried fields of trance. (Quoted in Iyengar, *Sri Aurobindo*, p. 309).
121. Richard Crashaw.
122. See *The Renaissance Philosophy of Man*, ed. by Cassirer, tr. by Forbes (University of Chicago Press).
123. Sir John Woodroffe, *Is India Civilised?*, p. 33.
124. *Aurora*, vii, 7 (Quoted in Stoudt, *Sunrise to Eternity*, p. 61).
125. *The Synthesis of Yoga*, pp. 59-60.
126. *Poetry as a Means of Grace*, p. 49.
127. *The Conquest of Illusion*, pp. 40-1.
128. *Savitri*, p. 623.

129. Book VI (Jaico Edition, 1949, p. 104).
130. *St. Matthew*, I, I-II and *St. Luke*, IV, I. 13; also see, for a modern version, William Faulkner's *A Fable* (Random House, 1954), pp. 341-56.
131. *Paradise Regained*, Book IV, II. 368-72.
132. *ibid.*, 1. 576.
133. *Julius Caesar*, II, i, 11. 66-9.
134. *The Allegory of Love*, pp. 68-9. Lewis himself, in his 'cosmic trilogy' of novels, has presented vividly the temptation of Eve, the grapple between his hero, Ransom, and the Tempter, and various other peripheral struggles. It is also interesting to note that Dorothy Richardson the novelist has presented the life of her heroine, Miriam Henderson, as a 'Pilgrimage' which of course includes 'struggles' on the way.
135. *The English Epic and Its Background*, p. 398.
136. *On Yoga*, II, Tome Two, p. 58.
137. Quoted in Iyengar, *Sri Aurobindo*, pp. 338-9.
138. *Letters of Sri Aurobindo* Second Series, pp. 68-9.
139. *Sri Aurobindo Mandir Annual*, No.7 (1948), pp. 191-2.
140. Introduction to *One Hundred Poems of Kabir*, ed. by Rabindranath Tagore, p. xix.
141. *Savitri*, p. 829.
142. *ibid.*, p. 831.
143. *ibid.*, p. 852.
144. See Sri Aurobindo, *On Yoga*, II, Tome Two, Section on 'Visions and Symbols', pp. 55-103.
145. *Savitri*, p. 828.
146. *ibid.*, pp. 908-9.
147. *ibid.*, p. 821.
148. *Mā niṣāda pratiṣṭhāṁ tvamagamaḥ śaś vatīḥ samāh,*
Yatkraucamithunā dekamavadhīḥ kāma mohitam.
"Oh hunter, as you have killed one of these love-intoxicated birds, you will wander homeless all your long years." (Tr. by C. Rajagopalchari).
149. Act II, Sc. 2 (p. 52).
150. *Collected Poems and Plays*, Vol. II, pp, 114-5.
151. *Savitri*, p. 822.
152. *ibid.*, p. 639.
153. *ibid.*, p. 650.
154. *ibid.*, pp. 10-11.
155. *ibid.*, p. 17.
156. *The Future Poetry*, pp. 192-7.
157. *Savitri*, p. 18.
158. *ibid.*, p. 22.
159. *ibid.*, p. 25.
160. *ibid.*, p. 19.
161. *ibid.*, p. 47.
162. *ibid.*, p. 47.
163. *ibid.*, p. 103.
164. *ibid.*, p. 19.
165. *ibid.*, p. 87.
166. *ibid.*, p. 721.
167. *ibid.*, p. 741.
168. *ibid.*, p. 764.
169. *ibid.*, p. 46.
170. *ibid.*, p. 821.
171. *ibid.*, p. 727.
172. *Literary Essays*, p. 183.
173. Sri Aurobindo admits that he has accepted in the present version of *Savitri*, "several of the freedoms established by the modernists including internal rhyme, exact assonance of syllable, irregularities introduced into the iambic run of the metre and others which would have been equally painful to an earlier taste." (*Savitri*, p.846).
174. *Mysticism*, p.79.
175. *Savitri*, p. 155.
176. *ibid.*, p. 171.
177. *ibid.*, p. 196. *Cf.* Tennyson:
Yet all experience is an arch wherethro'
Gleams that untravell'd world whose margin fades
Forever and forever when I move. (*Ulysses*).
178. *ibid.*, pp. 80-1.
179. *ibid.*, p. 549.
180. *ibid.*, p. 561.
181. *ibid.*, p. 561.
182. *ibid.*, p. 666.
183. *ibid.*, p. 618.

184. *ibid.*, pp. 593-4.
185. *ibid.*, p. 19. Sri Aurobindo has paraphrased this simile as follows: "It is as if one said: 'as might a soul like a hunted bird take refuge from the world in the peace of the Infinite and feel that as its own remembered home, so could one take refuge in her as in a haven of safety and like the tired bird reconstitute one's strength so as to face the world once more.'" (*ibid.*, pp. 870-1).
186. *ibid.*, pp. 213-4.
187. *ibid.*, p. 262.
188. See Wellek & Warren, *Theory of Literature*, pp.202-3.
189. *Countries of the Mind*, Second Series, p. 2. Murry also says that, "it seems impossible to regard metaphors and similies as different in any essential property: metaphor is compressed simile."(*ibid.*, p. 3).
190. *Savitri.*, p. 556.
191. *ibid.*, p. 6; also Sri Aurobindo's comment on p. 859.
192. *ibid..*, p. 623.
193. *ibid.*, p. 659.
194. *ibid.*, p. 683.
195. *ibid.*, p. 559. Some other examples are: A long lone line of hesitating hue… (p. 4) Never a rarer creature bore his shaft…(p. 18).
Pause or pass slowly through that perilous space... (p.238).
A bull-throat bellowed with its brazen tongue... (p.245).
Neighbouring proud palaces of perverted Power... (p.240).
196. *The Adventure of the Apocalypse*, Introduction, p. vi.
197. P. Lal, Introduction to Modern Indo-Anglian Poetry, pp. ii-iii.
198 *The Common Reader*, I Series, pp. 225-7.
199. *Savitri.*, p. 901.
200. *Mother India*, September 1956, p. 4.
201. *Arya*, July 1918.
202. *Savitri*, pp. 824-5.
203. *ibid.*, p. 826.
204. *ibid.*, p. 3.
205. Max Muller, *Rammohan to Ramakrishna*, p. 29.
206. See Cox, *Mythology of the Aryan Nations*, pp. 227-8, and p. 230.
207. *On the Veda*, p. 336.
208. Sri Aurobindo, (Tr. from the original Bengali by Niranjan), *Mother India*, July 1958, p. 7.
209. *The House of the Titans*, p. 71.
210. *Sri Aurobindo Circle*, Number V, p. 1.
211. *Collected Poems and Plays*, Vol I, pp. 39-40. It has been pointed out that like the description of Dawn in *Savitri*, the description of the descent of Rishi Narad at the beginning of Book VI, canto I, from the world of Immortals to the earth has so much more of the overhead afflatus than a similar description in Magha's *Naishadam* (A. B. Purani, *Savitri*: *An Approach and A Study*, p. 381).
212. *Ilion*, p. 1.
213. *Savitri*, p. 4.
214. *ibid.*, p. 829. *Cf.* R.L. Megroz: "Science is a fragmentary statement of experience; poetry a multitudinous presentation of beauty; but mysticism is a self-consistent orientation of the whole personality, which may exclude much of the field of science, though not necessarily." (Francis Thompson, p. 189).
215. *ibid.*, p. 856; also pp. 830-1 "… to me they are realities, concrete powers whose resistance is present everywhere and at all times in its tremendous and boundless mass… The Inconscient comes in persistently in the cantos of the First Book of *Savitri*: e.g.
Opponent of the glory of escape,
The black Inconscient swung its dragon tail
Lashing a slumberous Infinite by its force
Into the deep obscurities of form."
216. *ibid.*, p. 5-6.
217. *The Man of Letters in the Modern World*, pp. 333-4.
218. *Savitri*, p. 853. The comment really

referred to the 1936 version of the line as, "A slow miraculous gesture dimly came."
219. *ibid.*, pp. 828-9.
220. *ibid.*, p. 7.
221. *Cf.*:
"it seemed, so still the valleys were,
As if the whole world knelt at prayer..."
But this was an experience the poet had, not at dawn, but at night.
222. *Savitri*, p. 903.
223. *ibid.*, pp. 903-4.
224. *ibid.*, pp. 860, 904.
225. *ibid.*, p. 3
226. *ibid.*, pp. 18, 863.
227. *ibid.*, pp. 18-9. Commenting on this passage, K. D. Sethna writes: "The rhythm has an overpowering fidelity to the inner thrill of the experience suggested and symbolised. Here are the figures and values of a superhuman state of consciousness at the very top, breaking upon us in their own stuff and vibrancy through the medium of language. This is not the mind imagining the highest it can beyond itself. This is an Overmind actually holding all the magnitudes that are pictured; its vision is from within, composed of its own substance and lit up with its own vast vitality."(*The Poetic Genius of Sri Aurobindo*, pp. 140-1).
228. '*Savitri*': *An Approach and a Study*, Appendix II.
229. *Savitri*, p. 392.
230. *ibid.*, pp. 422-4.
231. *ibid.*, p. 476.
232. *ibid.*, pp. 746-7.
233. Personal Notes (Unpublished).
234. See K. D. Sethna's article on 'The Poet of Integralism' in *The Integral Philosophy of Sri Aurobindo*, edited by Haridas Chaudhuri and Frederic Spiegelberg (1960).

SAVITRI: A COSMIC EPIC

1. *The Hungry Eye: An Introduction to Comic Art*, pp. 131-2.
2. *Principles of Poetry*, pp. xciv-xcv.
3. *From Virgil to Milton*, p. 5
4. *The Idea of Great Poetry*, pp. 72-3.
5. *Heroic Poetry*, Preface, p. v.
6. (Italics mine) Sri Aurobindo, *Foundations of Indian Culture*, pp. 330-1; also see his *Vyasa and Valmiki*, p. 53.
7. Iyengar, *The Indian P.E.N.*, June 1956, p.178. Donald Davie's recent poem, *The Forests of Lithuania*, is admittedly adapted from *Pan Tadeusz*.
8. Originally published in 1938, it has now been translated from modern Greek into English verse by Kimon Friar (1959).
9. *The Future Poetry*, pp. 376-7. A.B. Purani also reports that to a question whether the epic, after Milton, will tend to be more subjective, Sri Aurobindo answered: "Yes, it is so. The idea that an epic requires a story has been there for long, but the story as a subject for an epic *poem* seems to be exhausted. It will have to be more subjective and the element of interpretation will have to be admitted." (*Evening Talks*, First Series, p. 282. See also the chapter on 'Early Epic and Modern Poetry' in John Holloway's *The Charted Mirror* (1960).
10. *The English Epic and its Background*, pp. 5-12.
11. *From Virgil to Milton*, p. 15.
12. Ezra Pound, *The Spirit of Romance*, p. 127.
13. Dante's *Other World*, p. 73.
14. *Possibility*, p. 27.
15. *The Figure of Beatrice*, p. 195.
16. *The Lusiads* (The Penguin Translation), pp. 40-1.
17. *ibid.*, Introduction, p. 26. Ezra Pound, however, says that the real weakness of the poem is that, "it is the epic of a cross section, and voices a phase, a fashion of a people, and not their humanity." (*The Spirit of Romance*, p. 216).

18. *ibid.*, p. 177.
19. *Collected Essays in Criticism*, p. 59.
20. *From Virgil to Milton*, p. 176.
21. *The Classical Tradition*, p. 159.
22. *Paradise Lost*, V, II. 571-4.
23. Quoted in Hugh Kenner, *The Poetry of Ezra Pound*, p. 279.
24. *The Future Poetry*, pp. 117-9.
25. *Savitri*, pp. 821-2.
26. *Mother India*, 19 May 1951.
27. *The Future Poetry*, pp. 211-2.
28. *ibid.*, p. 212.
29. Louis Untermeyer, *Modern American Poetry: A Critical Anthology* (1936), p. 36
30. Whitman, *Leaves of Grass*, p. 76.
31. 'Towards an American Epic' (*The Hudson Review*, Autumn 1959) p. 366.
32. Quoted in Beevers, *World Without Faith*, p. 12.
33. *Savitri*, p. 891.
34. Louis Untermeyer, *Modern American Poetry*, p. 588.
35. *ibid.*, p. 500.
36. *Collected Essays*, pp. 351, 354, 355.
37. *ibid*, p. 533.
38. Hugh Kenner, *The Poetry of Ezra Pound*, pp. 261-2.
39. *ibid.*, p. 314.
40. *ibid.*, pp. 332-3.
41. Canto VI.
42. Canto XX.
43. Canto XLVII.
44. *Collected Essays*, p. 354. It is rather surprising that Mr. W.B. Stanford should make no reference whatsoever to the *Cantos* in his otherwise exhaustive study, *The Ulysses Theme* (1954).
45. *The Poetry of Ezra Pound*, p. 317.
46. G. S. Fraser, in his *Ezra Pound* (1960), compares the pattern of the *Cantos* with that of *The Divine Comedy*, *The Pisan Cantos* being "a kind of Purgatorio" (p. 70).
47. Canto LXXXVII.
48. Roy Harvey Pearce, *The Hudson Review*, Autumn 1959, p. 370.
49. A. Alvarez, *The Shaping Spirit*, p. 70.
50. Untermeyer, *Modern American Poetry*, p. 336.
51. *The Hudson Review*, Autumn 1957, p. 377.
52. The contrast between Hamlet, father and son, has been brilliantly brought out by Peter Alexander in his Northcliffe Lectures on this subject.
53. C. Day Lewis, *The Aeneid of Virgil*, p. 137
54. *The English Epic*, p. 83.
55. *The Sewanee Review*, Summer 1954, pp. 426-7. In his more exhaustive survey, *The Ulysses Theme*, W.B. Stanford has brought together Leopold Bloom in Joyce's *Ulysses* and Kazantzakis's *Odysseus* and drawn some interesting points of similarity and contrast. (pp. 222-39).
56. *Opus Posthumous*, p. 100.
57. Cf. Browning: *What does, what knows, what is*; three souls, one man. ('A Death in the Desert') Quiller-Couch makes this line the text of the first of his Cambridge Lectures on the *Art of Reading*.
58. *Opus Posthumous*, pp. 101, 103.
59. *Poetry*, December 1959, p. 140.
60. Quoted from his 'Credo' in Kimon Friar's Introduction to *The Odyssey*, p. xxiii.
61. *ibid.*, p. xxi.
62. Tennyson's *Ulysses.*
63. Kipling's fine story, 'The Miracle of Purun Bhagat', is a moving tribute to this Indian tradition.
64. Rex Warner in his review (*The London Magazine*, July 1959, p. 65).
65. James Dickey, in his review of Kazantzakis' poem in *The Sewance Review*, Summer 1959, p. 518.
66. *A Heifer of the Dawn*, pp. vii-viii. Cf. Virgil:
    And now was Aurora, leaving the saffron bed of Tithonus,
    Beginning to shower upon earth the light of another day (C. Day Lewis' translation).
67. *The Odyssey: A Modern Sequel*, p. 1.
68. *ibid.*, p. 776.
69. *ibid.*, pp. 150-1.

70. *ibid.*, pp. 30-1.
71. *ibid.*, pp. 35-6.
72. *ibid.*, pp. 41-2.
73. *ibid.*, p. 44.
74. *ibid.*, p. 31.
75. *Savitri*, p. 873.
76. *ibid.*, p. 869.
77. *ibid.*, p. 863.
78. *The Odyssey: A Modern Sequel*, pp. 513-4. *Cf.* W.B. Stanford: "The Lonely One: here is the nemesis of absolute freedom...Kazantzakis sends his hero, when he has freed himself in turn from the Ego, the Race, and the World, to a much more desolate place—to the wastes of polar ice...The Odysseus of Kazantzakis has pursued personal liberty to the zero-point of the earth." (*The Ulysses Theme*, p. 236).
79. Quoted in *Towards Standards of Criticism*, ed. by F.R. Leavis, p. 107.
80. *Poetry*, December 1959, p. 181.
81. *The Use of Poetry and the Use of Criticism*, p. 152.
82. *The Idea of Great Poetry*, pp. 147-8.
83. *The Listener*, 2 February 1950.
84. Preface to *Laureate of Peace*, p. vii.
85. *The Crown of Life*, p. 225.
86. *Coleridge on Imagination*, p. 163.
87. *People, Places and Books*, p. 80.
88. *Cf.* William James: "In mystical literature such self-contradictory phrases as 'dazzling obscurity', 'whispering silence', 'teeming desert', are continually met with. They prove that not conceptual speech, but music rather, is the element through which we are best spoken to by mystical truth. Many mystical scriptures are indeed little more than musical compositions." (*Varieties of Religious Experience*, pp. 420-1).
89. In his essay on 'The Relation of Time and Eternity', J. McT. Ellis McTaggart gives twenty-eight definitions of Time and Eternity! (*Philosophical Studies*, pp. 132-5).
90. *Countries of the Mind*, Second Series, p. 47.
91. *ibid.*, p. 59.
92. *Medieval Panorama* (Quoted in Sansom, *The World of Poetry*, p.121).
93. I am indebted to K.R.Srinivasa Iyengar's essay on Wordsworth (*Journal of the University of Bombay*, May 1937, p.41) for this and the following quotation. See also 'Q' Art of Writing (Guild Books), p. 33.
94. *Selected Essays.*, pp. 258, 271. Writing of Lucretius' *De Rerum Natura* and its basis on the materialistic philosophy of Democritus and Epicurus, Santayana writes: "Suppose.... Lucretius is quite wrong in his science...His poem would then lose its pertinence to our lives and personal convictions; it would not lose its imaginative grandeur.
    We could still conceive a world as he describes." (*Three Philosophical Poets*, p. 36).
95. *ibid.*, p. 271.
96. *The Divine Comedy*, Paradise, Canto XXXIII. This is the Temple Classics rendering; Cary's is: "Three orbs of triple hue, clipt in one bound."
97. *Collected Essays*, p. 420.
98. *Selected Essays*, p. 252.
99. *The Spirit of Romance*, p. 154.
100. See Iyengar, *Sri Aurobindo*, p.108; also fn.1 on the same page.
101. *ibid.*, pp.159-60. This experience is also referred to in the first chapter as well as the previous chapter, 'Overhead Poetry and *Savitri*'.
102. *Prayers and Meditations* of the Mother (Tr. from the original French) pp. 88-9. She has also stated elsewhere: "As soon as I saw Sri Aurobindo, I recognised him as the well-known being whom I used to call Krishna,...and this is enough to explain why I am fully convinced that my place and my work are near him in India." (Quoted in A.B. Purani, *Life*, p. 170).
103. *On the Mother*, p. 62.
104. See K.D. Sethna on 'The Passing of Sri Aurobindo' in *Mother India*, January 1951.

105. *Mother India*, 19 May 1951.
106. It was perhaps this or one of the early versions that Sri Aurobindo read to Amrita in 1913. (Vide A.B. Purani, *Life*, p. 155).
107. *Cf.* Iyengar:"...a devoted and widely-read Roman Catholic thinks that *The Life Divine* reminds him often of the structure as well as the thought-content of St Thomas Aquinas' *Summa Theologica*..." (Sri Aurobindo, p. 258).
108. Nirodbaran, *Mother India*, 19 May 1951.
109. T.S. Eliot, 'Dante' (*Selected Essays*, p. 272).
110. *Collected Essays*, p. 421.
111. *Savitri*, pp. 822-3.
112. *ibid.*, p. 823.
113. *Sri Aurobindo*, p. 64.
114. *Collected Poems and Plays*, Vol. I, p. 76.
115. *ibid.*, p. 82.
116. Sir Edwin Arnold gave this title, *Love and Death*, to his verse translation of the *Mahabharata* story of Savitri. It is an interesting coincidence that Sri Aurobindo should have followed up his *Love and Death* with his own first version of *Savitri*.
117. *Collected Poems and Plays*, Vol., I p. 100.
118. *ibid.*, pp. 105-6.
119. *The Poetic Genius of Sri Aurobindo*, p.31. Mr.W.H. Auden sees in the symbolic situations in some of Tennyson's best poems an archetypal pattern consisting of three elements:
    i. Death, threatened or actual;
    ii. Temptation; and
    iii. Rescue or rebirth.

    This applies no less to Sri Aurobindo's *Urvasie*, *Love and Death* and *Savitri*. (See Introduction to *A Selection from the Poems of Alfred, Lord Tennyson*, 1946. p.xv).
120. *Savitri*, p. 827.
121. *ibid.*, p. 917.
122. *Cf.* S.K. Maitra's article on 'Faust and Savitri' in *The Meeting of the East and the West in Sri Aurobindo's Philosophy*.
123. *Letters of Sri Aurobindo*, Third Series, pp. 305-6. It is also interesting to recall Sri Aurobindo's youthful tribute to Goethe:
    A perfect face amid barbarian faces,
    A perfect voice of sweet and serious rhyme,
    Traveller with calm, inimitable paces,
    Critic with judgment absolute to all time,
    A complete strength when men were maimed and weak,
    German obscured the spirit of a Greek. (*Collected Poems and Plays*, Vol. I, p. 9).
124. *Oxford Lectures on Poetry*, p. 174.
125. *Faust* (Bohn's series: 1919), p. 412.
126. *ibid.*, p. 416.
127. *Goethe's Major Plays* (1959), p. 166.
128. *Christian Mysticism*, p. 132.
129. *Plays and Poems*: 1948-58. *Cf.*: "Man as the intersection of two worlds suffers because he partakes of the nature of animals, and of God", Rudd, *Divided Image*, p. 203.
130. *A Modern Prelude*, p. 297.
131. See Johnson, *The Imprisoned Splendour*, p. 174.
132. *God*, pp. 22, 85.
133. Mackenzie, *Cosmic Problems*, p. 113.
134. *God*, p. 44.
135. See Mackenzie, *Cosmic Problems*, p. 113.
136. See Stace, *Time and Eternity*, p. 75.
137. *Space, Time and Deity*, Vol. II, p. 345.
138. Quoted in Johnson, *The Imprisoned Splendour*, p. 148.
139. *My Philosophy*, p. 21.
140. *The Secret of the Golden Flower*, ed. by Richard Wihelm and C.G. Jung, p. 99.
141. *ibid.*, p. 93.
142. See Stoudt, *Sunrise to Eternity*, p. 230.
143. Quoted in Johnson's *The Imprisoned Splendour*, pp. 403-4.
144. *Prayers and Meditations*, pp. 61-2.
145. *God*, p. 69.
146. *Collected Poems and Plays*, Vol. I, pp. 138-9.

147. *Mother India*, September 1957, p. 7. Again, in *The Advent* (April 1960), M.V. Seetaraman has pointed out the parallelism between the sonnet entitled *The Divine Worker* and certain passages in *Savitri.*
148. *Last Poems*, p. 48.
149. *ibid.*, p. 47.
150. *ibid.*, p. 3.
151. *ibid.*, p. 8.
152. *ibid.*, p. 21. *Cf.* also:
My dumb abysses are His screened abode;
In my heart's chamber lives the unworshipped God. (p. 35)
153. *ibid.*, p. 22. *Cf.* Dorothy Sayers: "The intention of creation was to create, that is, a joy that could rejoice in its own being, each creature after its own manner, and reflect back to God the joy and gifts that He bestowed upon it." *Further Papers on Dante*, p. 91).
154. *ibid.*, p. 12.
155. *ibid.*, p. 7.
156. *ibid.*, p. 9.
157. *Essays*, p. 96.
158. 17 January 1942.
159. 14 September 1958.
160. *Savitri*, pp. 797-798
161. *God*, p. 18.
162. *The Figure of Beatrice*, p. 56.
163. *Savitri*, pp. 869,823,863.
164. *ibid.*, p. 494.
165. *ibid.*, p. 746.
166. *ibid.*, p. 748.
167. *ibid.*, pp. 771-77.
168. *Humanity and Deity*, p. 464.
169. Williams, *The Figure of Beatrice*, p. 195.
170. *Existentialism*, Tr. by E.M. Cocks, pp. 49-50.
171. T.S. Eliot, *Burnt Norton.*
172. *Savitri*, p. 835.
173. See *A Heifer of the Dawn*, pp. 19-21.
174. P. Lal, Introduction to *Modern Indo-Anglian Poetry*, pp. ii-iii.
175. Quoted in Purani, *Savitri: An Approach and a Study*, p. 2.
176. *Savitri*, p. 323.
177. *ibid.*, p. 892.
178. *ibid.*, p. 838.
179. *ibid.*, pp. 390-1.
180. *ibid.*, pp. 391-2. I have purposely omitted the marvellous lines that give a preview of the glory that is to be incarnated as Savitri; my point is that even the apparently 'rhetorical' lines sound right and are properly evocative in the given context.
181. See *The Autobiography of Maharshi Debendranath Tagore*, p. 150.
182. *Essays and Studies* (1959), p. 1.
183. *Savitri*, p. 32.
184. *ibid.*, p. 110.
185. *ibid.*, p. 804.
186. *ibid.*, p. 276.
187. July-September, 1954
188. *God*, p. 203.
189. *The Crown of Life*, p. 225.
190. *Sri Aurobindo Mandir Annual.* No. 7, p.
191. Sri Krishnaprem is the Hindu name assumed by Ronald Nixon, an Englishman and a former Professor of English in an Indian University.
191. *ibid.*, p. 190 fn.
192. *ibid.*, pp. 191-2.

SELECT BIBLIOGRAPHY

I. BOOKS BY SRI AUROBINDO

Collected Poems and Plays, Vols. I and II (Sri Aurobindo Ashram, Pondicherry, 1942).
Ilion : An Epic in Quantitative Hexameters (Ashram, 1957).
Poems, Past and Present (Ashram, 1946).
Last Poems (Ashram, 1952).
More Poems (Ashram, 1958).
Poems from Bengali (Ashram, 1956).
Songs of Vidyapati (Ashram, 1956).
Vasavadutta (Ashram, 1957).
Rodogune (Ashram, 1958).
The Viziers of Bassora (Ashram, 1959).
Eric (Ashram, 1960).
Prince of Edur (Ashram, 1961).
Savitri: A Legend and a Symbol (Ashram, 1995)
The Future Poetry (Ashram, 1953).
Vyasa and Valmiki (Ashram, 1956).
Kalidasa (Arya Publishing House, Calcutta, 1929).
Bankim-Tilak-Dayananda (Arya Publishing House, Calcutta, 1940).
Heraclitus (Arya Publishing House, Calcutta, 1941).
Hymns to the Mystic Fire (Ashram, 2nd Edition, 1952).
On the Veda (Ashram, 1956).
Eight Upanishads (Ashram, 1953).
Isha Upanishad (Ashram, 1951).
Kena Upanishad (Ashram, 1952).
Essays on the Gita (Sri Aurobindo Ashram Library Inc., New York, 1950)
The Foundations of Indian Culture (Sri Aurobindo Library Inc., New York, 1953).
The Renaissance in India (Arya Publishing House, Calcutta, 1947).
The Life Divine (Sri Aurobindo Library Inc., New York, 1951).
The Mother (Arya Publishing House, Calcutta, 3rd Impression, 1940).
The Synthesis of Yoga (On Yoga I), (Ashram 1955).
On Yoga II : Tomes One and Two (Ashram 1958).
The Human Cycle (Sri Aurobindo Library Inc., New York, 1950).

The Ideal of Human Unity (Sri Aurobindo Library Inc., New York, 1950).
Letters, First Series (Sri Aurobindo Circle, Bombay, 1947).
Letters, Second Series (Sri Aurobindo Circle, Bombay, 1949).
Letters, Third Series (Ashram, 1949).
Letters, Fourth Series (Ashram, 1950).
Speeches (Arya Publishing House, Calcutta, 1922).
Thoughts and Aphorisms (Ashram, 1958).
On Himself and on the Mother (Ashram, 1953).
A System of National Education (Arya Publishing House, Calcutta, 1924).
Sri Aurobindo's Vedic Glossary, compiled by A.B. Purani (Ashram, 1962).
(Note : The editions actually used by me are listed here, but the books published by Sri Aurobindo Library Inc., New York, and Arya Publishing House, Calcutta, have now been reissued by Sri Aurobindo Ashram, Pondicherry.)

II. BOOKS BY OTHERS

Abercrombie, Lascelles. *The Idea of Great Poetry* (Martin Secker, London, 3rd Impression, 1926).
A.E. *Voices of the Stones* (Macmillan, London, 1925). *The House of the Titans* (Macmillan, London, 1934).
Aiyangar, Narayan. *Essays on Indo-Aryan Mythology* (Bangalore, 1898).
Alexander,S. *Space, Time and Deity*, Vols. I & II (Macmillan, London, 1927).
Alvarez,A. *The Shaping Spirit : Studies in Modern English and American Poets* (Chatto & Windus, London, 1958).
Arnold, Sri Edwin. *The Light of Asia : and the Indian Song of Songs* (Jaico Books, Bombay, 1949).
Auden, W.H. (Ed.) *The Criterion Book of Modern American Verse* (Criterion Books, New York, 1956).
Bain, F.W. *A Heifer of the Dawn* (Methuen, London, 13th Impression, 1927).
Baker, James Volant : *The Sacred River : Coleridge's Theory of the Imagination* (Louisiana State University Press, 1957).
Beevers, John. *World Without Faith* (Hamish Hamilton, London, 1935).
Berdyaev, Nicolas. *The Meaning of History* : translated from the original Russian by George Reavey (Geoffrey Bles, London, 3rd Reprint, 1949).
Blackstone, Bernard. *The Consecrated Urn : An Interpretation of Keats in terms of Growth and Form* (Longmans, London, 1959).
Boodin, John Elof. *God : A Cosmic Philosophy of Religion* (Macmillan Company, New York, 1934).
Bowman, Archibald Allan. *A Sacramental Universe*, the Vanuxem Lectures edited by J.W. Scott (Princeton University Press, 1939).
Bowra, C.M. *From Virgil to Milton* (Macmillan, London, 1945). *Heroic Poetry* (Macmillan, London, 1952).
Brockington, A. Allen. *Mysticism and Poetry on a Basis Of Experience* (Chapman & Hall, London, 1934).
Brooks, Cleanth, & Robert Penn Warren. *Understanding Poetry* (Henry Holt, New York, 1955).
Brough, John. *Selections from Classical Sanskrit Literature*, with English translation and Notes (Luzac, Londan, 1951).
Buchanan, Scott. *Possibility* (Kegan Paul, London, 1927).
Bullett, Gerald. *The English Mystics* (Michael Joseph, London, 1950).

Camoens, Luis Vas De. *The Lusiads,* translated by William Atkinson (Penguin Books, London, 1952).

Cassirer, Ernst. *Language and Myth,* translated by Susanne K. Langer (Dover Publications Inc., New York, 1946).

Chardin, Pierre Teilhard de. *The Phenomenon of Man,* translated by Bernard Wall (Collins, London, 1960).

Letters from a Traveller (Collins, London, 1962).

Chaudhuri, Haridas, *The Philosophy of Integralism, or the Metaphysical Synthesis inherent in the Teaching of Sri Aurobindo* (Sri Aurobindo Pathmandir, Calcutta, 1954).

Chaudhuri, Haridas, & Frederic Spiegelberg (Eds.) *The Integral Philosophy of Sri Aurobindo* (George Allen & Unwin, London, 1960).

Cox, Sir George W. *The Mythology of the Aryan Nations* (Kegan Paul, London, 1903).

Croce, Benedetto. *Aesthetic: As Science of Expression and General Linguistic.* Translated by Douglas Ainslie (Macmillan, London, 1929).

Cruickshank, John. *Albert Camus, and the Literature of Revolt* (Oxford University Press, London, 1959).

Dante, Alighieri. *The Vision: or Hell, Purgatory, and Paradise*, translated by Henry Francis Cary (Oxford University Press, London, 1923).

The Divine Comedy, translated by Charles Eliot Norton (*Great Books of the Western World,* William Benton, Chicago, 1952).

Das, Abinas Chandra. *Rig-Vedic India,* Vol. I (The University of Calcutta, 1921).

Deshmukh, P.S. *The Origin and Development of Religion in Vedic Literature* (Oxford University Press, 1933).

Diwakar, R.R. *Mahayogi* (Bharatiya Vidya Bhavan, Bombay, 1954).

Dixon, W. Macneile. *English Epic and Heroic Poetry* (Dent & Sons, London, 1912).

Donnelly, M. *Founding the Life Divine. An Introduction to the Intergral Yoga of Sri Aurobindo* (Rider, London, 1955).

Eastman. Max. *The Literary Mind* (Charles Scribner's Sons, New York, 1932).

Eaton, Gai. *The Richest Vein: Eastern Tradition and Modern Thought* (Faber & Faber, London, 1949).

Eliot, T.S. *Selected Essays* (Faber Faber, London, 1944).

The Use of Poetry and the Use of Criticism (Faber & Faber, London, 1955).

Fausset, Hugh I'Anson. *A Modern Prelude* (Jonathan Cape, London, 1933).

Frazer, Sri James George. *Man, God and Immortality: Thoughts on Human Progress* (Macmillan, London, 1927).

Gayley, C.M. *Methods and Materials of Literary Criticism: Lyric, Epic, and allied forms of Poetry* (New York, 1919). *The Principles of Poetry* (New York, 1904).

Gilson, Etienne. *Dante the Philosopher,* translated by David Moore (Sheed & Ward, London, 1952).

Goethe, Johann Wolfgang von. *Faust,* (Bohn's Series, Bell, London, 1919).

Gore, Charles. *The Philosophy of the Good Life* (John Murray, London, 1930).

Graves, Robert. *The White Goddess: A Historical Grammar of Poetic Myth* (Farrar Straus & Cudahy, New York, 1948).

Grierson, H.J.C. (Ed.) *Essays and Studies,* Vol. XVI (The Clarendon Press, Oxford, 1931).

Gupta, J.N. *Life and Work of Romesh Chunder Dutt* (Dent & Sons, London, 1911).

Gupta, Nolini Kanta. *The Yoga of Sri Aurobindo,* Parts I-VIII (Sri Aurobindo Ashram, Pondicherry).

Haas, William S. *The Destiny of the Mind: East and West* (Faber & Faber, London, 1956).

Highet, Gilbert. *The Classical Tradition* (Oxford University Press, London, 1951). *People, Places and Books* (Oxford University Press, London, 1953).

Housman, A.E. *The Name and Nature of Poetry* (Cambridge University Press, London, 1933).

Hudson, Derek (Ed.) *English Critical Essays, XX Century*, Second Series (Oxford University Press, London, 1958).

Inge, W.R. *Christian Mysticism* (Methuen, London, 6th Edition, 1925.)

Isaacs, J. *The Background of Modern Poetry* (Bell, London, 1951)

Iyengar, K.R. Srinivasa. *Sri Aurobindo* (Arya Publishing House, Calcutta, 2nd Edition, 1950).

Sri Aurobindo: An Introduction (Rao & Raghavan, Mysore, 1961).

On the Mother (Sri Aurobindo Ashram, Pondicherry, 1952).

Gerard Manley Hopkins: The Man and the Poet (Oxford University Press, London, 1948).

Indian Writing in English (Asia Publishing House, Bombay, 1962).

The Adventure of Criticism (Asia Publishing House, Bombay, 1962).

Jacobi, Jolande. *Complex, Archetype, Symbol:* in the Psychology Of C.G. Jung, translated from the German by Ralph Manheim (Routledge, London, 1959).

James, William, *The Varieties of Religious Experience* (Longmans, London, 37th Impression, 1929).

Johnson, Raynor C. *The Imprisoned Splendour* (Hodder & Stoughton, London, 1954).

Jones, Phyllis M. (Ed.) *English Critical Essays*, XX Century (Oxford University Press, London, 1933).

Kazantzakis, Nikos. *The Odyssey : A Modern Sequel,* translated into English verse, with Introduction, Synopsis and Notes by Kimon Friar (Secker & Warburg, London, 1958).

Kellett, E.E. *Reconsiderations* (Cambridge University Press, London, 1928).

Kenner, Hugh. *The Poetry of Ezra Pound* (New Directions, New York, 1951).

Ker, W.P. (ed.) *Essays and Studies,* Vol. III (The Clarendon Press, Oxford, 1912).

Knight, G. Wilson. *The Crown of Life* : *Essays in Interpretation of Shakespeare's Final Plays* (Methuen, London, 1958).

Laureate of Peace : *on the Genius of Alexander Pope* (Routledge, London, 1954).

Kurtz, Benjamin P. *The Pursuit of Death* (Oxford University Press, London, 1933).

Lal, P. & K. Raghavendra RAO. *Modern Indo-Anglian Poetry* (Kavita, Delhi, 1959).

Langley, G.H. *Sri Aurobindo : Indian Poet, Philosopher and Mystic* (David Marlowe, London, 1949).

Leavis, F.R. (Ed.) *Towards Standards of Criticism* (Wishart, London, 1933).

Leeuw,J.J. Van Der. *The Conquest of Illusion* (Alfred A. Knopf, New York, 1928).

Leuba, James H. *The Psychology of Religious Mysticism* (Kegan Paul, London, 1925).

Levy, G.R. *The Sword from the Rock* (Faber & Faber, London, 1953).

Lewis, C. Day. *The Aeneid of Virgil* (The Hogarth Press, London, 1954).

A Hope for Poetry (Basil Blackwell, Oxford, 1934).

The Poet's Way to Knowledge (Cambridge University Press, London, 1957).

Lodge, Sri Oliver. *My Philosophy* (Ernest Benn, London, 1933).

Longinus. *On the Sublime,* translated by A. O. Prickard (The Clarendon Press, Oxford, 1930).

Macdonnel, A.A. *A Vedic Reader for Students* (Oxford University Press, London, 1917).

Mackenzie, J.S. *Cosmic Problems* : *An Essay on Speculative Philosophy* (Macmillan, London, 1931).

Matthiessen, F.O. *American Renaissance* : *Art and Expression in the Age of Emerson and Whitman* (Oxford University Press, London, 1946).

Mctaggart, J. McT. Ellis. *Philosophical Studies* (Edward Arnold, London, 1934).

Megroz, R.L. *Francis Thompson : The Poet of Earth in Heaven* (Faber & Gwyer, London, 1927).
Meyerhoff, Hans. *Time in Literature* (University of California Press, 1955).
Miller, Henry. *The Air-Conditioned Nightmare* (New Directions, New York, 1945).
Mitra, Sisirkumar. *The Dawn Eternal : The Secret of India's Evolution* (Sri Aurobindo Ashram, Pondicherry, 1954).
The Liberator : Sri Aurobindo, India and the World (Jaico Books, Bombay, 1955).
Montague, William Pepperell. *The Ways of Knowing* (Allen & Unwin, London, 4th Impression, 1953).
Morgan, Charles. *Liberties of the Mind* (Macmillan, London, 1951).
Mother, The. *Prayers and Meditations*, translated from the French (Sri Aurobindo Ashram, Pondicherry, Revised edition, 1948).
Words of the Mother (Sri Aurobindo Ashram, Pondicherry, 3rd Edition, 1946).
Mukerjea, S.V. *Disjecta Membra : Studies in Literature and Life* (Indian Institute of World Culture, Bangalore, 1959).
Muller, Max. *Auld Lang Syne : Second Series—My Indian Friends* (Longmans, London, 1899).
Rammohan to Ramkrishna (Susil Gupta, Culcutta, 1952).
Murry, John Middleton. *Countries of the Mind,* Second Series (Oxford University Press, London, 1931).
Nandakumar, Prema. *Bharati in English Verse* (Higginbothams, Madras, 1958).
Noyes, Alfred. *The Torch-Bearers*, Vol. II, *The Book of Earth* (Blackwood & Sons, 1925).
Osgood, Charles Grosvenor. *Poetry as a Means of Grace* (Princeton University Press, Princeton, 1946).
Pandit, M.P. *Where the Wings of Glory Brood* (Sri Aurobindo Ashram, Pondicherry, 1961).
Sadhana in Sri Aurobindo's Yoga (Sri Aurobindo Ashram, Pondicherry, 1962).
Pasternak, Boris. *An Essay in Autobiography,* translated by Manya Harari (Collins & Harvill, London, 1959).
Payne, M.A. *Creative Education* (William Maclellan, Glasgow, 1958).
Pearson, N. *Sri Aurobindo and the Soul Quest of Man* (Allen & Unwin, London, 1952).
Pinto, Vivian de Sola. *Crisis in English Poetry : 1880-1940* (Hutchinson, London, 1951).
Pound, Ezra. *The Canto* 1-84 (New Directions, New York).
Section : Rock-Drill, 85-95 (New Directions, New York).
Thrones : 96-109 (New Directions, New York, 1959).
The Spirit of Romance (New Directions, New York).
ABC of Reading (New Directions, New York).
Press, John. *The Fire and the Fountain* (Oxford University Press, London, 1955).
The Chequer'd Shade : Reflections on Obscurity in Poetry (Oxford University Press, London, 1958).
Purani, A.B. *Evening Talks with Sri Aurobindo,* First and Second Series (Sri Aurobindo Ashram, Pondicherry, 1959, 1960).
Life of Sri Aurobindo (Sri Aurobindo Ashram, Pondicherry, 1958).
Sri Aurobindo's 'Savitri' : An Approach and a Study (Sri Aurobindo Ashram, Pondicherry, 2nd Edition, 1956).
Technical Terms in Sri Aurobindo's Philosophy (Sri Aurobindo Karyalaya, Anand, 1949).
Ray, Prithwis Chandra. *Life and Times of C. R. Das* (Oxford University Press, Bombay, 1927).
Read, Sri Herbert. *Collected Essays in Literary Criticism* (Faber & Faber, London, 1938).
Richards, I.A. *Coleridge on Imagination* (Routledge, London, 2nd Edition, 1950).
Science and Poetry (Kegan Paul, London, 1926).

Rilke, Rainer Maria. *Poems* 1906 to 1926, translated with an Introduction by J. B. Leishman (The Hogarth Press, London, 1957).

Rishabhchand. *The Integral Yoga of Sri Aurobindo* (Sri Aurobindo Ashram, Pondicherry, 1959).

Roy, Dilip Kumar. *Among the Great* (Nalanda Publications, Bombay, 1946).

Sri Aurobindo Came to Me (Sri Aurobindo Ashram, Pondicherry, 1952).

Roy, Pratap Chandra. *The Mahabharata*, Vol. II, *Vana Parva*, English Translation (Datta Bose & Co., Calcutta).

Rudd, Margaret. *Divided Image : A Study of William Blake and W. B. Yeats* (Routledge, London, 1953).

Ruggiero, Guido de. *Existentialism,* translated from the original Italian by E. M. Cocks (Secker & Warburg, London, 1946).

Sansom, Clive. (Ed.) *The World of Poetry* : *Poets and Critics on Art and Functions of Poetry* (Phoenix House, London, 1959).

Santayana, George. *Essays in Literary Criticism*, Selected and edited by Irving Singer (Charles Scribner's Sons, New York, 1956).

Three Philosophical Poets : *Lucretius, Dante, and Goethe* (Harvard University Press, Cambridge, 1935).

Sarma, D.S. *Studies in the Renaissance of Hinduism in the 19th and 20th centuries* (Benares Hindu University, Benares, 1944).

Sayers, Dorothy L. *Further Papers on Dante* (Methuen, London, 1957).

Sen, Kshitimohan. *Medieval Mysticism of India,* translated from the Bengali of Manmohan Ghosh (Luzac, London, 1935).

Sethna, K.D. *The Adventure of the Apocalypse* (Sri Aurobindo Circle, Bombay, 1949).

The Poetic Genius of Sri Aurobindo (Sri Aurobindo Circle, Bombay, 1947).

Smith, Jay. (Ed.) *Pioneer of the Supramental Age* (Sri Aurobindo Ashram, Delhi Branch, 1958).

Smith, G.C. Moore. (Ed.) *Essays and Studies*, Vol. VIII (The Clarendon Press, Oxford, 1922).

Spurgeon, Caroline E. *Mysticism in English Literature* (Cambridge University Press, Cambridge, 1927).

Stace, W.T. *Time and Eternity* : *An Essay in the Philosophy of Religion* (Princeton University Press, Princeton, 1952).

Stambler, Bernard. *Dante's Other World* : *The 'Purgatorio' as Guide to the 'Divine Comedy'* (Peter Owen, London, 1958).

Stanford, W.B. *The Ulysses Theme* : *A Study in the Adaptability of a Traditional Hero* (Basil Blackwell, Oxford, 1954).

Stevens, Wallace. *Collected Poems* (Alfred A. Knopf, New York, 1957).

Opus Posthumous (Alfred A. Knopf, New York, 1957).

Stoudt, John Joseph. *Sunrise to Eternity* : *A Study in Jacob Boehme's Life and Thought* (University of Pennsylvania Press, Philadelphia, 1957).

Strachey, Lytton. *Biographical Essays* (Chatto Windus, London, 1948).

Literary Essays (Chatto Windus, London, 1948).

Strong, L.A.G. *Common Sense About Poetry* (Victor Gollancz, London, 1934).

Tagore, Rabindranath. *Personality* (Macmillan, London, 1948). *The Religion of Man* (Allen & Unwin, London, 2nd Impression, 1932).

Collected Poems and Plays of Tagore (Macmillan, 1936).

Tagore, Satyendranath, & Indira Devi. (Trs.) *The Autobiography of Maharshi Devendranath Tagore*, Introduction by Evelyn Underhill (Macmillan, London, 1916).

Tate, Allen. *Poems* : *1920-1945* (Eyre & Spottiswoode, London, 1947).

The Man of Letters in the Modern World (Thames Hudson, London, 1957).
Collected Essays (Alan Swallow, Denver, 1959).
Tate, Allen, (in collaboration with David Cecil). *Modern Verse in English : 1900-1950* (Eyre & Spottiswoode, London, 1958).
Tillyard, E.M.W. *The English Epic and its Background* (Chatto & Windus, London, 1954).
Underhill, Evelyn. *Mysticism* (Methuen, London, 12th Edition, 1930).
Untermeyer, Louis. *Modern American Poetry : Modern British Poetry, A Critical Anthology* (Harcourt Brace & Co., New York, 1936).
Urban, Wilbur Marshall. *Humanity and Deity* (Allen & Unwin, London, 1951).
Vivas, Elisco. *Creation and Discovery : Essays in Criticism and Aesthetics* (The Noonday Press, New York, 1955).
Yeats, W.B. *Essays* (Macmillan, London, 1924).
Yutang, Lin. *The Wisdom of India* (Michael Joseph, London, 1948).
Wain, John. *Preliminary Essays* (Macmillan, London, 1957).
Walker, Kenneth. *A Study of Gurdjieff's Teaching* (Jonathan Cape, London, 1957).
Wellek, Rene, & Austin Warren. *Theory of Literature* (Jonathan Cape, London, 1953).
Whitman, Walt. *Leaves of Grass* (Everyman's Edition, Dent & Sons, London, 1949).
Wilhelm, Richard. (Tr.) *The Secret of the Golden Flower: A Chinese Book of Life.* Translated & explained by Richard Wilhelm ; with a European commentary by C.G. Jung; translated into English by Cary F. Baynes (Kegan Paul, London, 1932).
Williams, Charles. *The Figure of Beatrice : A Study of Dante* (Faber & Faber, London, 6th Impression, 1953).
Reason and Beauty in the Poetic Mind (The Clarendon Press, Oxford, 1933).
Wimsatt JR., William K, & Cleanth Brooks. *Literary Criticism : A Short History* (Alfred A. Knopf, New York, 1957).
Winternitz, M. *A History of Indian Literature*, Vol. I, Translated from the German by Mrs. S. Ketkar (University of Calcutta, 1927).
Woodroffe, Sir John. *Is India Civilized ?* (Ganesh & Co., Madras, 1918).
The World as Power (Ganesh & Co., Madras, 1956).
Woolf, Virginia. *The Common Reader*, First Series (The Hogarth Press, London, 1951).

III. MAGAZINES AND PERIODICALS

Sri Aurobindo Mandir Annual. Published by the Sri Aurobindo Pathmandir, Calcutta, every year since 1942, on 15 August.
Loving Homage. Special Commemoration Volume Published by the Sri Aurobindo Pathmandir, Calcutta, on 15 August 1958.
Sri Aurobindo Circle. Annual Numbers published since 1945 on behalf of the Sri Aurobindo Circle, Bombay.
The Advent, Quarterly Journal, published since 1944, first from Madras and now from Pondicherry.
Mother India. First published as a fortnightly from Bombay (since February 1949), and subsequently converted into a monthly and published from Pondicherry.
Bulletin of Sri Aurobindo International Centre of Education. Originally published (since February 1949) as the *Bulletin of Physical Education*: now issued quarterly as an Anglo-French-Hindi illustrated Journal; published by Sri Aurobindo Ashram, Pondicherry.

APPENDIX

A KEY TO ASWAPATI'S TRAVELS IN THE WORLD-STAIR

GROSS MATTER
(Canto II)

SUBTLE MATTER
(Canto II)

Material Paradise

LITTLE LIFE
(Cantos III, IV, V)

Insect, Animal, Early Man

GREATER LIFE
(Canto VI)

Kingdom of the Morning Star:
The Heroic Age

SELF OF MIND
(Canto XIII)
Centre of
Silence

WORLD-SOUL
(Canto XIV)
Purusha
Prakriti

HEAVENS OF THE IDEAL
(Canto XII)
The Rose & the Flame

GREATER MIND
(Canto XI)

Higher mind, Illumined Mind,
Intuitive mind

LITTLE MIND
(Canto X)
Pigmy Thought, Intelligence, Reason

NIGHT

(Cantos VII, VIII)
Mother of Falsehood
& Sons of Darkness

DAY

(Cantos IX)
The Life-Gods:
The Gandharva World

INDEX